Treating **Depression, Anxiety,** and **Stress**
in *Ethnic* and *Racial Groups*

CULTURAL, RACIAL, AND ETHNIC PSYCHOLOGY BOOK SERIES

Treating **Depression, Anxiety, and Stress** in *Ethnic and Racial Groups*

Cognitive Behavioral Approaches

Edited by

**Edward C. Chang, Christina A. Downey,
Jameson K. Hirsch,** and **Elizabeth A. Yu**

AMERICAN PSYCHOLOGICAL ASSOCIATION
Washington, DC

Published by
American Psychological Association
750 First Street, NE
Washington, DC 20002
www.apa.org

APA Order Department
P.O. Box 92984
Washington, DC 20090-2984
Phone: (800) 374-2721; Direct: (202) 336-5510
Fax: (202) 336-5502; TDD/TTY: (202) 336-6123
Online: http://www.apa.org/pubs/books
E-mail: order@apa.org

In the U.K., Europe, Africa, and the Middle East, copies may be ordered from
Eurospan Group
c/o Turpin Distribution
Pegasus Drive
Stratton Business Park
Biggleswade Bedfordshire
SG18 8TQ United Kingdom
Phone: +44 (0) 1767 604972
Fax: +44 (0) 1767 601640
Online: https://www.eurospanbookstore.com/apa
E-mail: eurospan@turpin-distribution.com

Typeset in Goudy by Circle Graphics, Inc., Columbia, MD

Printer: Sheridan Books, Chelsea, MI
Cover Designer: Mercury Publishing Services, Inc., Rockville, MD

Library of Congress Cataloging-in-Publication Data
Names: Chang, Edward C. (Edward Chin-Ho), editor. | Downey, Christina A.,
    editor. | Hirsch, Jameson K., editor. | Yu, Elizabeth A., editor. |
    American Psychological Association, issuing body.
Title: Treating depression, anxiety, and stress in ethnic and racial groups:
    cognitive behavioral approaches / edited by Edward C. Chang, Christina A.
    Downey, Jameson K. Hirsch, and Elizabeth A. Yu.
Other titles: Cultural, racial, and ethnic psychology book series.
Description: Washington, DC : American Psychological Association, [2018] |
    Series: Cultural, racial, and ethnic psychology book series | Includes
    bibliographical references and index.
Identifiers: LCCN 2017061650| ISBN 9781433829215 | ISBN 1433829215
Subjects: | MESH: Depressive Disorder—therapy | Cognitive Therapy—methods |
    Anxiety Disorders—therapy | Stress, Psychological—ethnology | Depressive
    Disorder—ethnology | Anxiety Disorders—ethnology | Cultural Competency
Classification: LCC RC537 | NLM WM 171.5 | DDC 616.85/27—dc23 LC record available at
https://lccn.loc.gov/2017061650

British Library Cataloguing-in-Publication Data
A CIP record is available from the British Library.

Printed in the United States of America
First Edition

http://dx.doi.org/10.1037/0000091-000

10 9 8 7 6 5 4 3 2 1

This book is dedicated to all those who played a formative role in helping me develop as a practitioner and as a scientist during my graduate years at SUNY Stony Brook. In particular, I wish to thank Ed Katkin, who, as one of my clinical supervisors, dared to call me a behavioral therapist during one of our sessions together! This is also dedicated to the two who make me go each day, Stephanie and Olivia. I'll see the two of you at Mount Otemanu!

—*Edward C. Chang*

I would like to dedicate this book to my husband, Chad. It's a good, good life. Thank you.

—*Christina A. Downey*

I dedicate this book to my wife, Kittye, and my sons, Clint and Gabe, who give meaning to my life and my work and who give me a reason to be the best me I can be.

—*Jameson K. Hirsch*

For my mentor, Edward Chang, whose steadfast dedication to his work has never failed to inspire me; for my supervisors, whose invaluable guidance has molded my early training in providing culturally informed clinical interventions; and for my parents, for Emily, and for Chris, whose support for me has never wavered.

—*Elizabeth A. Yu*

CONTENTS

CONTRIBUTORS

Cristina Adames, BA, Clinical Psychology Doctoral Program, Psychology Department, University of Puerto Rico, Rio Piedras Campus, San Juan

Elom Amuzu, MA, Department of Psychology, Southern Illinois University at Carbondale

Jiwoon Bae, BA, Department of Psychology and Neuroscience, University of North Carolina at Chapel Hill

Holly Batchelder, MS, Pacific Graduate School of Psychology, Palo Alto University, Palo Alto, CA

Guillermo Bernal, PhD, Presidency Department, Carlos Albizu University, San Juan Campus, San Juan, PR

Donte L. Bernard, MA, Department of Psychology and Neuroscience, University of North Carolina at Chapel Hill

Beth Boyd, PhD, Psychology Department, University of South Dakota, Vermillion

Elizabeth Brondolo, PhD, Department of Psychology, St. John's University, Queens, NY

Esteban V. Cardemil, PhD, Frances L. Hiatt School of Psychology, Clark University, Worcester, MA

Michele M. Carter, PhD, Department of Psychology, American University, Washington, DC

Courtney P. Chan, BA, Department of Psychology, Claremont McKenna College, Claremont, CA

Edward C. Chang, PhD, Department of Psychology, University of Michigan, Ann Arbor

Joyce Chu, PhD, Pacific Graduate School of Psychology, Palo Alto University, Palo Alto, CA

Christina A. Downey, PhD, Indiana University Kokomo

Lisa M. Edwards, PhD, Department of Counselor Education and Counseling Psychology, Marquette University, Milwaukee, WI

Jacqueline S. Gray, PhD, Department of Population Health, University of North Dakota School of Medicine and Health Sciences, Grand Forks

Tawanda M. Greer, PhD, Department of Psychology, Southern Illinois University at Carbondale

Jameson K. Hirsch, PhD, Department of Psychology, East Tennessee State University, Johnson City

Leslie C. Ho, BA, Department of Psychology, University of California–Berkeley

Janie J. Hong, PhD, Redwood Center for Cognitive Behavior Therapy and Research and University of California–Berkeley

Kristyne K. Hong, BA, Department of Psychology, Claremont McKenna College, Claremont, CA

Ryan Hunsaker, PhD, Wyoming State Hospital, Evanston

Wei-Chin Hwang, PhD, Department of Psychology, Claremont McKenna College, Claremont, CA

Gayle Y. Iwamasa, PhD, HSPP, Department of Veterans Affairs, VA Central Office, Lafayette, IN

Amandeep Kaur, MA, Department of Psychology, St. John's University, Queens, NY

Tess Kilwein, MA, Department of Psychology, University of Wyoming, Laramie

Frederick T. L. Leong, PhD, Department of Psychology, Michigan State University, East Lansing

Karina T. Loyo, MEd, Department of Counselor Education and Counseling Psychology, Marquette University, Milwaukee, WI

Kelvin Mariani, BA, Industrial Psychology Doctoral Program, Psychology Department, University of Puerto Rico, Rio Piedras Campus, San Juan

John McCullagh, PhD, Psychology Department, College of Mount Saint Vincent, New York, NY

J. Douglas McDonald, PhD, Department of Psychology, University of North Dakota, Grand Forks

Jeanne Miranda, PhD, Department of Psychiatry and Biobehavioral Sciences at the David Geffen School of Medicine at University of California, Los Angeles; Center for Health Services and Society, Los Angeles, CA

Jeralys Morales, Department of Biology, University of Puerto Rico, Río Piedras Campus, San Juan

Enrique W. Neblett, Jr., PhD, Department of Psychology and Neuroscience, University of North Carolina at Chapel Hill

Tamara Nelson, MPH, Frances L. Hiatt School of Psychology, Clark University, Worcester, MA

Victoria K. Ngo, PhD, RAND Corporation; Department of Psychiatry and Biobehavioral Sciences at the David Geffen School of Medicine at University of California, Los Angeles, Santa Monica

Gabrielle Poon, PhD, Pacific Graduate School of Psychology, Palo Alto University, Palo Alto, CA

Royleen Ross, PhD, Department of Psychology, University of North Dakota, Grand Forks

Emily Sargent, MA, Department of Psychology, University of North Dakota, Grand Forks

Tracy Sbrocco, PhD, Department of Medical & Clinical Psychology, Uniformed Services University of the Health Sciences, Bethesda, MD

Effua E. Sosoo, MA, Department of Psychology and Neuroscience, University of North Carolina at Chapel Hill

Henry A. Willis, MA, Department of Psychology and Neuroscience, University of North Carolina at Chapel Hill

Elizabeth A. Yu, MS, doctoral candidate, Department of Psychology, University of Michigan, Ann Arbor

SERIES FOREWORD

As series editor of the American Psychological Association's (APA's) Division 45 (Society for the Psychological Study of Culture, Ethnicity, and Race) Cultural, Racial, and Ethnic Psychology book series, it is my pleasure to introduce another volume in the series: *Treating Depression, Anxiety, and Stress in Ethnic and Racial Groups: Cognitive Behavioral Approaches*, edited by Edward C. Chang, Christina A. Downey, Jameson K. Hirsch, and Elizabeth A. Yu.

As Paul Pedersen[1] observed, "multiculturalism" is the fourth force in psychotherapy. The first three were psychoanalysis, behaviorism, and humanism. Each had been developed in part to counter the problems and deficits in the previous approach. Behaviorism arose in response to the highly introspective and unscientific foundations of psychoanalysis, and humanist approaches to psychotherapy in turn criticized the mechanistic and simplistic stimulus–response formulations of behaviorism. Pedersen's observations about multiculturalism being the fourth force or latest approach to psychotherapy were predicated on the previous approaches' tendencies to minimize or ignore

---

[1]Pedersen, P. (1998). *Multiculturalism as a fourth force*. New York, NY: Brunner/Mazel.

cultural differences in psychotherapy models. Of course, there was also the "cognitive revolution" within behaviorism that criticized radical behaviorism for having "thrown the baby out with the bath water" by ignoring cognition or the mind. This brings us to the present day, where various forms of cognitive behavior therapy (CBT) approaches to psychotherapy have become the dominant paradigm with the strongest empirical foundations.

Yet, Pedersen's critique remains valid, and the current volume edited by Chang, Downey, Hirsch, and Yu will become part of the fourth force by advancing our understanding of the impact of cultural influences in CBT. The editors of this pioneering volume have assembled experts in CBT who also understand the nuances of culture as they play out in the psychotherapy enterprise. In a sense, this volume is also an answer to Henrich, Heine, and Norenzayan's[2] critique that too much of our scientific bases in psychology has been built on Western, Educated, Industrialized, Rich, Democratic (WEIRD) samples. Whether framed as a biased sample of WEIRD countries or the advent of a new approach to psychotherapy in the fourth force, the underlying issue is that psychology in general, and psychotherapy in particular, have tended to ignore cultural factors.

Since Eysenck's[3] mistaken conclusion that psychotherapy is not effective, the field has come a long way in recognizing the complexity of the issue. The critical research question is now, What works for whom, when, and under what conditions? This volume actively engages that question to examine when and under what conditions would CBT work for culturally diverse samples. Therefore, this new volume is a welcome addition that aligns perfectly with the mission of our series to explore cultural, racial and ethnic factors in the science and practice of psychology. The contributors address not only the relevance and needed adaptations of CBT for specific racial and ethnic groups, but they also do so across a range of disorders from depression to anxiety to stress. In many respects, this volume represents a state-of-the-art review of applications of CBT with racial and ethnic minority groups with a culturally sensitive lens. It will no doubt prove highly useful to both researchers and practitioners in the field of CBT.

For newcomers to the book series, it is worth pointing out that our Cultural, Racial, and Ethnic Psychology series was designed to advance theory, research, and practice regarding this increasingly crucial subdiscipline. It will focus on, but not be limited to, the major racial and ethnic groups in the United States (i.e., African Americans, Latin Americans, Asian

---

[2]Henrich, J., Heine, S. J., & Norenzayan, A. (2010). The weirdest people in the world? *Behavioral and Brain Sciences, 33,* 1–75.

[3]Eysenck, H. J. (1952). The effects of psychotherapy: An evaluation. *Journal of Consulting Psychology, 16,* 319–324.

Americans, and American Indians) and will include books that examine a single racial or ethnic group, as well as books that undertake a comparative approach. The series will also address the full spectrum of related methodological, substantive, and theoretical issues, including topics in behavioral neuroscience, cognitive and developmental psychology, and personality and social psychology. Other volumes in the series will be devoted to cross-disciplinary explorations in the applied realms of clinical psychology and counseling, as well as educational, community, and industrial–organizational psychology. Our goal is to commission state-of-the art volumes in cultural, racial, and ethnic psychology that will be of interest to both practitioners and researchers. The work of recruiting and reviewing proposals for the book series is carried out by members of the editorial board who represent the leading scholars in the field.

Frederick T. L. Leong
Series Editor

FOREWORD

GAYLE Y. IWAMASA

It is a distinct honor to introduce this book to readers, and I thank the editors for the invitation to do so. In reflecting on the work in this volume, I found myself thrilled thinking about the amount of progress that has been made in the field of psychology in the past 30 years. In the late 1980s when I was in graduate school, I found myself realizing that I had embarked on a professional journey where there was little empirical research on the effectiveness of psychotherapy with ethnic minority populations. And that realization didn't even occur to me until after I discovered that because of my own ethnicity, my experience of being a psychologist and therapist was likely going to be different than those of my nonethnic minority classmates. Thank goodness there were pioneer ethnic minority psychologists at the time, whose hard work and mentoring opened doors to those of us starting our psychology careers with the hope of how we could improve mental health services for people of color. I vividly remember reading Sue and Zane's (1987) article "The Role of Culture and Cultural Techniques in Psychotherapy,"[1] and saying to myself, "Yes! This is what I want to work on as a psychologist!" Sue

[1]Sue, S., & Zane, N. (1987). The role of culture and cultural techniques in psychotherapy: A critique and reformulation. *American Psychologist*, *42*, 37–45. http://dx.doi.org/10.1037/0003-066X.42.1.37

and Zane's concepts of the cultural roles of credibility and giving in therapy are still highly relevant in today's world. Their work, and that of other pioneers such as Lillian Comas-Díaz, Spero Manson, Thomas Parham, and Dick Suinn, just to name a few, inspired me, solidified my interests, and confirmed that indeed, one's ethnicity is an important aspect not only of oneself, but of one's work as a psychologist.

Early in my career, I wrote an article that considered the lack of research on culturally diverse populations in the field of behavior therapy at that time (Iwamasa, 1997).[2] In that article, I noted that, as the United States population continued to become more culturally diverse, the demand for mental health services by people of color would also increase and researchers and practitioners of behavior therapy would need to commit to focusing on this neglected component of society. Fast forward to the late 2010s. Recent Substance Abuse and Mental Health Services Administration (SAMHSA) estimates are that people of color currently comprise about one third of the United States population, and will likely become the majority by 2050 (SAMHSA, 2016),[3] confirming the ethnic minority population projections I read about early in my career. Has there been a commitment to increased research on (cognitive) behavior approaches to treatment? This book demonstrates that now there is an actual body of psychological research literature on the major ethnic minority groups in the United States—Asian Americans, Latinos, African Americans, and Native Americans/American Indians—and even enough research and clinical work in cognitive behavior therapy (CBT) with these ethnic minority groups to review and summarize. Clearly, there is a continuing need for mental health providers to be prepared to provide treatment to the growing population of people of color and to ameliorate continued racial and ethnic disparities in mental health care. This book indicates that many researchers in psychology have committed to studying people of color and that their work provides a solid foundation for understanding ethnic minority populations and how CBT approaches have been, and could be, customized and individualized for ethnic minority clients experiencing depression, anxiety, and stress.

The focus of this book on CBT with ethnic minorities is important. CBT, a treatment that is grounded in an individualized and collaborative approach to therapy, emphasizes the importance of one's environmental context in addition to an individual's belief systems and behaviors as major considerations for treatment. Indeed, the theoretical principles of cognitive and behavioral models of understanding human behavior have unmatched

---

[2]Iwamasa, G. Y. (1997). Behavior therapy and a culturally diverse society: Forging an alliance. *Behavior Therapy, 28*, 347–358. http://dx.doi.org/10.1016/S0005-7894(97)80080-9
[3]Substance Abuse and Mental Health Services Administration. (2016). *Racial and ethnic minority populations*. Retrieved from https://www.samhsa.gov/specific-populations/racial-ethnic-minority

empirical support across the globe. While the main focus of most chapters is on reviewing the literature, some of the chapters provide readers with vignettes to illustrate the cultural implications of ethnicity in CBT work. A strength of each chapter is the list of suggestions for future research, which provides our field with many excellent questions and ideas for continued research on improving therapeutic treatments for people of color. Finally, the editors provoke readers to recognize that ethnicity is only one facet of who we are as people; understanding culture in context, appreciating that socioeconomic status is intimately entwined with race and ethnicity, and that at the core, understanding your clients as human beings, are all integral to being an effective therapist, cognitive behavioral or otherwise. I expect that this volume will inspire a new generation of future psychologists to continue this important work.

PREFACE

A few years ago, three of the coeditors of this book proposed (and later published) a volume to examine issues related to research, theory, assessment, and practice at the intersectionality of positive psychology and race and ethnicity. At that same time, we developed another proposal paralleling this framework—namely, a volume that would focus on the intersectionality of cognitive behavior therapy and race and ethnicity. As trained clinical psychologists, it was evident to us that the same lack of attention given to race and ethnicity in positive psychology was also present in one of the most dominant forms of mental health intervention to emerge over the past half-century. Thus, it was our great fortune that Dr. Frederick Leong not only considered both of our proposals but also took an active role in supporting them for inclusion in the American Psychological Association's (APA's) Cultural, Racial, and Ethnic Psychology Book Series. We are greatly indebted to both him and to Susan Reynolds at APA for their support throughout the process of publishing both our volumes in this series. We thank them for their trust in our vision of greater inclusivity and understanding.

A note for the reader: Our decision to put a spotlight on cognitive behavioral strategies should not suggest we necessarily believe such strategies represent optimal approaches to working with diverse populations. Cognitive behavioral approaches have become compelling, if not dominant, in the models, measures, and treatments they have proffered to both scientists and practitioners interested in promoting positive mental health. But we must all remind ourselves that even these promising and robust approaches, including those presented in this volume, are themselves predicated on assumptions and values that may not necessarily map harmoniously or indigenously onto those that foster meaningful living across members of different ethnoracial groups. Accordingly, it is important for readers to not only consider how cognitive behavioral strategies can be adapted or modified to work better for diverse ethnoracial groups but also to consider when other models and strategies might prove as useful or meaningful in addition to cognitive behavioral models and strategies. Overall, we hope this volume helps facilitate greater and more complex discourse, research, and practice among practitioners, researchers, and scholars interested in identifying effective ways to promote positive mental health for all individuals, regardless of race or ethnicity.

Last, we would like to thank the wonderful contributors to this volume for sharing not only their clinical wisdom and insights with us but also their passion for finding ways to positively affect those who are often disenfranchised or not well-represented in the scientific enterprise of understanding and treating mental health problems. We hope readers of this volume will be inspired to learn from these expert contributors and gain a greater appreciation for the complexity, inclusivity, and connectedness between the models that sometimes guide us, the measures that sometimes define us, and the treatments we hope always promote us.

Treating **Depression, Anxiety,** and **Stress** in *Ethnic* and *Racial Groups*

INTRODUCTION: COGNITIVE BEHAVIORAL MODELS, MEASURES, AND TREATMENTS IN ETHNORACIAL GROUPS

EDWARD C. CHANG, CHRISTINA A. DOWNEY,
JAMESON K. HIRSCH, AND ELIZABETH A. YU

As history has repeatedly shown, the complex process of science, like all human endeavors, changes as the values and visions of society change across time (Kuhn, 1962). Thus, it should not be surprising that systematic efforts to understand and treat psychological problems experienced by individuals have themselves changed considerably over the past century. In the modern era, one of the most dominant paradigms to emerge for understanding and treating psychological problems has been the cognitive behavioral paradigm.

THE RISE OF THE COGNITIVE BEHAVIORAL PARADIGM IN MODERN DAY PSYCHOLOGY

In historical context, the behavioral paradigm emerged in response and reaction to earlier psychoanalytic models that both pioneered and influenced the way mental health professionals treated psychological problems.

http://dx.doi.org/10.1037/0000091-001
Treating Depression, Anxiety, and Stress in Ethnic and Racial Groups: Cognitive Behavioral Approaches,
E. C. Chang, C. A. Downey, J. K. Hirsch, and E. A. Yu (Editors)

In contrast to the use of highly subjective techniques like introspection, free association, and dream analysis, the initiation of behavioral therapies in the early to mid-1900s was founded on the principles of operant and classical conditioning, which posited the learning of overt behaviors through processes involving conditioning and reinforcement. Within the behavioral framework was the basic assumption that the causes of psychological disturbances were rooted in learning and the contexts that maintained those maladaptive behavior patterns.

However, by the 1970s, psychology, along with other disciplines (e.g., philosophy, neuroscience, anthropology, linguistics, computer science), experienced developments in what would later be known as the *cognitive revolution* (Miller, 2003), the result of a collective synergy among multidisciplinary efforts that emphasized the role of cognition and cognitive processes in how individuals engaged with their world (Robins, Gosling, & Craik, 1999). In many ways, this change represented a return to psychology's founding mission. Specifically, the scientific understanding of how the content and function of human consciousness defined human experience had been the original aim of the new "mind science" as conceptualized by its earliest pioneers (Downey & Henderson, 2017). Within psychology, the cognitive approach focused largely on the individual's cognitions, such as beliefs, attributions, expectations, or appraisals, and psychological problems were viewed as being caused by maladaptive thoughts and dysfunctional thought processes associated with the self, world, or future.

During this time, the behavioral and cognitive paradigms remained somewhat separate from each other. However, by the late 1970s, behaviorists and cognitive psychologists began to recognize a growing need to integrate these two conceptually disparate approaches to garner a richer and more meaningful understanding of human behavior. One substantive example of this recognition was the development of Bandura's (1977, 1986) triadic reciprocal determinism model that implicated the important and dynamic interplay between behavior, cognitions, and environment. Indeed, so compelling was the pressure to identify with the positive value of integrating behavioral and cognitive approaches that the Association for Advancement of Behavioral Therapies established in 1966 was later renamed in 2005 as the Association for Behavioral and Cognitive Therapies. Alternatively, theories and therapies that were once almost exclusively cognitive evolved to increasingly incorporate behavioral processes and principles, as evidenced by the rebranding of rational-emotive therapy (Ellis, 1962) to rational emotive behavior therapy 3 decades later (Ellis, 1995).

In turn, the emergence of integrative theories that examined the confluence of behavioral and cognitive factors on psychological problems helped give rise to treatments that pointed to targeting and changing both behavioral and cognitive elements, namely, cognitive behavior therapies (for a comprehensive historical review, see Dobson & Dozois, 2010). Cognitive behavior therapies include a diverse set of therapeutic techniques whose common aim is to improve psychological functioning through the modification of beliefs, perceptions, knowledge, and/or emotional experience, as well as the behaviors that accompany them in mental health conditions. As cognitive behavioral theories were developed and tested in practice, they, in turn, fueled further refinements to help mental health professionals identify those strategies and techniques that were both high in efficacy and efficiency. So useful have cognitive behavioral approaches become in the treatment of a spectrum of psychological problems, that a large proportion of practitioners readily identify themselves as aligned with a cognitive behavioral orientation (Norcross & Rogan, 2013). Indeed, with extensive empirical support over the past several decades, cognitive behavioral models, measures, and treatments (CBMMTs) have been widely used to conceptualize, assess for, and treat commonly experienced psychological problems, including depression, anxiety, and stress. That said, however, the validity and utility of cognitive behavioral approaches for working with ethnoracially diverse populations, although promising, have gone largely unexamined (Hofmann, 2006; Iwamasa, 1996).

ON THE NEED TO INTEGRATE ETHNORACIAL FACTORS IN COGNITIVE BEHAVIORAL MODELS, MEASURES, AND TREATMENTS: REMINDING OURSELVES THAT SPECIFICITY ALWAYS MATTERS

Despite the well-established use of CBMMTs for treating psychological problems, we were deeply troubled by a dearth of CBMMTs targeted for use with diverse ethnoracial groups (e.g., Asian Americans, Latin Americans, African Americans, American Indians). We found this problematic for a number of reasons. First, Asian Americans, Latin Americans, African Americans, and American Indians represent approximately 40% of the current United States population, and according to projected rates for 2060 by the U.S. Census Bureau, these groups will make up more than half of the U.S. population (Colby & Ortman, 2015).

Second, sociocultural factors such as ethnoracial discrimination and acculturative stress pose different trajectories of risk for the development of psychological problems compared with risk factors affecting non-Hispanic Whites. As cognitive behavioral approaches were developed from within a Western cultural context and strongly predicated on European American values (Hall, Hong, Zane, & Meyer, 2011; Hays, 2009), it is likely that these approaches may not be as useful for non-European American groups that adhere to other cultural values and visions.

Third, although ethnoracial disparities in mental health services have decreased over the years, findings from a meta-analysis of over 130 research studies and over 4 million clients found worrisome racial differences in mental health service use. For example, Asian Americans were just 51% as likely as White European Americans to use mental health resources. In addition, Hispanics/Latinos were only 25% as likely as Whites to use such resources, and African Americans were a mere 21% as likely to use mental health resources as Whites were (Smith & Trimble, 2016). Possible reasons for why this disparity prevails may include how many of the available empirically supported treatments, such as cognitive behavioral interventions, are not as effective for individuals from diverse ethnoracial groups. Also, the conceptualization of their experiences with mental health concerns is not effectively captured by the available traditional, nonculturally adapted cognitive behavioral models and assessment measures of psychological problems. Last, but not least, the dearth of CBMMTs for working with diverse ethnoracial groups is inconsistent with a central tenet underlying cognitive behavior therapy (CBT)—namely, the importance of appreciating the specifics of the complex clinical situation. This emphasis on clinical precision is not limited to an appreciation of the particulars of the presenting psychological problem (e.g., phenomenology, duration, severity) but also includes an appreciation of the particular characteristics embodied and brought forward by the client (e.g., race, culture, language, and socioeconomic background; Flaskerud, 1986; López, 1989). Yet, the inclusion of ethnoracial considerations has remained limited, if not disconnected, from the mainstream of CBMMTs (Cardemil, 2010), paralleling similar disparate patterns evidenced across areas in psychology and psychiatry (Chang, Downey, Hirsch, & Lin, 2016; Chang & Kwon, 2014).

OVERVIEW OF POPULATIONS OF FOCUS

It is important as we open this volume to share key factual details about each racial/ethnic group being discussed within so that the findings presented can be contextualized appropriately. Many of our contributing authors added their perspectives to these descriptions as noted.

Asian Americans

The 2010 United States Census revealed that between 2000 and 2010, the population of Asian Americans grew more quickly than any other racial group in the nation (Hoeffel, Rastogi, Kim, & Shahid, 2012). According to the Census assessment, Asian Americans include any U.S. citizen of Chinese, Japanese, Korean, Filipino, Vietnamese, Cambodian, Thai, Asian Indian, Pakistani, Native Hawaiian, Guamanian or Chamorro, Samoan, or other Asian or Pacific Islander background. Clearly, this is an extremely diverse group of individuals, many of whom come from nations within East Asia, South Asia, and the Pacific Island regions, which have historically seen themselves as utterly distinct and sometimes even as enemies. These diverse cultures and histories make speaking about this group as monolithic a challenge and have crucial implications for mental health treatment (Abe-Kim et al., 2007). However, the American approach to racial classification typically overlooks such differences in determining the size, geographic distribution, and needs of these individuals across the country.

The census report on Asian Americans placed the official population of this group at 14.7 million in 2010, up from 10.2 million in 2000 (an increase of 43%). When counting individuals who listed Asian as among their racial group memberships, the total population was 17.3 million, 46% higher than 10 years prior, accounting for 5.6% of the total U.S. population (Hoeffel et al., 2012). By 2015, growth had accelerated again, as this group had grown to 20.4 million. Chinese (24%), Asian Indian (20%), and Filipino (19%) groups represent the largest proportions of Asian Americans by nationality (Pew Research Center, 2017). This explosive population growth was most apparent in the American West, with nearly half of all Asian Americans residing in this region (and about a third of all Asians residing in California alone; Hoeffel et al., 2012). Because this group is largely growing due to immigration rather than birth, the median age of Asian Americans is older than Latin Americans (36.3 years vs. 28.1 years; Pew Research Center, 2014). By 2055, it is projected that Asian Americans will surpass Latin Americans to become the largest immigrant group in the country (Pew Research Center, 2017).

Generally speaking, Asian Americans fare relatively well economically, educationally, and socially. For example, their median household income is $73,060, 36% higher than the national average; their poverty rate is 3% lower than average at 12.1%; and just over half of Asian Americans hold a bachelor's degree or higher (20% above the national average). However, these outcomes vary radically by national origin, with certain groups (e.g., Asian Indians, Filipinos, Japanese) experiencing substantially better outcomes than others (e.g., Bangladeshi, Nepalese, Burmese). This also relates to the means by which Asian Americans become citizens; as a population that is more immigrant than native born, well-being is largely determined by the circumstances under which these individuals came to the United States. Thus, Asians arriving as refugees are much more challenged than those arriving as educated individuals seeking high-level opportunities and often lack access to sufficient medical and mental health care as a result. This may explain in some part why mental health service use is lower in Asian American populations than in the U.S. population at large (Abe-Kim et al., 2007).

Latin Americans

Latino is an umbrella term that includes individuals with heritage from any Spanish-speaking country in North, Central, or South America, excluding European countries. The Latino population is the largest minority group in the United States, numbering more than 53 million, or 17.1% of the U.S. population, in 2013 (Pew Research Center, 2013). The Latino American population comes from every country in Latin America, with Mexican Americans making up the largest group (64.1% of all U.S. Latinos) and Puerto Ricans (9.5% of all U.S. Latinos) the second largest, followed by Cuban and Salvadorans, each making up less than 4% of the Latino population (as contributed by Ngo & Miranda, Chapter 2, this volume). As noted by Bernal, Adames, Mariani, and Morales (Chapter 6, this volume), the Latino population is expected to reach 128.8 million by 2060, when it will constitute 31% of the total U.S. population. Therefore, the Latino community is currently one of the fastest growing ethnic or racial groups in the United States. Of the 54 million Latinos in the United States as of 2013, 32.36% are under the ages of 18, 26.42% are between the ages of 18 and 33, 22.29% are between 34 and 39, 14.45% are between 50 and 68, and 4.47% are 69 years old and older (Pew Research Center, 2014). Indeed, this diverse population is expected to grow exponentially, from a minority to probably a numerical majority in the United States.

Although many Latinos share a heritage in terms of language, culture, and religion, there is also a great deal of diversity in terms of race (White, African, American Indian, and Asian), and national origin. In addition, history of migration to the United States and the experience of conquest and submission are important to consider, as in the examples of Mexico and Puerto Rico (Bernal & Enchautegui-de-Jesús, 1994). In another example, many Central Americans fled their homelands because of guerrilla warfare, counterinsurgency activities, and other war-related conditions (Lichter & Johnson, 2009). As such, themes of loss and trauma, as well as the stress of acculturation and poverty, are particularly important considerations for Central Americans. Undocumented immigrants have particularly difficult social and economic conditions.

Ngo and Miranda (Chapter 2, this volume) add that because 40% of the Latino American community is foreign born, Latino health is often shaped by factors such as low-income status, language and cultural barriers, lack of access to preventive care, lack of health insurance, and citizenship. For example, Latinos continue to have the highest uninsured rates of any racial or ethnic group within the United States and account for nearly a third of the total nonelderly uninsured population. Although the Affordable Care Act (ACA) has been improving health care coverage by 11.8% for Latinos, noncitizens, including lawfully present and undocumented immigrants, who make up nearly half the uninsured Latino population, will continue to face eligibility restrictions for health coverage under the ACA (Uberoi, Finegold, & Gee, 2016). These sociopolitical factors are critical access barriers to health care for the Latino community and therefore are important considerations when providing mental health services.

Despite the heterogeneity in their migration history and sociocultural context, Latinos as a whole share certain sociodemographic characteristics related to their minority status; language access; exposure to poverty and adversities associated with poverty, such as inadequate housing; and a high rate of single-parent households. As immigrants, they also face discrimination and racism in addition to the acculturative stress of adjusting to the U.S. majority culture. These contextual factors shape the living context and mental health needs of this diverse community and may affect the expression of depression and its assessment and treatment.

African Americans

The Black or African American population of the United States includes individuals whose ancestry traces to the continent of Africa or the Afro Caribbean islands who self-identify as part of this racial and ethnic group. Although the total U.S. population grew by 9.7% between 2000 and 2010, the Black population grew by 15% to a total of 42 million people (13.6% of the U.S. population; Rastogi, Johnson, Hoeffel, & Drewery, 2011). Within the United States, the majority of Black people are descended from enslaved West African people brought to this continent during the colonial period; however, Black immigration to the United States has increased significantly in the last 30 years, such that now a record 3.8 million Blacks in the United States are foreign-born (Pew Research Center, 2015). African Americans are a relatively young population, with over 40% being under the age of 26 and only 10% over the age of 65 (compared with 30% and 17% of Whites, respectively; Duckett & Artiga, 2013). African Americans are largely concentrated in the South, with 55% of these individuals living in this geographic region. Thus, they make up a full 20% of the Southern population but only between 6% and 13% of the population in other regions, and they are further concentrated in every region in large metropolitan areas. African Americans are more likely than any other racial or ethnic group to live within the limits of large cities (rather than in suburbs, exurbs, or rural areas; Rastogi, Johnson, Hoeffel, & Drewery, 2011), making this group the most likely to experience the challenges of high population density, urban decay, and neighborhood gentrification.

Disparities in education, income, wealth, and personal health between Whites and Blacks in the United States have existed since the country's founding. However, since the Great Recession of 2008, Blacks have seen the erosion of indices of well-being relative to Whites, with their wealth gap having been set back to levels not seen in the United States since the early 1990s. Holding wealth that is 1/13th that of Whites, Blacks experience the greatest measured wealth disparity by race in U.S. society (Kochhar & Fry, 2014). About one in four African Americans lives in poverty, a rate much higher than the national rate of 14.3%. High rates of poverty among Blacks can be found in all regions of the United States, with several states across the Upper Plains and Midwest and in the South evidencing poverty rates of 30% or more among Blacks (Macartney, Bishaw, & Fontenot, 2013).

African Americans are overrepresented in the uninsured population generally, and uninsured rates for Blacks are actually highest in states with the highest proportion of Blacks as residents (i.e., in the South). For example, only 9% of Blacks in Delaware are uninsured, whereas 30% of Blacks in Louisiana are (Duckett & Artiga, 2013). Accordingly, very good or excellent self-reported health among Blacks lags behind that of Whites by about 5%, and significantly higher obesity, hypertension, and mortality rates are also in evidence for Blacks (Kochanek, Murphy, Xu, & Tejada-Vera, 2016). With so many challenges, it is not surprising that mental health needs among African Americans are great; rates of depression and anxiety are high in this population (estimated at 36.9% and 66.6% of Black psychiatric patients, respectively). However, access to mental health care is an ongoing issue, particularly care aligned with minimum recommendations for effectiveness (Hines, Cooper, & Shi, 2017).

Native Americans

Boyd and Hunsaker (Chapter 12, this volume) describe the demographics of American Indian and Alaska Native (AI/AN) people as a proportionally small but extremely diverse group. Approximately 5.4 million people, or 1.7% of the total U.S. population, self-identify as AI/AN (Norris, Vines, & Hoeffel, 2012). Approximately 60% of American Indian people in the United States currently live in metropolitan areas, with 22% on tribal reservations or territories and the greatest concentrations residing in the West, Southwest, and Midwest (Norris, Vines, & Hoeffel, 2012; U.S. Department of the Interior, Indian Affairs, 2015). Young people under the age of 18 make up about 30% of the AI/AN population (U.S. Department of Health & Human Services Office of Minority Health, 2012). AI/ANs are a heterogeneous group: There are currently 566 federally recognized AI/AN groups in the United States, with more than 100 additional state-recognized tribes. Each tribal group is unique, with its own distinct culture, language, traditions, histories, and identities. Almost 200 different Native languages are still spoken in the United States (U.S. Department of the Interior, Indian Affairs, 2015), but the number of fluent speakers and the level of acculturation to Western culture varies widely across tribal groups.

McDonald, Ross, Kilwein, and Sargent (Chapter 4, this volume) note that before European contact, the indigenous population was as high as 18 million and consisted of at least 600 different tribes (Graham, 2002). Decades of war and disease decimated the Native American population by the late 1800s (McDonald & Chaney, 2003). The Native population has since significantly increased from an estimated low of 248,253 in 1890 to around 2.9 million, or 0.9% of the total American population (U.S. Census Bureau, 2011).

One third of American Indians live in poverty. The annual median income for Native Americans is estimated at $35,192, in comparison with $50,502 for the nation as a whole (U.S. Census Bureau, 2012). As McCullagh and Gray note in Chapter 8 of this volume, AI/ANs are more likely to struggle with homelessness and unemployment, live in substandard housing, and have lower levels of educational attainment (Freeman & Fox, 2005) than other ethnic groups. AI/ANs also tend to be uninsured at higher rates compared with the general population, which results in reduced physical and mental health care use (Gone & Trimble, 2012; Zuckerman, Haley, Roubideaux, & Lillie-Blanton, 2004). For example, in 2015, over one in five American Indian people were without health care coverage (Centers for Disease Control and Prevention, 2015). Many of the communities in which AI/ANs live are characterized by poor infrastructure and extremely limited access to mental health services. The multiple social problems, minimal access to mental health resources, poverty, and legacy of historical trauma are all believed to contribute to contemporary mental health disparities among AI/ANs. AI/ANs are more likely to suffer from alcohol abuse and dependence and posttraumatic stress disorder (PTSD), and to have a greater prevalence of conduct disorders among children and adolescents, higher suicide rates among adolescents, and greater likelihood of experiencing physical and sexual violence, compared with the general population (Beals et al., 2005; Gone & Trimble, 2012; Gray & McCullagh, 2014; Indian Health Service, 2011; Wahab & Olson, 2004).

OVERVIEW OF THIS VOLUME

To meet the needs of the predicted change in the diversity of our society and to prevent the disparity in mental health services for members of ethnoracial groups from growing larger, it is essential to improve evidence-supported models, measures, and treatments by understanding how they work for specific ethnoracial groups. It was from this realization that we developed this volume. The book is divided into three main sections, each focusing on a robust concern for mental health treatment—namely, working with individuals experiencing clinically significant symptoms of depression, anxiety, or stress. We focused on these conditions because they represent some of the most common conditions for which individuals seek mental health treatment. Within each section, separate chapters are devoted to the discussion of depression, anxiety, or stress specific to Asian Americans, Latin Americans, African Americans, and American Indians.

Part I focuses on CBMMTs of depressive disorders. In Chapter 1, Hwang, Ho, Chan, and Hong examine CBMMTs for depressive disorders among Asian Americans. Focusing on findings from large epidemiological surveys, the important challenges to consider in conceptualizing and assessing for depression in Asian Americans are discussed. Furthermore, Hwang et al. review methods of assessing depression in Asian American populations and note the dearth of research examining treatment efficacy with Asian Americans. The chapter concludes with notes on the importance of culturally adapting CBT and provides suggestions for future clinical and research directions on how to best culturally adapt CBMMTs.

In Chapter 2, Ngo and Miranda discuss CBMMTs for treating depressive disorders among Latin Americans. They discuss depression prevalence and risk factors, as well as cultural-specific expressions of mental health distress. Also central to the chapter is the discussion of validated measures of depression for use with Latino Americans and noted cautions for interpretations of assessment results. Ngo and Miranda end the chapter with a review of extant cognitive behavioral models and interventions for Latino Americans and note that although CBMMTs should take into account the diverse individual differences of Latino American culture, interventions and measurements that have been common to European American, White populations appear to be largely effective for Latinos.

In Chapter 3, Neblett, Sosoo, Willis, Bernard, and Bae discuss CBMMTs for depressive disorders in African Americans. The authors begin with an overview of depressive disorders among this population and note the factors (e.g., exposure to racism) that may contribute to greater risk for experiences of depression and depressive disorders among African Americans despite lower prevalence rates of depression according to epidemiological studies. Neblett et al. comment on the shortage of cognitive behavioral models specific to understanding depressive disorders in African Americans and that take into account the sociocultural characteristics, social, and/or cultural values and perspectives of African Americans. The authors provide distinctions between, and examples of, traditional, culturally adapted, and culturally tailored cognitive behavioral models of depressive disorders for African Americans. Furthermore, they review common assessment measures and treatments of depressive disorders for use with African Americans.

Finally, in Chapter 4, McDonald, Ross, Kilwein, and Sargent examine CBMMTs for depressive disorders in American Indians. Having an understanding of how wellness, body, mind, and spirit are conceptualized within the American Indian population is imperative for providing and/or creating culturally congruent measures and treatments of depression for use with American Indians. To illustrate the important considerations when conceptualizing, measuring, and treating depression in American Indians, McDonald and his colleagues provide a vignette in the chapter to show cultural adaptations to traditional cognitive behavioral approaches for depression and argue for the importance of future research and assessment to ensure the effectiveness of culturally adapted CBMMTs of depression.

Part II focuses on the review of CBMMTs of anxiety disorders. In Chapter 5, Hong examines CBMMTs for anxiety disorders in Asian Americans, with a primary focus on the sociocultural influences and maintenance factors related to social anxiety. Hong describes cognitive behavioral models for understanding anxiety disorders in Asian Americans and notes how existing models of anxiety disorders may not take into account sociocultural influences. The author reviews cognitive behavioral measures of anxiety disorders in Asian Americans and describes cognitive behavioral treatments of anxiety disorders for Asian Americans. Given the dearth of data, Hong argues that there is no clear understanding of which cultural adaptations would be most useful for anxiety disorders in Asian Americans; the chapter ends with a discussion of possible future directions for CBMMTs for anxiety disorders in Asian Americans.

In Chapter 6, Bernal, Adames, Mariani, and Morales review CBMMTs for anxiety disorders in Latino Americans. In this chapter, Bernal and colleagues examine through a systematic review of the literature whether available treatments for anxiety that are delivered to Latinos in the United States are effective. They review the CBT models and treatment manuals used in the identified studies from their systematic review and also review cognitive behavioral assessment instruments for use with Latinos. Bernal et al. note that although cognitive behavioral treatments for anxiety appear to be effective for the treatment of anxiety conditions in Latinos, effectiveness may depend on a number of factors (e.g., acculturation more research is needed to test the effectiveness of CBT in this population).

In Chapter 7, Carter and Sbrocco examine CBMMTs for anxiety disorders in African Americans. The authors discuss traditional cognitive behavioral models of anxiety disorders as well as cognitive behavioral models of anxiety that have included cultural influences on anxiety for African Americans.

The authors describe useful and validated measures of general anxiety experiences as well as specific anxiety disorders for African Americans, and they also note some inconsistencies in the efficacy of other measures of anxiety. Furthermore, Carter and Sbrocco discuss findings from treatment outcome studies to examine whether extant cognitive behavioral treatments are effective for treating anxiety among African Americans.

In Chapter 8, McCullagh and Gray review CBMMTs for anxiety disorders in American Indian and Alaska Natives. The authors begin with a discussion of the context of mental health concerns among American Indian and Alaskan Natives. They discuss culturally congruent models of treatment and healing through which cognitive behavioral models could be adapted. McCullagh and Gray report on appropriate assessment measures of anxiety for use with American Indians and Alaska Natives, as well as their limitations. The authors note some important considerations for how clinicians can establish stronger therapeutic relationships with American Indian and Alaska Native clients, as well as how to integrate important cultural factors and values into treatment.

The focus of Part III is on CBMMTs for stress. In the first chapter of this part, Chapter 9, Chu, Batchelder, and Poon review CBMMTs for stress in Asian Americans. The authors begin with a brief overview of stress itself, stress as it relates to Asian Americans, and barriers to mental health treatment use by Asian Americans. Main stress theories and models are presented, followed by a review of various cultural factors and how they may influence or be valuable to incorporate into existing stress theories. Taking into account the number of cultural variables that contribute to stress and affect the expression of stress and the coping methods used by Asian Americans, the authors comment on the applicability of cognitive behavioral treatments for stress in these groups. Chu et al. provide some useful cultural considerations and adaptations to cognitive behavioral approaches to reduce barriers to seeking or engaging in treatment.

In Chapter 10, Cardemil, Edwards, Nelson, and Loyo write about CBMMTs for stress in Latino Americans. This chapter begins with an overview of stress in Latinos and describes current as well as historical contexts that may contribute to stress in this population. Cardemil and colleagues address the models and theories used to understand PTSD and acculturative stress in Latinos. They review useful assessment measures of PTSD and acculturative stress. The chapter concludes with some future directions for CBMMT for stress in Latinos—namely, the need for more research to fill gaps in the literature and the development and evaluation of assessment measures and interventions for stress in Latinos.

In Chapter 11, Greer, Brondolo, Amuzu, and Kaur review CBMMTs for stress in African Americans. The authors begin with an overview of the racial disparities in stress exposure that then contribute to disparities in other life areas. To conceptualize stress, the authors discuss the relationship between racism exposure and stress and describe useful measurements of race-related stress. Cognitive conceptualizations of stress that take into account how individuals within the African American community appraise threat and harm are reviewed. Greer et al. address benefits and limitations to cultural adaptations of cognitive behavioral treatments and discuss alternative treatment approaches to CBTs (e.g., meditation, yoga) for stress reduction in African Americans.

In the last chapter of Part III, Chapter 12, Boyd and Hunsaker discuss CBMMTs for stress in American Indians and Alaska Natives. The authors first briefly describe the AI/AN population, the stressors they face, important health disparities, and the historical trauma that contributes to the contextual understanding of stress in this population. After describing general stress and models of stress, Boyd and Hunsaker provide more detailed information on specific stressors for AI/ANs (e.g., psychological strains of historical trauma, environmental stressors). In addition, the importance of addressing stress in relation to other health concerns prevalent in the AI/AN population (e.g., diabetes, cardiovascular disease) is noted.

In Chapter 13, we conclude the book with an overview of common themes and concepts addressed in previous chapters. Specifically, in the interaction of culture with context, factors that are important to consider in relation to CBMMTs for racial and ethnic groups may be factors such as acculturation, language, cultural history, historical trauma, and stigma of mental illness. We argue for the importance of understanding the context and specific circumstances involved with the expression and experience of depression disorders, anxiety disorders, and stress disorders in the groups of focus for the book. In addition, we discuss the interaction of race and ethnicity with social class that may influence access to treatment and, particularly, culturally sensitive treatments that, in turn, may add to the mental health disparities that were mentioned in the previous chapters. Finally, we raise considerations and challenges for the notion that underlying cognitive behavioral concepts may not always adequately correspond to concepts of depression, anxiety, and stress in diverse groups.

CONCLUDING THOUGHTS

Although this volume focuses on cognitive behavioral approaches, we are mindful that there are many other approaches to conceptualizing, measuring, and treating psychological problems (Rotheram-Borus, Swendeman, & Becker, 2014). We are also mindful of the dangers associated with ascribing privilege to any singular theory or paradigm for understanding human behavior (Scarr, 1985) because this may hinder the development of innovative theories and paradigms in the near future (Govrin, 2014). That said, it was more than 20 years ago in one of the earliest publications to highlight the need to consider ethnoracial factors in applying CBT that Hays (1995) provided the following forethought:

> As the number of psychologists of minority cultures and groups increases, it is likely that cognitive-behavior therapy will become increasingly attentive to cultural influences and minority groups. The attention will no doubt lead to the recognition of an even more diverse range of helping strategies. Moreover, it should contribute to the improved effectiveness of cognitive-behavior therapy with specific groups of people whose mental health needs have been neglected. (p. 313)

In this context, we hope that this volume can play an instrumental role in helping all mental health professionals, regardless of their ethnoracial status and background, to find value and guidance when working with diverse adults, and we hope that researchers and practitioners will come to value the rich spectrum of CBMMTs provided here. This would include finding ways to apply some of these situated conceptualizations and techniques to ultimately help facilitate greater growth and meaning for all individuals seeking to improve the conditions and contexts of their lives. Finally, we hope that readers of this volume will also appreciate the wealth of opportunities to cross-fertilize the diverse ideas, methods, and techniques presented herein as we move toward a society that is becoming increasingly rich in diversity and complexity.

REFERENCES

Abe-Kim, J., Takeuchi, D. T., Hong, S., Zane, N., Sue, S., Spencer, M. S., . . . Alegría, M. (2007). Use of mental health-related services among immigrant and US-born Asian Americans: Results from the National Latino and Asian American Study. *American Journal of Public Health, 97*, 91–98. http://dx.doi.org/10.2105/AJPH.2006.098541

Bandura, A. (1977). Self-efficacy: Toward a unifying theory of behavioral change. *Psychological Review, 84*, 191–215. http://dx.doi.org/10.1037/0033-295X.84.2.191

Bandura, A. (1986). *Social foundations of thought and action: A social cognitive theory.* Englewood Cliffs, NJ: Prentice-Hall.

Beals, J., Manson, S. M., Whitesell, N. R., Spicer, P., Novins, D. K., & Mitchell, C. M. (2005). Prevalence of *DSM–IV* disorders and attendant help-seeking in 2 American Indian reservation populations. *Archives of General Psychiatry, 62*, 99–108. http://dx.doi.org/10.1001/archpsyc.62.1.99

Bernal, G., & Enchautegui-de-Jesús, N. (1994). Latinos and Latinas in community psychology: A review of the literature. *American Journal of Community Psychology, 22,* 531–557. http://dx.doi.org/10.1007/BF02506892

Cardemil, E. V. (2010). Cultural adaptations to empirically supported treatments: A research agenda. *The Scientific Review of Mental Health Practice, 7,* 8–21.

Centers for Disease Control and Prevention. (2015). *Summary Health Statistics: National Health Interview Survey, 2015.* Retrieved from https://ftp.cdc.gov/pub/Health_Statistics/NCHS/NHIS/SHS/2015_SHS_Table_P-11.pdf

Chang, E. C., Downey, C. A., Hirsch, J. K., & Lin, N. J. (Eds.). (2016). *Positive psychology in racial and ethnic groups: Theory, research, and practice.* Washington, DC: American Psychological Association. http://dx.doi.org/10.1037/14799-000

Chang, E. C., & Kwon, P. (2014). Special issue on psychopathology in Asians and the DSM–5: Culture matters. *Asian Journal of Psychiatry, 7,* 66–67. http://dx.doi.org/10.1016/j.ajp.2013.12.001

Colby, S. L., & Ortman, J. M. (2015). *Projections of the size and composition of the U.S. Population: 2014 to 2060: Population estimates and projections.* Retrieved from https://www.census.gov/content/dam/Census/library/publications/2015/demo/p25-1143.pdf

Dobson, K. S., & Dozois, D. J. A. (2010). Historical and philosophical bases of the cognitive-behavioral therapies. In K. S. Dobson (Ed.), *Handbook of cognitive-behavioral therapies* (3rd ed., pp. 3–38). New York, NY: Guilford Press.

Downey, C. A., & Henderson, R. E. (2017). Speculation, conceptualization, or evidence? A history of positive psychology. In C. R. Snyder, S. J. Lopez, L. M. Edwards, & S. C. Marques (Eds.), *The Oxford handbook of positive psychology* (3rd ed.). New York, NY: Oxford University Press. Advance online publication. http://dx.doi.org/10.1093/oxfordhb/9780199396511.013.57

Duckett, P., & Artiga, S. (2013). *Health coverage for the Black population today and under the Affordable Care Act.* Retrieved from the Henry J. Kaiser Family Foundation website: https://www.kff.org/disparities-policy/fact-sheet/health-coverage-for-the-black-population-today-and-under-the-affordable-care-act/

Ellis, A. (1962). *Reason and emotion in psychotherapy.* New York, NY: Lyle Stuart.

Ellis, A. (1995). Changing rational-emotive therapy (RET) to rational emotive behavior therapy (REBT). *Journal of Rational-Emotive & Cognitive-Behavior Therapy, 13,* 85–89. http://dx.doi.org/10.1007/BF02354453

Flaskerud, J. H. (1986). The effects of culture-compatible intervention on the utilization of mental health services by minority clients. *Community Mental Health Journal, 22,* 127–141. http://dx.doi.org/10.1007/BF00754551

Freeman, C., & Fox, M. (2005). *Status and trends in the education of American Indians and Alaska Natives.* Washington, DC: National Center for Education Statistics.

Gone, J. P., & Trimble, J. E. (2012). American Indian and Alaska Native mental health: Diverse perspectives on enduring disparities. *Annual Review of Clinical Psychology, 8,* 131–160. http://dx.doi.org/10.1146/annurev-clinpsy-032511-143127

Govrin, A. (2014). The vices and virtues of monolithic thought in the evolution of psychotherapy. *Journal of Psychotherapy Integration, 24*, 79–90. http://dx.doi.org/10.1037/a0035972

Graham, T. L. C. (2002). Using reasons for living to connect to American Indian healing traditions. *Journal of Sociology and Social Welfare, 29*, 55–75.

Gray, J. S., & McCullagh, J. A. (2014). Suicide in Indian country: The continuing epidemic in rural Native American communities. *Journal of Rural Mental Health, 38*, 79–86. http://dx.doi.org/10.1037/rmh0000017

Hall, G. C. N., Hong, J. J., Zane, N. W. S., & Meyer, O. L. (2011). Culturally competent treatments for Asian Americans: The relevance of mindfulness and acceptance-based psychotherapies. *Clinical Psychology: Science and Practice, 18*, 215–231. http://dx.doi.org/10.1111/j.1468-2850.2011.01253.x

Hays, P. A. (1995). Multicultural applications of cognitive-behavior therapy. *Professional Psychology: Research and Practice, 26*, 309–315. http://dx.doi.org/10.1037/0735-7028.26.3.309

Hays, P. A. (2009). Integrating evidence-based practice, cognitive-behavior therapy, and multicultural therapy: Ten steps for culturally competent practice. *Professional Psychology: Research and Practice, 40*, 354–360. http://dx.doi.org/10.1037/a0016250

Hines, A. L., Cooper, L. A., & Shi, L. (2017). Racial and ethnic differences in mental healthcare utilization consistent with potentially effective care: The role of patient preferences. *General Hospital Psychiatry, 46*, 14–19. http://dx.doi.org/10.1016/j.genhosppsych.2017.02.002

Hoeffel, E. M., Rastogi, S., Kim, M. O., & Shahid, H. (2012). *The Asian population: 2010*. Retrieved from https://www.census.gov/prod/cen2010/briefs/c2010br-11.pdf

Hofmann, S. G. (2006). The importance of culture in cognitive and behavioral practice. *Cognitive and Behavioral Practice, 13*, 243–245. http://dx.doi.org/10.1016/j.cbpra.2006.07.001

Indian Health Service. (2011). *American Indian/Alaska Native behavioral health briefing book*. Retrieved from https://www.ihs.gov/newsroom/includes/themes/newihstheme/display_objects/documents/201_Letters/AIANBHBriefingBook.pdf

Iwamasa, G. Y. (1996). Introduction to the special series: Ethnic and cultural diversity in cognitive behavioral practice. *Cognitive and Behavioral Practice, 3*, 209–213. http://dx.doi.org/10.1016/S1077-7229(96)80014-9

Kochanek, K. D., Murphy, S. L., Xu, J., & Tejada-Vera, B. (2016). *Deaths: Final data for 2014*. Retrieved from https://www.cdc.gov/nchs/data/nvsr/nvsr65/nvsr65_04.pdf

Kochhar, R., & Fry, R. (2014). *Wealth inequality has widened along racial, ethnic lines since end of Great Recession*. Retrieved from http://www.pewresearch.org/fact-tank/2014/12/12/racial-wealth-gaps-great-recession/

Kuhn, T. S. (1962). *The structure of scientific revolutions*. Chicago, IL: University of Chicago Press.

Lichter, D. T., & Johnson, K. M. (2009). Immigrant gateways and Hispanic migration to new destinations. *The International Migration Review, 43*, 496–518. http://dx.doi.org/10.1111/j.1747-7379.2009.00775.x

López, S. R. (1989). Patient variable biases in clinical judgment: Conceptual overview and methodological considerations. *Psychological Bulletin, 106*, 184–203. http://dx.doi.org/10.1037/0033-2909.106.2.184

Macartney, S., Bishaw, A., & Fontenot, K. (2013). *Poverty rates for selected detailed race and Hispanic groups by state and place: 2007–2011*. Retrieved from http://www.mrclotzman.com/handouts/acsbr11-17.pdf

McDonald, J. D., & Chaney, J. (2003). Resistance to multiculturalism: The "Indian Problem." In J. S. Mio & G. Y. Iwamasa (Eds.), *Multicultural mental health research and resistance: Continuing challenges of the new millennium* (pp. 39–53). New York, NY: Brunner-Routledge.

Miller, G. A. (2003). The cognitive revolution: A historical perspective. *Trends in Cognitive Sciences, 7*, 141–144. http://dx.doi.org/10.1016/S1364-6613(03)00029-9

Norcross, J. C., & Rogan, J. D. (2013). Psychologists conducting psychotherapy in 2012: Current practices and historical trends among Division 29 members. *Psychotherapy, 50*, 490–495. http://dx.doi.org/10.1037/a0033512

Norris, T., Vines, P. L., & Hoeffel, E. M. (2012). *The American Indian and Alaska Native Population: 2010*. Retrieved from https://www.census.gov/prod/cen2010/briefs/c2010br-10.pdf

Pew Research Center. (2013). *A nation of immigrants: A portrait of the 40 million, including 11 million unauthorized*. Retrieved from http://www.pewhispanic.org/2013/01/29/a-nation-of-immigrants/

Pew Research Center. (2014). *U.S. Hispanic and Asian populations growing, but for different reasons*. Retrieved from http://www.pewresearch.org/fact-tank/2014/06/26/u-s-hispanic-and-asian-populations-growing-but-for-different-reasons/

Pew Research Center. (2015). *A rising share of the U.S. Black population is foreign born*. Retrieved from http://www.pewsocialtrends.org/2015/04/09/a-rising-share-of-the-u-s-black-population-is-foreign-born/

Pew Research Center. (2017). *Key facts about Asian Americans, a diverse and growing population*. Retrieved from http://www.pewresearch.org/fact-tank/2017/09/08/key-facts-about-asian-americans/

Rastogi, S., Johnson, T. D., Hoeffel, E. M., & Drewery, M. P., Jr. (2011). *The Black population: 2010*. Retrieved from https://www.census.gov/prod/cen2010/briefs/c2010br-06.pdf

Robins, R. W., Gosling, S. D., & Craik, K. H. (1999). An empirical analysis of trends in psychology. *American Psychologist, 54*, 117–128. http://dx.doi.org/10.1037/0003-066X.54.2.117

Rotheram-Borus, M. J., Swendeman, D., & Becker, K. D. (2014). Adapting evidence-based interventions using a common theory, practices, and principles. *Journal of Clinical Child and Adolescent Psychology, 43*, 229–243. http://dx.doi.org/10.1080/15374416.2013.836453

Scarr, S. (1985). Constructing psychology: Making facts and fables for our times. *American Psychologist, 40*, 499–512. http://dx.doi.org/10.1037/0003-066X.40.5.499

Smith, T. B., & Trimble, J. E. (2016). *Foundations of multicultural psychology: Research to inform effective practice.* Washington, DC: American Psychological Association. http://dx.doi.org/10.1037/14733-000

Uberoi, N., Finegold, K., & Gee, E. (2016). *Health insurance coverage and the Affordable Care Act, 2010–2016.* Retrieved from https://aspe.hhs.gov/sites/default/files/pdf/187551/ACA2010-2016.pdf

U.S. Census Bureau. (2011). *American Indian and Alaska Native Heritage Month: November 2011.* Retrieved from https://www.census.gov/newsroom/releases/archives/facts_for_features_special_editions/cb11-ff22.html

U.S. Census Bureau. (2012). *American Indian and Alaska Native Heritage Month: November 2012.* Retrieved from https://www.census.gov/newsroom/releases/archives/facts_for_features_special_editions/cb12-ff22.html

U.S. Department of Health and Human Services Office of Minority Health. (2012). *Profile: American Indian/Alaska Native.* Retrieved from https://minorityhealth.hhs.gov/omh/browse.aspx?lvl=3&lvlid=62

U.S. Department of the Interior, Indian Affairs. (2015). *Frequently asked questions.* Retrieved from https://www.bia.gov/frequently-asked-questions

Wahab, S., & Olson, L. (2004). Intimate partner violence and sexual assault in Native American communities. *Trauma, Violence, & Abuse, 5*, 353–366. http://dx.doi.org/10.1177/1524838004269489

Zuckerman, S., Haley, J., Roubideaux, Y., & Lillie-Blanton, M. (2004). Health service access, use, and insurance coverage among American Indians/Alaska Natives and Whites: What role does the Indian Health Service play? *American Journal of Public Health, 94*, 53–59. http://dx.doi.org/10.2105/AJPH.94.1.53

I

COGNITIVE BEHAVIORAL MODELS, MEASURES, AND TREATMENTS FOR DEPRESSIVE DISORDERS

1

COGNITIVE BEHAVIORAL MODELS, MEASURES, AND TREATMENTS FOR DEPRESSIVE DISORDERS IN ASIAN AMERICANS

WEI-CHIN HWANG, LESLIE C. HO, COURTNEY P. CHAN, AND KRISTYNE K. HONG

Major depressive disorder (MDD) is a worldwide, recurrent health problem that ranks as one of the world's top leading causes of disability (Burcusa & Iacono, 2007). Unfortunately, there is a dearth of research on depression for Asian heritage populations. Nevertheless, mood disorders continue to be the most prevalent psychiatric problem among Asian Americans and the main reason for seeking treatment (Barreto & Segal, 2005; Takeuchi et al., 1998). Because of stigma, Asian Americans delay seeking treatment and evidence lower help-seeking rates compared with White Americans (Abe-Kim et al., 2007; Alegría et al., 2008; Le Meyer, Zane, Cho, & Takeuchi, 2009). They are also more likely to present with greater psychiatric impairment at treatment entry (Hwang et al., 2015; Kalibatseva & Leong, 2011; Nguyen & Bornheimer, 2014). Naturalistic studies on Asian Americans have found lower treatment satisfaction, higher dropout rates, and worse treatment outcomes when compared with White Americans (Alegría et al., 2008; Leong

http://dx.doi.org/10.1037/0000091-002
Treating Depression, Anxiety, and Stress in Ethnic and Racial Groups: Cognitive Behavioral Approaches,
E. C. Chang, C. A. Downey, J. K. Hirsch, and E. A. Yu (Editors)

& Lau, 2001; Zane, Enomoto, & Chun, 1994). In this chapter, we provide an overview of depression among Asian Americans (e.g., prevalence, etiology, and help seeking), discuss cultural issues in the assessment and measurement of depression, and conclude by discussing the cultural adaptation of cognitive behavior therapy (CBT) for Asian Americans.

PREVALENCE AND RISK FACTORS FOR MAJOR DEPRESSION

Two major epidemiological studies have assessed the prevalence and risk factors for depression among Asian Americans: the Chinese American Psychiatric Epidemiological Survey (CAPES; Takeuchi et al., 1998) and the National Latino and Asian American Survey (NLAAS; Alegría et al., 2004). The CAPES study was the first large-scale study conducted on Chinese Americans using rigorous diagnostic criteria and a longitudinal design (Hwang, Myers, & Takeuchi, 2000; Takeuchi et al., 1998). Participants included 1,747 Chinese Americans (ages 18–65) who resided in Los Angeles County between 1993 and 1994. MDD was diagnosed using the University of Michigan's Composite International Diagnostic Interview (UM-CIDI). Lifetime and 12-month prevalence MDD rates were 6.9% and 3.4%, respectively (Takeuchi et al., 1998). Although the rates found were lower than in the National Comorbidity Survey (lifetime rate of 17.1% and 12-month rate of 10.3%), which used similar methodology and assessment instruments (Kessler et al., 1994), it is important to note that epidemiological methods of assessing prevalence may underestimate rates in groups for which mental health is highly stigmatized. Asian Americans are collectivistic and may be reluctant to disclose personal information to strangers (e.g., researchers) because of stigma (Hwang, 2006).

Like other populations, risk factors associated with MDD in Chinese Americans include previous history of depression, psychiatric comorbidity, stress, poor health, and decreased social support (Hwang & Myers, 2007; Hwang et al., 2000; Takeuchi et al., 1998). Unlike in other studies conducted in the general U.S. population, Chinese American women were not significantly more likely to become depressed than Chinese American men (Hwang et al., 2000; Takeuchi et al., 1998). However, subsequent analyses found that acculturation moderated this effect, with more highly acculturated women evidencing greater risk than men and less acculturated women. In addition, age of onset for MDD is complicated by acculturation issues, with those growing up in the United States evidencing similar adolescent and young adult risk as other Americans and those immigrating at later developmental stages demonstrating greater risk at time of immigration (Hwang, Chun, Takeuchi, Myers, & Siddarth, 2005). Acculturation has also been found to moderate the effects of stress, with the more highly acculturated exhibiting greater stress vulnerability (Hwang & Myers, 2007).

The NLAAS was conducted in conjunction with the National Comorbidity Survey-Replication (NCS-R) using similar instruments and methodology (Alegría et al., 2004; Kessler et al., 2003). Both studies used the World Health Organization's World Mental Health Composite International Diagnostic Interview (WMH-CIDI) to assess depression. Data were collected in English, Mandarin, Cantonese, Tagalog, and Vietnamese. The final Asian American sample consisted of Chinese Americans ($n = 600$), Filipino Americans ($n = 508$), Vietnamese Americans ($n = 520$), and other Asians ($n = 467$). Asian American lifetime and 12-month MDD rates were 9.1% (Hong, Walton, Tamaki, & Sabin, 2014) and 4.6%, respectively (J. Kim & Choi, 2010). This is lower compared with the lifetime (16.2%) and 12-month (6.6%) prevalence of MDD among all Americans (Kessler et al., 2003). Asian Americans between the ages of 18 and 29 showed greater risk for 12-month MDD than Asian Americans in other age groups (J. Kim & Choi, 2010).

Compared with foreign-born Asian Americans, U.S.-born Asian Americans evidenced higher lifetime MDD rates (13.0% and 8.0%, respectively; Hong et al., 2014), providing evidence for the cultural assimilation hypothesis that higher acculturation increases the risk for mental illness such as depression (Hwang et al., 2005). Age and gender moderated these effects, such that U.S.-born Asian American women were at the highest risk, and young immigrant women demonstrated higher risk than older immigrant women (Hong et al., 2014; Takeuchi et al., 2007). Perceived discrimination was also positively correlated to MDD for Vietnamese and Filipino Americans (Ai, Nicdao, Appel, & Lee, 2015).

The NLAAS was also the first study that provided a national sample to understand suicidal ideation and behaviors among Asian Americans. Lifetime prevalence for suicidal ideation, planning, and attempts were 8.6%, 3.3%, and 2.5%, respectively (Duldulao, Takeuchi, & Hong, 2009). These rates are lower than those found in the NCS-R, in which suicidal ideation, planning, and attempt rates were 13.5%, 3.9%, and 4.6% (Kessler, Borges, & Walters, 1999). Risk factors for suicidal ideation and attempts included female gender, family conflict, perceived discrimination, and lifetime depressive or anxiety disorders (J. K. Y. Cheng et al., 2010). Among Asian Americans in the NLAAS, those between the ages of 18 and 34 evidenced the highest risk for suicidal thoughts (11.9%), intent (4.4%), and attempts (3.8%; Duldulao et al., 2009), which supports the growing body of literature indicating Asian American youth are at especially high risk for depression and suicidality because of family, academic, and financial stress (Wong, Brownson, & Schwing, 2011). Because the NLAAS did not include respondents who were more than 65 years old, suicidality among elderly Asian Americans was not assessed. Nevertheless, there is a growing body of research indicating that elderly Asian American women have the highest suicide ideation and completion rates among all women between the ages of 65 and 84 (Heron, 2011; Xu, Kochanek, Murphy, & Tejada-Vera, 2010). Differences emerged along nativity status, with U.S.-born Asian Americans of both genders demonstrating higher lifetime suicidal ideation (12.2%) than foreign-born Asian Americans (7.5%) but with no differences in attempts. U.S.-born Asian American women (15.9%) were at higher risk than foreign-born Asian American women (7.9%) for rate of suicidal ideation, which was slightly higher compared with the general U.S. population in the NCS-R (13.5%; Kessler et al., 1999).

CONCEPTUALIZATION AND ASSESSMENT OF DEPRESSION

There are a number of complexities involved with assessing depression across cultures. Key challenges include (a) developing a sophisticated understanding of how conceptualizations of depression may vary across cultures and (b) evaluating whether extant assessment instruments developed on predominantly White populations demonstrate positive psychometric properties across cultures.

Conceptualizing Depression Across Cultures

A limitation of our conceptualization of depression is the assumption of culture universality in the recognition, experience, reporting, expression, and the understanding of causality of depressive symptoms. Key to this discussion is also the concepts of *etic* (culture-universal) and *emic* (culture-specific) conceptualizations of depression (Hwang & Ting, 2013a, 2013b). The fact that most instruments were developed for and tested on White Americans leads to potential cultural biases when this top-down ethnocentric approach is applied to other groups. Specifically, there may be an assumed culture universality of the primary symptoms of depression identified in Western diagnostic systems, when in actuality they may reflect a culture-specific classification that is imposed on cultural others. For example, there may be cultural variations in the willingness to report or endorse the nine primary depression symptoms, or differences in cognitive recognition and understanding of illness.

Cross-national studies have found that Asian countries (i.e., Taiwan and Korea) evidence low prevalence of depression compared with Western countries (Weissman et al., 1996). Prevalence of depression may be influenced by stigma and methodological issues associated with epidemiology research (e.g., cultural differences in stigma and willingness to discuss psychiatric issues with strangers who call or knock on their doors). Also examined was the extent to which at least 60% of individuals from various countries endorsed different depressive symptoms. Although there may be culture universality in the experience of some symptoms across nations (i.e., insomnia and loss of energy), there can also be symptoms that are more primary in some countries but not others (i.e., 60% of those from Asian countries reported poor appetite, but those from Western countries did not). Understanding cultural variations in the current diagnostic symptoms can be important because this may affect whether people meet criteria for diagnosis and insurance coverage. For example, those from some cultures may express a narrower range of symptoms and may not meet the five out of nine symptom criteria but evidence greater severity in the symptoms they do endorse. Future research should examine these variations among different Asian and Asian American groups.

Moreover, there may also be variations in symptoms of depression that are not captured in current diagnostic criteria. Specifically, are there symptoms of depression that are common in Asian cultures but are not included in the current nine symptoms of major depression? Two examples of this issue are the notions of somatization and culture-bound syndromes. There is an abundant amount of research indicating that Asians and Asian Americans tend to express somatic symptoms of depression (e.g., headaches, stomachaches, shortness of breath, muscle weakness, bodily pains) more so than those from Western populations (Hwang, 2006). These symptoms are currently not listed in the *Diagnostic and Statistical Manual of Mental Disorders* (DSM; American Psychiatric Association, 2013). Taking a bottom-up approach to conceptualizing depression across cultures may, in fact, help us understand the culture universality and specificity of symptomatology. For example, do those from Western backgrounds place a more primary emphasis on the cognitive experience of depression whereas those from Asian heritage populations experience their depression more somatically? If so, what are the implications for cognitive conceptualizations and treatment planning, and what does this mean in terms of ordering of emphasis and types of skills building implemented in treatment?

Relatedly, the idea of cultural idioms of distress or culture-bound syndromes also has to be better understood. There is a growing body of research documenting the presence of many Asian culture-bound syndromes related to depression (e.g., neurasthenia [Chinese], Hwabyung [Korean]) and anxiety (e.g., Taijin kyofusho [Japanese], Dhat [Asian Indian], and Koro [evident in many Asian cultures]), which tend to be highly comorbid with depression (for descriptions of these syndromes, see Glossary of Cultural Concepts of Distress, American Psychiatric Association, 2013). If these disorders are not recognized by Western criteria, how do those who express their distress in these cultural manifestations access and receive parity in insurance coverage?

What ethical dilemma does this place on clinicians who treat these populations when it comes time to assigning diagnosis and submitting billing? From a CBT perspective, how do we conceptualize and develop a treatment plan if patients experience their depression in somatic and culture-specific ways? Is it appropriate to focus on cognitive reframing when the patient and clinician perspectives on the cause of the illness may differ (i.e., "My thinking is not the problem; my husband and my physical health is the issue I want to address in treatment")?

These questions raise another important quandary related to assessment and treatment. Specifically, how do we take into account the patient's explanatory model of illness when understanding their problems and planning out treatment strategies (Kleinman, 1980)? An explanatory model of illness includes a person's conceptualizations about the nature of the problem they are having, what they believe to be the cause, and their notions about what might be appropriate strategies for treatment. For example, Yeung, Chang, Gresham, Nierenberg, and Fava (2004) found that most of the depressed Chinese American patients seeking help in a primary care setting did not believe they had depression but instead referred to their problems as somatic concerns, nerves, stress, worry, or social problems. CBT heavily weights diagnostic psychoeducation and the cognitive etiology of depression. If patients do not feel they have depression and react adversely to the diagnosis, how does the therapist proceed? Moreover, if they do not feel their depression is caused by irrational thoughts but instead feel they have stress problems and social conflict, is it appropriate to focus on changing cognitions, or would it be more appropriate to focus on problem solving and improving first? How do we bridge cognitive explanatory models with patient explanatory models of illness, and how do we preserve the working alliance when patient and clinician perspectives differ? These issues have to be further studied as clinicians learn how to apply CBT to other cultures.

Common Instruments Used to Assess Depression Across Cultures

Although the aforementioned issues still have to be further understood, clinical researchers are often placed in a dilemma of what instruments to use when assessing and diagnosing depression. This can be especially challenging because grant and peer reviewers expect cultural variations to be addressed, but at the same time, few resources have been made available to research these issues or to examine the cross-cultural validity of existing measures. Creating new measures and testing their validity against extant measures can be expensive and time consuming. Use of instruments developed on White populations raises questions of internal and external validity on Asian American populations. Moreover, when assessing depression among Asian Americans, instruments have to undergo rigorous translation procedures (e.g., forward and back translation) to ensure accuracy and conceptual validity. These multiple additional demands are challenging for those interested in conducting cultural research.

Although it is beyond the scope of this chapter to review all these issues, we provide an overview of major instruments that have demonstrated adequate reliability and validity in assessing depression among Asian Americans. It is important to note that the majority of research conducted has focused on Chinese Americans, the largest Asian American group in the United States. Due to complexities in translation, cost, and funding, the dearth of research and examinations of the psychometric properties among other Asian American groups still have to be evaluated. Some Asian countries have begun using and evaluating these instruments, with the majority of this research conducted on Chinese international populations. However, the review of international studies goes beyond the scope of this chapter. Next, we discuss various types of instruments. Planning out which scale and what assessment method (i.e., self-report vs. clinician administered) to use can be especially important because prevalence rates can vary widely depending on the type of instrument used (H. J. Kim, Park, Storr, Tran, & Juon, 2015). See Kalibatseva, Wu, and Leong (2014) for a more comprehensive review of depression assessment measures.

Self-Report Instruments

The Beck Depression Inventory–II (BDI-II) is one of the most widely used assessment tools to diagnose severity of depression in both adolescents and adults (Beck, Steer, & Brown, 1996). It assesses 21 symptoms and attitudes over the preceding 2 weeks that are rated in intensity from 0 to 3. Although there are too many studies to cite here, the BDI and BDI-II have been translated into many different Asian languages and in general have been shown to have good reliability and validity among Asian Americans and Asians internationally.

Zheng and Lin (1991) noted the important limitation of using Western instruments with Asians and developed the Chinese Depression Inventory (CDI). The CDI is a 48-item questionnaire derived from several different depression instruments. Specifically, an initial 32 items were chosen from the Chinese translations of the BDI (Beck, Ward, Mendelson, Mock, & Erbaugh, 1961), Zung Self-Rating Depression Scale (Zung, 1965), and the Hamilton Depression Rating Scale (Hamilton, 1960). Sixteen items were eliminated after testing for face validity. In the process of reevaluating the remaining 16 items, the authors generated 32 additional equivalent phrases for keywords (e.g., depressed, guilty, indecisiveness, helplessness, lack of interest, suicidal ideation). The final scale of 48 items was finalized by Chinese psychiatrists.

It demonstrates good psychometric properties with both Chinese and Chinese American samples (Yeung et al., 2002; Zheng & Lin, 1991).

The Hamilton Depression Inventory (HDI) is a 23-item self-report inventory version of the 17-item Hamilton Depression Rating Scale (Dozois, 2003; Hamilton, 1960, 1967; Reynolds & Kobak, 1995). The HDI uses ratings over the preceding 2 weeks with an intensity of 0–2 or 0–4 to generate clinical cutoff scores for depression. There is strong support for the reliability and validity of the self-report HDI for assessment of the severity of depression in multiethnic samples (Hwang & Ting, 2008; Hwang & Wood, 2009; Hwang, Wood, & Fujimoto, 2010).

The Geriatric Depression Scale (GDS) is a 30-item self-report screening tool designed to identify depressive symptoms in the elderly (Brink et al., 1982). The GDS assesses the affective and cognitive domains and can be administered as a paper and pencil questionnaire or orally. It has demonstrated adequate reliability and validity for screening use in Chinese, Japanese, and Korean populations (Kalibatseva et al., 2014).

The Center for Epidemiological Studies Depression Scale (CES-D) is a widely used self-report instrument that measures depression in the general community (Radloff, 1977). The CES-D is a 20-item questionnaire that assesses depression during the preceding week using a four-point Likert-type response scale from *rarely or none of the time* (less than 1 day) to *most all of the time* (5–7 days). Although the CES-D was originally developed for use in epidemiological studies, it has now become a common tool for assessing depression in community samples. The CES-D has demonstrated sufficient reliability and validity for use in Asian and Asian American populations (S. T. Cheng & Chan, 2005; Cheung, Liu, & Yip, 2007; Herman et al., 2011; Okazaki, 2000; Ying, 1988). However, some research also indicates that the factorial structure may vary for Asians and Asian Americans.

Brief Screening Tools

The Patient Health Questionnaire-9 (PHQ-9) is used to diagnose MDD in primary care patients (Spitzer, Kroenke, Williams, & the Patient Health Questionnaire Primary Care Study Group, 1999). It consists of one item for each of the nine *DSM–IV* diagnostic criteria and is scored from 0 to 3 for intensity and presence of symptoms over the preceding 2 weeks. It has been validated as a screening instrument for Asian American patients in a number of studies (Chen, Huang, Chang, & Chung, 2006; Huang, Chung, Kroenke, Delucchi, & Spitzer, 2006) and has also been used in a number of studies in international Asian populations. Yeung et al. (2008) translated the PHQ-9 into Chinese and administered it side by side with the original English version, calling it the Chinese Bilingual Patient Health Questionnaire-9.

Clinician-Administered Interviews

The Structured Clinical Interview for *DSM–5* (SCID-5) is the most widely used semi-structured diagnostic interview for making *DSM–5* diagnoses (First, Williams, Karg, & Spitzer, 2015). The SCID-5 assesses the presence of the nine depression symptoms within the preceding 2 weeks. The Chinese version of the SCID-IV has demonstrated good psychometric properties when used with Chinese and CA populations (Hsu, Wan, & Adler, 2005; Hwang et al., 2015; So et al., 2003; Yeung et al., 2008).

The semi-structured Hamilton Depression Rating Scale (HDRS) is one of the most common measures for assessing MDD (Hamilton, 1960). It contains 17 items that are scored from 0–4 or 0–2. The HDRS has been successfully translated, validated, and used with Chinese and Chinese American populations (Hwang et al., 2015; Zheng et al., 1988), as well as some international Asian populations.

Epidemiological Instruments

The primary diagnostic measure for depressive disorders used in the CAPES study was the UM-CIDI, a structured interview schedule based on the Diagnostic Interview Schedule (DIS) designed to be used by trained non-clinician lay interviewers (Kessler et al., 1994). The UM-CIDI generates diagnoses according to both the *DSM–III–R* (American Psychiatric Association, 1987) and the *International Classification of Diseases* systems (World Health Organization, 1992). Although the validity of the UM-CIDI had not been previously tested in a Chinese sample, the Chinese translation of the DIS has shown good reliability and validity (Hwu, Yeh, Chang, & Yeh 1986; Hwu, Yeh, & Chang, 1989).

The NLAAS study used the WMH-CIDI (Kessler et al., 2003), which has demonstrated good concordance between *DSM–IV* diagnoses based on the WMH-CIDI and the SCID for international populations (Haro et al., 2006). Despite the high validity of both measures, there remains a potential underreporting bias with epidemiological studies, which have assessed the prevalence of disorders through random phone or door-to-door surveys. Stigma and cultural norms may affect the extent to which participants will disclose sensitive information to strangers.

COGNITIVE BEHAVIOR THERAPY FOR DEPRESSED ASIAN AMERICANS

Unfortunately, there continues to be a dearth of research examining treatment outcomes for Asian Americans (Miranda et al., 2005). Specifically, out of the 9,266 participants who participated in the clinical trials used to form the treatment guidelines for major psychiatric disorders, only 11 were Asian American or Pacific Islander (U.S. Department of Health and Human Services, 2001). For MDD only two out of 3,860 were Asian Americans. These numbers highlight that Western psychotherapies have not been sufficiently evaluated for their effectiveness with Asian Americans. To date, only two studies have examined CBT depression outcomes for Asian Americans. The first tested an 8-week brief CBT program for elderly Chinese Americans with minor depression (Dai et al., 1999). The treatment consisted of an eight-session informational videotape followed by discussion, whereas the control condition consisted of an 8-week wait followed by a four-session abbreviated lesson. Although the intervention was somewhat effective in reducing depressive symptoms (as measured by the HDRS), the study had no random assignment, recruitment from multiple sources with low participant rates, a limited sample size ($N = 20$), a waitlist control that was followed by unequal length of treatment, and no reported diagnostic outcomes or screening.

More recently, Hwang et al. (2015) conducted the first randomized controlled trial testing the effectiveness of CBT and culturally adapted CBT (CA-CBT) for treating depressed Chinese American adults (18–65 years old) seeking care at community mental health clinics. This was also the first randomized controlled trial to investigate psychiatric outcomes in Asian American adults using evidence-based research methods recommended for clinical trials, addressing the efficacy–effectiveness gap by treating patients in real-world community settings. Fifty Chinese Americans who sought treatment and met criteria for major depression were randomly assigned to 12 sessions of CBT or CA-CBT. The models and frameworks used to culturally adapt CBT, as well as specific examples of what was culturally modified, are provided later in this chapter.

Therapy and assessments were conducted in the patient's language of choice (English, Mandarin, or Cantonese). The SCID-IV and the HDRS were used to screen and diagnose depression. The primary outcomes were dropout rates and changes in depressive symptoms measured at baseline, Session 4, Session 8, and Session 12. Participants in CA-CBT evidenced a dropout rate of 7% ($n = 2$), whereas those in CBT dropped out at a rate of 26% ($n = 6$). Moreover, participants in CA-CBT demonstrated a greater overall decrease in depressive symptoms than those in CBT (with an average decrease in HDRS score of 10 vs. 5, respectively). Although the treatment effect size for both conditions was quite large (1.54 and 2.96 for CBT and CA-CBT, respectively), the majority in both treatment conditions remained depressed.

Participants evidenced a much greater depression severity than that typically seen in other racial groups, indicating that stigma toward mental illness and its treatment can delay help seeking and complicate recovery because of differences in clinical severity at point of entry. Although patients were randomly assigned, the CA-CBT participants were slightly more depressed than the CBT group at baseline. Moreover, even though the rate of depression change was steeper for the CA-CBT group, depression severity was only slightly lower by Session 12, making it unclear whether differences in initial depression severity led to a greater rate of improvement. Nevertheless, results indicate that CBT can be effective in treating depressed Chinese American immigrants. Results also indicate that short-term treatments may not be sufficient for treating the higher clinical severity of Asian American clients when they do seek help and that more intensive and longer treatments may be needed. Cultural adaptations may confer additional treatment benefits, facilitate treatment engagement, and reduce dropout.

The Importance of Culturally Adapting Cognitive Behavior Therapy

The notion of culturally adapting psychotherapy as a method of providing culturally effective care is an important "hot" topic that is garnering a lot of attention. As-is approaches to disseminating evidence-based treatments (EBTs) to culturally diverse groups such as Asian Americans may not be sufficient to address cultural differences. Even if as-is treatments are found to be beneficial, there is the question of whether cultural adaptations can further improve effectiveness. Developing new culture-specific EBTs for every ethnic group may be unrealistic because of cost and the difficulties of training practitioners to deliver multiple types of treatments. Culturally adapting EBTs may be the most practical strategy because core effective therapeutic elements can be retained, while modifications to address culture can be implemented.

Unfortunately, there are few frameworks to guide the adaptation of EBTs. In response, Hwang (2006, 2009, 2012) developed an integrative top-down and bottom-up community-participatory approach. The psychotherapy adaptation and modification framework (PAMF) and formative method for adapting psychotherapy (FMAP) were used to culturally adapt CBT for Chinese Americans in the randomized controlled trial discussed earlier (Hwang et al., 2015). In addition to developing these frameworks, Hwang, Wood, Lin, and Cheung (2006) also developed 18 principles for modifying CBT for Chinese Americans that fall into three core areas: general principles for adapting CBT, strengthening the client–therapist relationship, and understanding Chinese notions of self and mental illness. Readers are welcome to read the referenced article along with the application of these principles to a clinical case study.

The FMAP and the PAMF form an integrative and flexible framework that can be used to modify mental and physical health treatments for multiple groups. The top-down empirical and theoretically driven PAMF was formulated first and highlighted six core domains in which cultural adaptations can take place (Hwang, 2006). These domains include (a) observing dynamic issues and cultural complexities; (b) orienting clients to psychotherapy and increasing mental health awareness; (c) understanding cultural beliefs about mental illness, its causes, and what constitutes appropriate treatment; (d) improving the client–therapist relationship; (e) understanding cultural differences in the expression and communication of distress; and (f) addressing cultural issues specific to the population. In addition, therapeutic principles and corresponding rationales augment each domain. The initial conceptualization for culturally adapting psychotherapy for Asian Americans consisted of 25 therapeutic principles.

Subsequently, the FMAP framework was formulated (Hwang, 2009, 2012; Hwang et al., 2015) to help integrate top-down theory and research knowledge with information developed through community-participatory formative processes. The FMAP includes five phases: (a) generating knowledge and collaborating with stakeholders, (b) integrating generated information with theory and empirical and clinical knowledge, (c) reviewing the initial culturally adapted clinical intervention with stakeholders and revising the culturally adapted intervention, (d) testing the culturally adapted intervention, and (e) finalizing the adapted intervention.

During Phase I of treatment development, seven 4-hour focus groups were conducted at community mental health centers that specialize in treating Asian Americans. These clinics included Asian Americans for Community Involvement in San Jose, Asian Community Mental Health Services in Oakland, Asian Pacific Counseling and Treatment Center in Los Angeles, Asian Pacific Mental Health Services in Gardena, and Chinatown North Beach Service Center in San Francisco. Several clinics were involved in encapsulating a breadth of viewpoints and perspectives. Focus group discussions focused on what cultural adaptations they made when working with Asian Americans, what modifications they believed would be helpful when using a CBT framework, what they wished they would have learned about working with Asian Americans during their graduate training program, and what changes to a nonadapted CBT manual could potentially be made to help improve client engagement and outcomes. In addition, interviews were also conducted with Buddhist monks and nuns, spiritual and religious Taoist masters, and traditional Chinese medicine (TCM) practitioners to understand traditional Chinese notions of mental illness.

Phase II integrated information generated from community-based focus groups with theory, empirical, and prior clinical knowledge. The most common and salient themes were used by the author in writing the treatment manual, which also integrated his clinical experience across a variety of treatment settings. During Phase III, the culturally adapted clinical intervention was reviewed by community mental health therapists. Seven additional 4-hour focus groups were conducted. Feedback was used to finalize the CA-CBT manual before clinical trial implementation. Phase IV involved testing the culturally adapted CBT manual (Hwang, 2016) against the nonadapted CBT manual (Miranda et al., 2006). Phase V involved synthesizing stakeholder feedback and finalizing the culturally adapted intervention. Clients who finished the treatment were asked to participate in an interview to elicit feedback regarding their experiences, what they found useful, what they did not like, and their recommendations for improving the intervention. Therapists also participated in individual and group exit interviews.

Highlights of Potential Cognitive Behavior Therapy Cultural Adaptations

The integrative FMAP combines new information with extant knowledge. A few of the core areas where cultural adaptations can take place are highlighted next. Although these are not exhaustive, they represent key issues that can be considered when modifying CBT for Asian Americans. For a more comprehensive understanding of cultural adaptations, please see references on the FMAP and PAMF, as well as a recently released book on culturally adapting psychotherapy for Asian heritage populations (Hwang, 2016). Four key dimensions of cultural adaptation that can be taken into account when conceptualizing cases are (a) increasing the focus on psychoeducation and therapy orientations, (b) addressing Eastern and Western differences in cultural value orientations, (c) prioritizing a problem-solving approach to align with client goals, and (d) integrating cultural metaphors to bridge clinical concepts and reinforce extant cultural strengths.

Increasing the Focus on Psychoeducation and Therapy Orientations

CBT is one of the most psychoeducationally focused therapies. When working with Asian Americans, placing an even greater importance on psychoeducation is necessary because the notion and availability of psychotherapy is not part of most Asian health care systems. Mental illness and its treatment are heavily stigmatized, and there is much lack of awareness and fear of social judgment for being "crazy." Consequently, orienting clients to therapy, educating about mental illness, and reducing stigma to help clients feel comfortable in treatment should be part of case conceptualization and planning. The CA-CBT manual targets a number of clinical–cultural issues and provides more extensive psychoeducation and therapy orientation than traditional CBT.

An entire session is spent on helping clients understand mental health treatment, including the purpose, course, and timeline; confidentiality and privacy; facts and fallacies; roles and responsibilities of clients and therapists; how and why therapy may be helpful; why therapy can sometimes increase stressful thoughts; the identification of goals and markers of treatment progress; how to handle emergencies; how to address stigma; and premature dropout versus planned therapeutic endings. A second session educates clients about the prevalence and causes of depression, the benefits of psychotherapy and antidepressants, indigenous medicines, and the differentiation of physical, mental, and social symptoms of depression.

This more extensive therapy orientation may help promote treatment engagement and stigma reduction and help reduce premature treatment failure; this can be critically important with less acculturated Asian Americans who have less positive attitudes toward seeking help than those who are more acculturated (Suinn, 2010). Because Asian Americans may vary in acculturation and familiarity with treatment, it is important to assess the client's place of birth, English and heritage language proficiency, length of residence in the United States, age of immigration, and family migration history. This information provides valuable insight for case conceptualization and a better understanding of the family context in problem development, stressors and supports available, and the extent to which family and social expectations complicate individual goals.

Addressing Eastern and Western Differences in Cultural Value Orientations

Eastern and Western cultures are significantly different in their cultural value orientations. Asian heritage populations are predominately collectivistic, whereas Western cultures tend to be more individualistic (Triandis, Bontempo, Villareal, Asai, & Lucca, 1988). In addition, Asian cultures use interdependent self-construals, and Westerners are often described as being independent in self-construals (Markus & Kitayama, 1991). As a result, Asian Americans may have different treatment goals and priorities than White Americans that have to be taken into account by the CBT therapist. Family obligations and duties may take precedence over individual goals and desires. There may be a greater emphasis on self-restraint, the preservation of interpersonal harmony, and avoidance of conflict. This means that the CBT therapist may have to balance social versus personal needs in the treatment plan, explain that to help resolve problems we sometimes have to talk about them more before they can truly be let go, be patient and encourage clients to discuss their problems and express their emotions, and assess and reassess information because clients may share more when they get to know the therapist better.

Traditional CBT models may also need some modification to adjust for cultural orientation and concepts of self. For example, Beck's cognitive triad (i.e., negative thoughts about the self, world, and future) is a core concept in CBT (Beck, 1979). However, this triad was formulated from a predominantly individualistic and independent self-construal perspective. When adapting the triad for Asian Americans, incorporating collectivistic and interdependent notions of self may help CBT align with client goals and reduce the possibility of cultural incongruence that can exacerbate social and familial conflict. When conceptualizing the case and using therapeutic tools such as cognitive reframing, therapists may have to address self–other differentiation in thought processes. For example, negative thoughts about the self can be modified to include negative thoughts and critical thoughts toward other people and critical thoughts others may have toward the client. Cognitive skills building can also focus on interpersonal thoughts rather than just individual thoughts (e.g., "My mother wants me to be hardworking like my cousin" vs. "I am worthless"). This helps ensure that the client's cognitive reframing is more ecologically and socially valid and effective and bridges the patient's worldview with cognitive models.

For example, research has shown that Asian Americans may be more likely to use an interdependent perceptual filter when appraising and regulating emotional experiences (Soto, Levenson, & Ebling, 2005). Moreover, culture-bound syndromes such as the Japanese *taijin kyufusho* manifest as severe social phobia about offending or hurting others through one's bodily odors or exaggerated physical defects (Kleinknecht, Dinnel, Kleinknecht, Hiruma, & Harada, 1997). This self–other focus is distinctly different from social anxiety in a Western sense, which focuses on fears of being laughed at, made fun of, or appearing incompetent in front of others. These differences result in cultural variation in direct emotional verbalization and disclosure of private feelings to others and can also affect help seeking and comfort in treatment because of fears and avoidance of social judgment and blame. As a result, Asian Americans may not only be culturally different but also more clinically severe when they finally do seek help, necessitating also adapting the treatment to address greater clinical severity issues.

Family expectations may have to be effectively addressed to balance individual needs and goals, as well as family expectations and pressures. Therapists should be conscientious that they too come from a cultural system and may possess individualistic and independent self-construal biases, which when imposed on a client from a collectivistic background may actually increase family conflict. For example, many therapists focus on client rights from a Western perspective but fail to understand that these rights have to be differentially balanced and conceptualized differently when working with collectivistic family expectations and responsibilities. Imposing individualistic values and too much focus on the self may derail family contextual demands and incur even greater family distancing, conflict, and labeling of the client as selfish. Because Asian American families are typically hierarchical, therapists also have to properly address and respect parental authority. Learning how to collaborate effectively with Asian American families can be especially challenging if a therapist does not know how to address these dynamics and conceptualize the case from a more interdependent family systems perspective.

Prioritizing a Problem-Solving Approach to Align With Client Goals

Two dynamics interact to increase the problem-solving focus for Asian Americans when they finally do seek help: the Asian cultural focus on problem-solving and stigma toward treatment. Consequently, clients want therapists to help them immediately solve their problems, especially when they delay help seeking and arrive with severe symptoms. Their goals may not align well with the initial CBT focus of cognitive restructuring and education about irrational thoughts. Discussing cognitive reframing and changing their internal dialogue too early in the treatment process can be culturally incongruent because clients may not conceptualize their cognitions as being related to their problems. Instead, they often want to change other people or the stressful situations they believe are the cause of their problems, and acceptance of cognitive reframing may also be associated with blame for causing one's own problems. Many clients often come in with the expectation that treatment will be quick and effective and want the therapist to take charge and tell them what to do and not what or how to think.

An initial focus on problem solving can strengthen the client–therapist working alliance. Helping clients differentiate between short-, intermediate-, and long-term goals can be important and provides concrete directions for those who may feel uncomfortable with the open-ended nature of psychotherapy. This contrasts with traditional Asian medicines for which the doctor takes an authoritarian role and tells the patient what to do. Helping clients understand the course of therapy can also be beneficial. For example, normalizing that advice is typically not provided as much during the beginning stages of therapy can help address clients' expectations that the therapist will tell them what to do. The treatment manual addresses this issue by using the "map of the city metaphor," which helps clients to understand that therapists have to understand contextual issues before providing advice. Providing the rationale that therapists should not lead clients astray by giving clients advice too early (e.g., waste time and gas or driving around in circles or down a one-way street) can be important and help clients feel more aware and comfortable in treatment.

Integrating Cultural Metaphors to Bridge Clinical Concepts and Extant Cultural Strengths

To address the client's initial problem-solving goals, cultural metaphors can be used to bridge clinical and cultural concepts. The theme of the culturally adapted CBT manual is a Chinese saying that aligns with many Asian American client goals when they do seek help and demonstrates how CBT can help them achieve their goals. The Chinese characters are "山不轉路轉; 路不轉人轉;人不轉心轉," pronounced shān bù zhuǎn lù zhuǎn, lù bù zhuǎn rén zhuǎn, rén bù zhuǎn xīn zhuǎn in Mandarin Chinese, which translates to, "If the mountain doesn't turn, the road turns; if the road doesn't turn, the person turns; if the person doesn't turn, the heart/mind turns."

Metaphorically, it means that when one encounters a problem (i.e., the mountain) and one cannot move or change the people or situation, one has to use another strategy to address the problem (i.e., find a road around it). If that does not work, one may have to modify one's approach further (i.e., go off the beaten path or try an alternative strategy). If after exhausting various options the problem still has not resolved, one may have to change the way one thinks and feels about it. This provides an excellent example of how traditional CBT ordering of interventions may have to be culturally adapted for Asian Americans. After clients have gone through the process of trying to solve a problem in multiple ways, they are much more willing to engage in cognitive reframing as a tool to address their problems.

Cultural metaphors and symbols can also be used to link cognitive models with cultural beliefs. For example, the tai chi diagram (commonly known as a yin-yang diagram) carries great cultural, spiritual, and religious meaning for many different Asian groups. Taoist beliefs have been infused with Asian culture and possess philosophical meaning (which is more focused on TCM concepts of balance, energy, qi, and health) that can be interpreted separately from its religious meaning (which involves deities, spirits, ghosts, and demons). Interviewing Taoist masters helped reveal the deep therapeutic meaning of the tai chi diagram that goes beyond the traditional light and dark, male and female, positive and negative, solar and lunar, and balance. The tai chi diagram is a cultural and religious symbol that can help heal mental illness and cultivate inner peace, balance, awareness, and acceptance. The line is curvy rather than straight because it teaches people about the ups and downs of life. There is a small light circle in the dark and dark circle in the light because no matter how good life is something bad will likely happen, and no matter how bad life is something good can always happen. Linking this cultural symbol with cognitive reframing can help with accepting and normalizing stressful events, letting go of intense feelings when nothing can be done to change a particular situation, and understanding the impermanence of life.

Moreover, establishing this cultural–clinical bridge between client beliefs and therapeutic mechanisms can be further driven home by asking clients how they might think, act, and behave differently given this new understanding—a core component of CBT.

The tai chi diagram is inherently linked with the cultural and TCM emphasis on qi, or energy, and is recognized all throughout Asia. A specific adaptation to culturally bridge the concept of energy with behavioral activation and cognitive reframing can be implemented. The "sitting in the sun" exercise was developed and focuses on the TCM philosophy of strengthening a deficit in solar energy (pronounced as yángqì in Mandarin Chinese—陽氣) and reducing an overabundance of lunar energy (pronounced as yinqì in Mandarin Chinese—陰氣) when depressed. The yang in yángqì means *sun*, so clients are essentially cultivating solar energy to light up the darkness. Sitting in the sun can help clients feel more centered, relaxed, and rejuvenated. Therapists help clients focus on the positive energy of the sun warming up their body, energizing their life, and soothing their emotions, while at the same time letting go of their worries or reframing them as they imagine the sun healing their mind, body, and spirit. For those who do not believe in energy, this exercise can still be therapeutic. When clients go outside and meditate in the sun, it is also an effective form of behavioral activation.

CONCLUSION

In this chapter we reviewed the prevalence and risk factors for depression in Asian Americans, as well as contextual issues that cause and influence help seeking, which has important implications for understanding the clinical presentation, mental health beliefs, and establishment of culturally congruent treatment goals. Understanding how cultural issues may influence the reporting, experiencing, and assessing of symptoms is important if we are to accurately diagnose and address client concerns. We also reviewed the limited CBT treatment outcome studies conducted on Asian Americans, pointing out the need for future research in this arena.

Understanding the impact of cultural issues on mental health processes is important when conceptualizing client problems from a CBT framework, evaluating which cognitive interventions to use, and knowing when they might be most appropriate. Key to culturally adapting CBT is to evaluate whether to emphasize more heavily or deemphasize certain aspects of CBT and to determine whether there are extant cultural strengths that can be integrated into existing cognitive models or bridged with cognitive concepts to improve client–treatment congruency. We concluded by identifying four key dimensions where cultural adaptation can take place and that can be readily incorporated in case conceptualization and treatment planning to improve CBT's effectiveness with Asian Americans.

REFERENCES

Abe-Kim, J., Takeuchi, D. T., Hong, S., Zane, N., Sue, S., Spencer, M. S., . . . Alegría, M. (2007). Use of mental health-related services among immigrant and US-born Asian Americans: Results from the National Latino and Asian American Study. *American Journal of Public Health, 97*, 91–98. http://dx.doi.org/10.2105/AJPH.2006.098541

Ai, A. L., Nicdao, E. G., Appel, H. B., & Lee, D. H. J. (2015). Ethnic identity and major depression in Asian American subgroups nationwide: Differential findings in relation to subcultural contexts. *Journal of Clinical Psychology, 71*, 1225–1244. http://dx.doi.org/10.1002/jclp.22214

Alegría, M., Chatterji, P., Wells, K., Cao, Z., Chen, C. N., Takeuchi, D., . . . Meng, X. L. (2008). Disparity in depression treatment among racial and ethnic minority populations in the United States. *Psychiatric Services, 59*, 1264–1272. http://dx.doi.org/10.1176/ps.2008.59.11.1264

Alegría, M., Takeuchi, D., Canino, G., Duan, N., Shrout, P., Meng, X. L., . . . Gong, F. (2004). Considering context, place and culture: The National Latino and Asian American Study. *International Journal of Methods in Psychiatric Research, 13*, 208–220. http://dx.doi.org/10.1002/mpr.178

American Psychiatric Association. (1987). *Diagnostic and statistical manual of mental disorders* (3rd ed., rev.). Washington, DC: Author.

American Psychiatric Association. (2013). *Diagnostic and statistical manual of mental disorders* (5th ed.). Arlington, VA: Author.

Barreto, R. M., & Segal, S. P. (2005). Use of mental health services by Asian Americans. *Psychiatric Services, 56*, 746–748. http://dx.doi.org/10.1176/appi.ps.56.6.746

Beck, A. T. (Ed.). (1979). *Cognitive therapy of depression.* New York, NY: Guilford Press.

Beck, A. T., Steer, R. A., & Brown, G. K. (1996). *Manual for the BDI-II.* San Antonio, TX: The Psychological Corporation.

Beck, A. T., Ward, C. H., Mendelson, M., Mock, J., & Erbaugh, J. (1961). An inventory for measuring depression. *Archives of General Psychiatry, 4*, 561–571. http://dx.doi.org/10.1001/archpsyc.1961.01710120031004

Brink, T. L., Yesavage, J. A., Lum, O., Heersema, P. H., Adey, M., & Rose, T. L. (1982). Screening tests for geriatric depression. *Clinical Gerontologist, 1*, 37–43. http://dx.doi.org/10.1300/J018v01n01_06

Burcusa, S. L., & Iacono, W. G. (2007). Risk for recurrence in depression. *Clinical Psychology Review, 27*, 959–985. http://dx.doi.org/10.1016/j.cpr.2007.02.005

Chen, T. M., Huang, F. Y., Chang, C., & Chung, H. (2006). Using the PHQ-9 for depression screening and treatment monitoring for Chinese Americans in primary care. *Psychiatric Services, 57*, 976–981. http://dx.doi.org/10.1176/ps.2006.57.7.976

Cheng, J. K. Y., Fancher, T. L., Ratanasen, M., Conner, K. R., Duberstein, P. R., Sue, S., & Takeuchi, D. (2010). Lifetime suicidal ideation and suicide attempts in Asian Americans. *Asian American Journal of Psychology, 1*, 18–30. http://dx.doi.org/10.1037/a0018799

Cheng, S. T., & Chan, A. C. M. (2005). The Center for Epidemiologic Studies Depression Scale in older Chinese: Thresholds for long and short forms. *International Journal of Geriatric Psychiatry, 20*, 465–470. http://dx.doi.org/10.1002/gps.1314

Cheung, Y. B., Liu, K. Y., & Yip, P. S. F. (2007). Performance of the CES-D and its short forms in screening suicidality and hopelessness in the community. *Suicide & Life-Threatening Behavior, 37*, 79–88. http://dx.doi.org/10.1521/suli.2007.37.1.79

Dai, Y., Zhang, S., Yamamoto, J., Ao, M., Belin, T. R., Cheung, F., & Hifumi, S. S. (1999). Cognitive behavioral therapy of minor depressive symptoms in elderly Chinese Americans: A pilot study. *Community Mental Health Journal, 35*, 537–542. http://dx.doi.org/10.1023/A:1018763302198

Dozois, D. J. (2003). The psychometric characteristics of the Hamilton Depression Inventory. *Journal of Personality Assessment, 80*, 31–40. http://dx.doi.org/10.1207/S15327752JPA8001_11

Duldulao, A. A., Takeuchi, D. T., & Hong, S. (2009). Correlates of suicidal behaviors among Asian Americans. *Archives of Suicide Research, 13*, 277–290. http://dx.doi.org/10.1080/13811110903044567

First, M. B., Williams, J. B., Karg, R. S., & Spitzer, R. L. (2015). *Structured clinical interview for DSM–5 disorders (SCID-5-CV): Clinician version.* New York, NY: Biometrics Research, New York State Psychiatric Institute.

Hamilton, M. (1960). A rating scale for depression. *Journal of Neurology, Neurosurgery & Psychiatry, 23*, 56–62. http://dx.doi.org/10.1136/jnnp.23.1.56

Hamilton, M. (1967). Development of a rating scale for primary depressive illness. *British Journal of Social & Clinical Psychology, 6*, 278–296. http://dx.doi.org/10.1111/j.2044-8260.1967.tb00530.x

Haro, J. M., Arbabzadeh-Bouchez, S., Brugha, T. S., de Girolamo, G., Guyer, M. E., Jin, R., . . . Kessler, R. C. (2006). Concordance of the composite international diagnostic interview version 3.0 (CIDI 3.0) with standardized clinical assessments in the WHO World Mental Health surveys. *International Journal of Methods in Psychiatric Research, 15*, 167–180. http://dx.doi.org/10.1002/mpr.196

Herman, S., Archambeau, O. G., Deliramich, A. N., Kim, B. S., Chiu, P. H., & Frueh, B. C. (2011). Depressive symptoms and mental health treatment in an ethnoracially diverse college student sample. *Journal of American College Health, 59*, 715–720. http://dx.doi.org/10.1080/07448481.2010.529625

Heron, M. (2011). Deaths: Leading causes for 2007. *National Vital Statistics Reports, 59*, 1–95.

Hong, S., Walton, E., Tamaki, E., & Sabin, J. A. (2014). Lifetime prevalence of mental disorders among Asian Americans: Nativity, gender, and sociodemographic correlates. *Asian American Journal of Psychology, 5*, 353–363. http://dx.doi.org/10.1037/a0035680

Hsu, G. K., Wan, Y. M., & Adler, D. D. (2005). Detection of major depressive disorder in Chinese Americans in primary care. *Hong Kong Journal of Psychiatry, 15*, 71–76.

Huang, F. Y., Chung, H., Kroenke, K., Delucchi, K. L., & Spitzer, R. L. (2006). Using the Patient Health Questionnaire-9 to measure depression among racially and ethnically diverse primary care patients. *Journal of General Internal Medicine, 21*, 547–552. http://dx.doi.org/10.1111/j.1525-1497.2006.00409.x

Hwang, W.-C. (2006). The psychotherapy adaptation and modification framework: Application to Asian Americans. *American Psychologist, 61*, 702–715. http://dx.doi.org/10.1037/0003-066X.61.7.702

Hwang, W.-C. (2009). The Formative Method for Adapting Psychotherapy (FMAP): A community-based developmental approach to culturally adapting therapy. *Professional Psychology: Research and Practice, 40*, 369–377. http://dx.doi.org/10.1037/a0016240

Hwang, W.-C. (2012). Integrating top-down and bottom-up approaches to culturally adapting psychotherapy: Application to Chinese Americans. In G. Bernal & M. M. Domenech Rodríguez (Eds.), *Cultural adaptations: Tools for evidence-based practice with diverse populations* (pp. 179–198). Washington, DC: American Psychological Association. http://dx.doi.org/10.1037/13752-009

Hwang, W.-C. (2016). *Culturally adapting psychotherapy for Asian heritage populations: An evidence-based approach.* San Diego, CA: Academic Press.

Hwang, W.-C., Chun, C. A., Takeuchi, D. T., Myers, H. F., & Siddarth, P. (2005). Age of first onset major depression in Chinese Americans. *Cultural Diversity and Ethnic Minority Psychology, 11*, 16–27. http://dx.doi.org/10.1037/1099-9809.11.1.16

Hwang, W.-C., & Myers, H. F. (2007). Major depression in Chinese Americans: The roles of stress, vulnerability, and acculturation. *Social Psychiatry and Psychiatric Epidemiology, 42*, 189–197. http://dx.doi.org/10.1007/s00127-006-0152-1

Hwang, W.-C., Myers, H. F., Chiu, E., Mak, E., Butner, J. E., Fujimoto, K., . . . Miranda, J. (2015). Culturally adapted cognitive-behavioral therapy for Chinese Americans with depression: A randomized controlled trial. *Psychiatric Services, 66*, 1035–1042. http://dx.doi.org/10.1176/appi.ps.201400358

Hwang, W.-C., Myers, H. F., & Takeuchi, D. T. (2000). Psychosocial predictors of first-onset depression in Chinese Americans. *Social Psychiatry and Psychiatric Epidemiology, 35*, 133–145. http://dx.doi.org/10.1007/s001270050196

Hwang, W.-C., & Ting, J. Y. (2008). Disaggregating the effects of acculturation and acculturative stress on the mental health of Asian Americans. *Cultural Diversity*

& *Ethnic Minority Psychology, 14,* 147–154. http://dx.doi.org/10.1037/ 1099-9809.14.2.147

Hwang, W.-C., & Ting, J. Y. (2013a). Emic. In K. D. Keith (Ed.), *The encyclopedia of cross-cultural psychology* (Vol. II, pp. 466–469). Chichester, England: Wiley. http://dx.doi.org/10.1002/9781118339893.wbeccp189

Hwang, W.-C., & Ting, J. Y. (2013b). Etic. In K. D. Keith (Ed.), *The encyclopedia of cross-cultural psychology* (Vol. II, pp. 515–518). Chichester, England: Wiley. http://dx.doi.org/10.1002/9781118339893.wbeccp209

Hwang, W.-C., & Wood, J. J. (2009). Acculturative family distancing: Links with self-reported symptomatology among Asian Americans and Latinos. *Child Psychiatry and Human Development, 40,* 123–138. http://dx.doi.org/10.1007/ s10578-008-0115-8

Hwang, W.-C., Wood, J. J., & Fujimoto, K. (2010). Acculturative family distancing (AFD) and depression in Chinese American families. *Journal of Consulting and Clinical Psychology, 78,* 655–667. http://dx.doi.org/10.1037/a0020542

Hwang, W.-C., Wood, J. J., Lin, K. M., & Cheung, F. (2006). Cognitive-behavioral therapy with Chinese Americans: Research, theory, and clinical practice. *Cognitive and Behavioral Practice, 13,* 293–303. http://dx.doi.org/10.1016/ j.cbpra.2006.04.010

Hwu, H. G., Yeh, E. K., & Chang, L. Y. (1989). Prevalence of psychiatric disorders in Taiwan defined by the Chinese Diagnostic Interview Schedule. *Acta Psychiatrica Scandinavica, 79,* 136–147. http://dx.doi.org/10.1111/j.1600-0447.1989.tb08581.x

Hwu, H. G., Yeh, E. K., Chang, L. Y., & Yeh, Y. L. (1986). Chinese diagnostic interview schedule: II. A validity study on estimation of lifetime prevalence. *Acta Psychiatrica Scandinavica, 73,* 348–357. http://dx.doi.org/10.1111/ j.1600-0447.1986.tb02695.x

Kalibatseva, Z., & Leong, F. T. L. (2011). Depression among Asian Americans: Review and recommendations. *Depression Research and Treatment, 2011,* Article ID 320902. http://dx.doi.org/10.1155/2011/320902

Kalibatseva, Z., Wu, I. C., & Leong, F. L. (2014). Assessing depression and suicidality in Asian-Americans. In L. T. Benuto, N. S. Thaler, B. D. Leany, L. T. Benuto, N. S. Thaler, & B. D. Leany (Eds.), *Guide to psychological assessment with Asians* (pp. 181–198). New York, NY: Springer.

Kessler, R. C., Berglund, P., Demler, O., Jin, R., Koretz, D., Merikangas, K. R., . . . the National Comorbidity Survey Replication. (2003, June 18). The epidemiology of major depressive disorder: Results from the National Comorbidity Survey Replication (NCS-R). *JAMA, 289,* 3095–3105. http://dx.doi.org/10.1001/ jama.289.23.3095

Kessler, R. C., Borges, G., & Walters, E. E. (1999). Prevalence of and risk factors for lifetime suicide attempts in the National Comorbidity Survey. *Archives of General Psychiatry, 56,* 617–626. http://dx.doi.org/10.1001/archpsyc.56.7.617

Kessler, R. C., McGonagle, K. A., Zhao, S., Nelson, C. B., Hughes, M., Eshleman, S., . . . Kendler, K. S. (1994). Lifetime and 12-month prevalence of *DSM–III–R* psychiatric disorders in the United States: Results from the National Comorbidity Survey. *Archives of General Psychiatry, 51*, 8–19. http://dx.doi.org/10.1001/archpsyc.1994.03950010008002

Kim, H. J., Park, E., Storr, C. L., Tran, K., & Juon, H. S. (2015). Depression among Asian-American adults in the community: Systematic review and meta-analysis. *PLoS One, 10*(6), e0127760. http://dx.doi.org/10.1371/journal.pone.0127760

Kim, J., & Choi, N. G. (2010). Twelve-month prevalence of *DSM–IV* mental disorders among older Asian Americans: Comparison with younger groups. *Aging & Mental Health, 14*(1), 90–99. http://dx.doi.org/10.1080/13607860903046461

Kleinknecht, R. A., Dinnel, D. L., Kleinknecht, E. E., Hiruma, N., & Harada, N. (1997). Cultural factors in social anxiety: A comparison of social phobia symptoms and *Taijin kyofusho*. *Journal of Anxiety Disorders, 11*, 157–177. http://dx.doi.org/10.1016/S0887-6185(97)00004-2

Kleinman, A. (1980). *Patients and healers in the context of culture: An exploration of the borderland between anthropology, medicine, & psychiatry*. Berkeley: University of California Press.

Le Meyer, O., Zane, N., Cho, Y. I., & Takeuchi, D. T. (2009). Use of specialty mental health services by Asian Americans with psychiatric disorders. *Journal of Consulting and Clinical Psychology, 77*, 1000–1005. http://dx.doi.org/10.1037/a0017065

Leong, F. T., & Lau, A. S. (2001). Barriers to providing effective mental health services to Asian Americans. *Mental Health Services Research, 3*, 201–214. http://dx.doi.org/10.1023/A:1013177014788

Markus, H. R., & Kitayama, S. (1991). Culture and the self: Implications for cognition, emotion, and motivation. *Psychological Review, 98*, 224–253. http://dx.doi.org/10.1037/0033-295X.98.2.224

Miranda, J., Bernal, G., Lau, A., Kohn, L., Hwang, W. C., & LaFromboise, T. (2005). State of the science on psychosocial interventions for ethnic minorities. *Annual Review of Clinical Psychology, 1*, 113–142. http://dx.doi.org/10.1146/annurev.clinpsy.1.102803.143822

Miranda, J., Woo, S., Lagomasino, I., Hepner, K. A., Watkins, K. E., & Wiseman, S. (2006). *A manual for group cognitive-behavioral therapy of major depressions*. San Francisco, CA: San Francisco General Hospital.

Nguyen, D., & Bornheimer, L. A. (2014). Mental health service use types among Asian Americans with a psychiatric disorder: Considerations of culture and need. *The Journal of Behavioral Health Services & Research, 41*, 520–528. http://dx.doi.org/10.1007/s11414-013-9383-6

Okazaki, S. (2000). Asian American and White American differences on affective distress symptoms: Do symptom reports differ across reporting methods? *Journal of Cross-Cultural Psychology, 31*, 603–625. http://dx.doi.org/10.1177/0022022100031005004

Radloff, L. S. (1977). The CES-D Scale: A self-report depression scale for research in the general population. *Applied Psychological Measurement, 1,* 385–401. http://dx.doi.org/10.1177/014662167700100306

Reynolds, W. M., & Kobak, K. A. (1995). *HDI—Hamilton Depression Inventory: A Self-report version of the Hamilton Depression Rating Scale, professional manual.* Odessa, FL: Psychological Assessment Resources.

So, E., Kam, I. I., Leung, C. M., Chung, D., Liu, Z., & Fong, S. (2003). The Chinese-bilingual SCID-I/P project: Stage 1—Reliability for mood disorders and schizophrenia. *Hong Kong Journal of Psychiatry, 13,* 7–18.

Soto, J. A., Levenson, R. W., & Ebling, R. (2005). Cultures of moderation and expression: Emotional experience, behavior, and physiology in Chinese Americans and Mexican Americans. *Emotion, 5,* 154–165. http://dx.doi.org/10.1037/1528-3542.5.2.154

Spitzer, R. L., Kroenke, K., Williams, J. B., & the Patient Health Questionnaire Primary Care Study Group. (1999, November 10). Validation and utility of a self-report version of PRIME-MD: The PHQ primary care study. *JAMA, 282,* 1737–1744. http://dx.doi.org/10.1001/jama.282.18.1737

Suinn, R. M. (2010). Reviewing acculturation and Asian Americans: How acculturation affects health, adjustment, school achievement, and counseling. *Asian American Journal of Psychology, 1,* 5–17. http://dx.doi.org/10.1037/a0018798

Takeuchi, D. T., Chung, R. C. Y., Lin, K. M., Shen, H., Kurasaki, K., Chun, C. A., & Sue, S. (1998). Lifetime and twelve-month prevalence rates of major depressive episodes and dysthymia among Chinese Americans in Los Angeles. *The American Journal of Psychiatry, 155,* 1407–1414. http://dx.doi.org/10.1176/ajp.155.10.1407

Takeuchi, D. T., Zane, N., Hong, S., Chae, D. H., Gong, F., Gee, G. C., . . . Alegría, M. (2007). Immigration-related factors and mental disorders among Asian Americans. *American Journal of Public Health, 97,* 84–90. http://dx.doi.org/10.2105/AJPH.2006.088401

Triandis, H. C., Bontempo, R., Villareal, M. J., Asai, M., & Lucca, N. (1988). Individualism and collectivism: Cross-cultural perspectives on self-ingroup relationships. *Journal of Personality and Social Psychology, 54,* 323–338. http://dx.doi.org/10.1037/0022-3514.54.2.323

U.S. Department of Health and Human Services. (2001). *Mental health: Culture, race and ethnicity—A supplement to mental health: A report of the Surgeon General.* Rockville, MD: U.S. Department of Health and Human Services, Public Health Service, Office of the Surgeon General.

Weissman, M. M., Bland, R. C., Canino, G. J., Faravelli, C., Greenwald, S., Hwu, H. G., . . . Yeh, E. K. (1996). Cross-national epidemiology of major depression and bipolar disorder. *JAMA, 276,* 293–299. http://dx.doi.org/10.1001/jama.1996.03540040037030

Wong, Y. J., Brownson, C., & Schwing, A. E. (2011). Risk and protective factors associated with Asian American students' suicidal ideation: A multicampus, national study. *Journal of College Student Development, 52*, 396–408. http://dx.doi.org/10.1353/csd.2011.0057

World Health Organization. (1992). *The ICD–10 classification of mental and behavioural disorders: Clinical descriptions and diagnostic guidelines.* Geneva, Switzerland: Author.

Xu, J., Kochanek, K. D., Murphy, S. L., & Tejada-Vera, B. (2010). Deaths: Final data for 2007. *National Vital Statistics Reports, 58*, 1–19.

Yeung, A., Chang, D., Gresham, R. L., Jr., Nierenberg, A. A., & Fava, M. (2004). Illness beliefs of depressed Chinese American patients in primary care. *Journal of Nervous and Mental Disease, 192*, 324–327. http://dx.doi.org/10.1097/01.nmd.0000120892.96624.00

Yeung, A., Fung, F., Yu, S. C., Vorono, S., Ly, M., Wu, S., & Fava, M. (2008). Validation of the Patient Health Questionnaire-9 for depression screening among Chinese Americans. *Comprehensive Psychiatry, 49*, 211–217. http://dx.doi.org/10.1016/j.comppsych.2006.06.002

Yeung, A., Neault, N., Sonawalla, S., Howarth, S., Fava, M., & Nierenberg, A. A. (2002). Screening for major depression in Asian-Americans: A comparison of the Beck and the Chinese Depression Inventory. *Acta Psychiatrica Scandinavica, 105*, 252–257. http://dx.doi.org/10.1034/j.1600-0447.2002.1092.x

Ying, Y. W. (1988). Depressive symptomatology among Chinese-Americans as measured by the CES-D. *Journal of Clinical Psychology, 44*, 739–746. http://dx.doi.org/10.1002/1097-4679(198809)44:5<739::AID-JCLP2270440512>3.0.CO;2-0

Zane, N., Enomoto, K., & Chun, C. A. (1994). Treatment outcomes of Asian and White American clients in outpatient therapy. *American Journal of Community Psychology, 22*, 177–191. http://dx.doi.org/10.1002/1520-6629(199404)22:2<177::AID-JCOP2290220212>3.0.CO;2-7

Zheng, Y. P., & Lin, K. M. (1991). Comparison of the Chinese depression inventory and the Chinese version of the Beck Depression Inventory. *Acta Psychiatrica Scandinavica, 84*, 531–536. http://dx.doi.org/10.1111/j.1600-0447.1991.tb03189.x

Zheng, Y. P., Zhao, J. P., Phillips, M., Liu, J. B., Cai, M. F., Sun, S. Q., & Huang, M. F. (1988). Validity and reliability of the Chinese Hamilton Depression Rating Scale. *The British Journal of Psychiatry, 152*, 660–664. http://dx.doi.org/10.1192/bjp.152.5.660

Zung, W. W. K. (1965). A self-rating depression scale. *Archives of General Psychiatry, 12*, 63–70. http://dx.doi.org/10.1001/archpsyc.1965.01720310065008

2

COGNITIVE BEHAVIORAL MODELS, MEASURES, AND TREATMENTS FOR DEPRESSIVE DISORDERS IN LATIN AMERICANS

VICTORIA K. NGO AND JEANNE MIRANDA

Depression is a leading health care burden worldwide (Ferrari et al., 2013; Mathers, Lopez, & Murray, 2006; Murray et al., 2013) with untreated depression resulting in detrimental effects on quality of life, relationships, productivity, economic outcomes, morbidity, and mortality. Yet, the treatment gap for depression worldwide remains unacceptably large (Hyman, 2014). Because of the growing public health concern, the last few decades have seen a surge in depression intervention research. One of the most studied psychological interventions is cognitive behavior therapy (CBT), which has a significant body of literature demonstrating its effectiveness for a range of mental health conditions, including depression (Beltman, Voshaar, & Speckens, 2010; Butler, Chapman, Forman, & Beck, 2006; Hofmann, Asnaani, Vonk, Sawyer, & Fang, 2012). Although CBT for depression is well established, CBT and other evidence-based interventions are not easily accessible to ethnic minorities (Alegría et al., 2007; González et al., 2010;

http://dx.doi.org/10.1037/0000091-003
Treating Depression, Anxiety, and Stress in Ethnic and Racial Groups: Cognitive Behavioral Approaches,
E. C. Chang, C. A. Downey, J. K. Hirsch, and E. A. Yu (Editors)

U.S. Department of Health and Human Services, 2001). Furthermore, the quality of mental health care for ethnic minorities is often poor because many minorities reside in low-income communities where care systems are often underresourced and have severe shortages of trained providers, particularly those who are bilingual or ethnic minority themselves. In addition, significant barriers to care exist for ethnic minorities, including low depression literacy and mental health stigma, as well as obstacles related to transportation, childcare, cost, legal status, and lack of insurance coverage (Alegría, Canino, Rios, & African, 2002; Santiago, Kaltman, & Miranda, 2013). As a result, significant racial and ethnic disparities in mental health care access and outcomes persist (McGuire & Miranda, 2008).

Following the U.S. Department of Health and Human Services 2001 supplement to the Surgeon General's report, *Mental Health: Culture, Race, and Ethnicity*, which highlighted the limited access and quality of mental health care for ethnic minorities, greater attention has been paid to stimulate research and improve quality of evidence-based practices for ethnic minorities. In this chapter, we review the state of the science in assessment measures and CBT for depression for Latino Americans, who make up the largest ethnic minority group in the United States. To this end, we briefly describe key cultural concepts relevant to the mental health needs of this diverse community. Our review of the validity of depression measures and evidence base for CBT briefly summarizes existing reviews and provides greater detail about more recent developments in the field. We conclude with the implications for future research and practice.

DEPRESSION IN THE LATINO COMMUNITY

Depression disorders are considered comparably prevalent across cultural groups, with higher risk among women and patients with comorbid health conditions (Alegría et al., 2004; Andrade et al., 2003; Kessler et al., 2003). Despite their greater exposure to poverty, discrimination, and acculturative stress, which are known to have harmful effects on mental health (Lorant et al., 2003; Rogler, Cortes, & Malgady, 1991), epidemiological data show protective effects of Latino culture and the deleterious effects of acculturation on psychiatric morbidity (Alegría et al., 2004, 2007; Grant et al., 2004; Vega et al., 1998). In general, Latinos compared with their White counterparts, are more resilient to poor health and mental health outcomes, a phenomenon termed *Hispanic paradox* (Palloni & Morenoff, 2001). *Acculturation*, or the level of adaptation to mainstream American cultural values and beliefs, has been found to increase the incidence of depression for Latino individuals (Burnam, Hough, Karno, Escobar, & Telles, 1987; Escobar,

Hoyos Nervi, & Gara, 2000). The protective effect of Latino culture may be related to values such as *personalismo, espiritualidad,* and *familismo* that promote two-parent households, close-knit extended families, and community networks, as well as religious involvement and spirituality, all of which tend to diminish in the migration and acculturation process (Escobar, 1998; Mulvaney-Day, Alegría, & Sribney, 2007; Plant & Sachs-Ericsson, 2004).

Although earlier epidemiological studies (Epidemiologic Catchment Study: Hough, Karno, Burnam, Escobar, & Timbers, 1983; National Comorbidity Survey: Kessler et al., 1994) were more inconsistent regarding rates of depression among Latino subgroups due to sampling and methodological limitations (Blazer, Kessler, McGonagle, & Swartz, 1994; Burnam et al., 1987; Kessler et al., 1994), later epidemiological studies (National Latino and Asian American Study [NLAAS: Alegría et al., 2004], National Epidemiological Survey on Alcohol and Related Conditions [NESARC]: Grant et al., 2004) using more culturally valid instruments and Spanish interviews and including a more representative sample of Latinos support the Hispanic paradox.

Both NLAAS and NESARC found a converging pattern for ethnic background, as well as acculturation and proxy variables such as English language and nativity, such that those who are more similar to White Americans in terms of speaking English and being born in the United States had higher rates of psychiatric morbidity, including depression. Depression rates were less than half the rate observed for White Americans and were similar to that of African Americans. Increased rates were also found among U.S.-born, highly English proficient, and third generation Latino individuals (Alegría et al., 2007; Grant et al., 2004). The protective effect of Latino culture extended to Cuban Americans (Narrow, Rae, Mościcki, Locke, & Regier, 1990; Ortega, Rosenheck, Alegría, & Desai, 2000) but not Puerto Ricans, who had the highest rate of depression among subpopulations of Latinos; there was no difference between those born in Puerto Rico and the United States (Alegría, Canino, Stinson, & Grant, 2006; Canino, Bird, Shrout, Rubio-Stipec, Bravo, Martinez, Sesman, & Guevara, 1987; Shrout et al., 1992). Central Americans have also been found to have more symptoms of depression, greater migration-related stress, and a higher incidence of posttraumatic stress disorder (Cervantes, Salgado de Snyder, & Padilla, 1989) than Mexican Americans. However, they are understudied and often not represented in epidemiologic studies.

In the Latino culture, idioms of distress, or culturally specific ways of addressing mental health distress (Kleinman, 2004), have been identified, including *nervios, ataque de nervios, decaimiento, susto,* and *agitamiento,* all reflecting expressions that have somatic symptoms associated with the distress (Guarnaccia et al., 2010; Salgado de Snyder, Diaz-Perez, & Ojeda,

2000). In an epidemiological study of *nervios* in a rural sample of Mexican adults, 15% met criteria for *nervios*, which is defined as a generalized condition of distress expressed with a variety of somatic and psychological symptoms. However, only a small portion (17%–21%) of those with *nervios* met criteria for any *Diagnostic and Statistical Manual of Mental Disorders* (*DSM*; third ed., rev.; American Psychiatric Association, 1987) mood or anxiety disorder, which raises questions about the adequacy of capturing all models of distress using standard *DSM* criteria for diagnosis (Salgado de Snyder et al., 2000).

Ataque de nervios is probably the most prominent idiom of distress, particularly for Latinos in the Caribbean, with symptoms such as headaches, inability to perform activities of daily living, irritability, stomach problems, nervousness, inability to concentrate, dizziness, tingling sensations, and crying spells. It is also associated with a feeling of vulnerability related to stressful life circumstances and has been most extensively studied in the Puerto Rican community, where 15% of the island population reported experiencing *ataques de nervios*. Of these individuals, 63% met criteria for anxiety and affective disorders, which were most common among women from low-income backgrounds who reported marital disruption (Guarnaccia et al., 1993). Later studies on Puerto Ricans and Dominicans from New York also found a similar overlap with anxiety and affective disorders (Guarnaccia, Rivera, Franco, & Neighbors, 1996; Lewis-Fernández et al., 2002; Liebowitz et al., 1994; Salmán et al., 1998). The only population-based study on a representative and diverse sample of Latinos, the NLAAS study, found similar rates for Puerto Ricans (15%), higher than other Latino groups (7%–9%; Guarnaccia et al., 2010).

MEASURES

Validated measures available for assessing depression include the Beck Depression Inventory (Beck, Ward, Mendelson, Mock, & Erbaugh, 1961), Center for Epidemiologic Studies Depression Scale (Radloff, 1977), and Patient Health Questionnaire (Kroenke, Spitzer, & Williams, 2001). Diagnostic interviews include the Structured Clinical Interview for *DSM–IV* (Spitzer, Williams, Gibbon, & First, 1992), Composite International Diagnostic Interview (Kessler & Üstün, 2004), and the Mini International Neuropsychiatric Interview (Sheehan et al., 1998). These measures and diagnostic interviews are used widely across diverse populations and are available in numerous languages, including Spanish. In this review, we discuss the studies that have evaluated the cross-cultural validity of both English and Spanish versions for Latino Americans and include only tools that reflect diagnostic criteria of the *DSM–IV* (American Psychiatric Association, 1994) or later versions of the *DSM*.

Scale Measures

The Beck Depression Inventory (BDI) is a self-report, 21-item multiple-choice measure developed by Aaron Beck (Beck et al., 1961) to measure the severity of depression. The BDI and BDI-II have been used and studied in the Latino population and have shown adequate psychometric properties (Azocar, Areán, Miranda, & Muñoz, 2001; Bonilla, Bernal, Santos, & Santos, 2004; Novy, Stanley, Averill, & Daza, 2001; Wiebe & Penley, 2005). Psychometric evaluation of the Spanish version of the BDI found high internal consistency and a similar two-factor structure, a somatic factor and an affective factor, for both the Spanish and English versions (Azocar et al., 2001; Bernal, Bonilla, & Santiago, 1995). Although mean differences were not found, differential item functioning (DIF) analyses found four BDI items (punishment, tearfulness appearance, inability to work) to exhibit bias when comparing different language versions. These results suggest that cultural differences may alter the responses or expressions of depressive symptoms; however, additional research on DIF is needed. Although the authors concluded that the BDI was an adequate measure of depressive symptomatology for Spanish-speaking Latinos, they urged test administrators to use caution when interpreting scores and to gather more information before making a diagnosis (Azocar et al., 2001).

The Center for Epidemiologic Studies Depression Scale (CES-D; Radloff, 1977) scale is another well-established 20-item self-report scale that was designed to emphasize the affective component of depression. An initial factor analytic study found four factors (depressed affect, positive affect, somatic, and interpersonal) consistently across three groups of participants and concluded that the CES-D was suitable for use with English-speaking populations across many different ages and economic ranges (Radloff, 1977). However, several studies have found different mean levels and factor structures across diverse populations, including Latinos. Garcia and Marks (1989) compared responses on the CES-D from Mexican American and Caucasian adults and found that hopelessness about the future, lack of enjoyment from life, and depreciation of self in relation to others were more prevalent with Mexican American adults. They also found a different factor structure for the Mexican Americans and Caucasians and identified a unique factor for the Mexican American group that encompassed items that dealt with loneliness, sadness, and crying (Garcia & Marks, 1989). Different factor structures were also found across different Latino subpopulations (Puerto Rican, Mexican American, and Cuban adults) using the Hispanic Health and Nutrition Examination Survey, which suggest social and cultural differences in the expression of depressive symptoms and depressive affect within the Latino community (Guarnaccia, Angel, & Worobey, 1989). Although adequate reliability and sensitivity were found for the Spanish version, the CES-D exhibited limited specificity for detecting depression (Mościcki, Locke, Rae, & Boyd, 1989; Roberts, Vernon, & Rhoades, 1989). Overall, the CES-D may not be an appropriate measure to be used with the Latino population because of potential inconsistencies of factor structures found across ethnicities (Garcia & Marks, 1989; Guarnaccia et al., 1989). Even Radloff (1977) cautioned against using the CES-D with bilingual participants because of complex wording and colloquial phrases that may be confusing to some bilingual individuals.

The Patient Health Questionnaire-9 (PHQ-9; Kroenke et al., 2001) is a brief self-administered questionnaire consisting of nine items based on the *DSM–IV* diagnostic criteria. Its validity and reliability as a diagnostic measure as well as its utility in assessing depression severity and monitoring treatment response are well-established (Löwe et al., 2004). The only study that evaluated the cultural validity of the PHQ-9 across ethnic groups, comprehensively evaluated both factor structures and DIF across Chinese Americans, Latino Americans, African Americans, and White Americans. Using a large sample of 5,053 primary care patients, they found a single underlying factor with alphas ranging from .79 to .89 across the four groups. Minor group differences in the mean level of endorsement of some symptoms and DIF were found when minority groups were compared with non-Hispanic Whites. For Latinos, a higher endorsement rate and DIF was found for anhedonia; however, this difference was largely accounted for once sociodemographic covariates, including language, were controlled. The authors concluded that the scale functioned fundamentally the same across the four groups and that the screening threshold need not be adjusted, despite minor changes in symptom profiles. In contrast to previous studies on the CES-D and BDI, which recommended threshold adjustments, they did not find mean total score differences or factor invariance between Latinos and Whites and did not recommend threshold changes for Latinos (Huang, Chung, Kroenke, Delucchi, & Spitzer, 2006).

Diagnostic Interviews

Several well-established diagnostic interviews have been used in large-scale epidemiological studies in the Latino population, including the Diagnostic Interview Schedule (DIS; Robins, Helzer, Croughan, & Ratcliff, 1981), Composite International Diagnostic Interview (CIDI; Kessler & Ustün, 2004) and the Mini International Neuropsychiatric Interview (MINI; Sheehan et al., 1998), and have been subjected to psychometric evaluation for Latino Americans. Although the DIS has been evaluated in the Latino population (Burnam, Karno, Hough, Escobar, & Forsythe, 1983; Canino, Bird, Shrout, Rubio-Stipec, Bravo, Martinez, Sesman, Guzman, et al., 1987), we only reviewed the CIDI and MINI because they are based on *DSM–IV* criteria. Other well-established tools include the Structured Clinical Interview for *DSM* disorders (SCID; Spitzer et al., 1992) and the Schedule for Affective Disorders and Schizophrenia (Endicott & Spitzer, 1978); however, they have not been studied in the Latino population, although Spanish language versions are available.

The CIDI (Kessler & Ustün, 2004) is a fully structured interview designed by the World Health Organization to be used internationally to assess a range of *DSM–IV* disorders, including mood disorders such as major depressive disorder, dysthymia, and bipolar I and II. It was adapted from the DIS and modified to be used by trained lay interviewers. The CIDI is available in numerous languages and is probably the most widely used structured diagnostic interview outside the United States, as well as in research focused on Latino American populations. An earlier revision (Version 2.1), developed by an international advisory committee, specifically examined each item for cultural applicability (Andrews & Peters, 1998). Several large-scale epidemiological studies have used the English and Spanish versions of the CIDI (Alegría et al., 2004; Kessler et al., 1994, 2003), but only one study has evaluated the validity for Latino populations (Alegría et al., 2009). On the basis of data from the NLAAS study, the CIDI–SCID concordance for depression was adequate; however, the CIDI did present problems for accurately assessing posttraumatic stress disorder and generalized anxiety disorder for Latinos (Alegría et al., 2009).

The MINI (Sheehan et al., 1998) is a brief structured diagnostic instrument for evaluation of *DSM–IV* Axis I disorders. It can be administered by a trained non-mental health care provider and takes approximately 10 to 25 minutes to complete. Its reliability, sensitivity, and specificity have been examined in clinical populations, and it has been found to be equivalent to longer psychiatric diagnostic interviews such as the CIDI and the SCID (Lecrubier et al., 1997; Sheehan et al., 1997, 1998). The tool has been used in over 100 studies and has been translated into 30 different languages, including Spanish (Bobes, 1998). In a validation study of the Spanish version of the MINI with 126 primary care patients, acceptable agreement between the MINI and psychiatrists' diagnostic judgment across a range of common psychiatric diagnoses was found, as were acceptable levels of sensitivity, specificity, and positive and negative predictive values (Bobes, 1998).

With the exception of CES-D, studies that have evaluated well-established depression measures show that psychometric properties have been acceptable for Latino Americans. The limited cultural validation studies on diagnostic tools that do exist show that they function similarly across ethnic groups. Although DIF or measurement nonequivalence has been found for the BDI and CES-D, studies have not always been consistent in their directionality, have used different methodologies, and have been conducted on relatively small samples. In addition, studies evaluating DIF often explain cultural differences post hoc rather than using a theoretical framework to test cultural effects. The most rigorous study evaluating DIF on the PHQ-9 for multiple populations did not recommend threshold changes for the depression cutoff score and maintained that depression is functionally similar across ethnic groups. In conclusion, symptom measures and diagnostic tools available are valid for Latinos. More research is needed to link DIF to other factors associated with ethnic difference or language difference.

COGNITIVE BEHAVIOR INTERVENTIONS

CBT is an evidence-based model of therapy that was developed for depression but has been applied to a variety of mental health disorders and conditions. The model focuses on using therapeutic strategies to change maladaptive cognitions to decrease emotional distress and problematic behaviors. At the core of CBT is cognitive restructuring, interpersonal skills training, and engagement in pleasant activities, which is achieved through a collaborative process in which the patient is an active participant in examining and modifying their maladaptive thought and behavior patterns to achieve symptom reduction, functioning improvement, and depression remission (Beck, Rush, Shaw, & Emery, 1979).

CBT is the most commonly investigated psychotherapy, with over 269 meta-analytic studies of CBT for a variety of conditions (Hofmann et al., 2012). For depression, CBT has consistently been found to be effective relative to control or no treatment. However, no meta-analytic studies have focused specifically on Latino adults. Literature reviews summarizing the broader range of evidence-based treatments for Latinos (Cabassa & Hansen, 2007; Organista & Munoz, 1996) and ethnic minorities generally (Miranda et al., 2005; Ward, 2007) have all concluded that CBT is effective for Latinos. Latinos have unique histories in the United States, such as legal status and immigrant backgrounds and differences in mental health literacy and awareness, which could result in the need for adaptation of CBT specifically for them. Because of their unique histories, Latinos tend to be poorer, on average, than White Americans (U.S. Census Bureau, 2013) and tend to perceive more discrimination in their lives (Kessler, Mickelson, & Williams, 1999). Cultural differences in mental health understanding and expression of distress potentially could make psychotherapeutic interventions differently effective for Latinos. Although data are limited, culturally adapted engagement strategies for Latinos improve outcomes in terms of their effect on recruitment and treatment engagement (Griner & Smith, 2006; Miranda et al., 2005).

There have been eight randomized controlled trials (RCTs) focused on the implementation of CBT for Latino populations, including low-income primary care patients (Alegría et al., 2014; Miranda, Azocar, Organista, Dwyer, & Areane, 2003; Miranda, Duan, et al., 2003; Wells et al., 2004), women (Miranda, Chung, et al., 2003), women with perinatal depression (Le, Perry, & Stuart, 2011), and HIV-positive individuals (Simoni et al., 2013). The studies varied in terms of settings, providers, and whether they were delivered in group or individually, in person or over the phone.

The best studied CBT model for Latinos to date is the Munoz and Miranda (1986) English-language version and the Munoz, Aguilar-Gaxiola, and Guzman (1986) Spanish-language version, which has been empirically tested in a number of studies in health care settings and shown to be effective when delivered by therapists in health care and community settings (Miranda, Azocar, et al., 2003; Miranda, Chung, et al., 2003; Miranda, Duan, et al., 2003). It was also adapted and found to be effective for adolescents (Ngo et al., 2009) and perinatal populations (Le et al., 2011) and has been piloted with text messaging enhancements (Aguilera & Muñoz, 2011). This model of CBT adapted the standard treatment by making it more suitable for those with low levels of education and by simplifying the concepts of CBT (Lewinsohn & Amenson, 1978; Lewinsohn, Antonuccio, Steinmetz Breckenridge, & Teri, 1984) that focus on the influence of thoughts (Sessions 1–4), pleasant activities (Sessions 5–8), and interpersonal interactions (Sessions 9–12) on mood over 12 weekly sessions. In addition, it was translated into Spanish.

The Munoz and Miranda (1986) and Munoz, Aguilar-Gaxiola, and Guzman (1986) CBT protocol was first evaluated by Miranda, Azocar, and colleagues (2003) in a randomized trial in which group CBT was compared with group CBT combined with case management to address psychosocial stressors (e.g., housing difficulties, problems with immigration status) for low-income ethnic minority medical patients (39% Latino). A positive effect for case management was found for greater retention in care across all patients (60% CBT alone vs. 83% CBT + case management), but only Latinos improved in symptoms and functioning. Specifically, a 30% symptom reduction was found for Spanish-speaking patients who received both CBT and case management compared with only an 18% reduction for those who received only CBT. Case management may be a particularly important aspect of depression care for Spanish-speaking individuals who may need support in handling their affairs in an English-speaking country.

Partners in Care, a large quality improvement study, focused on insured minority populations (Wells et al., 2004). CBT was part of a collaborative care model in which either CBT and/or guideline medications for depression were offered as part of quality improvement (QI) efforts across six managed health care systems. QI was found to be more effective than usual care and resulted in improvements in depression over time, with effects strongest for ethnic minorities. Specifically, the interventions significantly decreased the likelihood that Latinos and other minorities would report probable depression at 6 and 12 months, whereas no difference in depression was found between QI and usual care conditions for the White sample at either follow-up. Five years after implementation, the participants in the intervention arms of this study had improved outcomes relative to those in usual care (Wells et al., 2004). Furthermore, disparities in outcomes were reduced through markedly improving health outcomes and lowering the unmet need for appropriate care among Latinos relative to Whites (Miranda, Schoenbaum, Sherbourne, Duan, & Wells, 2004).

In the Women Entering Care study, CBT was compared with paroxetine (switched to bupropion if clinically necessary) and community referral for Latina and African American women (Miranda, Chung, et al., 2003). The women were largely working poor women (half the sample were Latina), and culturally sensitive methods, including availability of Spanish language access, and accommodations related to childcare and transportation were made to engage women into care. Guideline care in both medication and CBT was effective over and above community care for treatment engagement, decreasing depressive symptoms, and improving functioning of these women. A higher proportion of women assigned to medication received guideline care (66/88), whereas a third received six or more CBT sessions (32/90), and only 17% (15/89) referred to community care attended at least one mental health session. By 6 months, 44% of medication patients, 32% of psychotherapy patients, and 28% of referred patients were asymptomatic. There were no interactions of treatment with ethnicity on outcomes, and all ethnic groups responded to treatment equally. At 1-year follow-up, 50.9% assigned to antidepressants, 56.9% assigned to CBT, and 37.1% assigned to community referral were no longer clinically depressed (Miranda et al., 2006). Furthermore, Siddique, Chung, Brown, and Miranda (2012) found that among depressed women with moderate baseline depression and anxiety, medication was superior to CBT at 6 months, but the difference was not sustained at 1 year. Among women with severe depression, there was no significant treatment group difference at 6 months, but CBT was superior to medication at 1 year. No ethnic differences were observed in this follow-up study (Siddique et al., 2012).

The Munoz and Miranda (1986) and Munoz, Aguilar-Gaxiola, and Guzman (1986) CBT protocol was also adapted for perinatal populations, and efficacy was evaluated with 217 high-risk Latinas (Le, Zmuda, Perry, & Muñoz, 2010). The study found that intervention participants had significantly fewer depressive symptoms and fewer cases of moderate depression than usual care participants posttreatment during pregnancy, but the differences did not persist into postpartum despite added booster sessions. Effects were stronger for women who participated for four or more sessions. The authors concluded that a CBT intervention for low-income, high-risk Latinas reduced depressive symptoms during pregnancy but not during the postpartum period.

Although the Munoz and Miranda (1986) intervention is not considered a culturally adapted model of CBT, it was modified to simplify language and to provide examples relevant to low-income populations. It has also been delivered in research and community contexts in which a variety of barriers for Latino populations, such as language access, transportation, and even childcare, are addressed.

Marchand, Ng, Rohde, and Stice (2010) conducted an RCT of a four-session CBT group intervention across two samples ($n_1 = 167$, $n_2 = 134$) of English-speaking ethnically diverse high school and university students (Asian Americans, African Americans, Latino Americans, and White Americans) and found reductions in depressive symptoms for intervention participants versus waitlist controls. Although the study was powered to detect ethnic effect, no ethnic differences were found in either trial (Marchand et al., 2010).

Simoni et al. (2013) focused on integrating depression treatment directly into HIV primary care, but this preliminary trial was small ($N = 40$) and not powered for tests of statistical significance. However, findings were promising, supporting the effectiveness of CBT for depression and antiretroviral therapy adherence posttreatment (Simoni et al., 2013).

Two studies evaluating telephone-delivered CBT (Alegría et al., 2014; Dwight-Johnson et al., 2010). Alegría et al. (2014) found that both telephone and face-to-face versions of engagement and counseling for Latinos (ECLA), interventions culturally tailored to Latinos, were more effective than usual care. Researchers used interviews with the target population to condense and modify standard CBT materials; add visual aids, culturally relevant metaphors, values, and proverbs; and lower health literacy requirements. In this trial, there was a higher treatment initiation for the telephone versus face-to-face intervention (89.7% vs. 78.8%), which suggests that telephone-based care may improve both access and quality of care. Dwight-Johnson et al. (2010) found a positive nonsignificant trend in which patients who received CBT by phone were more likely to experience improvement in depression scores over the 6-month follow-up period compared with patients who received enhanced usual care.

Several small-scale pilot or case studies evaluated culturally adapted versions of CBT for Latinos (Aguilera & Muñoz, 2011; Interian, Allen, Gara, & Escobar, 2008; Piedra & Byoun, 2012). A pilot evaluation of a culturally adapted 12-session individual CBT protocol in a primary care setting, which was based on cross-cultural considerations described in the literature, such as *simpatico* and *respeto*, and offered *dichos* or sayings to complement explanations of therapeutic techniques, found posttreatment change in a small sample of 15 Latino adults. Specifically, they found a 57% reduction in depressive symptoms at posttreatment and 54% from baseline to 6-month follow-up (Interian et al., 2008). In another pilot study of a 10-week group CBT program called *vida alegra*, cultural adaptations included incorporation of cultural examples and constructs, as well as a module focused on acculturative stress and its impact on relationships (Piedra & Byoun, 2012). The pilot study evaluated symptom change for 19 patients and found significant reduction of depression symptoms at posttreatment and 3-month follow-up. These studies of culturally adapted CBT for Latinos show promise; however, they have not been evaluated in large RCTs nor have they been compared with standard CBT delivered in Spanish.

With the exception of the Marchand et al. (2010) study, which was conducted on more acculturated English-speaking college students, all RCT studies incorporated minimum cultural considerations to increase language access (e.g., facilitating the interventions or making materials available in Spanish) or staff training to address cultural and contextual issues. Only one RCT has made significant cultural adaptations of CBT for Latinos (Alegría et al., 2014), although a few pilot feasibility studies have shown promise (Interian et al., 2008; Piedra & Byoun, 2012). In general, the RCTs revealed that standard CBT delivered in ways that are accessible to Latinos is equally effective, or more effective, for Latinos compared with non-Latino White populations in a variety of settings and special populations. Interventions that culturally adapt the CBT or address barriers to care may have greater effect on treatment engagement, particularly when access is made available by phone.

Two meta-analytic studies have evaluated the effects of culturally adapted interventions for ethnic minorities and have found mixed results. Griner and Smith (2006) conducted a meta-analysis of 76 studies, including pilot and RCT studies, to compare the effects of culturally adapted interventions for four ethnic minority groups (African Americans, Asian Americans, Latino Americans, and Native Americans; Griner & Smith, 2006). They found that the most common adaptations were related to inclusion of cultural concepts (84%) and language match (74%). Other types of modifications included ethnic match between client and therapist (61%); explicit focus on culturally diverse patients in the clinic or organization (41%); explicit collaboration and consultation with individuals familiar with the clients' culture (38%); outreach efforts to recruit underserved clients (29%); provision of extra services designed to increase client retention (24%), such as childcare during sessions; oral administration of written materials for illiterate clients (21%); cultural sensitivity training for professional staff (17%); and referrals to additional service agencies (15%). They concluded that interventions targeting a specific cultural group were four times more effective ($d = .45$) than interventions provided to groups consisting of clients from a variety of cultural backgrounds, and interventions provided in clients' native language were twice as effective as those provided in English. Studies that focused on Latino populations ($N = 18$) found a slightly higher effect size of .56 and suggested that Latino clients with low levels of acculturation appeared to benefit greatly from culturally adapted mental health interventions. However, these conclusions have been questioned because of the methodological limitations of many studies included in their analyses. Furthermore, no study has compared the effect of standard CBT provided in Spanish versus a culturally adapted CBT provided in Spanish.

In contrast, Huey and Polo's (2008) meta-analytic analysis of evidence-based treatments for ethnic minority youth, which evaluated 30 studies (eight of which had a considerably large Latino sample) did not find differences between studies that included culturally responsive considerations and those that did not. However, such variables as acculturation, language, and ethnic identity were not part of the meta-analysis; the definition of culturally responsive features was broad.

According to our review, CBT is effective for Latinos, particularly when available in Spanish and case management or efforts to address socioeconomic stressors and treatment barriers are provided. When treatment is made more accessible by phone, it appears to have greater benefit for recruitment and treatment engagement. Although cultural adaptations may have promise, the studies that focused on cultural adaptations have generally been single sample pilot studies without comparison groups (standard CBT vs. adapted CBT) or controls for language access (e.g., testing both versions in Spanish), which is a key confounding factor in distinguishing the effect of language access and cultural adaptation.

The effectiveness of CBT for Latinos may be related to its cultural fit for Latinos. Traditionally oriented Latinos of low socioeconomic status may be receptive to interventions that result in immediate symptom relief, guidance and advice, and a problem-centered approach. They may also prefer counseling over medication treatments (Cabassa & Hansen, 2007). Short-term, directive, problem-solving therapies are also more consistent with expectations of low-income groups whose life circumstances frequently demand immediate attention and interfere with long-term treatment. The didactic style of CBT helps to quickly orient patients to treatment by educating them about mental disorders and how CBT is used to conceptualize and treat their problems. Not only does this educational approach "demystify" psychotherapy but it is also consistent with "role preparation," in which patients unaccustomed to therapy are taught what they can expect and what will be expected of them in the attempt to prevent dropout and enhance treatment (Orlinsky & Howard, 1986). The common use of groups, therapy manuals, homework assignments, and chalkboards may also help Latino patients think of therapy as more of a classroom experience, further alleviating the stigma attached to therapy.

Following their review of Latino mental health, Organista and Munoz (1996) provided guidelines for a culturally responsive application of CBT that emphasizes the development of a culturally sensitive relationship between therapist and patient and attention to salient Latino values that affect engagement in therapy. They encouraged paying respect or *respeto*, which is practiced by formally addressing patients with their last names and by maintaining a humble para *servirle* ("to serve you") attitude. They also encouraged providers to display *personalismo* by taking time to engage in self-disclosure and small talk to build *confianza*, or trust, with Latino patients. These concepts have also been applied to interventions that focus on client engagement, such as that developed by Alegría et al. (2014) in the ECLA trial.

Other aspects of Organista and Munoz's (1996) culturally responsive framework include streamlining and simplification of cognitive restructuring because of low mental health literacy and lack of exposure to therapy and according to mental health concepts common in the Latino community. An example of this is provided in Munoz and Miranda's (1986) manual: Simplification of cognitive restructuring is achieved by collapsing various levels of maladaptive cognitions (i.e., automatic thoughts, beliefs, and core schemas) into harmful thoughts that are not true, complete, or balanced. Another example in the Munoz and Miranda manual is the "Yes, but . . ." technique that teaches patients about problematic thinking that is incomplete. The goal is to teach them how to turn these "half-truths" into "whole-truths." They also teach the difference between "harmful" and "helpful" thoughts and focus on initiating adaptive behaviors. Rather than talking about "disputing dysfunctional thoughts," they teach patients to "catch it, check it, change it." These modifications were made for multicultural groups of low-income patients with low education levels.

Another recommendation involves recognizing differences in cultural values and norms. An example is in social skills and communication training that promotes assertiveness. Traditional Latino culture does not promote assertiveness, particularly among women. Munoz and Miranda (1986) recommended helping patients strive for a more bicultural orientation by helping them understand how assertiveness may be a more effective communication skill in mainstream America in areas such as work, school, agency settings, and interpersonal relationships. Last, they recommended the acknowledgment of the socioeconomic context of Latino patients and promotion of activities that are free or low cost, as well as focused on practical rather than insight-oriented outcomes.

CONCLUSION

Latinos are a diverse group of Americans that are affected by factors such as migration history and racism in the United States. Despite their overall higher rates of poverty compared with other ethnic Americans, Latinos, particularly immigrants, are robust in terms of depression. In particular, Mexican and Cuban immigrants have lower rates of depression than do either their U.S.-born counterparts or non-Latino Americans.

There is growing research evaluating psychometric properties of commonly used depression measures, such as the PHQ-9, BDI, and CES-D, for Latinos that have found adequate psychometric properties for this group. Self-report measures generally work well, although there are inconsistencies in factor structures and DIF has been found.

Structured diagnostic instruments, such as the CIDI and the MINI appear to function well across diverse groups. Studies comparing psychometric properties and validation have found cultural equivalence for depressive disorders.

Recently, a number of studies have examined the impact of CBT for Latinos, with robust evidence that CBT is effective for treating depression in diverse Latino populations. The question remains regarding the importance of culturally adapting CBT specifically for Latinos. Accessible CBT appears to work well with Latino populations, whether or not it has been culturally tailored. To date, no large study has compared the impact of high-quality CBT that is not culturally adapted with high-quality CBT that is adapted. However, several studies have found that when CBT is offered in Spanish, with patient materials also available in Spanish, Latinos respond favorably. Studies of CBT interventions that have been especially adapted for this population may have better recruitment and retention rates. Of particular note, a recent study of CBT by telephone suggested that this is a particularly good way to recruit and retain Latinos in depression treatment (Dwight-Johnson et al., 2011).

Overall, both measurement and intervention strategies common to the White population appear generally effective for Latinos, when provided in the Spanish language when appropriate. Culturally sensitive strategies for engaging Latinas in care appear effective.

REFERENCES

Aguilera, A., & Muñoz, R. F. (2011). Text messaging as an adjunct to CBT in low-income populations: A usability and feasibility pilot study. *Professional Psychology: Research and Practice, 42*, 472–478. http://dx.doi.org/10.1037/a0025499

Alegría, M., Canino, G., Rios, R., & African, L. (2002). Inequalities in use of specialty mental health services among and non-Latino whites. *Psychiatric Services, 53,* 1547–1555. http://dx.doi.org/10.1176/appi.ps.53.12.1547

Alegría, M., Canino, G., Stinson, F. S., & Grant, B. F. (2006). Nativity and *DSM–IV* psychiatric disorders among Puerto Ricans, Cuban Americans, and non-Latino Whites in the United States: Results from the National Epidemiologic Survey on Alcohol and Related Conditions. *The Journal of Clinical Psychiatry, 67,* 56–65. http://dx.doi.org/10.4088/JCP.v67n0109

Alegría, M., Ludman, E., Kafali, E. N., Lapatin, S., Vila, D., Shrout, P. E., . . . Canino, G. (2014). Effectiveness of the Engagement and Counseling for Latinos (ECLA) intervention in low-income Latinos. *Medical Care, 52,* 989–997. http://dx.doi.org/10.1097/MLR.0000000000000232

Alegría, M., Mulvaney-Day, N., Torres, M., Polo, A., Cao, Z., & Canino, G. (2007). Prevalence of psychiatric disorders across Latino subgroups in the United States. *American Journal of Public Health, 97,* 68–75. http://dx.doi.org/10.2105/AJPH.2006.087205

Alegría, M., Shrout, P. E., Torres, M., Lewis-Fernández, R., Abelson, J. M., Powell, M., . . . Canino, G. (2009). Lessons learned from the clinical reappraisal study of the Composite International Diagnostic Interview with Latinos. *International Journal of Methods in Psychiatric Research, 18,* 84–95. http://dx.doi.org/10.1002/mpr.280

Alegría, M., Takeuchi, D., Canino, G., Duan, N., Shrout, P., Meng, X. L., . . . Gong, F. (2004). Considering context, place and culture: The National Latino and Asian American Study. *International Journal of Methods in Psychiatric Research, 13,* 208–220. http://dx.doi.org/10.1002/mpr.178

American Psychiatric Association. (1987). *Diagnostic and statistical manual of mental disorders* (3rd ed., rev.). Washington, DC: Author.

American Psychiatric Association. (1994). *Diagnostic and statistical manual of mental disorders* (4th ed.). Washington, DC: Author.

Andrade, L., Caraveo-Anduaga, J. J., Berglund, P., Bijl, R. V., De Graaf, R., Vollebergh, W., . . . Wittchen, H. U. (2003). The epidemiology of major depressive episodes: Results from the International Consortium of Psychiatric Epidemiology (ICPE) Surveys. *International Journal of Methods in Psychiatric Research, 12,* 3–21. http://dx.doi.org/10.1002/mpr.138

Andrews, G., & Peters, L. (1998). The psychometric properties of the Composite International Diagnostic Interview. *Social Psychiatry and Psychiatric Epidemiology, 33,* 80–88. http://dx.doi.org/10.1007/s001270050026

Azocar, F., Areán, P., Miranda, J., & Muñoz, R. F. (2001). Differential item functioning in a Spanish translation of the Beck Depression Inventory. *Journal of Clinical Psychology, 57,* 355–365. http://dx.doi.org/10.1002/jclp.1017

Beck, A. T., Rush, A. J., Shaw, B. F., & Emery, G. (1979). *Cognitive therapy of depression.* New York, NY: Guilford Press.

Beck, A. T., Ward, C. H., Mendelson, M., Mock, J., & Erbaugh, J. (1961). An inventory for measuring depression. *Archives of General Psychiatry, 4*, 561–571. http://dx.doi.org/10.1001/archpsyc.1961.01710120031004

Beltman, M. W., Voshaar, R. C. O., & Speckens, A. E. (2010). Cognitive-behavioural therapy for depression in people with a somatic disease: Meta-analysis of randomised controlled trials. *The British Journal of Psychiatry, 197*, 11–19. http://dx.doi.org/10.1192/bjp.bp.109.064675

Bernal, G., Bonilla, J., & Santiago, J. (1995). Confiabilidad interna y validez de construcción lógica de dos instrumentos para medir sintomatología psicológica en una muestra clínica: El inventario de depresión Beck y la Lista de Cotejo de Síntomas [Internal reliability and validity of the logical construction of two instruments to measure psychological symptomatology in a clinical trial: The Beck Depression Inventory and Symptoms Checklist]. *Revista Latinoamericana de Psicología, 27*, 207–209.

Blazer, D. G., Kessler, R. C., McGonagle, K. A., & Swartz, M. S. (1994). The prevalence and distribution of major depression in a national community sample: The National Comorbidity Survey. *The American Journal of Psychiatry, 151*, 979–986. http://dx.doi.org/10.1176/ajp.151.7.979

Bobes, J. (1998). A Spanish validation study of the mini international neuropsychiatric interview. *European Psychiatry, 13*, 198s–199s. http://dx.doi.org/10.1016/S0924-9338(99)80240-5

Bonilla, J., Bernal, G., Santos, A., & Santos, D. (2004). A revised Spanish version of the Beck Depression Inventory: Psychometric properties with a Puerto Rican sample of college students. *Journal of Clinical Psychology, 60*, 119–130. http://dx.doi.org/10.1002/jclp.10195

Burnam, M. A., Hough, R. L., Karno, M., Escobar, J. I., & Telles, C. A. (1987). Acculturation and lifetime prevalence of psychiatric disorders among Mexican Americans in Los Angeles. *Journal of Health and Social Behavior, 28*, 89–102. http://dx.doi.org/10.2307/2137143

Burnam, M. A., Karno, M., Hough, R. L., Escobar, J. I., & Forsythe, A. B. (1983). The Spanish Diagnostic Interview Schedule: Reliability and comparison with clinical diagnoses. *Archives of General Psychiatry, 40*, 1189–1196. http://dx.doi.org/10.1001/archpsyc.1983.01790100035005

Butler, A. C., Chapman, J. E., Forman, E. M., & Beck, A. T. (2006). The empirical status of cognitive-behavioral therapy: A review of meta-analyses. *Clinical Psychology Review, 26*, 17–31. http://dx.doi.org/10.1016/j.cpr.2005.07.003

Cabassa, L. J., & Hansen, M. C. (2007). A systematic review of depression treatments in primary care for Latino adults. *Research on Social Work Practice, 17*, 494–503. http://dx.doi.org/10.1177/1049731506297058

Canino, G. J., Bird, H. R., Shrout, P. E., Rubio-Stipec, M., Bravo, M., Martinez, R., Sesman, M., & Guevara, L. M. (1987). The prevalence of specific psychiatric disorders in Puerto Rico. *Archives of General Psychiatry, 44*, 727–735. http://dx.doi.org/10.1001/archpsyc.1987.01800200053008

Canino, G. J., Bird, H. R., Shrout, P. E., Rubio-Stipec, M., Bravo, M., Martinez, R., Sesman, M., Guzman, A., . . . Costas, H. (1987). The Spanish Diagnostic Interview Schedule: Reliability and concordance with clinical diagnoses in Puerto Rico. *Archives of General Psychiatry, 44*, 720–726. http://dx.doi.org/10.1001/archpsyc.1987.01800200046007

Cervantes, R. C., Salgado de Snyder, V. N., & Padilla, A. M. (1989). Posttraumatic stress in immigrants from Central America and Mexico. *Hospital & Community Psychiatry, 40*, 615–619.

Dwight-Johnson, M., Aisenberg, E., Golinelli, D., Hong, S., O'Brien, M., & Ludman, E. (2011). Telephone-based cognitive-behavioral therapy for Latino patients living in rural areas: A randomized pilot study. *Psychiatric Services, 62*, 936–942. http://dx.doi.org/10.1176/ps.62.8.pss6208_0936

Dwight-Johnson, M., Lagomasino, I. T., Hay, J., Zhang, L., Tang, L., Green, J. M., & Duan, N. (2010). Effectiveness of collaborative care in addressing depression treatment preferences among low-income Latinos. *Psychiatric Services, 61*, 1112–1118. http://dx.doi.org/10.1176/ps.2010.61.11.1112

Endicott, J., & Spitzer, R. L. (1978). A diagnostic interview: The schedule for affective disorders and schizophrenia. *Archives of General Psychiatry, 35*, 837–844. http://dx.doi.org/10.1001/archpsyc.1978.01770310043002

Escobar, J. I. (1998). Immigration and mental health: Why are immigrants better off? *Archives of General Psychiatry, 55*, 781–782. http://dx.doi.org/10.1001/archpsyc.55.9.781

Escobar, J. I., Hoyos Nervi, C., & Gara, M. A. (2000). Immigration and mental health: Mexican Americans in the United States. *Harvard Review of Psychiatry, 8*, 64–72. http://dx.doi.org/10.1080/hrp_8.2.64

Ferrari, A. J., Charlson, F. J., Norman, R. E., Patten, S. B., Freedman, G., Murray, C. J., . . . Whiteford, H. A. (2013). Burden of depressive disorders by country, sex, age, and year: Findings from the Global Burden of Disease study 2010. *PLoS Medicine, 10*, e1001547. http://dx.doi.org/10.1371/journal.pmed.1001547

Garcia, M., & Marks, G. (1989). Depressive symptomatology among Mexican-American adults: An examination with the CES-D Scale. *Psychiatry Research, 27*, 137–148. http://dx.doi.org/10.1016/0165-1781(89)90129-7

González, H. M., Vega, W. A., Williams, D. R., Tarraf, W., West, B. T., & Neighbors, H. W. (2010). Depression care in the United States: Too little for too few. *Archives of General Psychiatry, 67*, 37–46. http://dx.doi.org/10.1001/archgenpsychiatry.2009.168

Grant, B. F., Stinson, F. S., Hasin, D. S., Dawson, D. A., Chou, S. P., & Anderson, K. (2004). Immigration and lifetime prevalence of *DSM–IV* psychiatric disorders among Mexican Americans and non-Hispanic Whites in the United States: Results from the National Epidemiologic Survey on Alcohol and Related Conditions. *Archives of General Psychiatry, 61*, 1226–1233. http://dx.doi.org/10.1001/archpsyc.61.12.1226

Griner, D., & Smith, T. B. (2006). Culturally adapted mental health intervention: A meta-analytic review. *Psychotherapy: Theory, Research, Practice, Training, 43*, 531–548. http://dx.doi.org/10.1037/0033-3204.43.4.531

Guarnaccia, P. J., Angel, R., & Worobey, J. L. (1989). The factor structure of the CES-D in the Hispanic Health and Nutrition Examination Survey: The influences of ethnicity, gender and language. *Social Science & Medicine, 29*, 85–94.

Guarnaccia, P. J., Canino, G., Rubio-Stipec, M., & Bravo, M. (1993). The prevalence of ataques de nervios in the Puerto Rico disaster study. The role of culture in psychiatric epidemiology. *Journal of Nervous and Mental Disease, 181*, 157–165. http://dx.doi.org/10.1097/00005053-199303000-00003

Guarnaccia, P. J., Lewis-Fernandez, R., Martinez Pincay, I., Shrout, P., Guo, J., Torres, M., . . . Alegría, M. (2010). Ataque de nervios as a marker of social and psychiatric vulnerability: Results from the NLAAS. *International Journal of Social Psychiatry, 56*, 298–309. http://dx.doi.org/10.1177/0020764008101636

Guarnaccia, P. J., Rivera, M., Franco, F., & Neighbors, C. (1996). The experiences of ataques de nervios: Towards an anthropology of emotions in Puerto Rico. *Culture, Medicine and Psychiatry, 20*, 343–367. http://dx.doi.org/10.1007/BF00113824

Hofmann, S. G., Asnaani, A., Vonk, I. J. J., Sawyer, A. T., & Fang, A. (2012). The efficacy of cognitive behavioral therapy: A review of meta-analyses. *Cognitive Therapy and Research, 36*, 427–440. http://dx.doi.org/10.1007/s10608-012-9476-1

Hough, R., Karno, M., Burnam, M. A., Escobar, J., & Timbers, D. M. (1983). The Los Angeles Epidemiologic Catchment Area research program and the epidemiology of psychiatric disorders among Mexican Americans. *Journal of Operational Psychiatry, 14*, 42–51.

Huang, F. Y., Chung, H., Kroenke, K., Delucchi, K. L., & Spitzer, R. L. (2006). Using the Patient Health Questionnaire-9 to measure depression among racially and ethnically diverse primary care patients. *Journal of General Internal Medicine, 21*, 547–552. http://dx.doi.org/10.1111/j.1525-1497.2006.00409.x

Huey, S. J., Jr., & Polo, A. J. (2008). Evidence-based psychosocial treatments for ethnic minority youth. *Journal of Clinical Child and Adolescent Psychology, 37*, 262–301. http://dx.doi.org/10.1080/15374410701820174

Hyman, S. E. (2014). The unconscionable gap between what we know and what we do. *Science Translational Medicine, 6*, 253–259. http://dx.doi.org/10.1126/scitranslmed.3010312

Interian, A., Allen, L. A., Gara, M. A., & Escobar, J. I. (2008). A pilot study of culturally adapted cognitive behavior therapy for Hispanics with major depression. *Cognitive and Behavioral Practice, 15*, 67–75. http://dx.doi.org/10.1016/j.cbpra.2006.12.002

Kessler, R. C., Berglund, P., Demler, O., Jin, R., Koretz, D., Merikangas, K. R., . . . Wang, P. S., & the National Comorbidity Survey Replication. (2003). The epidemiology of major depressive disorder: Results from the National Comorbidity

Survey Replication (NCS-R). *JAMA, 289,* 3095–3105. http://dx.doi.org/10.1001/jama.289.23.3095

Kessler, R. C., McGonagle, K. A., Zhao, S., Nelson, C. B., Hughes, M., Eshleman, S., . . . Kendler, K. S. (1994). Lifetime and 12-month prevalence of *DSM–III–R* psychiatric disorders in the United States: Results from the National Comorbidity Survey. *Archives of General Psychiatry, 51,* 8–19. http://dx.doi.org/10.1001/archpsyc.1994.03950010008002

Kessler, R. C., Mickelson, K. D., & Williams, D. R. (1999). The prevalence, distribution, and mental health correlates of perceived discrimination in the United States. *Journal of Health and Social Behavior, 40,* 208–230. http://dx.doi.org/10.2307/2676349

Kessler, R. C., & Ustün, T. B. (2004). The World Mental Health (WMH) Survey Initiative Version of the World Health Organization (WHO) Composite International Diagnostic Interview (CIDI). *International Journal of Methods in Psychiatric Research, 13,* 93–121. http://dx.doi.org/10.1002/mpr.168

Kleinman, A. (2004, September 2). Culture and depression. *The New England Journal of Medicine, 351*(10), 951–953. http://dx.doi.org/10.1056/NEJMp048078

Kroenke, K., Spitzer, R. L., & Williams, J. B. (2001). The PHQ-9: Validity of a brief depression severity measure. *Journal of General Internal Medicine, 16,* 606–613. http://dx.doi.org/10.1046/j.1525-1497.2001.016009606.x

Le, H. N., Perry, D. F., & Stuart, E. A. (2011). Randomized controlled trial of a preventive intervention for perinatal depression in high-risk Latinas. *Journal of Consulting and Clinical Psychology, 79,* 135–141. http://dx.doi.org/10.1037/a0022492

Le, H. N., Zmuda, J., Perry, D. F., & Muñoz, R. F. (2010). Transforming an evidence-based intervention to prevent perinatal depression for low-income Latina immigrants. *American Journal of Orthopsychiatry, 80,* 34–45. http://dx.doi.org/10.1111/j.1939-0025.2010.01005.x

Lecrubier, Y., Sheehan, D. V., Weiller, E., Amorim, P., Bonora, I., Harnett Sheehan, K., . . . Dunbar, G. C. (1997). The Mini International Neuropsychiatric Interview (MINI). A short diagnostic structured interview: Reliability and validity according to the CIDI. *European Psychiatry, 12,* 224–231. http://dx.doi.org/10.1016/S0924-9338(97)83296-8

Lewinsohn, P. M., & Amenson, C. S. (1978). Some relations between pleasant and unpleasant mood-related events and depression. *Journal of Abnormal Psychology, 87,* 644–654. http://dx.doi.org/10.1037/0021-843X.87.6.644

Lewinsohn, P. M., Antonuccio, D. O., Steinmetz Breckenridge, J., & Teri, L. (1984). *The coping with depression course: A psychoeducational intervention for unipolar depression.* Retrieved from http://www.ori.org/files/Static%20Page%20Files/CWDC.pdf

Lewis-Fernández, R., Guarnaccia, P. J., Martínez, I. E., Salmán, E., Schmidt, A., & Liebowitz, M. (2002). Comparative phenomenology of ataques de nervios, panic attacks, and panic disorder. *Culture, Medicine and Psychiatry, 26,* 199–223. http://dx.doi.org/10.1023/A:1016349624867

Liebowitz, M. R., Salmán, E., Jusino, C. M., Garfinkel, R., Street, L., Cárdenas, D. L., . . . Klein, D. F. (1994). Ataque de nervios and panic disorder. *The American Journal of Psychiatry, 151,* 871–875. http://dx.doi.org/10.1176/ajp.151.6.871

Lorant, V., Deliège, D., Eaton, W., Robert, A., Philippot, P., & Ansseau, M. (2003). Socioeconomic inequalities in depression: A meta-analysis. *American Journal of Epidemiology, 157,* 98–112. http://dx.doi.org/10.1093/aje/kwf182

Löwe, B., Spitzer, R. L., Gräfe, K., Kroenke, K., Quenter, A., Zipfel, S., . . . Herzog, W. (2004). Comparative validity of three screening questionnaires for *DSM–IV* depressive disorders and physicians' diagnoses. *Journal of Affective Disorders, 78,* 131–140. http://dx.doi.org/10.1016/S0165-0327(02)00237-9

Marchand, E., Ng, J., Rohde, P., & Stice, E. (2010). Effects of an indicated cognitive-behavioral depression prevention program are similar for Asian American, Latino, and European American adolescents. *Behaviour Research and Therapy, 48,* 821–825. http://dx.doi.org/10.1016/j.brat.2010.05.005

Mathers, C. D., Lopez, A. D., & Murray, C. J. L. (2006). The burden of disease and mortality by condition: Data, methods, and results for 2001. In A. D. Lopez, C. D. Mathers, M. Ezzati, D. T. Jamison, & C. J. L. Murray (Eds.), *Global burden of disease and risk factors* (pp. 45–240). Washington, DC: The World Bank and Oxford University Press.

McGuire, T. G., & Miranda, J. (2008). New evidence regarding racial and ethnic disparities in mental health: Policy implications. *Health Affairs, 27,* 393–403. http://dx.doi.org/10.1377/hlthaff.27.2.393

Miranda, J., Azocar, F., Organista, K. C., Dwyer, E., & Areane, P. (2003). Treatment of depression among impoverished primary care patients from ethnic minority groups. *Psychiatric Services, 54,* 219–225. http://dx.doi.org/10.1176/appi.ps.54.2.219

Miranda, J., Bernal, G., Lau, A., Kohn, L., Hwang, W. C., & LaFromboise, T. (2005). State of the science on psychosocial interventions for ethnic minorities. *Annual Review of Clinical Psychology, 1,* 113–142. http://dx.doi.org/10.1146/annurev.clinpsy.1.102803.143822

Miranda, J., Chung, J. Y., Green, B. L., Krupnick, J., Siddique, J., Revicki, D. A., & Belin, T. (2003). Treating depression in predominantly low-income young minority women: A randomized controlled trial. *JAMA, 290,* 57–65. http://dx.doi.org/10.1001/jama.290.1.57

Miranda, J., Duan, N., Sherbourne, C., Schoenbaum, M., Lagomasino, I., Jackson-Triche, M., & Wells, K. B. (2003). Improving care for minorities: Can quality improvement interventions improve care and outcomes for depressed minorities? Results of a randomized, controlled trial. *Health Services Research, 38,* 613–630. http://dx.doi.org/10.1111/1475-6773.00136

Miranda, J., Green, B. L., Krupnick, J. L., Chung, J., Siddique, J., Belin, T., & Revicki, D. (2006). One-year outcomes of a randomized clinical trial treating depression in low-income minority women. *Journal of Consulting and Clinical Psychology, 74,* 99–111. http://dx.doi.org/10.1037/0022-006X.74.1.99

Miranda, J., Schoenbaum, M., Sherbourne, C., Duan, N., & Wells, K. (2004). Effects of primary care depression treatment on minority patients' clinical status and employment. *Archives of General Psychiatry, 61*, 827–834. http://dx.doi.org/10.1001/archpsyc.61.8.827

Mościcki, E. K., Locke, B. Z., Rae, D. S., & Boyd, J. H. (1989). Depressive symptoms among Mexican Americans: The Hispanic Health and Nutrition Examination Survey. *American Journal of Epidemiology, 130*, 348–360. http://dx.doi.org/10.1093/oxfordjournals.aje.a115341

Mulvaney-Day, N. E., Alegría, M., & Sribney, W. (2007). Social cohesion, social support, and health among Latinos in the United States. *Social Science & Medicine, 64*, 477–495. http://dx.doi.org/10.1016/j.socscimed.2006.08.030

Munoz, R. F., Aguilar-Gaxiola, S., & Guzman, J. (1986). *Manual de terapia de grupo para el tratamiento cognitivo-conductal de depression* [Manual for group cognitive behavioral therapy]. San Francisco, CA: San Francisco General Hospital Depression Clinic.

Munoz, R. F., & Miranda, J. (1986). *Group therapy for cognitive-behavioral treatment of depression.* San Francisco, CA: San Francisco General Hospital Depression Clinic.

Murray, C. J., Abraham, J., Ali, M. K., Alvarado, M., Atkinson, C., Baddour, L. M., . . . Bolliger, I. (2013). The state of US health, 1990–2010: Burden of diseases, injuries, and risk factors. *JAMA, 310*, 591–606.

Narrow, W. E., Rae, D. S., Mościcki, E. K., Locke, B. Z., & Regier, D. A. (1990). Depression among Cuban Americans. The Hispanic Health and Nutrition Examination Survey. *Social Psychiatry and Psychiatric Epidemiology, 25*, 260–268. http://dx.doi.org/10.1007/BF00788647

Ngo, V. K., Asarnow, J. R., Lange, J., Jaycox, L. H., Rea, M. M., Landon, C., . . . Miranda, J. (2009). Outcomes for youths from racial–ethnic minority groups in a quality improvement intervention for depression treatment. *Psychiatric Services, 60*, 1357–1364. http://dx.doi.org/10.1176/ps.2009.60.10.1357

Novy, D. M., Stanley, M. A., Averill, P., & Daza, P. (2001). Psychometric comparability of English- and Spanish-language measures of anxiety and related affective symptoms. *Psychological Assessment, 13*, 347–355. http://dx.doi.org/10.1037/1040-3590.13.3.347

Organista, K. C., & Munoz, R. F. (1996). Cognitive behavioral therapy with Latinos. *Cognitive and Behavioral Practice, 3*, 255–270. http://dx.doi.org/10.1016/S1077-7229(96)80017-4

Orlinsky, D. E., & Howard, K. I. (1986). The psychological interior of psychotherapy: Explorations with the Therapy Session Reports. In L. S. Greenberg & W. M. Pinsof (Eds.), *Guilford clinical psychology and psychotherapy series* (pp. 477–501). New York, NY: Guilford Press.

Ortega, A. N., Rosenheck, R., Alegría, M., & Desai, R. A. (2000). Acculturation and the lifetime risk of psychiatric and substance use disorders among Hispanics. *Journal of Nervous and Mental Disease, 188*, 728–735. http://dx.doi.org/10.1097/00005053-200011000-00002

Palloni, A., & Morenoff, J. D. (2001). Interpreting the paradoxical in the His-panic paradox: Demographic and epidemiologic approaches. *Annals of the New York Academy of Sciences, 954,* 140–174. http://dx.doi.org/10.1111/j.1749-6632.2001.tb02751.x

Piedra, L. M., & Byoun, S. J. (2012). Vida alegre: Preliminary findings of a depression intervention for immigrant Latino mothers. *Research on Social Work Practice, 22,* 138–150. http://dx.doi.org/10.1177/1049731511424168

Plant, E. A., & Sachs-Ericsson, N. (2004). Racial and ethnic differences in depres-sion: The roles of social support and meeting basic needs. *Journal of Consulting and Clinical Psychology, 72,* 41–52. http://dx.doi.org/10.1037/0022-006X.72.1.41

Radloff, L. S. (1977). The CES-D Scale: A self-report depression scale for research in the general population. *Applied Psychological Measurement, 1,* 385–401. http://dx.doi.org/10.1177/014662167700100306

Roberts, R. E., Vernon, S. W., & Rhoades, H. M. (1989). Effects of language and ethnic status on reliability and validity of the Center for Epidemiologic Studies-Depression Scale with psychiatric patients. *Journal of Nervous and Mental Disease, 177,* 581–592. http://dx.doi.org/10.1097/00005053-198910000-00001

Robins, L. N., Helzer, J. E., Croughan, J., & Ratcliff, K. S. (1981). National Insti-tute of Mental Health Diagnostic Interview Schedule: Its history, character-istics, and validity. *Archives of General Psychiatry, 38,* 381–389. http://dx.doi.org/10.1001/archpsyc.1981.01780290015001

Rogler, L. H., Cortes, D. E., & Malgady, R. G. (1991). Acculturation and men-tal health status among Hispanics: Convergence and new directions for research. *American Psychologist, 46,* 585–597. http://dx.doi.org/10.1037/0003-066X.46.6.585

Salgado de Snyder, V. N., Diaz-Perez, M. J., & Ojeda, V. D. (2000). The prevalence of nervios and associated symptomatology among inhabitants of Mexican rural communities. *Culture, Medicine and Psychiatry, 24,* 453–470. http://dx.doi.org/10.1023/A:1005655331794

Salmán, E., Liebowitz, M. R., Guarnaccia, P. J., Jusino, C. M., Garfinkel, R., Street, L., . . . Klein, D. F. (1998). Subtypes of ataques de nervios: The influ-ence of coexisting psychiatric diagnosis. *Culture, Medicine and Psychiatry, 22,* 231–244. http://dx.doi.org/10.1023/A:1005326426885

Santiago, C. D., Kaltman, S., & Miranda, J. (2013). Poverty and mental health: How do low-income adults and children fare in psychotherapy? *Journal of Clinical Psychology, 69,* 115–126. http://dx.doi.org/10.1002/jclp.21951

Sheehan, D. V., Lecrubier, Y., Sheehan, K. H., Amorim, P., Janavs, J., Weiller, E., . . . Dunbar, G. C. (1998). The Mini-International Neuropsychiatric Interview (M.I.N.I.): The development and validation of a structured diagnostic psychiatric interview for *DSM–IV* and *ICD–10. The Journal of Clinical Psychiatry, 59,* 22–33.

Sheehan, D. V., Lecrubier, Y., Sheehan, K. H., Janavs, J., Weiller, E., Keskiner, A., . . . Dunbar, G. C. (1997). The validity of the Mini International Neuropsychi-atric Interview (MINI) according to the SCID-P and its reliability. *European Psychiatry, 12,* 232–241. http://dx.doi.org/10.1016/S0924-9338(97)83297-X

Shrout, P. E., Canino, G. J., Bird, H. R., Rubio-Stipec, M., Bravo, M., & Burnam, M. A. (1992). Mental health status among Puerto Ricans, Mexican Americans, and non-Hispanic Whites. *American Journal of Community Psychology, 20,* 729–752. http://dx.doi.org/10.1007/BF01312605

Siddique, J., Chung, J. Y., Brown, C. H., & Miranda, J. (2012). Comparative effectiveness of medication versus cognitive-behavioral therapy in a randomized controlled trial of low-income young minority women with depression. *Journal of Consulting and Clinical Psychology, 80,* 995–1006. http://dx.doi.org/10.1037/a0030452

Simoni, J. M., Wiebe, J. S., Sauceda, J. A., Huh, D., Sanchez, G., Longoria, V., . . . Safren, S. A. (2013). A preliminary RCT of CBT-AD for adherence and depression among HIV-positive Latinos on the U.S.-Mexico border: The Nuevo Día study. *AIDS and Behavior, 17,* 2816–2829. http://dx.doi.org/10.1007/s10461-013-0538-5

Spitzer, R. L., Williams, J. B., Gibbon, M., & First, M. B. (1992). The Structured Clinical Interview for *DSM–III–R* (SCID): I. History, rationale, and description. *Archives of General Psychiatry, 49,* 624–629. http://dx.doi.org/10.1001/archpsyc.1992.01820080032005

U.S. Census Bureau. (2013). Poverty rates for selected detailed race and Hispanic groups by state and place: 2007–2011. Retrieved from https://www.census.gov/prod/2013pubs/acsbr11-17.pdf

U.S. Department of Health and Human Services. (2001). *Mental health: Culture, race, and ethnicity—A supplement to Mental Health: A Report of the Surgeon General.* Retrieved from http://amongourkin.org/2001%20mental%20health.pdf

Vega, W. A., Kolody, B., Aguilar-Gaxiola, S., Alderete, E., Catalano, R., & Caraveo-Anduaga, J. (1998). Lifetime prevalence of *DSM–III–R* psychiatric disorders among urban and rural Mexican Americans in California. *Archives of General Psychiatry, 55,* 771–778. http://dx.doi.org/10.1001/archpsyc.55.9.771

Ward, E. C. (2007). Examining differential treatment effects for depression in racial and ethnic minority women: A qualitative systematic review. *Journal of the National Medical Association, 99,* 265–274.

Wells, K., Sherbourne, C., Schoenbaum, M., Ettner, S., Duan, N., Miranda, J., . . . Rubenstein, L. (2004). Five-year impact of quality improvement for depression: Results of a group-level randomized controlled trial. *Archives of General Psychiatry, 61,* 378–386. http://dx.doi.org/10.1001/archpsyc.61.4.378

Wiebe, J. S., & Penley, J. A. (2005). A psychometric comparison of the Beck Depression Inventory–II in English and Spanish. *Psychological Assessment, 17,* 481–485. http://dx.doi.org/10.1037/1040-3590.17.4.481

3

COGNITIVE BEHAVIORAL MODELS, MEASURES, AND TREATMENTS FOR DEPRESSIVE DISORDERS IN AFRICAN AMERICANS

ENRIQUE W. NEBLETT, JR., EFFUA E. SOSOO, HENRY A. WILLIS, DONTE L. BERNARD, AND JIWOON BAE

The study of depressive disorders (DDs) in African Americans as a critical priority for research and practice is highlighted by the well-established association between depression and deleterious outcomes; the mixed findings regarding the risk, prevalence, and severity of depression; and reports of lesser access to quality care for depression among African Americans (Alegría et al., 2008; Breland-Noble et al., 2010). Although several psychiatric epidemiological studies have suggested lower prevalence rates of DDs for African Americans than Whites (Breslau et al., 2006; Somervell et al., 1989; Williams et al., 2007), DDs are among the most common psychological disorders for African Americans and are linked to compromised mental health functioning and disability (Breland-Noble, Sotomayor, & Burriss, 2015; Fortuna, Alegría, & Gao, 2010). Moreover, African Americans report more chronic major depressive disorder (MDD) and associated disability than Whites (Ward & Brown, 2015) and may be at greater risk for DDs due to higher

http://dx.doi.org/10.1037/0000091-004

Treating Depression, Anxiety, and Stress in Ethnic and Racial Groups: Cognitive Behavioral Approaches,
E. C. Chang, C. A. Downey, J. K. Hirsch, and E. A. Yu (Editors)

rates of chronic illness, functional disability, health problems, exposure to racism, financial strain, and poor neighborhood quality—all known risks for depression (Gitlin, Szanton, Huang, & Roth, 2014). In light of concerns regarding the absence of cultural considerations in conceptual models of DDs (Breland-Noble et al., 2015; Kennard, Stewart, Hughes, Patel, & Emslie, 2006), greater misdiagnosis and underdiagnosis of DDs (Baker & Bell, 1999), and limited treatment outcome studies with African American populations, in this chapter we consider cognitive behavioral models, measures, and treatments (CBMMTs) for DDs in African Americans.

COGNITIVE BEHAVIORAL MODELS FOR UNDERSTANDING DEPRESSIVE DISORDERS IN AFRICAN AMERICANS

What cognitive behavioral models guide our understanding of DDs in African Americans? Although there is no shortage of cognitive or cognitive behavioral models explaining vulnerability to depression (e.g., Abramson, Metalsky, & Alloy, 1989; Beck, 1987; Cole, Martin, & Powers, 1997; Rehm, 1977; Seligman, 1975), models specific to understanding DDs in African Americans are rare. In studies that contain guiding conceptual models or frameworks, oft-cited models of stress (e.g., Pearlin, Mullan, Semple, & Skaff, 1990; Pearlin & Schooler, 1978) or depression (e.g., Beck's cognitive theory of depression—Beck, 1987; social learning theory—see Lewinsohn, Hoberman, Teri, & Hautzinger, 1985; tripartite model—Clark & Watson, 1991) are common, whereas models considering the sociocultural characteristics and values or cultural and social perspectives of African Americans are limited. Next, we review several of the most commonly cited cognitive behavioral models in studies of DDs in African Americans, as well as recent adaptations of these models.

Beck's (1974) cognitive behavioral model of depression is arguably one of the most recognized models for depression. The model asserts that depression is a consequence of maladaptive cognitive styles or processes that are activated during stress (Hammen, Rudolph, & Abaied, 2014). These styles mediate the link between events and mood and include negative cognitive schemas that guide information processing, biases in thinking (e.g., automatic thoughts, cognitive errors), and the well-known "cognitive triad" characterized by maladaptive thinking patterns about oneself as inadequate, the world as mean and unfair, and the future as hopeless. Although some empirical studies of DDs in African Americans cite Beck's model as a critical conceptual framework for understanding depression in African Americans (e.g., Gregory, 2016; Jesse et al., 2015) and although Beck's theory enjoys wide acclaim in the clinical literature, little is known about its relevance in different cultural and ethnic groups in the United States (Kennard et al., 2006). Kennard and colleagues (2006) suggested that the model might overlook important cultural factors such as greater vulnerability to interpersonal difficulties (e.g., in ethnic groups that place emphasis on family and relationships) and differences in beliefs and coping strategies among different ethnic groups (e.g., increased reliance on spiritual and familial support) but ultimately concluded that Beck's model held equally across racial and ethnic groups.

In addition to Beck's and other commonly cited models of depression, several studies have contained adaptations of these models. These models fall somewhere between those that omit cultural considerations and those that fully consider contextual factors. In a study of the effects of telephone-based cognitive behavior therapy (CBT) and face-to-face CBT on changes in depressive affect and health status in African American dementia care-givers, Glueckauf et al. (2012) used a modified version of Pearlin and colleagues' stress process model (Pearlin et al., 1990; Pearlin & Schooler, 1978). According to the model, depression in African American dementia caregivers is shaped by caregiver (CG) and care recipient (CR) factors such as the type of CG–CR relationship (e.g., spouse vs. adult child of CR); CG gender, age, income, and education; CG stressors (e.g., CR problem behaviors such as angry outbursts and socially inappropriate responses, the extent to which the CR requires assistance in self-care activities); and CG appraisals of psycho-social resources (e.g., perceptions of informal social support and subjective burden; Glueckauf et al., 2012). This model acknowledges, at least superfi-cially, the relevance of various individual person characteristics (gender, age, income, education) and contextual variables that may be culturally relevant or salient (e.g., perceptions of social support) but does not explicitly invoke cultural factors or make specific reference to African Americans.

A third approach combines traditional models (e.g., Beck's cognitive behavioral model, social learning theory) with a conceptual framework that incorporates cultural factors relevant to the African American experience. In their examination of a culturally tailored CBT intervention to reduce risk of antepartum depression in a sample of rural, minority, pregnant, low-income African American women, Jesse and colleagues (2015) invoked Beck's model and Jesse's biopsychosocial–spiritual theory as overarching frameworks for the intervention. Jesse's model suggests that the interaction between an individual's biological underpinnings, psychological functioning, and socio-cultural environment determine subsequent mental health. Furthermore, spirituality is posited as a specific sociocultural factor contributing to the course of mental health by providing emotional support and bolstering inter-nal resources (e.g., self-esteem) to protect against negative mental health outcomes (e.g., depression). Although the model was not developed with African Americans in mind, research has suggested that religious involve-ment is a significant protective factor that may buffer the development of depression among African American adults (Ellison & Flannelly, 2009). Thus, Beck's theory combined with biopsychosocial–spiritual theory represents a hybrid approach to understanding depression (and DDs) in African Americans. Notably, we found only one such example, and as with the study of depressed African American dementia CGs, the focal population of the investigation was narrow (i.e., pregnant, low-income, rural African American women).

In our attempts to cull a sparse literature for models relevant to the treatment of DDs in African Americans, we also considered data-derived models with implications for cognitive behavioral approaches to DDs in African Americans. In a study of factors mediating the effects of a multicomponent CBT depression intervention on functional disability in older African Americans, Gitlin and colleagues (2014) found that behavioral activation, depression knowledge and symptom recognition, anxiety, and reduced depression symptoms might account for improvements in functional disability. Further, reduced depressive symptoms and enhanced depression knowledge and symptom recognition jointly mediated the effect of the intervention on functional disability. These results and others examining behavioral activation (e.g., Gitlin et al., 2013) suggest that emotional and physical activation, knowledge about depression, and anxiety are important correlates of both psychological and physical functioning and, as such, are possible treatment targets for older African Americans.

We have identified four types of conceptual models of depression in African Americans: classic models, modified models, culture-specific models, and empirically derived conceptual models. These models have focused on circumscribed African American populations (e.g., dementia CGs; pregnant, rural, low-income women) and none of the models was designed exclusively with the African American experience of DDs in mind (or even with African Americans' experiences as the focus of the model); plus, the models failed to provide a coherent synthesis of cultural factors that might influence DDs in African Americans. As a whole, the models confirm Kennard et al.'s (2006) assertion that few studies have examined cognitive models of depression across ethnic minority populations and suggest the need for future work to develop models to capture the African American experience of depression.

COGNITIVE BEHAVIORAL MEASUREMENT OF DEPRESSIVE DISORDERS IN AFRICAN AMERICANS

Accurate assessment could facilitate improved conceptual models of DDs in African Americans and treatment of these disorders. Although the psychometric properties of the most common measures of depression have been explored extensively, there are still concerns regarding the ability of these measures to adequately assess the depressive symptomatology of African Americans. As a result of the distinctive sociocultural history of this population in the United States (e.g., slavery and chronic racism-related stress), accurate psychological assessment of psychiatric symptoms may be clouded by clinician bias, negative stereotypes, and a lack of insight into the unique experiences of this population. Further, researchers have proposed that conscious and unconscious negative stereotype beliefs about this population may lead to differential interpretations of symptoms, contributing to misdiagnosis or underdiagnosis (Baker & Bell, 1999; Neighbors, Jackson, Campbell, & Williams, 1989). For example, previous analyses of case studies indicated that manic-depressive African American patients were often misdiagnosed as chronic undifferentiated schizophrenics (Bell & Mehta, 1980). In an attempt to understand the concerns regarding measurement of depression in this population, in this section, we first explore common measures used to assess depression, with a particular emphasis on measures whose psychometric properties have been investigated in African American populations. We then consider a novel measure for assessing depression in African Americans that takes into account the role of racial discrimination experiences.

Beck Depression Inventory

The Beck Depression Inventory (BDI), originally proposed by Beck, Ward, Mendelson, Mock, and Erbaugh (1961), is a 21-item measure that assumes that negative and distorted cognitions are the core characteristic of depression. In a review and meta-analysis of the BDI, as used between 1961 and 1986, the scale's internal consistency estimates yielded an average coefficient alpha of 0.81 for nonpsychiatric patients and 0.86 for psychiatric patients (Beck, Steer, & Carbin, 1988). Furthermore, the BDI has high concurrent validity with clinical ratings and similar rating scales of depression, such as the Hamilton Depression Scale (Hamilton, 1960). The most current version of the BDI, the BDI-II (Beck, Steer, & Brown, 1996), aligns more closely with the operationalized description of depression and depressive episodes put forth by the *Diagnostic and Statistical Manual of Mental Disorders* (*DSM*, fourth ed.; American Psychiatric Association, 1994) and does not reflect any specific theory of depression. A recent comprehensive review of the psychometric properties of the BDI-II in 118 studies found that the measure's internal consistency was around 0.9, and the test–retest reliability ranged from 0.73 to 0.96 (Wang & Gorenstein, 2013). Moreover, the BDI-II showed adequate sensitivity and specificity for detecting depression and is highly correlated with the original BDI.

Beck et al.'s (1996) original standardization sample for the BDI consisted of university students and a small, nonrepresentative portion of minorities. In response to this limitation, Sashidharan, Pawlow, and Pettibone (2012) examined differences in BDI-II scores between Caucasians and an equal number of African American college students. Using the Center for Epidemiologic Studies Depression Scale as a point of comparison, the researchers explored the assessment of depression in a sample of 278 students (composed of 35 African American men, 35 Caucasian men, 104 African American women, and 104 Caucasian women). There were no statistically significant differences between the two ethnic groups on income level, age, or mean years of education, and results indicated that the BDI-II was a valid measure of depression in this sample of African American college students. Although these results were based on a sample of college students with a particular level of educational attainment, other research has suggested that the BDI-II might have similar validity in other samples of African Americans (e.g., Grothe et. al., 2005; Tandon, Cluxton-Keller, Leis, Le, & Perry, 2012).

Joe, Woolley, Brown, Ghahramanlou-Holloway, and Beck (2008) examined the psychometric properties of the BDI-II in low-income African American suicide attempters ($N = 133$) who were participants in a randomized clinical trial examining the efficacy of cognitive therapy for suicide prevention. The mean age of this group was 35.23 ($SD = 9.85$, range 18–66), and it was composed of 83 females and 40 males. The reliability coefficient of the measure for this sample of African Americans was 0.94, and the authors concluded that the BDI-II had sufficient dimensionality, internal reliability, and convergent validity for this population. Although this study only included patients from a large urban hospital who had recently attempted suicide, it further suggests that the BDI-II is a psychometrically sound instrument for measuring depression in African Americans.

Center for Epidemiological Studies Depression Scale

Another popular measure of depressive symptoms, largely due to its open access nature and comparable properties to the BDI, is the Center for Epidemiological Studies Depression Scale (CES-D). Originally developed by Radloff (1977), the CES-D consists of four factors: absence of positive affect, depressed affect, somatic activity or inactivity, and interpersonal challenges. This measure has high internal consistency and adequate test–retest reliability and construct validity in a variety of samples (e.g., Devins et al., 1988; Hann, Winter, & Jacobsen, 1999; Radloff, 1977). However, recent reviews have called into question the reliability of this measure in different populations. For instance, Carleton et al. (2013) found sex biases in the CES-D, such that one item was found to inflate CES-D scores in women. Others have pointed out that the measure's original factor structure may not be valid when applied to various racial and ethnic groups (e.g., Long Foley, Reed, Mutran, & DeVellis, 2002) and that the measure may not accurately identify depression in minority populations (Baker, Velli, Friedman, & Wiley, 1995).

Carleton et al. (2013) found that only three factors of the CES-D were unbiased and in line with the diagnostic criteria for depression. Similarly, in a sample of older African Americans ($N = 227$, age range = 59–96), there was no distinction between depression and somatic complaints (Long Foley et al., 2002). This finding indicates that, for some African Americans, symptoms of depression and somatic complaints are similar and may represent one unidimensional construct rather than two independent factors as conceptualized by the CES-D. The results also indicate that the original four-factor structure may not be universally applicable when diagnosing depression among various populations. For instance, Carleton and colleagues (2013) identified a new factor specific to African Americans: social well-being, which comprised the social interactions of the sample, such as hopefulness, appetite, and talking. Contrary to these findings, however, others have found the four-factor model of the CES-D to be more valid than the three-factor model. Using a nationally representative study of African Americans ($N = 988$) and Whites ($N = 666$), Nguyen, Kitner-Triolo, Evans, and Zonderman (2004) found that the same four-factor model found in White populations could be replicated in two distinct African American samples. Furthermore, not only did the four-factor factor model hold across the White and African American groups but most items were also reliable, with standardized loadings greater than 0.50.

In a separate evaluation of the CES-D that used data collected through the National Survey of American Life (NSAL), a study designed to explore within- and between-group racial and ethnic differences in psychological functioning in African American and Black Caribbean adults living in the United States, Torres (2012) conducted a psychometric assessment of a shortened 12-item CES-D (CES-D-12). The construct validity of the CES-D-12 was supported for African American and Black Caribbean women, but findings were mixed for males. For African American men, construct validity was supported for MDD but not dysthymia. For Black Caribbean men, the results did not support construct validity of the CES-D-12 for MDD.

Finally, the CES-D may be more sensitive in White patients than in African American patients. The sensitivity of a measure, also called the *true positive rate*, measures the ability of an assessment tool to identify the proportion of individuals with a particular disorder correctly. In a study of the reliability of the CES-D for screening depression in 39 psychiatric patients age 50 or older who had already been diagnosed with the disorder, it was found that the measure's sensitivity in White patients was 85% but only 71% in

African American patients (Baker et al., 1995). Reasons why the sensitivity of the CES-D may be poorer among African American patients are unclear; however, it may be that the measure is less sensitive to subtle racial differences in the manifestation of depressive symptoms or depression between Blacks and Whites. Torres (2012) also observed that some items of the scale (e.g., "I felt like everything I did was an effort," "I felt that I was just as good as other people," and "I had trouble keeping my mind on what I was doing") had low interitem correlations with other scale items for African American and Black Caribbean men and women.

Geriatric Depression Scale

The Geriatric Depression Scale (GDS) was designed for assessing depression in elderly populations. During the validation and development of the measure, the GDS had an internal consistency of 0.94 (Yesavage et al., 1982). The GDS also had high test–retest reliability, and validity was established through the measure's ability to distinguish between groups of healthy, mildly depressed, and severely depressed patients. These initial psychometric findings are consistent across studies, yet it has been suggested that the sensitivity of this measure may vary depending on one's racial or ethnic background.

The GDS may be more reliable than the CES-D for older African American samples. Along these lines, Yesavage et al. (1982) noted that it does not include some of the items relating to somatic complaints and interpersonal problems assessed by the CES-D because it is assumed that some of these disturbances are common in older age and may not be reflective of true depressive symptoms. Using a short form of 15 items of the GDS in a sample of 401 African American adults over the age of 51, the measure had good internal consistency ($r = 0.71$) and adequate test–retest reliability over a 15-month interval ($r = 0.68$; Pedraza, Dotson, Willis, Graff-Radford, & Lucas, 2009). These findings support the notion that the GDS is a reliable, and perhaps more accurate, measure of depression for older African Americans. In contrast to these findings, others have noted that the GDS may not be a highly sensitive measure for this population. In Baker et al.'s (1995) assessment of the reliability of screening instruments mentioned earlier, the ability of the GDS to correctly identify depression in a sample of African American patients was only 53%, compared with 65% for White patients. Finally, it is worth noting that given that depression and somatic complaints may reflect a single dimension for older African Americans (Carleton et al., 2013; Long Foley et al., 2002) and given the importance of social support for African Americans, the omission of items related to somatic complaints and interpersonal problems from the GDS could be problematic.

Multiculturally Sensitive Mental Health Scale

To date, research has not adequately investigated how the assessment of depression may be directly affected by the unique experiences of African Americans, specifically racial discrimination. Racial discrimination is a common experience for African Americans (Kessler, Mickelson, & Williams, 1999) that has been associated with higher rates of depression for those who experience it (Borrell, Kiefe, Williams, Diez-Roux, & Gordon-Larsen, 2006; Sellers, Copeland-Linder, Martin, & Lewis, 2006). As such, it may be important to measure the two in tandem to yield a full portrait of factors contributing to depressive symptomatology.

In response to the need for multiculturally sensitive measures of mental health, specifically, measures that include African Americans' experiences of racism, Chao and Green (2011) created the Multiculturally Sensitive Mental Health Scale (MSMHS). The MSMHS includes items that assess the daily life stressors of racism, as well as mental health symptoms relating to depression, anxiety, and well-being. Chao and Green's final scale, developed using exploratory and confirmatory factor analyses, is composed of five stable subscales: Perceived Racism (coefficient alpha = 0.92), Depression (coefficient alpha = 0.88), Well-Being (coefficient alpha = 0.84), Anxiety (coefficient alpha = 0.82), and Suicidal Thoughts (coefficient alpha = 0.82). The sensitivity of the measures has not been documented, but the scale has exhibited adequate test–retest reliability over a 2-week period and high validity in that its Perceived Racism subscale and mental health subscales were significantly positively correlated with existing measures of racial discrimination experiences and mental health (i.e., the Index of Race-Related Stress, and the Outcome Questionnaire).

The MSMHS is unique in that it includes subscales that measure mental health concerns, such as depressive symptoms, providing clinicians with the ability to assess the relationship between perceived racial discrimination, psychological distress, and depressive symptoms in one measure. This approach acknowledges that African Americans' depressive symptomatology should be understood within a cultural context, especially given the link between racism-related stress experiences and depression outcomes.

Summary

To date, psychometric evaluations of the BDI-II and the GDS have supported the measures' ability to accurately assess depression in African Americans, whereas there is less definitive support for the psychometric stability of the CES-D. Many of the psychometric evaluations have been conducted using either secondary data or convenience samples (i.e., college students), and these findings might not be reflective of the measures' true reliability, validity, and predictive power in African Americans at large. Recent research has exposed an association between experiences of racial discrimination and levels of depression in African Americans. Novel measures that can assess perceived racial discrimination and symptoms of depression concurrently, such as the MSMHS, may yield a more comprehensive view of underlying and contributing factors to DDs in African American samples.

COGNITIVE BEHAVIORAL TREATMENTS FOR DEPRESSIVE DISORDERS IN AFRICAN AMERICANS

In this penultimate section of the chapter, we consider CBTs for DDs in African Americans. Our review of the literature identified (a) effectiveness studies of CBTs that examined depression (or depressive symptoms) and included African Americans and (b) cultural adaptations of CBTs for depression with African Americans in the sample. We describe recent meta-analytic work and empirical studies with the goal of providing readers with descriptions of CBT approaches for DDs and cultural adaptations of these treatments. Evidence has suggested the latter may yield more favorable treatment outcomes and better serve the mental health needs of marginalized populations (Ward & Brown, 2015).

Recent Findings

Several studies have examined the effectiveness of CBT among adult ethnic minorities with a variety of disorders, including depression, posttraumatic stress disorder, generalized anxiety disorder, and panic disorder (Horrell, 2008). In a study of CBT for depression in low-income ethnic minority medical patients (Organista, Muñoz, & González, 1994), participants ($N = 175$, 18% African American) were offered 12 sessions of CBT either individually or in a group setting or a combination of the two. Treatment focused on the role of thoughts, behaviors, and interpersonal interactions on mood and how to recognize and modify thoughts and behaviors related to depressed mood. Results indicated significant reductions in BDI scores from pre- to posttreatment; however, African Americans, Latinos, and Asians were analyzed together, making it difficult to draw conclusions about the effectiveness of the intervention for African Americans in particular. The study also had a fairly high dropout rate (58%), which appeared to be shaped by ethnicity, treatment modality (individual vs. group therapy), and age.

A second study also examined responses to a depression intervention in a sample of low-income women (Miranda et al., 2003). Participants were 267

Black, White, and Latina women ($M_{age} = 29.3$, $SD = 7.9$) randomly assigned to an antidepressant medication intervention, CBT, or referral to community mental health services. Participants in the 8-week CBT condition were seen either individually or in group sessions, depending on schedule, and were each given a manual and a therapy protocol that included doing homework, daily monitoring, engaging in pleasant activities, improving relationships with others, and cognitively managing mood. Women in the CBT and medication groups experienced a significant decrease in depressive symptoms and improvement in social functioning over time compared with the community referral group. There was no interaction between ethnicity and treatment type, suggesting that CBT is an efficacious treatment for African American, Latina, and White women with mild to moderate depressive symptoms.

In a randomized investigation of HIV-positive individuals with depressive symptoms, participants received up to 16 weeks of treatment with CBT, interpersonal psychotherapy, supportive psychotherapy, or imipramine plus supportive psychotherapy (Markowitz, Spielman, Sullivan, & Fishman, 2000). One hundred and one individuals participated; however, only 18 were African American and 88.9% of this group was male ($M_{age} = 37.5$). Analyses revealed a significant treatment-by-ethnicity interaction only for CBT: African Americans assigned to CBT had poorer outcomes than White, Hispanic, Asian American, or other-race individuals and had an increase in self-reported depressive symptoms. Though participants of other races improved over time, African Americans assigned to CBT markedly worsened. Markowitz et al. (2000), speculated that these results might have been due to therapists' lack of cultural competence or participants' perceptions of CBT as probing and confrontational; however, results should be interpreted cautiously because of the small sample size.

A recent meta-analysis by Gregory (2016) expanded on the aforementioned study by Miranda et al. (2003) to focus exclusively on studies with samples of adults of African descent (e.g., Caribbean Blacks, Black Africans, African Americans). It also required that these studies (a) used a measure of depression that had been validated in a study of individuals of African descent, (b) included results with a quantitative measure of depressive symptoms that could be used to estimate the effect size, (c) contained CBT that included "the evaluation of thoughts and/or beliefs to alter maladaptive emotions and/or behavior" (Gregory, 2016, p. 116), and (d) compared results with at least one other group (i.e., control, active treatment, or pretest–posttest design). Ten studies were included in the review: Five were randomized controlled trials (RCTs), four were pre–post designs, and one was quasi-experimental. Results indicated that CBT was associated with a significant decrease in depressive symptoms with a medium effect size. Though the number of studies included in the review was small, the meta-analysis was the first synthesized quantitative research specifically examining the effectiveness of CBTs in reducing depressive symptoms in African Americans.

Cultural Modifications of Cognitive Behavior Therapy

In addition to the findings discussed earlier, several recent studies examined cultural adaptations of CBTs for depressive symptoms in African Americans. For example, Kohn, Oden, Muñoz, Robinson, and Leavitt (2002) adapted a manualized CBT intervention to treat depressed low-income African American women experiencing multiple stressors. The modules focused on cognitions, activities, and relationships. The approach, referred to as African American CBT (AACBT), made several structural and didactic modifications to CBT, which included limiting the group to African American women, including experiential meditative exercises, and performing a termination ritual at the end of the intervention. In addition, therapists incorporated anecdotes from African American literature and used African American individuals as examples to illustrate concepts. Four culturally specific therapy modules were also added: creation of healthy relationships, spirituality, African American family issues, and African American female identity.

Participants were 12 African American general medical patients with chronic conditions (M_{age} = 47) who met criteria for MDD. Women were offered the choice of CBT or AACBT. Ten of the women opted for treatment in the AACBT group. Both interventions consisted of 16 weekly 90-minute group therapy sessions that included homework assignments designed to reinforce the therapeutic material. Results indicated that pretreatment, women in the AACBT and CBT groups demonstrated BDI scores in the severe range. Posttreatment, both groups experienced a decline in BDI scores; however, the AACBT group's average BDI scores decreased significantly more than that of the CBT group. Though women in the AACBT group experienced alleviation of symptoms twice the magnitude of the CBT group, it is important to note that the results are based on a small sample. Furthermore, because women were able to choose which treatment they preferred, it is possible that women who chose the AACBT group had certain characteristics that might have rendered them more likely to benefit from AACBT than CBT.

In a previously noted study comparing the effects of telephone-based CBT and face-to-face CBT, Glueckauf and colleagues (2012) examined cultural modifications of CBT. In the first phase of this study, focus groups were conducted with CBT counselors to provide guidance in modifying the treatment manuals, develop strategies for recruitment and retention, and select locations for the face-to-face intervention. On the basis of the recommendations of these groups, photos of African Americans were included in the CBT manual, ties were established with church leaders, and promotional materials were distributed over the course of the intervention to bolster retention.

Participants were 11 African American dementia CGs (M_{age} = 58.09, SD = 10.11) who reported at least moderate levels of depression, provided a minimum of 6 hours of care per week for at least 6 months to their CR, and reported specific caregiving problems. Participants in the telephone-based CBT group completed the intervention at their homes using a teleconference system, whereas those in the face-to-face group completed therapy in a conference room or in a soundproof room in a public library. Both groups completed 12 weekly 1-hour sessions, seven group sessions, and five individual goal-setting and implementation sessions. Telephone-based and face-to-face CBT groups reported declines in depressive symptoms. However, the impact of treatment was smaller for the face-to-face condition than for the telephone-based condition, even when accounting for location of treatment, age, gender, and relationship with CR. In telephone interviews conducted with study participants to assess elements of the session and their perceived utility, CGs expressed an appreciation of peer exchange of information, tips, and support. The authors suggested that peer interaction and group processes may play an important role in successful treatment outcomes. Although speculative, it could be that the slightly larger impact of treatment for the telephone-based CBT was due to the convenience of receiving treatment at home as opposed to contending with common sources of drop out and attrition (e.g., transportation difficulties).

Combining the cultural and technological modifications to CBT used by Kohn et al. (2002) and Glueckauf et al. (2012), Jesse and colleagues (2015) evaluated the feasibility and efficacy of Insight-Plus, a manualized, culturally tailored, and technology-enhanced cognitive behavioral intervention for rural low-income women at risk for antepartum depression. The manual included a section in the first chapter focusing on depression and women of color. Women were given preprogrammed MP3 players with playlists of homework assignments, positive affirmations and stress-reducing guided visualization, and inspirational music. In addition, the research team sought to reduce barriers to attending the intervention by providing transportation, childcare, ice-breaker games, fun activities, and snacks. The team was culturally and racially diverse, and the interviewers were trained in culturally competent interviewing techniques.

Participants were 146 African American, Caucasian, and Hispanic rural low-income pregnant women stratified as low–moderate or high risk for antepartum depression and randomized to either CBT or treatment as usual. African American women comprised 67.8% of the 146 participants (M_{age} = 25.05, SD = 5.49), and this subsample was examined separately from the larger sample in analyses. Depressive symptoms were assessed in the high and low–moderate risk groups, respectively, at baseline (T1), posttreatment (T2), and 1 month after treatment (T3). Those in the CBT intervention met for 2-hour sessions for a total of 6 weeks. Those in the treatment-as-usual group were offered routine social services. Results indicated that the mean reduction in depression scores from T2 to T3 was significantly greater for African American high-risk women in the intervention group than for the high-risk women in the treatment-as-usual group. The mean reduction in BDI-II scores from T1 to T2 was also significantly greater for low–moderate risk women in the intervention group than for low-risk women in the treatment-as-usual group. In other words, African American women at low risk and high risk for depression both had reductions in depression scores, and high-risk women were able to sustain these reductions 1 month after treatment. As with other studies, participant attrition was problematic. There was an 18% rate of attrition after randomization and before the intervention for the full sample. The intervention group had an attrition rate of 35% and the treatment-as-usual group a rate of 3%. Attrition rates in the CBT group were not associated with depressive symptoms but more likely to be influenced by conflicts with schedules and inability to reach women due to phones not working or being out of service (Jesse & Swanson, 2007).

Ward and Brown (2015) developed a culturally adapted depression intervention for African American adults experiencing MDD (Oh Happy Day Class [OHDC]). The OHDC was guided by the ecological validity framework, which proposes that language, culture, metaphors, content, concepts, goals, and context should guide cultural adaptation of treatments and interventions. The OHDC consisted of 12 weekly 2.5-hour sessions facilitated by African American counselors. Sessions used CBT, a support group format, and entailed a strong psychoeducation focus. Each session commenced with a light meal, offering participants an opportunity to bond with one another. The next hour focused on the use of CBT in a support group format. Participants would share psychosocial issues and elicit feedback from group facilitators and members. The final hour focused on psychoeducation. Specifically, participants would learn cognitive and behavioral strategies to enhance their use of healthy coping behaviors. The following topics were incorporated into each session: principles of Kwanzaa, depression and its impact on African Americans, treatment-seeking among African Americans, the relationship between medical conditions and depression, community resources, spiritual coping, and health benefits of forgiveness. On completion of the intervention, the researchers hosted a graduation celebration and reviewed key concepts discussed during the sessions. Three months later, participants reunited to share their challenges and progress and receive support.

In a pilot study of OHDC with 50 African American men and women (M_{age} = 51), the CES-D and the Hamilton Depression Rating Scale were used to assess the frequency and severity of depression symptoms in the preceding week. The measures were completed at baseline, Week 6 (midway through intervention), Week 12 (end of intervention), and Week 24 (postintervention follow-up). Sixty-six percent of the sample completed the entire intervention. Results indicated that depression symptoms decreased significantly from baseline across both genders, and there was no significant degradation to quality of life (as measured by the Short Form Health Survey) or attitudes toward seeking mental health services up to 12 weeks after the intervention.

Summary

Studies of CBTs for depressive symptoms and MDD, including meta-analyses, have suggested that CBT and cultural modifications to CBT interventions may be effective for African Americans. Yet, several concerns remain. First, the dearth of treatment outcome studies involving representative samples of non-White patients makes it difficult to draw meaningful conclusions about effectiveness in this population (Ward & Brown, 2015). Second, it is difficult to ascertain whether CBTs are similarly executed (with regard to content and emphasis) across studies. Only a few of the studies discussed delineated how CBT counselors were trained and expounded on precisely what participants experienced during each session of CBT (e.g., Glueckauf et al., 2012; Jesse et al., 2015; Ward & Brown, 2015). Third, the benefits of individual versus group CBT are unknown in treating DDs for African Americans. Organista and colleagues (1994) suggested that group therapy for depressed individuals may provide "an interpersonal context for normalizing depression and examining real examples of depressed thinking and attempts to apply CBT" (p. 247), which would seem to fit with the collective orientation (e.g., interdependence, cooperation) emphasized among many persons of African descent (Belgrave & Allison, 2014); yet, the mix of individual and group therapy (e.g., Glueckauf et al., 2012; Jesse et al., 2015; Miranda et al., 2003) within and across studies limits definitive conclusions.

THE FUTURE OF COGNITIVE BEHAVIORAL MODELS, MEASURES, AND TREATMENTS FOR DEPRESSIVE DISORDERS IN AFRICAN AMERICANS

Our review of the literature on CBMMTs for treating DDs in African Americans suggests that the extant knowledge in this area is in its infancy, with relatively few rigorous studies to date. Although our review highlights promise for the future of CBMMTs for DDs in African Americans, continued efforts to advance knowledge in this area are warranted. In this final section, we briefly consider recommendations and future directions for achieving this goal.

One of the most striking observations of our review was the relative absence of cultural considerations in conceptual models and treatment outcome studies of African Americans with DDs. This shortcoming (consistent with the rare mention of culture in the Depressive Disorders section of the *DSM–5*; American Psychiatric Association, 2013) is out of step with the rapid increase in racial, cultural, and socioeconomic diversity among individuals in the United States (Graham, Sorenson, & Hayes-Skelton, 2013) and the increasing emphasis on culture, race, and ethnicity in the field of clinical psychology (Hofmann, 2014). In our review of cognitive behavioral models relevant to DDs in African Americans, we observed that cultural considerations were often at the periphery of the models (i.e., briefly discussed in passing as possible factors that might play a role, if discussed at all). This tendency is surprising given that cultural variables such as race, ethnicity, and socioeconomic status are known correlates of many of the key determinants found in classic models of depression (e.g., thoughts, beliefs, stressors, early adverse experiences, perceptions of resources such as social support).

Although much has been written about differences in African Americans' attitudes and beliefs about effective treatment for DDs, preferences for treatment (e.g., same-race providers), mental health stigma, and mistrust of psychiatry and health providers (Cooper et al., 2003; Givens, Houston, Van Voorhees, Ford, & Cooper, 2007; Hankerson, Suite, & Bailey, 2015), we are unaware of any treatment models to substantively integrate these factors. Some African Americans have reported beliefs that (a) depression is a sign of personal weakness or being "crazy," a punishment from God, a normal part of aging, and/or a part of one's role as a Black woman; (b) treatment is unnecessary, and depression can remit without professional help; and (c) discussions about mental illness are inappropriate and should not be engaged in openly (Anglin, Alberti, Link, & Phelan, 2008; Chapman & Perry, 2008; Conner et al., 2010; Ward & Heidrich, 2009). Spirituality is also important to consider. Evidence suggests that, for some, faith and prayer are preferred strategies for coping with racism and, in some cases, thought to be the only ways to overcome mental disorders such as depression (Wittink, Joo, Lewis, & Barg, 2009). Though certainly not exhaustive, these examples highlight sociocultural factors that, in addition to racial bias, must be incorporated into CBMMTs for DDs in African Americans.

A growing body of research identifies a bevy of relevant factors and approaches for maximizing treatment of DDs in African Americans: incorporating cultural competence and warmth, inviting participants to be active and collaborative in the process (e.g., seeking direct feedback from clients), including kinship and extended social networks as part of treatment, inquiring about the role of religiosity and spirituality in the lives of African Americans, and timing intervention sessions with other health care visits to reduce missed visits (Connolly Gibbons et al., 2015; Hankerson et al., 2015; Jesse et al., 2015). Moreover, CBT might be further enhanced by talking about clients' experiences of racism (because they may be socialized not to talk about these experiences; Graham et al., 2013), tailoring psychoeducation to African Americans' lived experiences (e.g., barriers to health care, job experience of social injustice), incorporating these experiences into the case conceptualization, being aware of how those lived experiences might affect treatment adherence (e.g., a client working two jobs with a family might have difficulty engaging in therapy and completing assignments), and challenging negative self-talk instead of questioning the clients' experience as irrational or cognitive errors (which clients could experience as an invalidating microaggression; see Graham et al., 2013, for further discussion). A "culture-blind" approach seems inadvisable and, going forward, cultural considerations will have to be at the forefront and center of models describing pathways for DDs and their treatment in African Americans.

In the area of measurement, it will be important to identify valid measures of DDs for African Americans and clarify what is being assessed in available measures of DD. Youngstrom (2013) noted that it is imperative that we evaluate the utility of our measures according to their ability to "predict" a disorder, "prescribe" the most efficacious treatment, and track the "process" of recovery. In light of the relatively few measures validated in representative African American populations, the lack of consensus on the reliability and validity of some measures for depression and our evolving understanding of the impact of racial discrimination and other sociocultural factors on depressive symptoms, there is an immediate need for further explorations into the psychometric properties and evidence-based utility of common and novel measures (e.g., CES-D, MSMHS). Also worthy of consideration will be the considerable heterogeneity across measures with respect to what constitutes depression. Although we intended to frame the chapter around DDs, some studies examined depressive symptoms and not DDs per se, and few studies examined the full complement of DDs identified in the *DSM–5* (i.e., disruptive mood dysregulation disorder, MDD, persistent depressive disorder, premenstrual dysphoric disorder, substance or medication-induced depressive disorder). In light of findings from the NSAL suggesting differential factor structure for MDD versus persistent DD (dysthymia; Torres, 2012) and given mixed findings regarding somatization as distinct from cognitive or mood symptoms (Das, Olfson, McCurtis, & Weissman, 2006), future research is warranted. Differences in how DDs are conceptualized and operationalized may matter for assessment and treatment.

A final crosscutting issue to be addressed in future research is that of methodology and analysis. First, only a small number of studies, often with small sample sizes, have examined the treatment of DDs in African Americans, and there is limited data to support intervention effectiveness in the target population (Ward & Brown, 2015). More studies are needed, and the inclusion of representative samples of African Americans in treatment outcome studies is critical. Second, numerous design flaws compromise the ability to yield definitive conclusions regarding cultural adaptation of treatments and their effectiveness. Attrition was a problem in many of the studies we reviewed, but other problems included lack of randomization and control groups, heterogeneity of populations across a small number of studies with circumscribed African American populations (e.g., high- and low-risk pregnant mothers, dementia CGs older adults), the mixing of group and individual treatment within the same study, the comparison of conditions with closed versus rolling admissions, and unbalanced designs, among others. More rigorous investigation will be necessary to address these limitations while balancing the typical challenges of conducting this type of research.

From an analytic perspective, aggregating racial and ethnic groups together may be problematic because of differential experiences and history. Although this may be the most expedient approach given small sample sizes and power considerations, complex patterns exist (e.g., ethnicity by sex interactions for Black vs. Caribbean men and women for MDD vs. dysthymia; Breland-Noble et al., 2015) and greater understanding of how demographic, cultural, and psychological characteristics interact is important. Future studies should recognize that ethnic minorities and African Americans are not a monolithic group and examine race, ethnicity, socioeconomic status, and other cultural markers (e.g., age) as moderators in analyses. Finally, future studies should investigate mechanisms underlying DDs or treatment outcomes because few studies have done so to date. As Gitlin et al. (2014) noted, "Understanding the mechanisms by which one factor affects the other in a depression intervention can enhance the design of future interventions and guide clinical expectations when implementing an evidence-based depression program" (p. 2282).

The prospects for the future study of CBMMTs for DDs in African Americans are bright, and we challenge the field to bring cultural considerations (often relegated to the periphery or appearing as an afterthought, if at all) to the center of models and approaches examining DDs in African Americans. Second, measures of DDs in African Americans must be appropriately reliable, valid, and predictive in the populations in which they are used and may benefit from incorporating the African American experience (e.g., racism and discrimination) that influences the expression of DDs. Finally, we call for more treatment outcomes studies that include African American participants and for the use of rigorous and complex, methodological, and analytic approaches to capture the ways in which cultural factors intersect to influence the development and treatment of DDs. Together, these next steps can advance our understanding of DDs in African Americans and lessen the mental health suffering of African Americans with DDs.

REFERENCES

Abramson, L. Y., Metalsky, G. I., & Alloy, L. B. (1989). Hopelessness depression: A theory-based subtype of depression. *Psychological Review*, 96, 358–372. http://dx.doi.org/10.1037/0033-295X.96.2.358

Alegría, M., Chatterji, P., Wells, K., Cao, Z., Chen, C. N., Takeuchi, D., . . . Meng, X.-L. (2008). Disparity in depression treatment among racial and ethnic minority populations in the United States. *Psychiatric Services*, 59, 1264–1272. http://dx.doi.org/10.1176/ps.2008.59.11.1264

American Psychiatric Association. (1994). *Diagnostic and statistical manual of mental disorders* (4th ed.). Washington, DC: Author.

American Psychiatric Association. (2013). *Diagnostic and statistical manual of mental disorders* (5th ed.). Arlington, VA: Author.

Anglin, D. M., Alberti, P. M., Link, B. G., & Phelan, J. C. (2008). Racial differences in beliefs about the effectiveness and necessity of mental health treatment. *American Journal of Community Psychology*, 42(1-2), 17–24. http://dx.doi.org/10.1007/s10464-008-9189-5

Baker, F. M., & Bell, C. C. (1999). Issues in the psychiatric treatment of African Americans. *Psychiatric Services*, 50, 362–368. http://dx.doi.org/10.1176/ps.50.3.362

Baker, F. M., Velli, S. A., Friedman, J., & Wiley, C. (1995). Screening tests for depression in older Black vs. White patients. *The American Journal of Geriatric Psychiatry*, 3, 43–51. http://dx.doi.org/10.1097/00019442-199524310-00006

Beck, A. T. (1974). The development of depression: A cognitive model. In R. J. Friedman & M. M. Katz (Eds.), *The psychology of depression: Contemporary theory and research*. Oxford, England: John Wiley & Sons.

Beck, A. T. (1987). Cognitive models of depression. *Journal of Cognitive Psychotherapy*, 1, 5–37.

Beck, A. T., Steer, R. A., & Brown, G. K. (1996). *Manual for the Beck Depression Inventory–II*. San Antonio, TX: Psychological Corporation.

Beck, A. T., Steer, R. A., & Carbin, M. G. (1988). Psychometric properties of the Beck Depression Inventory: Twenty-five years of evaluation. *Clinical Psychology Review*, 8, 77–100. http://dx.doi.org/10.1016/0272-7358(88)90050-5

Beck, A. T., Ward, C. H., Mendelson, M., Mock, J., & Erbaugh, J. (1961). An inventory for measuring depression. *Archives of General Psychiatry*, 4, 561–571. http://dx.doi.org/10.1001/archpsyc.1961.01710120031004

Belgrave, F. Z., & Allison, K. W. (2014). *African American psychology: From Africa to America* (3rd ed.). Los Angeles, CA: Sage.

Bell, C. C., & Mehta, H. (1980). The misdiagnosis of Black patients with manic depressive illness. *Journal of the National Medical Association, 72,* 141–145.

Borrell, L. N., Kiefe, C. I., Williams, D. R., Diez-Roux, A. V., & Gordon-Larsen, P. (2006). Self-reported health, perceived racial discrimination, and skin color in African Americans in the CARDIA study. *Social Science & Medicine, 63,* 1415–1427. http://dx.doi.org/10.1016/j.socscimed.2006.04.008

Breland-Noble, A. M., Burriss, A., Poole, H. K., & the AAKOMA PROJECT Adult Advisory Board. (2010). Engaging depressed African American adolescents in treatment: Lessons from the AAKOMA PROJECT. *Journal of Clinical Psychology, 66,* 868–879. http://dx.doi.org/10.1002/jclp.20708

Breland-Noble, A. M., Sotomayor, J., & Burriss, F. A. (2015). Assessing mood disorders and suicidality in African Americans. In L. T. Benuto & B. D. Leany (Eds.), *Guide to psychological assessment with African Americans* (pp. 87–104). New York, NY: Springer. http://dx.doi.org/10.1007/978-1-4939-1004-5_7

Breslau, J., Aguilar-Gaxiola, S., Kendler, K., Su, M., Williams, D., & Kessler, R. C. (2006). Specifying race-ethnic difference in risk for psychiatric disorder in a USA national sample. *Psychological Medicine, 36,* 57–68. http://dx.doi.org/10.1017/S0033291705006161

Carleton, R. N., Thibodeau, M. A., Teale, M. J. N., Welch, P. G., Abrams, M. P., Robinson, T., & Asmundson, G. J. G. (2013). The Center for Epidemiologic Studies Depression Scale: A review with a theoretical and empirical examination of item content and factor structure. *PLoS ONE, 8*(3), e58067. http://dx.doi.org/10.1371/journal.pone.0058067

Chao, R. C.-L., & Green, K. E. (2011). Multiculturally Sensitive Mental Health Scale (MSMHS): Development, factor analysis, reliability, and validity. *Psychological Assessment, 23,* 876–887. http://dx.doi.org/10.1037/a0023710

Chapman, D. P., & Perry, G. S. (2008). Depression as a major component of public health for older adults. *Preventing Chronic Disease, 5*(1), A22.

Clark, L. A., & Watson, D. (1991). Tripartite model of anxiety and depression: Psychometric evidence and taxonomic implications. *Journal of Abnormal Psychology, 100,* 316–336. http://dx.doi.org/10.1037/0021-843X.100.3.316

Cole, D. A., Martin, J. M., & Powers, B. (1997). A competency-based model of child depression: A longitudinal study of peer, parent, teacher, and self-evaluations. *Journal of Child Psychology and Psychiatry and Allied Disciplines, 38,* 505–514. http://dx.doi.org/10.1111/j.1469-7610.1997.tb01537.x

Conner, K. O., Copeland, V. C., Grote, N. K., Rosen, D., Albert, S., McMurray, M. L., . . . Koeske, G. (2010). Barriers to treatment and culturally endorsed coping strategies among depressed African-American older adults. *Aging & Mental Health, 14,* 971–983. http://dx.doi.org/10.1080/13607863.2010.501061

Connolly Gibbons, M. B., Kurtz, J. E., Thompson, D. L., Mack, R. A., Lee, J. K., Rothbard, A., . . . Crits-Christoph, P. (2015). The effectiveness of clinician feedback in the treatment of depression in the community mental health system. *Journal of Consulting and Clinical Psychology, 83,* 748–759. http://dx.doi.org/10.1037/a0039302

Cooper, L. A., Gonzales, J. J., Gallo, J. J., Rost, K. M., Meredith, L. S., Rubenstein, L. V., . . . Ford, D. E. (2003). The acceptability of treatment for depression among African-American, Hispanic, and white primary care patients. *Medical Care, 41,* 479–489. http://dx.doi.org/10.1097/01.MLR.0000053228.58042.E4

Das, A. K., Olfson, M., McCurtis, H. L., & Weissman, M. M. (2006). Depression in African Americans: Breaking barriers to detection and treatment. *The Journal of Family Practice, 55,* 30–39.

Devins, G. M., Orme, C. M., Costello, C. G., Binik, Y. M., Frizzell, B., Stam, H. J., & Pullin, W. M. (1988). Measuring depressive symptoms in illness populations: Psychometric properties of the Center for Epidemiologic Studies Depression (CES-D) scale. *Psychology and Health, 2,* 139–156.

Ellison, C. G., & Flannelly, K. J. (2009). Religious involvement and risk of major depression in a prospective nationwide study of African American adults. *Journal of Nervous and Mental Disease, 197,* 568–573. http://dx.doi.org/10.1097/NMD.0b013e3181b08f45

Fortuna, L. R., Alegría, M., & Gao, S. (2010). Retention in depression treatment among ethnic and racial minority groups in the United States. *Depression and Anxiety, 27,* 485–494. http://dx.doi.org/10.1002/da.20685

Gitlin, L. N., Harris, L. F., McCoy, M. C., Chernett, N. L., Pizzi, L. T., Jutkowitz, E., . . . Hauck, W. W. (2013). A home-based intervention to reduce depressive symptoms and improve quality of life in older African Americans: A randomized trial. *Annals of Internal Medicine, 159,* 243–252. http://dx.doi.org/10.7326/0003-4819-159-4-201308200-00005

Gitlin, L. N., Szanton, S. L., Huang, J., & Roth, D. L. (2014). Factors mediating the effects of a depression intervention on functional disability in older African Americans. *Journal of the American Geriatrics Society, 62,* 2280–2287. http://dx.doi.org/10.1111/jgs.13156

Givens, J. L., Houston, T. K., Van Voorhees, B. W., Ford, D. E., & Cooper, L. A. (2007). Ethnicity and preferences for depression treatment. *General Hospital Psychiatry, 29,* 182–191. http://dx.doi.org/10.1016/j.genhosppsych.2006.11.002

Glueckauf, R. L., Davis, W. S., Willis, F., Sharma, D., Gustafson, D. J., Hayes, J., . . . Springer, J. (2012). Telephone-based, cognitive-behavioral therapy for African American dementia caregivers with depression: Initial findings. *Rehabilitation Psychology, 57,* 124–139. http://dx.doi.org/10.1037/a0028688

Graham, J. R., Sorenson, S., & Hayes-Skelton, S. A. (2013). Enhancing the cultural sensitivity of cognitive behavioral interventions for anxiety in diverse populations. *The Behavior Therapist, 36,* 101–108.

Gregory, V. L., Jr. (2016). Cognitive-behavioral therapy for depressive symptoms in persons of African descent: A meta-analysis. *Journal of Social Service Research, 42,* 113–129. http://dx.doi.org/10.1080/01488376.2015.1084973

Grothe, K. B., Dutton, G. R., Jones, G. N., Bodenlos, J., Ancona, M., & Brantley, P. J. (2005). Validation of the Beck Depression Inventory–II in a low-income African American sample of medical outpatients. *Psychological Assessment, 17*, 110–114. http://dx.doi.org/10.1037/1040-3590.17.1.110

Hamilton, M. (1960). A rating scale for depression. *Journal of Neurology, Neurosurgery, and Psychiatry, 23*, 56–62. http://dx.doi.org/10.1136/jnnp.23.1.56

Hammen, C. L., Rudolph, K. D., & Abaied, J. L. (2014). Childhood and adolescent depression. In E. J. Mash & R. A. Barkeley (Eds.), *Child psychopathology* (3rd ed., pp. 225–263). New York, NY: Guilford Press.

Hankerson, S. H., Suite, D., & Bailey, R. K. (2015). Treatment disparities among African American men with depression: Implications for clinical practice. *Journal of Health Care for the Poor and Underserved, 26*, 21–34. http://dx.doi.org/10.1353/hpu.2015.0012

Hann, D., Winter, K., & Jacobsen, P. (1999). Measurement of depressive symptoms in cancer patients: Evaluation of the Center for Epidemiological Studies Depression Scale (CES-D). *Journal of Psychosomatic Research, 46*, 437–443. http://dx.doi.org/10.1016/S0022-3999(99)00004-5

Hofmann, S. G. (2014). President's message: Culture matters. *The Behavior Therapist, 36*, 97–99.

Horrell, S. C. V. (2008). Effectiveness of cognitive-behavioral therapy with adult ethnic minority clients: A review. *Professional Psychology: Research and Practice, 39*, 160–168. http://dx.doi.org/10.1037/0735-7028.39.2.160

Jesse, D. E., Gaynes, B. N., Feldhousen, E. B., Newton, E. R., Bunch, S., & Hollon, S. D. (2015). Performance of a culturally tailored cognitive-behavioral intervention integrated in a public health setting to reduce risk of antepartum depression: A randomized controlled trial. *Journal of Midwifery & Women's Health, 60*, 578–592. http://dx.doi.org/10.1111/jmwh.12308

Jesse, D. E., & Swanson, M. S. (2007). Risks and resources associated with antepartum risk for depression among rural southern women. *Nursing Research, 56*, 378–386. http://dx.doi.org/10.1097/01.NNR.0000299856.98170.19

Joe, S., Woolley, M. E., Brown, G. K., Ghahramanlou-Holloway, M., & Beck, A. T. (2008). Psychometric properties of the Beck Depression Inventory–II in low-income, African American suicide attempters. *Journal of Personality Assessment, 90*, 521–523. http://dx.doi.org/10.1080/00223890802248919

Kennard, B. D., Stewart, S. M., Hughes, J. L., Patel, P. G., & Emslie, G. J. (2006). Cognitions and depressive symptoms among ethnic minority adolescents. *Cultural Diversity and Ethnic Minority Psychology, 12*, 578–591. http://dx.doi.org/10.1037/1099-9809.12.3.578

Kessler, R. C., Mickelson, K. D., & Williams, D. R. (1999). The prevalence, distribution, and mental health correlates of perceived discrimination in the United States. *Journal of Health and Social Behavior, 40*, 208–230. http://dx.doi.org/10.2307/2676349

Kohn, L. P., Oden, T., Muñoz, R. F., Robinson, A., & Leavitt, D. (2002). Adapted cognitive behavioral group therapy for depressed low-income African American women. *Community Mental Health Journal, 38,* 497–504. http://dx.doi.org/10.1023/A:1020884202677

Lewinsohn, P. M., Hoberman, H., Teri, L., & Hautzinger, M. (1985). An integrative theory of depression. In S. Reiss & R. Bootzin (Eds.), *Theoretical issues in behavior therapy* (pp. 331–359). New York, NY: Academic Press.

Long Foley, K., Reed, P. S., Mutran, E. J., & DeVellis, R. F. (2002). Measurement adequacy of the CES-D among a sample of older African-Americans. *Psychiatry Research, 109,* 61–69. http://dx.doi.org/10.1016/S0165-1781(01)00360-2

Markowitz, J. C., Spielman, L. A., Sullivan, M., & Fishman, B. (2000). An exploratory study of ethnicity and psychotherapy outcome among HIV-positive patients with depressive symptoms. *The Journal of Psychotherapy Practice and Research, 9,* 226–231.

Miranda, J., Chung, J. Y., Green, B. L., Krupnick, J., Siddique, J., Revicki, D. A., & Belin, T. (2003). Treating depression in predominantly low-income young minority women: A randomized controlled trial. *JAMA, 290,* 57–65. http://dx.doi.org/10.1001/jama.290.1.57

Neighbors, H. W., Jackson, J. S., Campbell, L., & Williams, D. (1989). The influence of racial factors on psychiatric diagnosis: A review and suggestions for research. *Community Mental Health Journal, 25,* 301–311. http://dx.doi.org/10.1007/BF00755677

Nguyen, H. T., Kitner-Triolo, M., Evans, M. K., & Zonderman, A. B. (2004). Factorial invariance of the CES-D in low socioeconomic status African Americans compared with a nationally representative sample. *Psychiatry Research, 126,* 177–187. http://dx.doi.org/10.1016/j.psychres.2004.02.004

Organista, K. C., Muñoz, R. F., & González, G. (1994). Cognitive-behavioral therapy for depression in low-income and minority medical outpatients: Description of a program and exploratory analyses. *Cognitive Therapy and Research, 18,* 241–259. http://dx.doi.org/10.1007/BF02357778

Pearlin, L. I., Mullan, J. T., Semple, S. J., & Skaff, M. M. (1990). Caregiving and the stress process: An overview of concepts and their measures. *The Gerontologist, 30,* 583–594. http://dx.doi.org/10.1093/geront/30.5.583

Pearlin, L. I., & Schooler, C. (1978). The structure of coping. *Journal of Health and Social Behavior, 19,* 2–21. http://dx.doi.org/10.2307/2136319

Pedraza, O., Dotson, V. M., Willis, F. B., Graff-Radford, N. R., & Lucas, J. A. (2009). Internal consistency and test–retest stability of the Geriatric Depression Scale-Short Form in African American older adults. *Journal of Psychopathology and Behavioral Assessment, 31,* 412–416. http://dx.doi.org/10.1007/s10862-008-9123-z

Radloff, L. S. (1977). The CES-D Scale: A self-report depression scale for research in the general population. *Applied Psychological Measurement, 1,* 385–401. http://dx.doi.org/10.1177/014662167700100306

Rehm, L. P. (1977). A self-control model of depression. *Behavior Therapy, 8,* 787–804. http://dx.doi.org/10.1016/S0005-7894(77)80150-0

Sashidharan, T., Pawlow, L. A., & Pettibone, J. C. (2012). An examination of racial bias in the Beck Depression Inventory–II. *Cultural Diversity and Ethnic Minority Psychology, 18,* 203–209. http://dx.doi.org/10.1037/a0027689

Seligman, M. E. P. (1975). *Helplessness: On depression, development, and death.* New York, NY: W. H. Freeman/Times Books/Holt.

Sellers, R. M., Copeland-Linder, N., Martin, P. P., & Lewis, R. L. (2006). Racial identity matters: The relationship between racial discrimination and psychological functioning in African American adolescents. *Journal of Research on Adolescence, 16,* 187–216. http://dx.doi.org/10.1111/j.1532-7795.2006.00128.x

Somervell, P. D., Kaplan, B. H., Heiss, G., Tyroler, H. A., Kleinbaum, D. G., & Obrist, P. A. (1989). Psychologic distress as a predictor of mortality. *American Journal of Epidemiology, 130,* 1013–1023. http://dx.doi.org/10.1093/oxfordjournals.aje.a115402

Tandon, S. D., Cluxton-Keller, F., Leis, J., Le, H. N., & Perry, D. F. (2012). A comparison of three screening tools to identify perinatal depression among low-income African American women. *Journal of Affective Disorders, 136,* 155–162. http://dx.doi.org/10.1016/j.jad.2011.07.014

Torres, E. (2012). Psychometric properties of the Center for Epidemiologic Studies Depression Scale in African American and Black Caribbean US adults. *Issues in Mental Health Nursing, 33,* 687–696. http://dx.doi.org/10.3109/01612840.2012.697534

Wang, Y.-P., & Gorenstein, C. (2013). Psychometric properties of the Beck Depression Inventory–II: A comprehensive review. *Revista Brasileira de Psiquiatria, 35,* 416–431. http://dx.doi.org/10.1590/1516-4446-2012-1048

Ward, E. C., & Brown, R. L. (2015). A culturally adapted depression intervention for African American adults experiencing depression: Oh, happy day. *American Journal of Orthopsychiatry, 85,* 11–22. http://dx.doi.org/10.1037/ort0000027

Ward, E. C., & Heidrich, S. M. (2009). African American women's beliefs about mental illness, stigma, and preferred coping behaviors. *Research in Nursing & Health, 32,* 480–492. http://dx.doi.org/10.1002/nur.20344

Williams, D. R., González, H. M., Neighbors, H., Nesse, R., Abelson, J. M., Sweetman, J., & Jackson, J. S. (2007). Prevalence and distribution of major depressive disorder in African Americans, Caribbean blacks, and non-Hispanic whites: Results from the National Survey of American Life. *Archives of General Psychiatry, 64,* 305–315. http://dx.doi.org/10.1001/archpsyc.64.3.305

Wittink, M. N., Joo, J. H., Lewis, L. M., & Barg, F. K. (2009). Losing faith and using faith: Older African Americans discuss spirituality, religious activities, and depression. *Journal of General Internal Medicine, 24,* 402–407. http://dx.doi.org/10.1007/s11606-008-0897-1

Yesavage, J. A., Brink, T. L., Rose, T. L., Lum, O., Huang, V., Adey, M., & Leirer, V. O. (1982). Development and validation of a geriatric depression screening scale: A preliminary report. *Journal of Psychiatric Research, 17*, 37–49. http://dx.doi.org/10.1016/0022-3956(82)90033-4

Youngstrom, E. A. (2013). Future directions in psychological assessment: Combining evidence-based medicine innovations with psychology's historical strengths to enhance utility. *Journal of Clinical Child and Adolescent Psychology, 42*, 139–159. http://dx.doi.org/10.1080/15374416.2012.736358

4

COGNITIVE BEHAVIORAL MODELS, MEASURES, AND TREATMENTS FOR DEPRESSIVE DISORDERS IN AMERICAN INDIANS

J. DOUGLAS McDONALD, ROYLEEN ROSS,
TESS KILWEIN, AND EMILY SARGENT

The presence of depression in Indian country is as long-standing as it is tragic. Aside from alcoholism and the stoic–savage dichotomy historically depicted in popular American media, the prevalence of depression amongst indigenous Americans is perhaps best known. Depression, as is well established, is often associated with domestic violence, substance abuse, and multiple somatic ailments for the peoples of all nations, but the depth and breadth of its hold on American Indians, however, is truly horrifying. Lest one might dismiss these statements as hyperbole, this chapter seeks to identify and discuss the aspects of Native Americans' experiences with depression that are culturally and historically distinct from other ethnic groups without minimizing its adverse impact on others. Many Americans believe because they passed "American" History in school, they, therefore, understand the history and status of the Native peoples of this continent. Few non-Indians invest the time and effort to fully investigate and begin to comprehend the

http://dx.doi.org/10.1037/0000091-005
Treating Depression, Anxiety, and Stress in Ethnic and Racial Groups: Cognitive Behavioral Approaches,
E. C. Chang, C. A. Downey, J. K. Hirsch, and E. A. Yu (Editors)

predictors and correlates contributing to the daily individual and group differences for America's smallest, yet only, original minority.

In this chapter, we seek to accomplish several objectives. First, we wish to share accurate and relevant historical information contributing to the development of depression and its psychopathological relatives for Native Americans. This is not an easy task, as the reader shall soon see. Second, we discuss the unique historical and contemporary status and stark health and health care-related realities experienced by American Indians and providers. Finally, in a poignant vignette we offer a potential merging of Western best practice and traditional Native approaches (i.e., cognitive behavior therapy) for treating American Indians experiencing depression.

AMERICAN INDIANS

Key Terms

The terms *Native American, American Indian, Native,* and *Indian* are considered equivalent and used interchangeably throughout this chapter. This practice is not intended to offend or confuse but to be inclusive of all viewpoints by appropriately identifying the indigenous peoples of North America. McDonald and Chaney (2003) detailed this controversy and its inconclusive outcomes.

History: Education—The Boarding School Era

Before the boarding school era, European Americans assumed American Indian communities lacked any educational practices within their tribes. Though American Indian education was not institution based or literate like European American practices, it included biology, botany, religion, literature, art, music, astronomy, agriculture, and mathematics. In addition, practical skills such as horticulture, gathering, hunting, fishing, and home and community building were emphasized, which equipped young tribal members with both the knowledge and skills to survive and thrive in their environments (McDonald & Chaney, 2003). As discussed in greater detail later in this chapter, in return for the cessation of hostilities between Native tribes and White settlers and communities, the federal government included in their treaties the promise to "educate" future generations of Native Americans. Seeking to find the cheapest means to fulfill this promise, the government gave birth to the boarding school era.

Originating initially with the Indian Civilization Act of 1819 government-run, off-reservation boarding schools began forcibly taking Native children from their families and transporting them, often long distances from home. The purpose of these schools was not education per se but to assimilate American Indian children into the larger European American society through forced replacement of language and culture, rejecting their ancestral heritage and traditional learning (Brophy & Aberle, 1966; Deloria, 1974; Duran & Duran, 1995; Dussias, 2008) and abandoning the customs and spirit of their culture (Witko, 2006). Even further, American Indian children were subjected to atrocious acts of emotional, physical, and sexual abuse and were not permitted to see their families, circumstances which contributed to lives of psychological, spiritual, and behavioral devastation that they inadvertently passed on to future generations.

Intergenerational Trauma—Postcolonialism

Traumatic events experienced by one generation have the power to affect future generations, a pattern that resonated among indigenous people living with historical trauma, often carrying forward the burden of traumas experienced by their ancestors (Duran & Duran, 1995; Evans-Campbell, 2008; Gone, 2009; Whitbeck, Adams, Hoyt, & Chen, 2004). Despite variations of the term *historical trauma*, it encompasses how the collective trauma of ancestors may contribute to the negative health and social outcomes among current indigenous people (Walters et al., 2011). Evans-Campbell (2008) acknowledged three distinctive characteristics of historically traumatic events: (a) the event was widespread among a specific group or population, with many group members being affected, (b) the event was perpetrated by outgroup members with purposeful and often destructive intent, and (c) the event generated high levels of collective distress in the victimized group.

In the late 19th century, government policies with the intent of assimilating indigenous people were established on the basis of the assumption that Whites were inherently superior to the "uncivilized Indian savages." To a great extent, these policies have contributed to the historical trauma brought on American Indian people (Bombay, Matheson, & Anisman, 2014), thereby contributing to the alarmingly high rates of abuse, depression, and household dysfunction (e.g., domestic violence, parental alcohol abuse) experienced on reservations today (Bombay et al., 2014).

Proliferation of stressors across generations continues to contribute to the distress experienced among American Indian offspring, such as greater childhood adversities and increased stress exposure as adults (Bombay et al., 2014; Duran & Duran, 1995), greater exposure to stressors and trauma experiences, and higher levels of criminality (Bombay et al., 2014). In addition, 30% of American Indians think about the historical losses experienced in their community (e.g., loss of culture, language, and respect for elders) yearly or at special times, and even more alarming, 25% think of these losses daily (Ehlers, Gizer, Gilder, Ellingson, & Yehuda, 2013). One need not be a behavioral health professional to understand how such distressing thoughts might lead to feelings of sadness or depressive symptoms.

Depression in Indian Country

It is often difficult, even for Native Americans themselves and researchers and clinicians, to discern the line where the stereotype of the "depressed American Indian" ends and the reality begins. As discussed previously, depression is an unfortunate and sometimes inescapable aspect of daily life, particularly for those with fewer financial and clinical resources. For many, growing up and living in a context of poverty, hopelessness, and helplessness fosters an overwhelming sense of learned helplessness that is difficult to escape (Duran, Duran, & Brave Heart, 1998; McDonald & Chaney, 2003). As we discuss in upcoming segments, even physical health care is often difficult to access for American Indians, with problems including sanitation, staffing, and health delivery procedures more commonly imagined in developing or Third World countries (Cano, 2016). Many non-Indians are shocked to learn the status of health care delivery in Indian country; yet, many reservation-dwelling natives have never known any different and therefore do not demand or even expect positive change. This ontological view of one's health care context may be a risk factor for the development of depressive symptomatology (McDonald & Gonzalez, 2006); for instance, previous research has suggested that even the perception of discrimination contributes to the risk of development of depression (Whitbeck, McMorris, Hoyt, Stubben, & LaFromboise, 2002).

Thus, we understand that intergenerational trauma can generate a sociocultural context within which both group and individual depressive symptomatology may thrive; indeed, this occurrence has even been described as a *soul wound* for the tribe as a whole, as well as for individual members (Duran et al., 1998). It should also be noted, however, that that sociocultural resilience and strength may also arise in response to intergenerational trauma (Whitbeck et al., 2002; Brave Heart & DeBruyn, 1998). As such, many native communities may react to this depressive context with positive and powerful efforts. These efforts may be generated by community programs, religious societies, or concerned individuals. An elder in the first author's family was often known to smile and say, "We may be down a lot of times, but we are never out!" Although this chapter focuses on individualized cognitive behavior therapy efforts for depression with Native clients and patients, we do wish to leave readers with the knowledge that native communities, despite being painfully aware of the sometimes intergenerationally transmitted depressive context, remain resilient, proud, and forward looking. Perhaps that point—at which Native communities strive to understand their situation and proactively defy the past and present pain with culturally competent research and best practices—is where the dividing line between stereotypes of misery and future hope and energy is defined.

Treaties and Health Care

Health care, and particularly behavioral health care resources, availability, and utilization opportunities, are different for American Indians than for any other ethnic group in America. As mentioned previously, the federal government promised, yet often retracted, provision of education and health care services, resulting in a chronically underfunded, poorly organized, highly politicized system. Thus, the options available to Indian people were, and continue to be, different and typically inadequate in terms of funding, cultural competence, and responsible oversight, fostering a culture of dependency and subsequent helplessness and distrust of the Western medical approach for many Natives. Nations of people who had assessed, diagnosed, and treated their own—and in their own ways—for thousands of years were now subjugated to reliance on what was deemed by White federal doctors and politicians as "best practices."

The pronounced and unavoidable humiliation of seeking health care from those who both despise and patronize them is impossible for non-Indians to understand and contributes not only to the historical trauma and subsequent depression in Native Americans but also to the continued misgivings they maintain about seeking assistance for physical and mental health concerns. This mistrust is paired with other barriers, such as geographical isolation and often a lack of even basic amenities such as electricity, safe drinking water, telephone service, and reliable transportation. Continuity of care is rare to nonexistent in not only rural and frontier areas but also for urban Natives, who are often unemployed and lack insurance; as a result, there are few private practitioners available to treat Native patients, given that the majority of their potential clients have no money.

CULTURAL ISSUES

Who Is Indian?

The question of who is Indian is a complicated and sensitive issue (Deloria, 2002). In accordance with treaty arrangements, the federal government charged every recognized tribe with maintaining their own citizenry without guidance.

Health care and other services are only available to tribally enrolled (or sometimes descended) members (Spruhan, 2006). So, who is Indian?

Most tribes have required (and still do) a certain percentage of Indian blood—*blood quantum*—for membership; however, one tribe may establish a blood quantum criterion of 50% for membership, whereas another tribe may set theirs at 5%, and still others may eschew blood quantum in favor of proven lineage (Spruhan, 2006). Given that federally recognized tribes are sovereign nations, the next incoming tribal government may vote to alter or even repudiate the previously existing enrollment criteria on a whim. Tribal membership as a qualifying variable affects other potential resources as well, in that some tribes who own casinos or oil, for example, may choose to dole out profits only to enrolled tribal members, denying those who do not meet the current enrollment criteria. Yet, the tribal government could meet and pass a new enrollment resolution that loosens standards, and immediately whole groups and generations of individuals would become qualified.

Identity Versus Competence

Another challenging aspect of contemporary mental health care for American Indians involves cultural identity and competence. Although some Native individuals may optimize their tribal worldview and its subsequent expected behaviors (*traditional*), others may hail from Native families who actively ignore or even suppress these ideals, choosing instead to embrace those of the majority culture (*assimilated*). Some choose to embrace both (*bicultural*), and still others grow up to embrace neither (*marginal*). Research and practical life experiences have shown cultural identification and competence to greatly determine or at least mediate environmental information processing and subsequent behavior (Oetting & Beauvais, 1991). More simply, a traditional Native person may consider and value Western majority culture behavioral health treatment modalities and opportunities extremely differently than their more assimilated brethren. More bicultural Native individuals may value and practice both treatment approaches equally, whereas those with little cultural competence in either realm may devalue or refuse treatment altogether. It is not uncommon for more traditional patients to suffer unnecessarily because of their mistrust of Western medical and behavioral resources and practices (McDonald, Morton, & Stewart, 1992).

Mental Health Implications: Measurement, Diagnosis, and Treatment Issues

Among the myriad challenges for any behavioral health practitioner is maintaining validity (Dana, 1993; McDonald & Chaney, 2003). Previous research has suggested that accurate assessment lends itself to accurate diagnoses and subsequent treatment. This concept forms the backbone of the "best practices" emphasis and movement of the past generation. Most American Psychological Association (APA)–accredited training programs espouse a scientist–practitioner training model, which suggests good science leads to good treatment, and vice versa. These same programs promote consistent adherence to the application of valid and reliable research in clinical practice. Although few would deny this, the unfortunate reality for Native Americans is that the "good" science regarding their behavioral health status and treatment is less prevalent than for any other cultural group. This lack of empirically generated direction makes valid and reliable navigation of competent clinical practice for American Indians extremely difficult and of questionable efficacy. Thankfully, more American Indian psychologists are being trained who, along with many majority-culture allies, are finally embracing the importance of large-scale, culturally competent clinical research that can inform American Indian clinical services (McDonald, 1994). Yet, much of the map remains unexplored.

NATIVE PERSPECTIVES OF "PSYCHOLOGY," MENTAL HEALTH, AND PSYCHOTHERAPY

Ambiguity of "Psychology" and "Mind"

Thawacin is one of several Lakota words for the human mind; however, it is neither a simple nor entirely accurate translation. *Thawacin* also speaks to one's thoughts and feelings and disposition. Adhering to a recurring theme throughout this chapter, any efforts to competently and effectively provide behavioral health services to Native Americans is complicated, yet not impossible. Despite the fact that these two words, *psychology* and *mind*, have differences, they also have important similarities. To therefore accept the worth and validity of both worlds simultaneously requires a flexible mind-set, tolerant of ambiguity, which is entirely natural for traditional and bicultural Native Americans and cognitively dissonant for many majority-culture behavioral scientists and practitioners. An example of this scenario can be found in many reservation Christian churches. It is commonplace to find the book of hymns translated into a Native language yet still considered equally valuable and authentic as its English version right next to it behind the pew (Smithsonian Center for Folklife and Cultural Heritage, 2004). Many non-Indian parishioners may find that confusing or even offensive. Yet, in their essence, and at their core, they both represent the same thing.

It might be argued that such a flexible and open-minded perspective lends itself to better understanding American Indians, their problems, and potential healing practices among Natives and non-Natives alike. An inflexible, concrete clinician or researcher (regardless of their heritage) may find it difficult to work effectively with Native clients and patients and, for that matter, anyone significantly different from themselves. We make this point primarily to provide a context for considering such related issues as wellness, illness, diagnosis, and treatment from an American Indian worldview. Other authors (McDonald & Chaney, 2003) provide a more comprehensive and detailed discussion of these points, but they can be summarized as follows.

Wellness and Illness

The degree to which an individual, or group, is experiencing wellness or illness is determined by assessing two important aspects. First, there must be recognition that individuals comprise three coexisting components: mind, body, and spirit. Some tribes and other indigenous groups may include other components, or even split aspects of this trinity, by considering "body" as "heart" and "brain," for example. The important thing to understand is that most Natives consider individuals as holistic beings comprising more than one aspect. The second foundational consideration is that of balance. Combined, the two notions (and according to many elders and healers) suggest a healthy person has achieved a balance between mind, body, and spirit and, correspondingly, an unwell person to be out of balance on one or more components. This explanation is vastly oversimplified and generalized, yet it does provide an overall framework within which many Natives conceptualize health. Historically, majority culture approaches have sought to distinguish these aspects and treat, for example, a physical ailment with the exclusion of the mental and spiritual aspects of the person on the examination table (Hodge, Limb, & Cross, 2009). An indigenous healer would never do this. Although most scientist–practitioner training programs teach the importance of considering some physical aspects of a patient's psychosocial history and behavioral observations, few emphasize the assessment of that patient's spiritual functioning or even acknowledge it as potentially diagnostically important. Such a treatment plan would be considered drastically incomplete by a traditional Native practitioner (McDonald & Chaney, 2003).

Traditional Versus Western Modalities

As mentioned previously, traditionalism does not necessarily imply a degree of blood quantum but rather refers to the extent to which an individual embraces his or her culture of origin over the dominant culture. Accordingly, *traditional medicine* is one term used to describe Native American healing beliefs and practices. Traditional medicine takes into account the union of traditional knowledge, traditional beliefs, collectivistic values, and obligatory tribal and community aspects (McDonald et al., 1992). Native traditionalists view the past as manifested in the present, known only through "spiritual sources, rituals, and oral tradition" (McGuire, 1992, p. 828). As a result, traditional American Indians are often unlikely to seek formal help from a therapist when experiencing a mental health disturbance, preferring instead to seek help from a traditional healer, highlighting why an understanding of the cultural aspects related to healing is crucial among health care providers.

It is important to recognize how critical cultural competency is in delivering effective services to Native Americans, primarily because this population tends to operate from a worldview that differs from the worldview of the dominant secular culture (McDonald & Gonzales, 2006). Unfortunately, this bridging task is more difficult than it might appear because most Western practitioners are unconsciously entrenched in a worldview that denies openness to practices outside rational, empirical thought processes (Duran & Duran, 1995).

Although much of traditional Indian medicine includes empirical observation, applying scientific inquiry involving blinded and controlled observations is absent from traditional healing (Rhoades & Rhoades, 2000). In contrast, Western approaches to medicine involve applying scientific principles developed by European American cultures, centered on the disease concept (Rhoades & Rhoades, 2000). In Western medicine, conventional health care providers use methods developed according to Western medical and scientific traditions in the treatment of medical conditions. This approach differs from traditional or alternative medicine in its approach to treatment, which heavily relies on medications and strict adherence to the formal scientific process. Though both traditional and Western approaches have an important place in healing, it is crucial to recognize the differences between the two and the impact they may have on American Indian people experiencing mental health disturbances and/or considering seeking treatment for their mental health condition.

COGNITIVE BEHAVIOR THERAPY AND AMERICAN INDIANS

Cognitive Behavior Therapy With Ethnic Minorities

The demand for both empirically supported and culturally sensitive therapies for ethnic minority populations has increased (Hall, 2001). As a result, mental health professionals often question how relevant cognitive behavior therapy (CBT) is for their clients belonging to ethnic minority groups. Although CBT has traditionally been empirically supported for primarily White European Americans, many question how well this generalizes to ethnic minorities (Alvidrez, Azocar, & Miranda, 1996). Surprisingly enough, few CBT-based treatments have been validated with ethnic minority individuals, despite the growing rate of the non-White population in the United States (Chen, Kramer, Chen, & Chung, 2005; Hall, 2001; Horrell, 2008). Our brothers and sisters of color discuss intersections of CBT and non-Indian cultural experiences in this book with eloquence and wisdom. In that regard, we speak from our own campfires and respectfully allow them to speak from theirs.

Cognitive Behavior Therapy With American Indians

The fundamental mechanism of CBT focuses on cognitive attributions relating to characteristics associated with Western European culture; therefore, the approach may not always be applicable to, or highly effective with, minority cultures (Jackson, Schmutzer, Wenzel, & Tyler, 2006; Schieffelin, 1985). Although there is a lack of empirical data, numerous clinicians have identified ways in which CBT may be cohesive with American Indian clients (McDonald & Gonzalez, 2006). For example, one important contributing factor is the emphasis on incorporating unique cultural facets into treatment plans, as well as studying the differences between each culture without assuming all minorities will respond the same (Jackson et al., 2006; Safren, 2001). Renfrey (1992) discussed how CBT's focus on action orientation, the present, and directiveness are all useful therapy characteristics, which are also consistent with American Indian cultural values. Several Native psychologists proposed that non-Indian therapists using CBT with American Indians should be extremely aware of their cultural sensitivity to minimize assumptions or interfering behaviors (McDonald & Gonzalez, 2006; Renfrey, 1992).

It is important to note that the degree to which an American Indian identifies with traditional values may play a vital role in the effectiveness of culturally sensitive provisions of CBT (Herring, 1990). For example, one identifying more with the traditional values may incorporate sweat-lodge ceremonies or other spiritual ceremonies into therapy. Fiferman (1989) conducted an empirical study of CBT acceptability with American Indians by creating a scenario of a potential client with a depressive disorder and providing college students with treatment rationales for CBT and traditional American Indian therapy. Findings showed that more acculturated American Indians and European Americans preferred CBT as a more acceptable approach than did traditional American Indian participants.

In addition, Jackson et al. (2006) investigated the applicability of CBT with a sample of both European Americans and American Indians. This study was the first to empirically evaluate which facets of CBT may have to be altered. Investigators hypothesized European American participants would favor CBT's focused in-session behavior, active stance, and structured therapy at a higher level compared with American Indians. It was also hypothesized that more acculturated American Indians would have similar scores to European Americans. Results indicated that European American participants gave higher ratings for the focused in-session behavior scale than the American Indian participants. One explanation for these results is that the majority culture emphasizes a linear and logical approach in relation to therapy, whereas American Indian individuals may explain behavior in terms of harmony with natural order or how humans should relate appropriately with their social and physical environment (Tyler, Cohen, & Clark, 1982). For instance, traditional American Indians may associate depression with disharmony in the natural order of the world and nature. Active stance (AS), the second CBT-AS factor scale, which measures the individuals desire for active participation both in and out of sessions, was rated equally acceptable by both American Indians and European Americans. These results may suggest that American Indians endorse CBT components of active stance such as active scheduling, present-focused treatment, provision of short-term treatment, and work completion but might not agree with the foundation of how CBT works. This explanation may have importance in relation to how clinicians demonstrate the treatment background for CBT for American Indians. Last, a structured therapeutic relationship, which—optimally—represents a client's acceptance of personal change and growth, was rated higher in desirability by European Americans than American Indians. Overall, European Americans rated CBT as more acceptable than did American Indians. However, the ratings of acculturated American Indians were more similar to those of European Americans than traditional American Indians. American Indians may demonstrate an external locus of control in problem solving, which may come across as passive or as seeming treatment noncompliance or even symptomatic of a depressed clinical presentation. The impending negative interpretation can be reversed if the clinician implements a more culturally sensitive type of CBT.

Substance abuse is often comorbid with depression and, historically, Indian Health Agencies (Indian Health Service, 1997) have documented that American Indians experience high rates of substance use disorders compared with the general population; yet, little treatment outcome research has been devoted to the American Indian community. In one study, Villanueva, Tonigan, and Miller (2007) compared CBT (Kadden et al., 2003), motivation and enhancement therapy (MET), and twelve-step facilitation (Nowinski,

Baker, & Carroll, 1992), finding that MET was more effective for promoting abstinent days and reducing number of drinks on drinking days. The authors suggested that MET might be more culturally compatible for Native groups than CBT in its current format. Thus, cultural adaptation and alignment with tribal customs is a necessary transition for CBT to be effective for treating correlates of depression in American Indians.

Assessment and Treatment Plan Development Considerations

Some fundamental differences between assessing the majority culture and American Indian clients and patients must be considered. Even at the most basic level, attempting to reduce and isolate reflections of one's individual, personal thoughts and beliefs can be more complicated for all collectivist-oriented groups and certainly for Native Americans. Some more traditional American Indians may struggle to identify purely individual aspects of "self," independent of the group (Trimble, 1987). More specifically, questions such as "Tell me some positive things about you" may cause some Natives to focus on what others might think of them first, rather than engaging in self-evaluation. Unawareness of potential cross-culturally related misunderstandings such as this may contribute to inaccurate assessments of schema and other factors (e.g., emotions) that are important to CBT treatment plan development.

Dana (1993) and others (McDonald et al., 1992) additionally suggested the importance of considering reading levels, normative samples, length, and cultural appropriateness when using assessment materials. These authors offered an example from an item in the Minnesota Multiphasic Personality Inventory—2 (MMPI–2; Butcher, Dahlstrom, Graham, Tellegen, & Kaemmer, 1989) that asks whether one has seen or heard things that others cannot. This item, if affirmed, contributes to a subscale suggestive of schizophrenia. Many persons, particularly more traditional Natives, might consider this a description of a sacred "vision" and mark "yes," thereby unintentionally increasing the likelihood of an invalid clinical picture. Some have even suggested using cultural identification as a means to adjust or modify findings from standardized assessments. Dana (1993, p. 102) suggested using cultural identification data as "moderator variables" to clarify testing scores for Native Americans. Above all, multicultural competence plays a pivotal role in an accurate and culturally informed assessment process. As stated previously, the validity of assessment data is key. For example, are negative self-statements derived from one's Beck Depression Inventory–II (BDI-II; Beck, Steer, & Brown, 1996) evaluation more reflective of that individual or their group (tribe), given a more traditional (collectivist) worldview? Practitioners of CBT will immediately recognize the quandary of engaging in such an important aspect of treatment if it is based on inaccurate results, which then may lead to a faulty or even harmful treatment plan.

CULTURAL APPROPRIATENESS OF COMMONLY USED STANDARDIZED INSTRUMENTS

A number of critically important and relevant scholarly works addressing the use of standardized psychological and educational tests with ethnic minorities have been published in the past (Hays, 2008; Helms, 2002; Sandoval, Frisby, Geisinger, Scheuneman, & Grenier, 1998). Entire books and even APA guidelines (APA, 2002) exist to inform practitioners about the thoughtful use and interpretation of standardized tests with non-majority culture patients and research participants. Interested readers are encouraged to consult these works for a more comprehensive discussion of this topic. Consensus regarding this issue is far from conclusive, yet any practitioner, regardless of his or her own racial, cultural, and ethnic background is not only encouraged but also required by Section 2 of the APA (2017) *Ethical Principles of Psychologists and Code of Conduct* to optimize the diversity of their clinical competence when using psychological tests with populations for which they may not have been sufficiently normed.

Readers seeking specifics such as lists of culturally acceptable standardized tests for use with all or any ethnic and cultural minorities will be disappointed. No such list and no such guidance exist. These, and many other scholarly works all boil down to the same suggestions: (a) honestly evaluate your own level of cultural competence and, if necessary, increase and adapt it appropriately; (b) exercise significant caution when choosing and using standardized tests insufficiently normed for those on which you intend to use them; (c) consider differential levels of cultural orientation and competence (and thereby the appropriateness) of the patients or participants you intend to assess with these instruments; and (d) indicate clearly in any dissemination of assessment findings the limitations of using such instruments on these particular patients or participants (APA, 2002; Dana, 1993; McDonald & Chaney, 2003). Although these suggestions are necessary, they are by no means sufficient to ensure the responsible and psychometrically sound use of standardized tests with American Indian patients or participants. We all understand, however, that these tests are being used with American Indians in clinical and research settings every day. Calling for a blanket moratorium on their use would, therefore, be impossible even if it were deemed necessary. Given these realities, we encourage readers to focus on the important steps and criteria discussed previously when considering or using standardized measures with American Indians.

Similar considerations should also guide appropriate treatment plan development when assessing depression in American Indians, again using cultural identification as a vital component. Several measures of cultural orientation exist, including the American Indian Biculturalism Inventory–Northern Plains (McDonald, Ross, & Rose, 2016). In the following section, we attempt to demonstrate an example of assessing, and incorporating, traditional Native aspects into the treatment of a young Native woman exhibiting symptoms of depression and related clinical concerns.

VIGNETTE

We present the following vignette as an example of an effective cultural adaptation of CBT for a young American Indian woman experiencing considerable depressive and other symptomatology. (Patient details have been disguised to maintain confidentiality.)

A Native American woman in her mid-20s presented in distress, feeling down and depressed most of the time, experiencing significant changes in her eating and sleeping habits, feeling anxious and irritable, and experiencing prejudicial attitudes and microaggressions in her professional occupation. She also felt she was a failure for letting her family and tribe down in feeling this way. She sought psychological intervention for moderate depression, potentially attributed to acculturation stress, with secondary anxiety. Before the intake, the BDI-II and MMPI–2 were administered. During the intake, acculturation was assessed through a psychosocial interview, and biopsychosocial information was obtained, revealing a bicultural orientation. The client was a commissioned state police officer. Before completing a rigorous 4-month police academy course with male recruits, serving as graduating valedictorian, and making state police history, she lived and worked on the reservation.

Since the department's inception in the 1930s, this district had never employed a woman, much less a Native American. She believed history, coupled with misogyny, was contributing to fabricated complaints regarding her professionalism and productivity. None of the alleged complaints were ever formally filed with the professional standards office. She noted the complainants were all middle-aged, White men. The patient sensed the overall sentiment in the community toward minorities was negative because many egregious incidents had occurred between the mostly rural Native American population and the metropolitan Caucasian population. Thus, although she felt a degree of pride in her unique accomplishments, she perceived her status as hopelessly and heavily influenced by racism and sexism, leaving her feeling helpless and insignificant. She reported nonspecific passive suicidal ideation, without intent or plan. Regarding her satisfaction with life, on a scale from 1 to 10, she reported being at a 3 most of the time. Although she had been an avid runner, this and other physical activity had been greatly reduced as well.

Assessment results suggested her BDI-II was significantly clinically elevated with Items 2 and 9 endorsed as "1," scoring in the severe depression range. On the MMPI–2, elevations on F, 2, 4, and 8 were noted, suggesting she may have recorded infrequent responses attributed to psychological distress and potential depressive, psychopathic deviant, and schizophrenic pathology. Neither assessment tool has been normed on the Native American population and, thus, were interpreted with caution because cultural considerations and bias may have been contributing factors to the elevated scores, specifically with the MMPI (Aponte, Rivers, & Wohl, 1995; Duran & Duran, 1995). Hill, Pace, and Robbins (2010) also found alternative interpretations of MMPI elevations for American Indian populations, contrasting with Graham (2002) and Greene (2000). In subsequent sessions, the patient was continually assessed for depressive symptomatology and suicidal ideation.

Session 1

Ninety minutes were reserved for the first session. The client was provided with psychoeducation about depressive and anxiety symptomatology. The agenda was set and her BDI-II and MMPI–2 scores were reviewed. She disclosed that one of her close relations had passed the previous year, and she had not gotten over this relative's death. She also expressed concern about the MMPI results and wondered whether her Native worldview and belief in traditional ceremonies and practices affected her results. A discussion about attitude formation from a classical conditioning perspective, the patient's worldview, and the patient's collectivistic orientation ensued. The patient expressed the importance of her cultural traditions and ceremonies; however, she had not participated for several years, which had left a significant void in her life. The patient was encouraged to discuss, in detail, the most troubling prejudicial scenario wherein the microaggressions were difficult and her reactions, thoughts, and feelings about the situation were didactic.

CBT was introduced. The patient's core beliefs and automatic thoughts were explored, resulting in a realization that the origin of those feelings of failure began in her childhood. A brief role playing exercise was used wherein the therapist read negative self-statements the patient made about herself when feelings of worthlessness emerged. The patient was instructed to counter the negative statements with a response containing positive attributes; however, she started the exercise with the perceptions of her by others. She struggled with separating herself, potentially attributable to a collectivistic orientation.

For homework, the patient was assigned to think of five positive traits she possessed, record them, and practice repeating the phrases or words used. Breathing and relaxation exercises were introduced. They were to be used before bedtime or if she awoke from her sleep, and she was to record the results in an activity log. Reconnecting with her traditional Native ways was highly recommended. She was also encouraged to set aside a half hour twice a week to exercise by walking.

Session 2

Ninety minutes were reserved for Session 2. Promoting autonomy from a collectivistic perspective was difficult and arose when homework was discussed. The session agenda was then set. The patient indicated that the breathing and relaxation techniques were effective and that her anxiety was less intense and frequent than previously experienced. She reported she had invited one of her colleagues to coffee, which had resulted in a conversation about their families and backgrounds. Overall, the interaction was positive, which helped to reduce some of the anxiety she felt at work. She had also arranged a meeting with a traditional healer, which helped to alleviate some of the spiritual void she felt. The patient explained that she had not had the opportunity to return to her hometown to participate in traditional ceremonies because of her job, which contributed to her negative mood. She also felt anxious about not participating in traditional activities because she had responsibilities and obligations to her family and community, a core belief. Though she was meeting her secular responsibilities, her traditional responsibilities were being neglected; she was having difficulty navigating two distinct cultural worlds.

The concepts of the cognitive triad were introduced, and the association between thoughts, feelings, and behavior was discussed. Thoughts at the automatic, intermediate, and core belief strata were also discussed. Follow-up on breathing and relaxation techniques occurred. The patient's homework was to, again, attempt to think of positive characteristics of herself aside from others. She was encouraged to maintain contact with the traditional healer and was asked to sign a release form allowing the therapist to maintain contact with the healer to facilitate an open dialogue about her case. She was also to record the frequency, duration, and the results of her use of the breathing technique and her engagement in exercise.

Sessions 3 Through 5

Sixty minutes each were set for Sessions 3 through 5. The client's homework was discussed with positive progress at each subsequent session. Within a cultural context, cognitive restructuring occurred because she was able to recognize positive self-traits that she identified as positive reflections of her family and community. Between Sessions 3 and 4, she also took a leave from work, returned to her hometown, and participated in traditional cultural activities. The patient reported that her interpersonal relations with fellow officers had improved and, between sessions, she had been invited to lunch by the day-shift officers and—rather than refusing their offers as before—she accepted. She experienced some anxiety when she arrived; however, she used her breathing and relaxation skills in her patrol car, which alleviated the symptoms.

She reported she had begun running again. She had been in frequent contact with the traditional healer and participated in healing ceremonies tailored to her specific presentation of symptoms. She reported feeling empowered and hopeful regarding her renewed spiritual and tribal focus and practices. Relaxation training was expanded in this and the remaining few sessions to use reciprocal inhibition by introducing increasingly distressing images from her past while she remained relaxed. She proved remarkably capable in developing this skill set. It was believed that her law enforcement training (which emphasized discipline), as well as her increased participation in traditional rituals and ceremonies at the direction of her elders, might have strongly and positively reinforced her skills acquisition.

The patient's homework consisted of practicing repeating positive attributes. She was also encouraged to engage in social activities with her colleagues. Termination was discussed in Session 5 and was scheduled to occur in Session 6.

Session 6

Sixty minutes were reserved for the termination session. The patient brought a basket filled with fruit and baked goods. She explained the offering as a traditional means of showing respect and thanks. The patient had participated in a traditional ceremony in Week 3; thus, discussions about feelings of the void the patient experienced, as well as debriefing and processing, occurred. She recognized her ongoing participation and involvement in traditional activities and traditional ways were significant to maintaining balance in her life. A release form was obtained, allowing the therapist to contact the traditional healer to ensure follow-up ceremonial practices indeed would occur.

Final homework was processed, with encouragement to continue practice repeating positive traits about herself. She reported participating in a 10K run the weekend before, which greatly enhanced her sense of well-being and physical health. She had also been invited to an annual barbeque hosted by one of her coworkers, which she attended. On arrival, she felt slightly anxious, but the breathing and relaxation skills alleviated the anxiety. The majority of department personnel were in attendance, and she reported talking with everyone and enjoying herself. Over the previous several weeks and during the outing, she had several conversations about her traditional background, which her colleagues found intriguing. They expressed a genuine desire to learn more about her culture and were more respectful in not making ethnic jokes in her presence any longer.

She reported that the microaggressions she had experienced had diminished. The patient seldom had feelings of worthlessness; however, when she did, through repeating positive phrases and words, the negative thoughts were replaced with positive thoughts. With regard to her depressive state and suicidal ideation, all symptoms were alleviated. Her BDI-II scores were in the nonclinical range. A discussion about scheduling a follow-up appointment in 6 months to a year occurred.

Follow-Up

At a 6-month 1-hour follow-up session, the patient reported she had not experienced any microaggressions from her colleagues. She had not experienced any negative thoughts of worthlessness in the previous 6 months. She had also continued to exercise and had begun a running regimen again, registering for a marathon the following month. With respect to her traditional cultural participation, she regularly went home and both participated in and attended traditional ceremonies.

CONCLUSION

American Indians remain the least researched and, consequently, the least understood ethnic and racial group in terms of their psychopathology and treatment. Yet, what has become clear from several generations of increased attention is that Native Americans experience depression-related disorders at an alarmingly higher rate than any other ethnocultural group in America. As we have discussed, many variables factor into that equation.

Despite the unique history and present-day challenges American Indians contend with, we hope we have made a case for the effectiveness of culturally appropriate applications of cognitive behavioral interventions for American Indians experiencing depression. The cognitive behavioral approach presents many positive aspects, with flexibility perhaps being its best asset. We contend that Native therapists and cross-culturally competent non-Native therapists can apply the CBT approach effectively in combating depressive symptomatology. We also hope to have conveyed that one cannot competently apply CBT in working with Native Americans without a clear and extensive understanding of their particular historical and contemporary experiences. We also wish to mention that many common, empirically derived aspects of CBT (e.g., deep breathing, cognitive restructuring) may be used similarly, if not exactly, as they are used with any other clients and patients. The expertise and competence of the clinician determine their appropriate application, as portrayed in the vignette. Finally, we wish again to emphasize that although depression is indeed disproportionately evidenced in Native communities, so too are cultural and community wellness and resiliency efforts and programs.

All marginalized groups in America, be they defined by ethnicity or other demographic, have tragic histories that haunt their contemporary existence. For those unfamiliar with the particular contributing hardships for American Indians, as well as their present-day struggles, understanding their problems may be difficult. However, one need not have been born Native, grown up around Natives, or married into a tribe to achieve sufficient understanding and compassion for their current health and well-being. Increasing one's cross-cultural competence toward another human group is a willful and honorable effort. Regardless of its motivation (be it personal or professional), the journey toward learning and experiencing more of life in our "other" brothers and sisters' moccasins brings us closer toward the spirit of the Lakota phrase *Mitakuye Oyasin*. This "amen"-type statement is spoken at the conclusion of prayers and ceremonies, yet is intended to reflect and celebrate so much more. The literal translation is effectively "all my relatives" and "we are all related," simultaneously. Those translations are far too simplistic. The elders speak of human beings as a "Rainbow Tribe," its members representing all nations, colors, and directions of the earth. It is our profound hope that we have, in our small and humble way, nudged us all closer to that vision.

REFERENCES

Alvidrez, J., Azocar, F., & Miranda, J. (1996). Demystifying the concept of ethnicity for psychotherapy researchers. *Journal of Consulting and Clinical Psychology, 64*, 903–908. http://dx.doi.org/10.1037/0022-006X.64.5.903

American Psychological Association. (2002). *Guidelines on multicultural education, training, research, practice and organizational change for psychologists.* Washington, DC: Author.

American Psychological Association. (2017). *Ethical principles of psychologists and code of conduct* (2002, Amended June 1, 2010, and January 1, 2017). Retrieved from http://www.apa.org/ethics/code/index.aspx

Aponte, J., Rivers, R., & Wohl, J. (1995). *Psychological interventions and cultural diversity*. New York, NY: Pearson.

Beck, A. T., Steer, R. A., & Brown, G. K. (1996). *Manual for the Beck Depression Inventory–II*. San Antonio, TX: Psychological Corporation.

Bombay, A., Matheson, K., & Anisman, H. (2014). The intergenerational effects of Indian residential schools: Implications for the concept of historical trauma. *Transcultural Psychiatry*, *51*, 320–338. http://dx.doi.org/10.1177/1363461513503380

Brave Heart, M. Y. H., & DeBruyn, M. (1998). The American Indian holocaust: Healing historical trauma and grief. *Journal of American Indian and Alaska Native Mental Health*, *56*, 56–64.

Brophy, W. A., & Aberle, S. D. (1966). *The Indian: America's unfinished business*. Norman: University of Oklahoma Press.

Butcher, J. N., Dahlstrom, W. G., Graham, J. R., Tellegen, A., & Kaemmer, B. (1989). *The Minnesota Multiphasic Personality Inventory—2 (MMPI–2): Manual for administration and scoring*. Minneapolis: University of Minnesota Press.

Cano, R. (2016, January 28). AP Newsbreak: Doctors detail serious issues in two hospitals in South Dakota providing care to Native Americans. *U.S. News & World Report*. Retrieved from https://www.usnews.com/news/us/articles/2016-01-28/ap-newsbreak-reports-detail-issues-at-reservation-hospitals

Chen, H., Kramer, E. J., Chen, T., & Chung, H. (2005). Engaging Asian Americans for mental health research: Challenges and solutions. *Journal of Immigrant Health*, *7*, 109–118. http://dx.doi.org/10.1007/s10903-005-2644-6

Dana, R. (1993). *Multicultural assessment perspectives for professional psychology*. Boston, MA: Allyn & Bacon.

Deloria, V. (1974). From Wounded Knee to Wounded Knee. In J. B. Billard (Ed.), *The world of the American Indian* (pp. 28–32). Washington, DC: National Geographic Society.

Deloria, V. (2002). *The Indian Reorganization Act: Congresses and bills*. Norman: University of Oklahoma Press.

Duran, E., & Duran, B. (1995). *Native American post-colonial psychology*. Albany: State University of New York Press.

Duran, E., Duran, B., & Brave Heart, M. Y. H. (1998). Native Americans: The trauma of history. In R. Thornton (Ed.), *Studying native America: Problems and perspectives* (pp. 60–78). Madison: University of Wisconsin Press.

Dussias, A. M. (2008). Indigenous languages under siege: The Native American experience. *Intercultural Human Rights Law Review*, *3*, 5.

Ehlers, C. L., Gizer, I. R., Gilder, D. A., Ellingson, J. M., & Yehuda, R. (2013). Measuring historical trauma in an American Indian community sample: Contributions of substance dependence, affective disorder, conduct disorder and PTSD. *Drug and Alcohol Dependence*, *133*, 180–187. http://dx.doi.org/10.1016/j.drugalcdep.2013.05.011

Evans-Campbell, T. (2008). Historical trauma in American Indian/Native Alaska communities: A multilevel framework for exploring impacts on individuals, families, and communities. *Journal of Interpersonal Violence, 23*, 316–338. http://dx.doi.org/10.1177/0886260507312290

Fiferman, L. A. (1989). *Native American and Anglo ratings of acceptability of four treatments for depression* (Unpublished doctoral dissertation). University of South Dakota, Vermillion.

Gone, J. P. (2009). A community-based treatment for Native American historical trauma: Prospects for evidence-based practice. *Journal of Consulting and Clinical Psychology, 77*, 751–762. http://dx.doi.org/10.1037/a0015390

Graham, T. L. C. (2002). Using reasons for living to connect to American Indian healing traditions. *Journal of Sociology and Social Welfare, 29*, 55–75.

Greene, R. L. (2000). *The MMPI–2: An interpretive manual* (2nd ed.). Needham Heights, MA: Allyn & Bacon.

Hall, G. C. N. (2001). Psychotherapy research with ethnic minorities: Empirical, ethical, and conceptual issues. *Journal of Consulting and Clinical Psychology, 69*, 502–510. http://dx.doi.org/10.1037/0022-006X.69.3.502

Hays, P. A. (2008). *Addressing cultural complexities in practice: Assessment, diagnosis, and therapy* (2nd ed.). Washington, DC: American Psychological Association. http://dx.doi.org/10.1037/11650-000

Helms, J. E. (2002). A remedy for the Black–White test-score disparity. *American Psychologist, 57*, 303–305.

Herring, R. D. (1990). Understanding Native American values: Process and content concerns for counselors. *Counseling and Values, 34*, 134–137. http://dx.doi.org/10.1002/j.2161-007X.1990.tb00918.x

Hill, J., Pace, D., & Robbins, T. (2010). Decolonizing personality assessment and honoring indigenous voices: A critical examination of the MMPI–2. *Cultural Diversity and Ethnic Minority Psychology, 16*, 16–25. http://dx.doi.org/10.1037/a0016110

Hodge, D. R., Limb, G. E., & Cross, T. L. (2009). Moving from colonization toward balance and harmony: A Native American perspective on wellness. *Social Work, 54*, 211–219. http://dx.doi.org/10.1093/sw/54.3.211

Horrell, S. C. V. (2008). Effectiveness of cognitive-behavioral therapy with adult ethnic minority clients: A review. *Professional Psychology: Research and Practice, 39*, 160–168. http://dx.doi.org/10.1037/0735-7028.39.2.160

Indian Health Service. (1997). *Alcoholism: A high priority health problem* (DHEW Publication No. HAS77-1001). Washington, DC: U.S. Government Printing Office.

Jackson, L. C., Schmutzer, P. A., Wenzel, A., & Tyler, J. D. (2006). Applicability of cognitive-behavior therapy with American Indian individuals. *Psychotherapy: Theory, Research, Practice, Training, 43*, 506–517. http://dx.doi.org/10.1037/0033-3204.43.4.506

Kadden, R., Carroll, K., Donovan, D., Cooney, N., Monti, P., Abrams, D., Litt, M., & Hester, R. (2003). *Cognitive-behavioral coping skills therapy manual: A clinical research guide for therapists treating individuals with alcohol abuse and dependence.* Rockville, MD: National Institute on Alcohol Abuse and Alcoholism.

McDonald, J. D. (1994). New frontiers in clinical training: The UND Indians Into Psychology Doctoral Education Program. *Journal of American Indian and Alaska Native Mental Health Research, 5,* 52–56.

McDonald, J. D., & Chaney, J. (2003). Resistance to multiculturalism: The "Indian Problem." In J. S. Mio & G. Y. Iwamasa (Eds.), *Multicultural mental health research and resistance: Continuing challenges of the new millennium* (pp. 39–54). New York, NY: Brunner-Routledge.

McDonald, J. D., & Gonzalez, J. (2006). Cognitive-behavioral therapy with American Indians. In P. Hays & G. Iwamasa (Eds.), *Culturally responsive cognitive-behavioral therapy* (pp. 23–45). Washington, DC: American Psychological Association. http://dx.doi.org/10.1037/11433-001

McDonald, J. D., Morton, R., & Stewart, C. (1992). Clinical issues with American Indian patients. *Innovations in Clinical Practice, 12,* 437–454.

McDonald, J. D., Ross, R., & Rose, W. (2016, August). *Development and scoring of the American Indian Biculturalism Inventory–Northern Plains.* Poster presented at the meeting of the American Psychological Association, Denver, CO.

McGuire, R. H. (1992). Archaeology and the first Americans. *American Anthropologist, 94,* 816–836. http://dx.doi.org/10.1525/aa.1992.94.4.02a00030

Nowinski, J., Baker, S., & Carroll, K. (1992). *Twelve step facilitation therapy manual: A clinical research guide for therapists treating individuals with alcohol and dependence.* Rockville, MD: National Institute on Alcohol Abuse and Alcoholism.

Oetting, E. R., & Beauvais, F. (1991). Orthogonal culture identification theory: The cultural identification of minority adolescents. *The International Journal of the Addictions, 25,* 655–685.

Renfrey, G. S. (1992). Cognitive-behavior therapy and the Native American client. *Behavior Therapy, 23,* 321–340. http://dx.doi.org/10.1016/S0005-7894(05)80161-3

Rhoades, E. R., & Rhoades, D. A. (2000). Traditional Indian and modern Western medicine. In E. R. Rhoades (Ed.), *American Indian health innovations in health care, promotion, and policy* (pp. 3–18). Baltimore, MD: The Johns Hopkins University Press.

Safren, S. A. (2001). The continuing need for diversity in cognitive-behavioral therapy training and research. *Behavior Therapist, 24,* 209.

Sandoval, J., Frisby, C. L., Geisinger, K. F., Scheuneman, J. D., & Grenier, J. R. (Eds.). (1998). *Test interpretation and diversity: Achieving equity in assessment.* Washington, DC: American Psychological Association. http://dx.doi.org/10.1037/10279-000

Schieffelin, E. L. (1985). The cultural analysis of depressive affect: An example from New Guinea. In A. Kleinman & B. Good (Eds.), *Culture and depres-*

sion: Studies in the anthropology and cross-cultural psychiatry of affect and disorder (pp. 101–134). Berkeley: University of California Press.

Smithsonian Center for Folklife and Cultural Heritage. (2004). *Beautiful beyond: Christian songs in Native languages*. Washington, DC: Smithsonian Pathways.

Spruhan, P. (2006). A legal history of blood quantum in American Indian Law. *South Dakota Law Review, 51*, 1–50.

Trimble, J. (1987). Self-perception and perceived alienation among American Indians. *Journal of Community Psychology, 15*, 316–333. http://dx.doi.org/10.1002/1520-6629(198707)15:3<316::AID-JCOP2290150305>3.0.CO;2-E

Tyler, J. D., Cohen, K. N., & Clark, J. S. (1982). Providing community consultation in a reservation setting. *Journal of Rural Community Psychology, 3*, 49–58.

Villanueva, M., Tonigan, J. S., & Miller, W. R. (2007). Response of Native American clients to three treatment methods for alcohol dependence. *Journal of Ethnicity in Substance Abuse, 6*(2), 41–48. http://dx.doi.org/10.1300/J233v06n02_04

Walters, K. L., Mohammed, S. A., Evans-Campbell, T., Beltrán, R. E., Chae, D. H., & Duran, B. (2011). Bodies don't just tell stories, they tell histories. *Du Bois Review, 8*, 179–189. http://dx.doi.org/10.1017/S1742058X1100018X

Whitbeck, L. B., Adams, G. W., Hoyt, D. R., & Chen, X. (2004). Conceptualizing and measuring historical trauma among American Indian people. *American Journal of Community Psychology, 33*, 119–130. http://dx.doi.org/10.1023/B:AJCP.0000027000.77357.31

Whitbeck, L. B., McMorris, B. J., Hoyt, D. R., Stubben, J. D., & LaFromboise, T. (2002). Perceived discrimination, traditional practices, and depressive symptoms among American Indians in the upper Midwest. *Journal of Health and Social Behavior, 43*, 400–418. http://dx.doi.org/10.2307/3090234

Witko, T. (2006). *Mental health care for urban Indians: Clinical insights from Native practitioners*. Washington, DC: American Psychological Association.

II

COGNITIVE BEHAVIORAL MODELS, MEASURES, AND TREATMENTS FOR ANXIETY DISORDERS

5

COGNITIVE BEHAVIORAL MODELS, MEASURES, AND TREATMENTS FOR ANXIETY DISORDERS IN ASIAN AMERICANS

JANIE J. HONG

Individuals with anxiety disorders experience excessive levels of both fear and anxiety and use maladaptive coping strategies to manage their distress. According to the *Diagnostic and Statistical Manual of Mental Disorders* (*DSM*; fifth ed.; American Psychiatric Association, 2013), *fear* is the emotional response felt when a person perceives an imminent threat (e.g., gun pointed at his head) and *anxiety* is the emotional anticipation of a future threat (e.g., waiting for the results of a tumor biopsy). The fears that define anxiety disorders are experienced by most (if not all) people at one time or another and can even be viewed as biologically favorable to experience. Stated in a different way, individuals are driven to respond to threat cues and feel safe.

Cognitive behavioral models of anxiety disorders focus on the overestimation of threat as the primary driver of pathological anxiety. Cognitive behavioral treatments flow directly from these models and teach patients

http://dx.doi.org/10.1037/0000091-006
Treating Depression, Anxiety, and Stress in Ethnic and Racial Groups: Cognitive Behavioral Approaches, E. C. Chang, C. A. Downey, J. K. Hirsch, and E. A. Yu (Editors)

ways to reappraise the actual threat level of their feared triggers. Smits, Julian, Rosenfield, and Powers (2012) conducted a systematic review of studies looking at the role of threat reappraisal in cognitive behavior therapy (CBT) for anxiety disorders and found strong support for a relationship between threat reappraisal and anxiety reduction. Moreover, among the studies that examined whether threat reappraisal mediated the relationship between CBT and anxiety reduction, all but one of them found that threat reappraisal played a statistically significant mediating role.

The overestimation of threat that characterizes anxiety disorders is inherently tied to contextual cues and expectations (Craske et al., 2008; Craske, Liao, Brown, & Vervliet, 2012). This suggests that beliefs about which situations are safe and what strategies increase feelings of safety will vary across cultures. The cultural shaping of threat cues holds particular relevance for Asian Americans. Cognitive behavioral models of the anxiety disorders originate from the United States and other Western cultural contexts and often reflect the cultural beliefs and norms of these contexts (Hall, Hong, Zane, & Meyer, 2011). Eastern cultures, such as those in Asia, typically promote values, beliefs (e.g., about the self, social norms, emotions), and behaviors that are different from and, at times, contrary to those promoted in Western cultures (for a review, see Markus & Kitayama, 1991). By definition, Asian Americans represent a heterogeneous group of individuals who identify with an Eastern cultural heritage but live in a Western culture. Asian Americans continually face the challenge of negotiating the tensions of two (often contradicting) cultural pulls and may react differently to the same triggers of the cultural pulls felt in a particular context. Indeed, research has indicated that Asian Americans have the ability to switch cultural frames and have a greater awareness than their monocultural counterparts of cultural differences between their heritage and U.S. cultures (e.g., Benet-Martínez, Lee, & Leu, 2006; Y. Y. Hong, Morris, Chiu, & Benet-Martínez, 2000).

Epidemiological research has indicated that the challenge of managing the cultural tension between one's heritage and one's host culture may increase the likelihood of having a psychiatric disorder (Lau et al., 2013; Takeuchi et al., 2007). Specifically, U.S.-born Asian Americans, when compared with their foreign-born counterparts, appear to be at greater risk of developing a psychiatric disorder. For example, Takeuchi and colleagues (2007) found that U.S.-born Asian women were significantly more likely than foreign-born Asians to have any lifetime anxiety or depression and had a significantly higher 12-month risk of any anxiety disorder. Nativity in Asian American men was associated with an increased lifetime risk of a substance abuse disorder.

Overall, the findings suggest that, for Asian Americans, being raised in a bicultural context increases awareness of conflicting cultural norms and promotes the development of pathological anxiety. It may be that the tension in cultural norms lowers the predictability of threat cues across contexts, which, in turn, raises the likelihood of chronically high anxiety and perceived danger. In this chapter, I examine the evidence for the cultural shaping of threat overestimation and pathological anxiety. In other words, do Asian Americans differ from White Americans in what they judge as threatening? Cultural differences in interpretations of threat suggest different mechanisms for the cognitive behavioral understanding and treatment of an anxiety disorder. I focus particular attention on social anxiety. Social anxiety is, by definition, inextricably tied to the social norms, expectations, and context in which it arises; thus, the triggering and maintaining factors are likely more susceptible to cultural influences. Relatedly, there are significantly more studies with Asian Americans on social anxiety than any other type of anxiety. I also examine the ways current cognitive behavioral measures and treatments may be culturally limited and conclude with recommendations on how to expand the cultural flexibility of cognitive behavioral treatments and with directions for potential future research to better understand and serve Asian Americans with anxiety disorders.

COGNITIVE BEHAVIORAL MODELS FOR UNDERSTANDING ANXIETY DISORDERS IN ASIAN AMERICANS

Underlying cognitive behavioral models are assumptions about what responses are normal and what are pathological. Specifically, each model holds assumptions about the cognitive processes (e.g., beliefs, biases, expectations) and behaviors that increase a person's vulnerability to develop and maintain anxiety disorder symptoms. To the extent that culture influences these assumptions, pathways to pathological anxiety may differ across cultural contexts. Specifically, it may be that existing cognitive behavioral models may not address the bicultural stress felt by Asians living in Western cultures.

Studies of Asian Americans with anxiety disorders have been primarily limited to epidemiological studies of disorder prevalence rates (e.g., Asnaani, Richey, Dimaite, Hinton, & Hofmann, 2010; Takeuchi et al., 2007) or treatment studies in which Asian Americans represent a small portion of the treated population (see Voss Horrell, 2008). Studies examining differences between Asian Americans and White Americans on factors identified in cognitive behavioral models of the anxiety disorders have focused exclusively on nonclinical (primarily undergraduate) populations. Findings with these nonclinical populations have, however, offered indirect support for the cultural shaping of fear and anxiety. In the following section, I review these studies, with a particular focus on high social anxiety.

Pathological Worry

Pathological worry is the core diagnostic feature of generalized anxiety disorder (GAD) and is defined by difficulties controlling the degree to which one worries and an inability to stop worrying even when it interferes with functioning (American Psychiatric Association, 2013). Scott, Eng, and Heimberg (2002) found that Asian Americans did not differ significantly from White Americans in the severity of their worry or the likelihood of meeting criteria for GAD, but they differed in the topics about which they worried. Specifically, Asian Americans reported significantly greater concerns about their ability to meet their goals and ambitions. Although Asian Americans reported worrying about all the presented domains to a similar degree, the White American group reported significantly greater worry about feeling insecure than having poor ambition or interpersonal difficulties. The differences found between the two groups and within the White American group are consistent with known East–West differences (e.g., Heine, Lehman, Markus, & Kitayama, 1999; Markus & Kitayama, 1991) and suggest that culture may play a greater role in shaping the focus of people's worries than determining the severity of them.

Saw, Berenbaum, and Okazaki (2013) directly examined whether group differences in worry content reflected differences in cultural values. Like Scott et al. (2002), they found no severity differences between Asian and White Americans in worry. As predicted, Asian Americans worried significantly more than their White American counterparts about domains typically valued in Asian cultures (i.e., academic achievement, maintaining family roles and obligations). Moreover, Asian Americans reported having higher personal standards and lower perceptions of living up to parental expectations in the school and family domains; the cultural differences in worry content were partially explained by the degree to which participants felt they were meeting these standards and expectations. Overall, the data suggest the same cultural values that help shape a person's goals also shape the content of his or her worries and fears. This combined with the lack of group difference in worry severity supports the idea that cultural differences lie in what a person finds threatening and not in the overall likelihood of experiencing pathological worry.

Cultural Differences in Social Anxiety

Social anxiety is the anxious response to social or performance situations when a person fears he or she will act in a way (or show anxiety symptoms) that will be embarrassing and/or lead to negative judgments by others (American Psychiatric Association, 2013). Cognitive behavioral models of social anxiety disorder (SAD) point to excessively high expectations of performance as one reason socially anxious individuals view social situations as threatening (Clark & Wells, 1995; Rapee & Heimberg, 1997). For example, someone who believes a pause in conversation is a sign of poor performance will feel more socially anxious than someone who sees it as a normal part of social conversation. These expectations lead to a hypervigilant monitoring of one's performance. The hypervigilance to potential mistakes coupled with high expectations of performance leads to extreme fears of social failure.

Among studies on anxiety with Asian Americans, the most consistent and well-studied finding is that Asian Americans report higher levels of social anxiety than their White American counterparts (for reviews, see Krieg & Xu, 2015; Woody, Miao, & Kellman-McFarlane, 2015). Woody et al. (2015) conducted a meta-analytic review of studies comparing individuals of Asian heritage with those of Caucasian heritage on at least one established measure of social anxiety. Among the 31 studies identified, 21 of them used Asian participant samples from a Western context (i.e., United States and Canada). Across the studies, the authors found the weighted mean effect size to be $d = 0.47$ (medium effect size) in the direction of individuals of Asian heritage having higher social anxiety scores. Krieg and Xu (2015) conducted a similar meta-analytic review and found that with studies using only self-report social anxiety measures ($N = 30$), 41 out of the 47 independent effect sizes were in the positive direction (i.e., Asians scoring higher than Whites) and 40 were statistically significant. None of the studies showed results in the negative direction.

Self-Construal and Social Anxiety

Several researchers have sought a cultural explanation for higher social anxiety ratings among Asians and Asian Americans. One frequently cited cultural difference between East Asian and Western cultures is how one views the self in relation to others (see Markus & Kitayama, 1991). East Asian cultures are thought to promote an interdependent view of the self (i.e., interdependent self-construal) that values group harmony and group needs over individual needs and emphasizes contextual cues (e.g., obligations, responsibilities, norms) in social decision making. By contrast, Western cultures promote an independent view of the self (i.e., independent self-construal) that emphasizes individual wants and needs and social decision making based on personal beliefs, values, and traits. Independent self-construal and interdependent self-construal are considered orthogonal constructs.

Krieg and Xu (2015) examined the potential mediating role of self-construal in the Asian European heritage difference in social anxiety. Using data from seven published studies that included individuals of Asian and

European heritage, a measure of self-construal, and at least one measure of social anxiety, they used structural equation models to test the mediating role of self-construal. They found the best model was one with independent self-construal partially mediating the relationship between ethnicity and social anxiety and interdependent self-construal, though related to both ethnicity and social anxiety, having no mediating role. The results suggest that part of the reason Asians report more social anxiety than their European heritage counterparts is their lower endorsement of beliefs associated with an independent self-construal (e.g., "My personal identity, independent of others, is very important to me").

Emotion Regulation and Social Anxiety

Another cultural difference implicated in Asians' social anxiety ratings is how individuals regulate their emotions. Given the collectivistic emphasis in Asian cultures on group and situational needs, individual emotions are less important for guiding behavior than contextual demands (e.g., obligations, norms, social hierarchy) of the situation (Kitayama, Karasawa, & Mesquita, 2004; Markus & Kitayama, 1991). Consistent with this, research has shown Asians and Asian Americans, when compared with their European American counterparts, to be worse at identifying negative emotions in others (Beaupré & Hess, 2005; Lau, Fung, Wang, & Kang, 2009) and in themselves (Dere, Falk, & Ryder, 2012; Ryder et al., 2008) and to be more likely to suppress emotions by resisting public display of them (Butler, Lee, & Gross, 2007; Gross & John, 2003; Matsumoto, Takeuchi, Andayani, Kouznetsova, & Krupp, 1998). Asian Americans are also more likely to report being socialized by their parents to suppress emotions (Lau et al., 2009; Saw & Okazaki, 2010; Wu et al., 2002). For example, Saw and Okazaki (2010) found that Asian Americans, when compared with White Americans, described their interactions with their parents as less open to discussion of (positive and negative) emotions and reported lower open expression of positive emotions by their parents.

In Western-based models of mental health, emotion suppression and poor emotion recognition are viewed as maladaptive and significant contributing factors to distress (e.g., Mennin, Heimberg, Turk, & Fresco, 2005; Mennin, Holaway, Fresco, Moore, & Heimberg, 2007; Taylor, 2000). Cognitive behavioral models of SAD assert emotion suppression is driven by fears of revealing negative aspects of the self to others and, as a result, being alienated from others. The use of this strategy backfires, however, because it prevents the development of intimate relationships and promotes further social withdrawal (Clark & Wells, 1995; Rapee & Heimberg, 1997). Given that the emotion-regulation strategies promoted in Asian cultures are found in anxiety disorder patients, there may be a relationship between these strategies and social anxiety ratings among Asian Americans.

Park and colleagues (2011) examined whether emotion suppression explained the relationship between self-construal and social anxiety in a large U.S. sample of Asian American undergraduates ($N = 784$). They found emotion suppression mediated the relationship between interdependent self-construal and social anxiety and, to a lesser extent, the relationship between independent self-construal and social anxiety. The results suggest the aspects of an interdependent self-construal that promote emotion suppression lead to elevations in social anxiety in Asian Americans.

Lau and colleagues (2009) tested whether emotional attunement, another emotion-regulation strategy shown to differ culturally between Asian and Western contexts, also helps to explain elevated social anxiety ratings in Asian Americans. The authors highlighted how individuals living in a collectivistic cultural context are socialized from a young age to be attuned to the needs of others and respond in ways that prevent shaming, loss of face, or negative evaluations from others (Lieber, Fung, & Leung, 2006; Wu et al., 2002; Zane & Yeh, 2002). Despite the emphasis on emotional attunement, Asians show poorer emotion recognition in others than do those of European heritage (Beaupré & Hess, 2005). The lack of accuracy in emotion recognition is thought to be a consequence of the cultural promotion of emotion suppression.

Emotion suppression reduces the utility of differentiating specific emotions to guide behavior, which then leads to a reduced need to develop the skill of recognizing specific emotions in others. Sensitivity to whether an interaction is going well is more important than understanding exactly what emotions others are feeling. Emotional attunement in East Asian cultures thus relies on perceived social expectations and rules and judgments of whether others are responding positively or negatively during the interaction. As predicted, Lau et al. (2009) found that Asian Americans, when compared with European Americans, reported significantly greater face-loss concerns and made more errors in classifying negative emotional stimuli; both of these factors mediated the ethnic difference in social anxiety. Overall, it appears the emotion-regulation strategies promoted in Asian contexts (i.e., emotion suppression, emotional attunement) lead to higher social anxiety ratings.

Given the relationship between social anxiety ratings and the values and beliefs promoted in Asian contexts, how do we interpret Asian American reports of greater social anxiety? One explanation is that the symptoms that characterize social anxiety in Western contexts are more culturally normative and less functionally impairing for Asians. There are some lines of research to support this view. Heinrichs et al. (2006) presented social vignettes and social anxiety measures to university students in eight different countries

($N = 909$). The vignettes described either socially assertive, attention-seeking behaviors or socially withdrawn, attention-avoidant behaviors and asked participants how favorably they viewed the behaviors and how appropriate the behaviors would be in their culture. They found that undergraduate participants from collectivistic countries (e.g., Japan, Korea) viewed socially withdrawn and reticent behavior as more culturally normative and reported more social anxiety and fear of blushing than participants from individualistic countries (e.g., United States, Canada, Australia). Moreover, individuals who judged socially extraverted behavior more favorably had lower fears of blushing and social anxiety. The findings suggest that higher social anxiety ratings and the behaviors associated with these ratings may be more culturally normative in Asian cultures than in Western ones.

There is also indirect evidence to suggest that higher social anxiety ratings do not translate into higher levels of impairment for Asian Americans. Epidemiological studies of SAD have shown lower 12-month and lifetime prevalence rates of SAD in Asian Americans than in White Americans (for a review, see J. J. Hong, 2012). For example, using data from the National Epidemiologic Survey on Alcohol and Related Conditions, Asian Americans showed lower prevalence rates of SAD than the White American group (12-month: 2.1% vs. 3.0%; lifetime: 3.3% vs. 5.5%; Grant et al., 2005).

Horng and Coles (2014) examined the discrepancy between higher social anxiety ratings and lower prevalence rates of SAD in Asian Americans when compared with White Americans. They initially screened Asian and White American undergraduates by having them complete a measure of social anxiety. For each ethnic group, they selected participants who scored either high or low in social anxiety and then used a structured clinical interview to assess for a SAD diagnosis. Consistent with past results, the authors found Asian Americans in the screening phase scored significantly higher in social anxiety than their White American counterparts, and a significantly higher proportion of the Asian American sample compared with the proportion of the White American sample met criteria for the high social anxiety group. Despite these differences, there were no significant ethnic group differences in the likelihood of being diagnosed with SAD in either the high or low social anxiety group. This further supports the idea that social anxiety ratings may be less predictive of impairment and more culturally normative for Asians and Asian Americans.

Hsu et al. (2012), however, argued against the idea that higher social anxiety ratings are a reflection of the culturally normative values of East Asian cultures. The authors asserted that their findings suggest Asians' elevated social anxiety ratings are due to the distress caused by a discrepancy in cultural values between their ethnic heritage culture and mainstream Western culture. Specifically, they cited the greater social anxiety bicultural Asians (i.e., Asians living in Canada) in their sample reported compared with their monocultural White (i.e., European Canadians living in Canada) and monocultural Asian counterparts (i.e., Koreans living in South Korea and Chinese living in China). Data supporting social anxiety ratings as culturally normative would have shown a linear increase in scores on social anxiety measures with increased exposure to East Asian cultural values. Specifically, monocultural White Canadians would have shown the lowest social anxiety scores, monocultural Asians would have had the highest scores, and bicultural Asian Canadians' scores would have fallen somewhere in the middle. Their findings are consistent with findings that suggest bicultural Asians may be more sensitive than monocultural individuals to the cultural pulls of their heritage culture and the Western culture in which they live (Benet-Martínez et al., 2006; Y. Y. Hong et al., 2000) and are at greater risk of developing mental health problems with increased Western (i.e., U.S.) cultural exposure (Takeuchi et al., 2007).

These findings suggest that it may be that Asian American parents socialize their children to see themselves and manage their emotions in ways that are consistent with Asian social norms and inconsistent with Western social norms. Asian Americans are then called to reconcile the beliefs and behaviors they are socialized to have with those promoted in the culture in which they live. By having an awareness of this cultural tension, they are also more aware that behaviors that are appropriate in one context may be unacceptable in another. This creates a social uncertainty unseen by their monocultural peers, which may then reduce social confidence and raise social anxiety levels.

Clinical Implications of High Social Anxiety Among Asian Americans

If Asian Americans are more likely to experience social anxiety than White Americans but just as likely (if not less likely) to be diagnosed with SAD, how do these findings translate in a clinical context? To date, I have not found studies of social anxiety in clinical samples of Asian Americans. Given this, I offer some possibilities based on observations from my clinical practice. Through my private practice at the Cognitive Behavior Therapy and Science Center (and previously at other CBT-focused group practices), I have treated over 30 Asian American patients seeking treatment for anxiety and/or depression. And, because I provide therapy in English, all my Asian American patients have spent the majority, if not all, of their lives in the United States. From my work with these patients, two clear patterns have emerged that distinguish them from my White American patients: (a) Every one of my (East) Asian American patients has had problems with social anxiety and/or assertiveness, regardless of his or her primary diagnosis and (b) none of my (East) Asian American patients sought treatment for only social anxiety or had a single diagnosis of SAD.

Despite the limited nature of these data, the findings are compelling and consistent with the research previously described. It may be that Asian Americans are indeed more likely to experience difficulties with social anxiety, but those who meet the criteria for SAD or have clinically significant levels of social anxiety are also more likely to experience other anxiety or mood disorder diagnoses. To the extent that this is true, cognitive behavioral models of anxiety disorders (and possibly other disorders as well) in Asian Americans would have to include ways to assess for and target social anxiety within the context of the primary disorder.

The following case is an example of how social anxiety can manifest in the context of another disorder and the need to incorporate strategies targeting these fears into the treatment. Mary[1] is a 31-year-old Chinese American married woman who teaches computer science at a local high school. Mary immigrated to the United States from Hong Kong with her parents when she was 9 years old; her parents moved back to Hong Kong when Mary left for college. She has struggled with symptoms of obsessive–compulsive disorder (OCD) since high school. When Mary came in for treatment, she was struggling with compulsive checking of door locks and with repeatedly checking different websites to verify the accuracy of her teaching materials. She shared how in the past she had struggled with compulsive cleaning (e.g., frequent hand washing), but not checking, and how these cleaning rituals stopped when she started dating her husband. She explained how she resisted cleaning in front of him out of fears of "looking crazy," and when they began living together, Mary felt unable to clean without "getting caught" and immediately stopped all cleaning compulsions. Similarly, she recounted a history of stopping or limiting her compulsions when her fears of disapproval grew too high.

In this example, Mary's social anxiety is closely tied to her OCD symptoms. When her social fears are triggered and are at odds with her OCD symptoms, she effectively eliminates her compulsions in service of easing her social anxiety. The clinician is left with questions about how to effectively target Mary's OCD without reinforcing social fears of the unacceptability of her compulsions and how to treat disapproval fears without alienating significant others by promoting values consistent with an independent self-construal.

---

[1]All identifying information has been changed to protect the confidentiality of this patient.

COGNITIVE BEHAVIORAL MEASUREMENT
OF ANXIETY DISORDERS IN ASIAN AMERICANS

Use of Measures in Cognitive Behavior Therapy for Anxiety Disorders

Integral to the cognitive behavioral approach is the development and use of standardized measures to assess the effectiveness of its treatments. Although cultural factors are acknowledged, the majority of this research has been conducted in Western contexts using measures validated with Western populations (e.g., United States, Canada, United Kingdom). One concern is whether these measures are valid or relevant to other cultural populations. For example, the Social Phobia and Anxiety Inventory (Turner, Beidel, Dancu, & Stanley, 1989) is a well-validated measure of social anxiety that has been used to show the social anxiety difference between Asian and White Americans. The questionnaire lists various social situations in which the respondent may experience anxiety (e.g., "I feel anxious when I am in a social situation and I become the center of attention") and asks the respondent to rate how frequently (anchored by *never* and *always*) he or she experiences anxiety in the listed situation. With Western populations, frequency of social anxiety is an excellent measure of symptom severity and a predictor of a social anxiety diagnosis. With Asians and Asian Americans, however, this may not be the case. I further review these and other measurement issues elsewhere (see J. J. Hong, 2012).

Measures as Part of Cognitive Behavior Therapy for Anxiety Disorders

Another core feature of CBT is the assignment of homework between sessions and the use of standardized measures and rating scales to help inform and drive the treatment (see Huppert, Roth Ledley, & Foa, 2006). For example, one of the first exercises in CBT is the identification of feared situations and the predicted intensity of anxiety in each of the identified situations. The list of situations is then used to choose the types of exposures to be conducted in the treatment (Goldfried & Goldfried, 1977), and the intensity ratings help order the exposures and provide a way for patients to communicate and monitor changes in their anxiety levels. Traditionally, intensity ratings have also been used during exposures to determine whether corrective learning is occurring (see Foa & Kozak, 1986; Foa & McNally, 1996; Rachman, 1980).

Another early goal is to develop the skill of self-monitoring and examining the evidence for reactions experienced in triggering situations. This skill is considered key to the hypothesis-testing approach underlying CBT protocols. Patients and therapists are continually developing hypotheses about the patients' problems (e.g., "My anxiety will never go down unless I escape from the situation"), testing these hypotheses (e.g., stay in the situation), and monitoring the outcomes of these tests (e.g., anxiety levels while in the situation). Typically, intensity ratings are used to help patients and therapists examine changes in distress associated with the exercises completed. Thus, assessing, monitoring, and measuring anxiety disorder symptoms are an integral part of the therapy and are taught as a necessary skill for symptom improvement.

There are two potential cultural concerns with the use of measures and self-monitoring tools with Asian Americans. First, as previously described, one of the early goals in CBT is to teach patients to self-monitor and become familiar with the nature of their anxiety. Implicit to this goal is the assumption that patients' anxiety symptoms and the factors that maintain them are relatively stable across situations and that patients can easily predict the severity of their fear response with only a few contextual cues.

In Western cultures, the self is seen as stable and distinct, with little change in core personality traits and beliefs across situations (i.e., "I am who I am"; Markus & Kitayama, 1991). By contrast, East Asian cultures tend to promote a sense of self that is more fluid and dependent on the contextual needs of the situation (i.e., "Who I am depends on who I am with"). Suh (2002) compared undergraduate students in Korea with those in the United States in how they rated themselves on different personality traits (e.g., affectionate, impulsive, nervous) in five different contexts (e.g., with parents, a close friend) and in general. Compared with the U.S. sample, Suh found that the Korean participants viewed themselves as significantly more inconsistent across different situations, and unlike the U.S. sample, this inconsistency was less important to subjective well-being. Given this cultural difference in perceptions of the self and one's traits, the simple exercise of rating levels of anxiety and understanding the nature of one's anxiety may be more complicated for Asian and Asian American patients.

Although the cultural importance of contextual cues has not been tested in clinical samples, my Asian American patients frequently show difficulties with rating anxiety levels when presented with generic descriptions of a situation (e.g., talking with a stranger) and marked inconsistencies in anxiety ratings during homework exposures to a seemingly similar situation (e.g., asking for directions from a stranger). These problems are consistent with the cultural importance of context in defining the self and one's reactions. The following example highlights how an emphasis on contextual cues can complicate an exercise that is standard to CBT.

> *Therapist:* How high would your anxiety be if you had to find a seat in a room where everyone was already seated?
>
> *Patient:* It depends. How many people are in the room?

Therapist:	Let's say 10 to 15.
Patient:	Who are these people? Do I know them?
Therapist:	Let's say you know them but not well.
Patient:	Is this for work or is it social? Are they mostly male or female? Where is this room? Why is everyone else already seated?

What typically takes other patients a few seconds to answer took this patient several minutes and made creating a fear hierarchy not only timely but also nearly impossible. Although there may be noncultural-related reasons for this patient's difficulty, I have found that a large proportion of my Asian American patients struggle with intensity ratings and other measures requiring a more stable view of the self, which can affect the delivery of CBT and monitoring of treatment progress.

The second concern with using self-monitoring tools with Asian Americans is the assumption that all individuals can accurately recognize and report on their internal experiences (e.g., thoughts, feelings). Answering questions such as, "What would you rate your anxiety on a 0 to 10-point scale?" or "What were your thoughts when that happened?" is critical to most CBT interventions; without an ability to answer such questions, patients are unable to develop the skills cognitive behavioral models assert as necessary for threat reappraisals and symptom reduction.

One trait that is closely tied to the ability to complete self-monitoring tools and records is alexithymia. *Alexithymia* is defined as a deficit in the ability to identify and describe emotion states (Taylor, 2000). It is multifaceted and characterized by (a) a difficulty identifying feelings and distinguishing them from physical sensations of emotional arousal, (b) a difficulty describing emotions to others, (c) a reduced capacity to imagine or engage in fantasy, and (d) an externally oriented thinking (EOT) style that emphasizes concrete stimuli rather than inner emotions (Taylor, 2000). Research has indicated that Asian Americans are significantly more alexithymic than their European American counterparts (Dere et al., 2012; Dion, 1996; Le, Berenbaum, & Raghavan, 2002; Lo, 2014).

One explanation for the group difference in alexithymia levels is the Eastern cultural emphasis on emotional restraint and external, contextual demands over internal, private experiences for making decisions about how to respond. Consistent with this, alexithymia, particularly the EOT factor, appears to be closely tied to differences in cultural values (Dere et al., 2012; Ryder et al., 2008). For example, Dere et al. (2012) compared Chinese Canadian and European Canadian undergraduates on an established measure of alexithymia and found the Chinese Canadian participants' total scores on the measure were significantly higher than those of the European Canadians. The authors also found that higher levels of endorsement of European

American values predicted lower EOT and that European American and Asian values fully mediated the group difference in EOT.

Given that Asian Americans show poorer ability to recognize emotions in themselves (e.g., Dere et al., 2012) and others (e.g., Lau et al., 2009), they may struggle with the internally focused exercises and measures introduced at the start of CBT. Moreover, Asian Americans' tendency to emphasize concrete, external cues (i.e., EOT) over their emotions and thoughts may lead to difficulties internalizing the cognitive (re)appraisals considered critical to change in CBT.

COGNITIVE BEHAVIORAL TREATMENTS OF ANXIETY DISORDERS IN ASIAN AMERICANS

Few studies have examined the effectiveness of CBT for anxiety disorders in Asian Americans. In a review of studies using CBT with ethnic minorities (Voss Horrell, 2008), none of the studies focused on Asian Americans with a *DSM–5* anxiety disorder. Similarly, Carter, Mitchell, and Sbrocco (2012) specifically examined the treatment outcome research for U.S. ethnic minorities experiencing one of the anxiety disorders and found only one study, by Pan, Huey, and Hernandez (2011), that focused on CBT for an anxiety disorder in Asian Americans. The remaining studies that examined CBT treatment outcomes in Asian Americans represented the work of Hinton and colleagues (2004, 2005) on Asian refugees experiencing a cultural variant of posttraumatic stress disorder.

Pan et al. (2011) conducted a small randomized controlled trial comparing the effectiveness of a culturally adapted exposure treatment for specific phobias with a standard exposure treatment protocol and with a self-help treatment condition. All participants were of East Asian descent and met criteria for a specific phobia. Individuals assigned to the exposure treatment conditions completed their individualized fear hierarchies in a single session (with a maximum session length of 3 hours). The culturally adapted treatment condition used the same treatment techniques as the standard treatment, but it focused on increasing patient engagement by reframing the rationale and delivery of the techniques in more culturally consistent ways. Individuals in the self-help condition received a self-help book on exposure.

The study collected posttreatment data 1 week and 6 months after treatment. At 1 week, but not 6 months, participants in the culturally adapted treatment showed significantly greater reduction in general fear and catastrophic thinking than those in the standard treatment and the self-help condition. This effect was moderated by acculturation status, with greatest reductions in general fear and catastrophic thinking occurring among Asian

Americans low in acculturation status who received the culturally adapted treatment. Although superior to the self-help control condition, participants in the culturally adapted and standard treatment conditions did not significantly differ on other indices of anxiety (e.g., self-report, behavioral approach, clinician ratings) at posttreatment.

Hinton, Rivera, Hofmann, Barlow, and Otto (2012) described 12 key ways they adapted CBT for posttraumatic stress disorder and panic disorder to meet the culturally unique needs of Southeast Asian refugees experiencing trauma-related anxiety. Their culturally adapted model focused on the role of trauma associations and increased anxiety sensitivity and included interventions for two culturally specific types of panic attacks: orthostatically triggered panic attacks and neck-focused panic attacks (Hinton et al., 2005). *Neck-focused panic* is characterized by worries that a neck vessel will rupture and is associated with autonomic arousal such as dizziness, blurry vision, and heart palpitations. *Orthostatic panic attacks* are associated with a sudden onset of dizziness and other somatic symptoms and fears of fainting, which leads the person to sit down. Several studies support the effectiveness of these adaptations (e.g., Hinton et al., 2004, 2005).

From the sparse data, it appears that cultural adaptations of CBT can be effective in treating anxiety disorders in Asian Americans. It is not clear, however, what adaptations (if any) would improve the cultural sensitivity of CBT for anxiety disorders in all Asian Americans and whether establishing such adaptations would act to only reify ethnic stereotypes. In the following section, I examine possible future directions for addressing cultural factors within a cognitive behavioral framework.

THE FUTURE OF COGNITIVE BEHAVIORAL MODELS, MEASURES, AND TREATMENTS FOR ANXIETY DISORDERS IN ASIAN AMERICANS

Recent Advances in the Cognitive Behavioral Treatment of Anxiety Disorders

One characteristic feature of CBT for the anxiety disorders is the use of exposure. *Exposure* refers to the practice of exposing patients to a feared situation (e.g., a crowded elevator) and having them stay in the feared situation until the fear subsides. Typically, exposures to one situation or trigger are repeated until the patient reports minimal anxiety or difficulty with that situation. Patients are then systematically exposed to situations of increasing difficulty until the fear response is no longer activated in situations they originally identified as most difficult (e.g., being locked in a small, dark closet).

The basic rationale is that when patients report minimal fear in the context of their exposures, it indicates corrective learning has occurred and patients no longer see the stimulus as threatening or dangerous (for a review, see Foa & Kozak, 1986; Foa & McNally, 1996; Rachman, 1980).

More recently, Craske and her colleagues (e.g., Craske et al., 2008, 2012; Craske, Treanor, Conway, Zbozinek, & Vervliet, 2014) questioned the proposed processes by which inhibitory learning (i.e., learning of safety) occurs during exposures and asserted that current models fail to incorporate factors that are more important to this learning than actual fear reduction during an exposure. In particular, Craske and colleagues underscored (among other factors) the importance of expectancies and contextual cues. Citing several lines of research with both clinical populations and animal learning models, they argued that to truly learn they are safe, patients must have multiple and varied experiences that violate their expectations of harm (however defined), and these expectancy violations must occur across a variety of contexts (e.g., not just limited to the therapeutic context). For example, patients with a height phobia are more likely to extinguish their height fears if they practice being on the roofs or top decks of a variety of buildings than practicing on just the rooftop of the building where they receive CBT.

Although Craske and colleagues (2008, 2012, 2014) did not mention the role of culture, their findings and the proposed mechanisms of fear reduction highlight the potential complexity of working with bicultural Asian Americans who, from their awareness of both Eastern and Western cultural frames, may have a greater variability in threat expectations across contexts than their monocultural counterparts. For Asian Americans, standard exposure practices may then be less effective in developing corrective learning across situations, and exposures would, instead, have to be carefully constructed to match the predicted fear outcomes of a particular situation and be clearly rooted in the cultural frame in which the fears are experienced.

Idiographic Approaches to Treating Anxiety Disorders

To address symptoms at the individual level, Zayfert (2008) proposed a more idiographic approach to responding to cultural concerns. In this approach, the clinician asks clients before the start of treatment open-ended questions about their ethnocultural context and uses those data to contextualize their presenting problems. Some example questions include "What is the individual's perspective on . . . the role of women's sexuality? . . . the centrality of family over the individual? . . . the meaning of seeking professional help outside of the family?" This approach provides a framework by which a clinician can culturally adapt treatments on a case-by-case basis and in a systematic manner. Zayfert also highlighted how this framework lends itself well to larger scale studies that could clarify the domains most relevant to an ethnocultural idiographic assessment for a particular disorder and, thus, provide guidance to clinicians on ways to adjust treatment delivery.

Despite its advantages, a limitation to this idiographic approach is the assumption that clients will have adequate psychological insight to respond to questions about their ethnocultural values and context and provide enough data at the start of treatment to structure the entire treatment plan. Most individuals do not spend time thinking about their cultural values and how they may be related to their problems. This is particularly true for Asians who are socialized to be more externally oriented and who show poorer awareness of their internal states (Dere et al., 2012; Ryder et al., 2008). Moreover, bicultural Asian Americans may find their views change as a function of context and the cultural demands of a situation. Thus, the likelihood a clinician or patient could identify all the different contexts in which culture shapes the patient's anxious appraisals or even distinguish the factors that influence the patient's decision making is zero.

How, then, does a clinician who is committed to evidence-based care incorporate cultural factors into treatment? As described elsewhere (J. J. Hong, 2013), one approach is to create an individually tailored treatment plan that continually reviews with the patient the cultural relevance and responsiveness of its interventions. I offer three strategies to do this. The strategies mirror the hypothesis-testing approach characteristic of CBT, but in an idiographic way. First, as a way to address the difficulty of directly assessing an individual's cultural values, I recommend using standardized measures of constructs that are relevant to the presenting problem and may be influenced by the client's ethnocultural context (e.g., emotional avoidance, alexithymia, perfectionism). This approach allows the clinician to collaboratively review the assessment data and discuss the functional and cultural meaning of score elevations with the client. This prevents the problem of clinicians presuming an Asian American patient's problems are influenced by their heritage cultural values just because he or she is Asian. It also creates a collaborative atmosphere in which the patient completes a measure, the clinician scores it, and both the patient and clinician discuss whether the significant elevations in the measure have functional relevance.

Second, a core feature of CBT is the use of psychoeducation to explain the reasons for a person's anxiety symptoms and to support the interventions proposed in the treatment. For example, in panic disorder, patients learn about the evolutionary basis for fight-or-flight sympathetic arousal and how an elevated sensitivity to this arousal (i.e., anxiety sensitivity) increases risk for panic attacks (e.g., Barlow & Craske, 2007). In a similar way, Asian American patients who may be struggling with the bicultural tension of their heritage culture and U.S. culture may benefit from psychoeducation of the

East–West cultural differences in values and how conflicts in these values can lead to increased distress. Educating Asian American patients on the cross-cultural research relevant to their problems offers a foundation—similar to that seen in CBT protocols—for discussing how to target difficulties they may be experiencing and for developing an awareness of why they respond to situations in a particular way and how that response may (or may not) be problematic.

Finally, and perhaps most important, I recommend a hypothesis-testing approach to treatment with frequent, systematic collection of behavioral and self-report data. These data help the clinician and patient (a) jointly develop hypotheses about the function of different behaviors, (b) create interventions based on the hypotheses, and (c) examine the effectiveness of the interventions. Although this recommendation is not new and is implicit to CBT protocols, it is particularly important when working to address cultural factors that are uniquely influencing an individual and when there is little external data on appropriateness of certain interventions. This approach also helps circumvent some of the previously outlined difficulties in using self-monitoring measures and tools with Asian Americans. For example, rather than creating a fear hierarchy, which requires patients to reflect and predict levels of anxiety in different situations, clinicians and patients may identify one or two situations that might create a certain level of anxiety in the patients—though insight into the actual level is not required—and the patients would then enter into the situation with the goal of behaving differently—though insight into thoughts and feelings is not required—and see whether they experience a more positive outcome than if they behaved in ways they normally do in the situation. After the exercise or experiment, the patient and therapist can review the outcome and discuss what the patient may have learned through the experience. This approach is consistent with recent assertions that corrective learning about actual threat levels is best achieved through experiences that violate expectancies and allow patients to infer safety across multiple contexts (Craske et al., 2008, 2014) and does not require patients to report on reductions in fear levels during an exposure.

Summary and Future Directions

According to cognitive behavioral theories, anxiety disorders are defined by an overestimation of threat that triggers an exaggerated fear response to a particular trigger. The disorders are maintained by maladaptive (cognitive and behavioral) responses that reinforce the fear and prevent patients from disconfirming their faulty appraisals. Research has indicated that contextual cues can be as powerful triggers of fear responses as the threat cues themselves and can help shape beliefs about how to respond (see Craske et al., 2008,

2014). Given this, the pathways to pathological anxiety will be influenced by the cultural context in which they develop. Specifically, the beliefs and values promoted in a cultural context help define what is considered safe and what is threatening.

Clinical research on cognitive behavioral models, measures, and treatments of anxiety disorders in Asian Americans is virtually nonexistent. Much of our understanding of how culture shapes processes related to pathological anxiety comes from nonclinical samples. Research on social anxiety in Asian Americans is relatively well-developed and has shown that elevated social anxiety ratings found in Asian Americans (when compared with White Americans) can be explained by cultural values typically promoted in Asian contexts (e.g., low independent self-construal, emotion suppression). Although the cultural pathways to increased social anxiety do not appear to translate to higher levels of impairment, bicultural Asian Americans who, by definition, must negotiate the pulls of their Eastern heritage and Western host cultures are more likely to report distress (Hsu et al., 2012) and develop an anxiety (or other *DSM*) disorder (Takeuchi et al., 2007) than their monocultural counterparts.

Given the lack of research, it remains unclear how the noted cultural shaping of anxiety translates in a clinical context. Existing cognitive behavioral measures and treatments do appear to hold assumptions about the pathways to good mental health that reflect the Western cultural contexts from which they were developed. According to my clinical observations, many of these assumptions do not translate well with Asian American patients with anxiety disorders, and the difficulties experienced appear to be related to culturally different beliefs about identity consistency and the importance of understanding and using internal information to guide decision making. Given this and the heterogeneity of Asian American populations, clinicians are encouraged to work with their Asian American clients on developing individualized treatment plans by taking existing CBT interventions and examining which interventions are most helpful and in what contexts. Future research should focus on examining the utility of individualized, hypothesis-driven cultural adaptations in Asian American clinical samples and whether such adaptations are superior to existing Western-based CBT protocols.

REFERENCES

American Psychiatric Association. (2013). *Diagnostic and statistical manual of mental disorders* (5th ed.). Arlington, VA: Author.

Asnaani, A., Richey, J. A., Dimaite, R., Hinton, D. E., & Hofmann, S. G. (2010). A cross-ethnic comparison of lifetime prevalence rates of anxiety disorders.

Journal of Nervous and Mental Disease, 198, 551–555. http://dx.doi.org/10.1097/NMD.0b013e3181ea169f

Barlow, D. H., & Craske, M. G. (2007). *Mastery of your anxiety and panic: Client workbook* (4th ed.). New York, NY: Oxford University Press.

Beaupré, M. G., & Hess, U. (2005). Cross-cultural emotion recognition among Canadian ethnic groups. *Journal of Cross-Cultural Psychology, 36*, 355–370. http://dx.doi.org/10.1177/0022022104273656

Benet-Martínez, V., Lee, F., & Leu, J. (2006). Biculturalism and cognitive complexity: Expertise in cultural representations. *Journal of Cross-Cultural Psychology, 37*, 386–407. http://dx.doi.org/10.1177/0022022106288476

Butler, E. A., Lee, T. L., & Gross, J. J. (2007). Emotion regulation and culture: Are the social consequences of emotion suppression culture-specific? *Emotion, 7*, 30–48. http://dx.doi.org/10.1037/1528-3542.7.1.30

Carter, M. M., Mitchell, F. E., & Sbrocco, T. (2012). Treating ethnic minority adults with anxiety disorders: Current status and future recommendations. *Journal of Anxiety Disorders, 26*, 488–501. http://doi.org/10.1016/j.janxdis.2012.02.002

Clark, D. M., & Wells, A. (1995). A cognitive model of social phobia. In R. G. Heimberg, M. R. Liebowitz, D. A. Hope, & F. R. Schneier (Eds.), *Social phobia: Diagnosis, assessment, and treatment* (pp. 69–93). New York, NY: Guilford Press.

Craske, M. G., Kircanski, K., Zelikowsky, M., Mystkowski, J., Chowdhury, N., & Baker, A. (2008). Optimizing inhibitory learning during exposure therapy. *Behaviour Research and Therapy, 46*, 5–27. http://dx.doi.org/10.1016/j.brat.2007.10.003

Craske, M. G., Liao, B., Brown, L., & Vervliet, B. (2012). Role of inhibition in exposure therapy. *Journal of Experimental Psychopathology, 3*, 322–345. http://dx.doi.org/10.5127/jep.026511

Craske, M. G., Treanor, M., Conway, C. C., Zbozinek, T., & Vervliet, B. (2014). Maximizing exposure therapy: An inhibitory learning approach. *Behaviour Research and Therapy, 58*, 10–23. http://dx.doi.org/10.1016/j.brat.2014.04.006

Dere, J., Falk, C. F., & Ryder, A. G. (2012). Unpacking cultural differences in alexithymia: The role of cultural values among Euro-Canadian and Chinese-Canadian students. *Journal of Cross-Cultural Psychology, 43*, 1297–1312. http://dx.doi.org/10.1177/0022022111430254

Dion, K. L. (1996). Ethnolinguistic correlates of alexithymia: Toward a cultural perspective. *Journal of Psychosomatic Research, 41*, 531–539. http://dx.doi.org/10.1016/S0022-3999(96)00295-4

Foa, E. B., & Kozak, M. J. (1986). Emotional processing of fear: Exposure to corrective information. *Psychological Bulletin, 99*, 20–35. http://dx.doi.org/10.1037/0033-2909.99.1.20

Foa, E. B., & McNally, R. J. (1996). Mechanisms of change in exposure therapy. In R. M. Rapee (Ed.), *Current controversies in the anxiety disorders* (pp. 329–343). New York, NY: Guilford Press.

Goldfried, M. R., & Goldfried, A. P. (1977). Importance of hierarchy content in the self-control of anxiety. *Journal of Consulting and Clinical Psychology, 45*, 124–134. http://dx.doi.org/10.1037/0022-006X.45.1.124

Grant, B. F., Hasin, D. S., Stinson, F. S., Dawson, D. A., June Ruan, W., Goldstein, R. B., . . . Huang, B. (2005). Prevalence, correlates, co-morbidity, and comparative disability of *DSM–IV* generalized anxiety disorder in the USA: Results from the National Epidemiologic Survey on Alcohol and Related Conditions. *Psychological Medicine, 35*, 1747–1759. http://dx.doi.org/10.1017/S0033291705006069

Gross, J. J., & John, O. P. (2003). Individual differences in two emotion regulation processes: Implications for affect, relationships, and well-being. *Journal of Personality and Social Psychology, 85*, 348–362. http://dx.doi.org/10.1037/0022-3514.85.2.348

Hall, G. C., Hong, J. J., Zane, N. W. S., & Meyer, O. L. (2011). Culturally competent treatments for Asian Americans: The relevance of mindfulness and acceptance-based psychotherapies. *Clinical Psychology: Science and Practice, 18*, 215–231. http://dx.doi.org/10.1111/j.1468-2850.2011.01253.x

Heine, S. J., Lehman, D. R., Markus, H. R., & Kitayama, S. (1999). Is there a universal need for positive self-regard? *Psychological Review, 106*, 766–794. http://dx.doi.org/10.1037/0033-295X.106.4.766

Heinrichs, N., Rapee, R. M., Alden, L. A., Bögels, S., Hofmann, S. G., Oh, K. J., & Sakano, Y. (2006). Cultural differences in perceived social norms and social anxiety. *Behaviour Research and Therapy, 44*, 1187–1197. http://dx.doi.org/10.1016/j.brat.2005.09.006

Hinton, D. E., Chhean, D., Pich, V., Safren, S. A., Hofmann, S. G., & Pollack, M. H. (2005). A randomized controlled trial of cognitive-behavior therapy for Cambodian refugees with treatment-resistant PTSD and panic attacks: A crossover design. *Journal of Traumatic Stress, 18*, 617–629. http://dx.doi.org/10.1002/jts.20070

Hinton, D. E., Pham, T., Tran, M., Safren, S. A., Otto, M. W., & Pollack, M. H. (2004). CBT for Vietnamese refugees with treatment-resistant PTSD and panic attacks: A pilot study. *Journal of Traumatic Stress, 17*, 429–433. http://dx.doi.org/10.1023/B:JOTS.0000048956.03529.fa

Hinton, D. E., Rivera, E. I., Hofmann, S. G., Barlow, D. H., & Otto, M. W. (2012). Adapting CBT for traumatized refugees and ethnic minority patients: Examples from culturally adapted CBT (CA-CBT). *Transcultural Psychiatry, 49*, 340–365. http://dx.doi.org/10.1177/1363461512441595

Hong, J. J. (2012). Anxiety disorders in Asians. In E. C. Chang (Ed.), *Handbook of adult psychopathology in Asians: Theory, diagnosis and treatment* (pp. 143–178). New York, NY: Oxford University Press. http://dx.doi.org/10.1093/med:psych/9780195179064.003.0007

Hong, J. J. (2013). An idiographic evidence-based approach to addressing cultural factors in treatment: A case example. *Behavior Therapist, 36*, 145–146.

Hong, Y. Y., Morris, M. W., Chiu, C. Y., & Benet-Martínez, V. (2000). Multicultural minds. A dynamic constructivist approach to culture and cognition. *American Psychologist, 55*, 709–720. http://dx.doi.org/10.1037/0003-066X.55.7.709

Horng, B., & Coles, M. E. (2014). Do higher self-reports of social anxiety translate to greater occurrence of social anxiety disorder in Asian Americans compared to Caucasian Americans? *Journal of Cognitive Psychotherapy, 28*, 287–302. http://dx.doi.org/10.1891/0889-8391.28.4.287

Horrell, S. C. V. (2008). Effectiveness of cognitive-behavioral therapy with adult ethnic minority clients: A review. *Professional Psychology: Research and Practice, 39*, 160–168. http://dx.doi.org/10.1037/0735-7028.39.2.160

Hsu, L., Woody, S. R., Lee, H.-J., Peng, Y., Zhou, X., & Ryder, A. G. (2012). Social anxiety among East Asians in North America: East Asian socialization or the challenge of acculturation? *Cultural Diversity and Ethnic Minority Psychology, 18*, 181–191. http://dx.doi.org/10.1037/a0027690

Huppert, J. D., Roth Ledley, D., & Foa, E. B. (2006). The use of homework in behavior therapy for anxiety disorders. *Journal of Psychotherapy Integration, 16*, 128–139. http://dx.doi.org/10.1037/1053-0479.16.2.128

Kitayama, S., Karasawa, M., & Mesquita, B. (2004). Collective and personal processes in regulating emotions: Emotion and self in Japan and the United States. In P. Philippot & R. S. Feldman (Eds.), *The regulation of emotion* (pp. 251–273). Mahwah, NJ: Erlbaum.

Krieg, A., & Xu, Y. (2015). Ethnic differences in social anxiety between individuals of Asian heritage and European heritage: A meta-analytic review. *Asian American Journal of Psychology, 6*, 66–80. http://dx.doi.org/10.1037/a0036993

Lau, A. S., Fung, J., Wang, S. W., & Kang, S.-M. (2009). Explaining elevated social anxiety among Asian Americans: Emotional attunement and a cultural double bind. *Cultural Diversity and Ethnic Minority Psychology, 15*, 77–85. http://dx.doi.org/10.1037/a0012819

Lau, A. S., Tsai, W., Shih, J., Liu, L. L., Hwang, W. C., & Takeuchi, D. T. (2013). The immigrant paradox among Asian American women: Are disparities in the burden of depression and anxiety paradoxical or explicable? *Journal of Consulting and Clinical Psychology, 81*, 901–911. http://dx.doi.org/10.1037/a0032105

Le, H.-N., Berenbaum, H., & Raghavan, C. (2002). Culture and alexithymia: Mean levels, correlates and the role of parental socialization of emotions. *Emotion, 2*, 341–360. http://dx.doi.org/10.1037/1528-3542.2.4.341

Lieber, E., Fung, H., & Leung, P. W. (2006). Chinese child-rearing beliefs: Key dimensions and contributions to the development of culture-appropriate assessment. *Asian Journal of Social Psychology, 9*, 140–147. http://dx.doi.org/10.1111/j.1467-839X.2006.00191.x

Lo, C. (2014). Cultural values and alexithymia. *SAGE Open, 4*, 1–6. http://dx.doi.org/10.1177/2158244014555117

Markus, H. R., & Kitayama, S. (1991). Culture and self: Implications for cognition, emotion, and motivation. *Psychological Review, 98,* 224–253. http://dx.doi.org/10.1037/0033-295X.98.2.224

Matsumoto, D., Takeuchi, S., Andayani, S., Kouznetsova, N., & Krupp, D. (1998). The contribution of individualism vs. collectivism to cross-national differences in display rules. *Asian Journal of Social Psychology, 1,* 147–165. http://dx.doi.org/10.1111/1467-839X.00010

Mennin, D. S., Heimberg, R. G., Turk, C. L., & Fresco, D. M. (2005). Preliminary evidence for an emotion dysregulation model of generalized anxiety disorder. *Behaviour Research and Therapy, 43,* 1281–1310. http://dx.doi.org/10.1016/j.brat.2004.08.008

Mennin, D. S., Holaway, R. M., Fresco, D. M., Moore, M. T., & Heimberg, R. G. (2007). Delineating components of emotion and its dysregulation in anxiety and mood psychopathology. *Behavior Therapy, 38,* 284–302. http://dx.doi.org/10.1016/j.beth.2006.09.001

Pan, D., Huey, S. J., Jr., & Hernandez, D. (2011). Culturally adapted versus standard exposure treatment for phobic Asian Americans: Treatment efficacy, moderators, and predictors. *Cultural Diversity and Ethnic Minority Psychology, 17,* 11–22. http://dx.doi.org/10.1037/a0022534

Park, I. J. K., Sulaiman, C., Schwartz, S. J., Kim, S. Y., Ham, L. S., & Zamboanga, B. L. (2011). Self-construals and social anxiety among Asian American college students: Testing emotion suppression as a mediator. *Asian American Journal of Psychology, 2,* 39–50. http://dx.doi.org/10.1037/a0023183

Rachman, S. (1980). Emotional processing. *Behaviour Research and Therapy, 18,* 51–60. http://dx.doi.org/10.1016/0005-7967(80)90069-8

Rapee, R. M., & Heimberg, R. G. (1997). A cognitive-behavioral model of anxiety in social phobia. *Behaviour Research and Therapy, 35,* 741–756. http://dx.doi.org/10.1016/S0005-7967(97)00022-3

Ryder, A. G., Yang, J., Zhu, X., Yao, S., Yi, J., Heine, S. J., & Bagby, R. M. (2008). The cultural shaping of depression: Somatic symptoms in China, psychological symptoms in North America? *Journal of Abnormal Psychology, 117,* 300–313. http://dx.doi.org/10.1037/0021-843X.117.2.300

Saw, A., Berenbaum, H., & Okazaki, S. (2013). Influences of personal standards and perceived parental expectations on worry for Asian American and White American college students. *Anxiety, Stress, and Coping, 26,* 187–202. http://dx.doi.org/10.1080/10615806.2012.668536

Saw, A., & Okazaki, S. (2010). Family emotion socialization and affective distress in Asian American and White American college students. *Asian American Journal of Psychology, 1,* 81–92. http://dx.doi.org/10.1037/a0019638

Scott, E. L., Eng, W., & Heimberg, R. G. (2002). Ethnic differences in worry in a nonclinical population. *Depression and Anxiety, 15,* 79–82. http://dx.doi.org/10.1002/da.10027

Smits, J. A. J., Julian, K., Rosenfield, D., & Powers, M. B. (2012). Threat reappraisal as a mediator of symptom change in cognitive-behavioral treatment of anxiety disorders: A systematic review. *Journal of Consulting and Clinical Psychology, 80*, 624–635. http://dx.doi.org/10.1037/a0028957

Suh, E. M. (2002). Culture, identity consistency, and subjective well-being. *Journal of Personality and Social Psychology, 83*, 1378–1391. http://dx.doi.org/10.1037/0022-3514.83.6.1378

Takeuchi, D. T., Zane, N., Hong, S., Chae, D. H., Gong, F., Gee, G. C., . . . Alegría, M. (2007). Immigration-related factors and mental disorders among Asian Americans. *American Journal of Public Health, 97*, 84–90. http://dx.doi.org/10.2105/AJPH.2006.088401

Taylor, G. J. (2000). Recent developments in alexithymia theory and research. *The Canadian Journal of Psychiatry/La Revue Canadienne de Psychiatrie, 45*, 134–142. http://dx.doi.org/10.1177/070674370004500203

Turner, S. M., Beidel, D. C., Dancu, C. V., & Stanley, M. A. (1989). An empirically derived inventory to measure social fears and anxiety: The Social Phobia and Anxiety Inventory. *Psychological Assessment, 1*, 35–40. http://dx.doi.org/10.1037/1040-3590.1.1.35

Woody, S. R., Miao, S., & Kellman-McFarlane, K. (2015). Cultural differences in social anxiety: A meta-analysis of Asian and European heritage samples. *Asian American Journal of Psychology, 6*, 47–55. http://dx.doi.org/10.1037/a0036548

Wu, P., Robinson, C. C., Yang, C., Hart, C. H., Olsen, S. F., Porter, C. L., . . . Wu, X. (2002). Similarities and differences in mothers' parenting of preschoolers in China and the United States. *International Journal of Behavioral Development, 26*, 481–491. http://dx.doi.org/10.1080/01650250143000436

Zane, N., & Yeh, M. (2002). The use of culturally-based variables in assessment: Studies on loss of face. In K. S. Kurasaki & S. Sue (Eds.), *Asian American mental health: Assessment, methods and theories* (pp. 123–138). New York, NY: Kluwer. http://dx.doi.org/10.1007/978-1-4615-0735-2_9

Zayfert, C. (2008). Culturally competent treatment of posttraumatic stress disorder in clinical practice: An ideographic, transcultural approach. *Clinical Psychology: Science and Practice, 15*, 68–73. http://dx.doi.org/10.1111/j.1468-2850.2008.00111

6

COGNITIVE BEHAVIORAL MODELS, MEASURES, AND TREATMENTS FOR ANXIETY DISORDERS IN LATINOS: A SYSTEMATIC REVIEW

GUILLERMO BERNAL, CRISTINA ADAMES, KELVIN MARIANI, AND JERALYS MORALES

There is a high incidence of anxiety disorders[1] in the Latino population, and cognitive behavior therapy (CBT) has been demonstrated to be an efficacious psychological treatment for a variety of anxiety conditions (Hofmann & Smits, 2008; Olatunji, Cisler, & Deacon, 2010; Stewart & Chambless, 2009). In this chapter, we examine the available evidence on the efficacy of CBT treatments for anxiety in Latinos. We also review the CBT models and measures used to evaluate outcomes in adult Latinos. Recently, an agenda for psychotherapy research with ethnic minorities was proposed by Lau, Chang, Okazaki, and Bernal (2016). A central question was the degree to which evidence-based treatments (EBTs) work with minorities. We refine the question further by examining the available evidence on the efficacy of CBT treatments for anxiety with Latinos.

---

[1]In a study of depression and anxiety in Latinos, Wassertheil-Smoller et al. (2014) found the prevalence of depression was 27%; depression and anxiety were highly correlated. The authors noted that anxiety symptoms followed a similar pattern as those for depression.

http://dx.doi.org/10.1037/0000091-007
Treating Depression, Anxiety, and Stress in Ethnic and Racial Groups: Cognitive Behavioral Approaches,
E. C. Chang, C. A. Downey, J. K. Hirsch, and E. A. Yu (Editors)

Literature searches were conducted from August 2013 to October 2014 using selected keywords in different online databases (e.g., EBSCO Host, Dialnet, JStor, OvidSp, ProQuest, PubMed, PsycNET, Scielo, and Science Direct). These queries were conducted independently for all years before December 2014. An update of the literature searches was performed and produced an additional study for 2016. Randomized controlled trials (RCTs) and open clinical trials (OCTs) were key selection criteria. Twenty-three studies met the inclusion criteria for cognitive treatments for anxiety with Latino adults. EBTs such as CBT and metacognitive therapy were commonly studied treatments. In this chapter, we examine the state of the science on the efficacy of CBT for Latino adults with anxiety. The introductory chapter to this volume provides context on the demographics of Latinos and their health equity status. Here, we review the literature on the efficacy of CBT to determine its consideration as a well-established treatment for Latinos based on the Chambless and Hollon (1998) criteria modified to consider the adequacy of the sample size for this population group. On the basis of our systematic review, we then examine the CBT models used followed by an examination of the primary measures used to assess outcome in the treatment of anxiety with Latinos.[2] We conclude with a discussion of the role of culture, language, cultural adaptation, and the availability and accessibility of EBTs for Latinos.

SETTING CONDITIONS FOR MENTAL HEALTH ISSUES AND CARE FOR LATINOS IN THE UNITED STATES

The prominence of the Latino population is evident in different spheres of U.S. society (e.g., culture, food, music, art, politics, government, science). Nevertheless, these communities continue to face major disparities with regard to health equity. The Centers for Disease Control and Prevention showed that 29.1% of Latinos lacked health insurance (Ward, Schiller, Freeman, & Peregoy, 2013). Also, Latinos were twice as likely as non-Latino Blacks and 3 times as likely non-Latino Whites to lack a regular health care provider. Most uninsured Latinos are between the ages of 18 and 64 (Cohen & Martinez, 2012). The high percentage of noninsured Latinos represents a serious public health concern because this community is not receiving adequate treatment for a wide range of health conditions, such as diabetes, heart disease, HIV/AIDS, and mental health disorders. Wassertheil-Smoller et al. (2014)

---

[2]We use the terms *Latino* and *Hispanic* to refer to people from Puerto Rico, Cuba, Central or South America, and other people from Spanish cultures or origins. *Hispanic* was a label adopted by the deferral government in the 1970s to classify census data and administering federal programs. It also emphasizes the Spanish roots of these groups, whereas the term *Latino* encompasses individuals who speak different languages and have diverse origins.

noted that depression and anxiety are generally not treated among Latinos who lack health insurance; these authors also reported a correlation of 0.71 between depression and anxiety disorders for this group. Clearly, it is essential to attend to the health needs of Latinos, providing equity in health and mental health care.

Latinos have less access or use fewer mental health treatments than the general population, and the rates for most mental disorders are similar to the overall population. However, Latinos and non-Hispanic Whites show higher prevalence rates of affective disorders (e.g., major depression, social phobia) compared with African Americans, who show a lower prevalence of major depression and dysthymia (Woodward et al., 2012). Also, rates of mental disorders vary among Latino subgroups; Alegría et al. (2007) found that Puerto Ricans showed the highest overall prevalence rate of mental illness among Latino subgroups and the highest prevalence for depressive symptoms (58% more likely; Albert Einstein College of Medicine, 2014). In addition, Puerto Ricans show higher anxiety rates (18.3, CI [17.9, 18.8]) compared with other Latinos (Wassertheil-Smoller et al., 2014).

A central question is whether the treatments delivered are effective with specific mental disorders, such as anxiety, in Latinos. To answer this question, we look at efficacy and effectiveness studies that make up the evidence base for treatments (Miranda et al., 2005) for adults. Efficacy studies serve as the foundation for identifying outcomes associated with well-defined treatments, whereas effectiveness studies help evaluate the impact of such treatments in real-world settings (Miranda et al., 2005). The issue of external validity is not trivial; there seems to be a bias in the use of basic principles of science (Sue, 1999) given the paucity of efficacy studies with minority populations. In fact, the U.S. Surgeon General's supplementary report noted that minorities are largely missing from efficacy trials (Office of the Surgeon General, Center for Mental Health Services, & National Institute of Mental Health, 2001). The paucity of diverse populations in efficacy studies has led investigators to question whether EBTs can be generalized to ethnic and racial minorities, including Latinos.

In 1998, the American Psychological Association (APA) Society of Clinical Psychology (Division 12) established a Task Force on Promotion and Dissemination of Psychological Procedures that exposed criteria (for EBTs) and identified a list of EBTs (CBT, behavioral therapy, and interpersonal psychotherapy) demonstrating efficacy superior to a placebo or another comparison control in the treatment of anxiety, stress, depression, health problems, childhood problems, marital discord, and sexual dysfunction (Hall, 2001). A concern with the list was that none of the treatments showed adequate empirical support for the efficacy of EBTs for ethnic minority groups, in part due to the scarcity of minorities represented in the sample (Hall, 2001). Similarly, Bernal and Scharró-del-Río (2001) noted that although they emphasized internal over external validity, most of the studies had little if any consideration of the cultural, interpretative, population, ecological, and construct validity of the intervention and the results reported, thus making these treatments unresponsive to the needs of EBTs for diverse groups. Various scholars have argued in favor of adapting psychotherapies for diverse populations that are based on both the evidence and the consideration of the culture, language, and context of the population in question (Bernal, Bonilla, & Bellido, 1995; Bernal & Domenech Rodríguez, 2012; Comas-Díaz, 2012; Hall, 2001; La Roche, 2012), including constructs such as the meaning of interdependence, spirituality, and discrimination, even if such constructs appear to be counter to mainstream values inherent in traditional psychotherapies.

Two decades after the publication of the Division 12 task force report, major challenges remain in generating studies with Latinos and other minorities. Mak, Law, Alvidrez, and Pérez-Stable (2007) examined the representation of ethnic minorities in studies of the National Institutes of Health. These authors found that less than half the studies provided complete ethnic information, ethnic minorities are still underrepresented (except African Americans) with no improvement in the last decade, subgroup analyses by specific ethnic groups were infrequently reported, and relatively small sample sizes of ethnic minorities in most studies were reported. Psychotherapy research has been slow to respond to the cultural aspect of therapy, considering psychotherapy as something that can be ethnocentric, decontextualized, ahistorical, and apolitical (Comas-Díaz, 2012). EBTs that are responsive to the demands of particular ethnic groups have been culturally adapted to focus on the specifics of language, ethnicity, culture, meanings, and values and have to be developed and tested (Bernal, Jiménez-Chafey, & Domenech Rodríguez, 2009; Miranda et al., 2005).

Latinos are one of the fastest growing ethnic minority groups and are projected to become the largest minority group in the United States, yet this population continues to face serious disparities in health and mental health care. Furthermore, it is not altogether clear whether psychological treatments that are considered "well-established" are available for this population group. Next, we turn to a description of the methods and results of the systematic review of the literature.

METHOD OF THE SYSTEMATIC REVIEW

Inclusion Criteria (Study Selection)

The studies included in this review met the following inclusion criteria: Outcome data were provided on mental health treatments for anxiety, the sample included any percentage of adult Hispanic and/or Latino participants, studies were either RCTs or OCTs, measures were taken at pretreatment and posttreatment, and cognitive therapies were the primary treatment. Articles that did not report client or patient demographic information and that were on children and adolescents were excluded.

Search Strategy for Identification of Studies

The research team defined the most appropriate search terms for the systematic review with the assistance of librarians at the University of Puerto Rico (UPR). For modality or type of treatment, the terms used were *clinical trials*, *psychotherapy*, *drug therapy*, *prevention*, *intervention*, *treatment*, and *therapy*. The terms *efficacy* and *effectiveness* were included, as well as *Latinos* and *Hispanics* for the observed population in searches for measures of outcome. These terms were used on searches conducted between August 2013 and December 2014 using revised and selected keywords in various combinations including a keyword for modality, measure of results, and population. These searches were later updated to reflect the literature available until March 2016. Searches were conducted for abstract title and keywords specifically and used Boolean operators and quotation marks for groups of words to be searched together. The databases Scielo, PubMed, PsycNET, Science Direct, Dialnet, Cochrane, OvidSP, JStor, EBSCOHost, and ProQuest were independently searched for all years. All references found were downloaded into different EndNote libraries and organized according to specific keyword combinations, dates searched, and the database from which the references were obtained.

Selection of Studies

Studies were included if the articles provided demographic data of Latino participants, interventions for anxiety and other anxiety symptoms, or quantitative data regarding mental health treatments. Studies with any percentage of Latino or Hispanic participants were included in the study.

The terms *treatment*, *intervention*, and *Latino* or *Hispanic* were defined for the relevance and inclusion criteria of this review. Terms such as *Latinos*, *Hispanics*, and *Spanish-speaking* were considered as different labels for the same individuals or groups considered part of a broad cultural, language, ethnic, racial, or national group. A treatment was defined as a "behavioral program focused on ameliorating nonnormative psychological distress," reducing problem behaviors, or increasing adaptive behavior by the use of counseling, psychotherapy, training programs, and so forth (Weisz, Doss, & Hawley, 2005, p. 338).

The titles, abstracts, and full text of all relevant articles were reviewed and identified in the database searches. These data were recorded in a spreadsheet documenting the reasons for inclusion or exclusion and read carefully for the reasons studies were or were not included. Percentage of Latinos or Hispanics was also recorded within the inclusion and exclusion spreadsheet. Data regarding type of study, mental health condition, and treatment for which the study was designed were included. Studies with a treatment model or intervention for anxiety and other anxiety symptoms were the only studies considered for inclusion and data analysis. The last inclusion criterion was the presence or absence of a treatment based on CBT ($N = 13$). Studies with treatments designed for any other treatment modality were excluded. Included studies were reassessed. The full texts were obtained independently by various team members through individual website search or the use of UPR's library system, each member in charge of an individual database. Figure 6.1 provides a summary of how the articles were obtained and selected.

Extraction of Data and Quality Assessment

Articles were selected on the basis of inclusion and exclusion criteria and were obtained in PDF form. Further analysis of the articles was conducted through tabulation in Excel spreadsheets of all study information, including author, title of article, year of publication, sample size (n), study design, condition, measures, experimental group, control group, pre and post measures, results, and percentage of Latino or Hispanic participants. For the experimental and control group categories, treatments and measures assigned to participants were identified. Data analysis was conducted through individual assessment of each of the articles and organized into the spreadsheets.

To evaluate the validity and quality of each study, the Cochrane risk of bias tool (modified) for quality assessment of RCTs was used (van Tulder, Furlan, Bombardier, & Bouter, 2003). This tool considers the external validity of treatments based on identifying, among other things, the use of randomization, concealment of allocation, and adequate blinding. The Cochrane system defines the validity and reliability of test results and/or treatments in a study according to the analysis of systematic errors and bias (Ryan, Hill, Prictor, & McKenzie, 2013).

Team members were trained on the use of the Cochrane tool, with each member responsible for carrying out quality assessment for RCTs. Quality assessments were performed independently, and the selection for each criterion of the Cochrane tool was coded, as well as the reason for its selection. To avoid bias, members could not comment or ask each other questions in relation to quality assessment or evaluation criteria. Once the evaluations were completed, members met and discussed the results, documenting

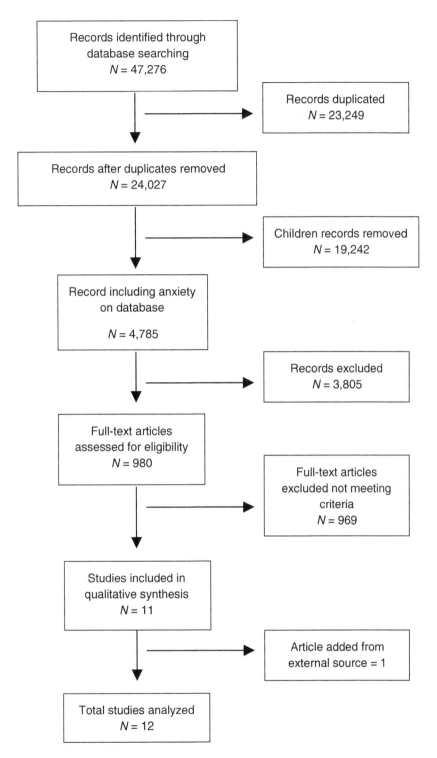

Figure 6.1. Article search and inclusion flowchart for cognitive behavior therapy studies with Latinos.

corrections and considering discrepancies in a new table. Corrections and discrepancies were also discussed with the rest of the team to finally determine whether the RCTs were rated as high risk, doubtful risk, or low risk of bias. For this coding process, the legend provided by the Cochrane rubric was used. It should be noted that the considerations based on Cochrane's criteria and guidance required a great deal of clarity and specificity to reach a determination. If details were omitted from an article (i.e., sequence generation, task concealment, blinding of both participants and personnel, data for incomplete results, reports of result selectivity, and other sources of bias) stipulated by the Cochrane rubric, the rater was bound to consider such omissions as a risk of bias.

The studies were also evaluated using the criteria developed by Chambless and Hollon (1998) based on the earlier work of the APA Task Force on the Promotion and Dissemination of Psychological Procedures, determining whether a treatment is well-established, probably efficacious, or experimental without sufficient evidence for efficacy. However, Chambless and Hollon did not provide a rubric, nor is there a detailed evaluation method to carry out the expected judgment (Weisz & Hawley, 1998). Using the task force criteria helped determine whether the treatments used had good designs with positive outcomes that were not due to other external factors. In this way, if the treatment were judged as efficacious, it could have been considered a study with high internal validity. To determine whether treatments used in each study were well-established treatments or probably efficacious treatments or neither, a team member studied the criteria established by the task force and extracted the treatments with their studies. These were organized in a table and were identified as well-established treatments, probably efficacious treatments, and treatments with limited evidence.

In addition to the criteria established by Chambless and Hollon (1998), we also considered the percentage of Latinos in the sample for the determination of a well-established treatment. On the basis of the distribution of the percentage of Latinos in treatment studies (Bernal et al., in press), we opted for the 60% mark as our cutoff point. Thus, we determined that for a designation of well-established treatment, there had to be at least two studies that demonstrated efficacy with over 60% Latino participation in the sample.

RESULTS AND DISCUSSION

The articles included in the systematic review are presented in Table 6.1. The information presented in summary form includes the author and year of publication, title of article, sample (n), percentage of Latino and Latina

TABLE 6.1

Cognitive Behavior Therapy Studies of Latinos/as for Anxiety by Author, Title, Sample Size, Percentage Latino/a, Design, Disorder/Treatment, Experimental/Control, and Results

Author (year)	Sample size	% Latinos	Design	Disorder/ treatment	Experimental/ control	Results
Barrios (2011)	279	18.90	RCT/OXO	PD, GAD, PTSD, SAD/CBT	CBT versus treatment as usual	CBT for anxiety disorders was effective in reducing anxiety symptoms, severity, and frequency of related depressive symptoms in both groups (Whites and Hispanics).
J. G. Beck et al. (2009)	44	2	RCT/OXO	PTSD/GCBT or MCC	GCBT ($n = 26$), MCC ($n = 18$)	GCBT did not appear to reduce comorbid anxiety and depressive disorders, unlike individual CBT.
Boden et al. (2012)	47	10.60		SAD/CBT	Immediate CBT or delayed CBT	CBT significantly mediated effects of SAD symptoms.
Bosic (1981)	30	10	RCT	Anxiety/RT	RT ($n = 15$), control ($n = 15$)	RT significantly reduced anxiety.
Chavira et al. (2014)	366	23.22	RCT	GAD/CBT versus UC	Meditation, CBT, or both/UC	Regression models showed no differences between Latino and NLW. CBT is effective for English-speaking Latinos.
Goldin et al. (2016)	108	9.3	RCT, OXO	Generalized SAD/group CBT versus MBSR	CBGT versus MBSR	CBGT and MBSR are both efficacious for treating SAD.

(continues)

TABLE 6.1
Cognitive Behavior Therapy Studies of Latinos/as for Anxiety by Author, Title, Sample Size, Percentage Latino/a, Design, Disorder/Treatment, Experimental/Control, and Results *(Continued)*

Author (year)	Sample size	% Latinos	Design	Disorder/ treatment	Experimental/ control	Results
Hinton et al. (2011)	24	100	RCT	PSTD/ CA-CBT	CA-CBT (n = 12), AMR (n = 12)	Both treatments showed improvements in all outcomes.
Olivares and García-López (2002)	30	100	OXO and follow-up	Phobia/CBT versus placebo	CBT/control (n = 14)	Those in CBT showed greater decrease in anxiety responses at posttest and 2-year follow-up.
Pérez Benítez et al. (2013)	11 (8 with post)	100	RCT/OXO	PTSD/CBT	CBT	CBT has the potential to be helpful to those experiencing PTSD symptoms.
Rodríguez Biglieri et al. (2007)	8	100	RCT, OXO	OCD in Ex/ PR and MT	Ex/PR versus MT	Both treatments showed clinical utility.
Roy-Byrne et al. (2010)	1004	19.5	RCT, OXO	GAD, social phobia, PTSD/ CALM	CBT versus UC	The CALM (CBT) group showed better improvement than the UC group.
Stanley et al. (2009)	134	12	RCT	UC/CBT versus EUC	CBT (n = 70), UC (n = 64)	No difference between CBT and EUC for GAD. CBT showed improvement in anxiety and depression.

Note. AMR = applied muscle relaxation; CA-CBT = culturally adapted CBT; CALM = coordinated anxiety learning and management; CBT = cognitive behavior therapy; EUC = enhanced usual care; Ex/PR = exposure and response prevention therapy; GAD = generalized anxiety disorder; GCBT = group cognitive behavior therapy; MBSR = mindfulness-based stress reduction; MCC = minimum contact comparison; MT = metacognitive therapy; NLW = non-Latino White; OCD = obsessive-compulsive disorder; OXO = pre–post evaluations; PD = panic disorders; PTSD = posttraumatic stress disorder; RCT = randomized controlled trial; RT = relaxation training; SAD = social anxiety disorder; UC = usual care.

participants, study design, anxiety condition and treatment, setting of the study, results, CBT model manuals, and measures used. The complete documents in PDF form were obtained for all studies that met the inclusion criteria. Of these 980 articles assessed for eligibility, 12 CBT studies were identified (Barrios, 2011; J. G. Beck, Coffey, Foy, Keane, & Blanchard, 2009; Boden et al., 2012; Bosic, 1981; Chavira et al., 2014; Dour et al., 2014; Goldin et al., 2016; Hinton, Hofmann, Rivera, Otto, & Pollack, 2011; Olivares & García-López, 2002; Pérez Benítez, Zlotnick, Gomez, Rendón, & Swanson, 2013; Rodríguez Biglieri, Vetere, & Keegan, 2007; Roy-Byrne et al., 2010; Stanley et al., 2009).

As can be seen in Table 6.1, there are four studies on anxiety conditions with a 100% Latino sample (Hinton et al., 2011; Olivares & García-López, 2002; Pérez Benítez et al., 2013; Rodríguez Biglieri et al., 2007). Despite their relatively small sample size ($n = 8, 11, 24, 30$, respectively), there are now four studies of CBT for anxiety with Latinos; this finding alone represents progress, given that not a single study on anxiety with adult Latinos was reported by Miranda et al. (2005).

Of the articles that had a 100% sample of Latinos, two studies (Hinton et al., 2011; Pérez Benítez et al., 2013) treated Latinos for posttraumatic stress disorder (PTSD), a third study (Olivares & García-López, 2002) provided treatment for the fear of public speaking (phobia), and a fourth (Rodríguez Biglieri et al., 2007) treated obsessive–compulsive disorder (OCD) with exposure and response prevention therapy and a metacognitive therapy. All these studies reported a decrease in anxiety responses and improvements in outcomes.

For well-established treatments, the first and second author evaluated the studies using the Chambless and Hollon (1998) criteria adapted to include at least one well-designed study with over 60% Latino participation. No study was identified as well-established for Latinos. However, CBT for PTSD was identified as a probably efficacious treatment, and CBT for OCD was identified as a treatment with limited empirical support.

The remaining eight studies had a varied sample size of Latino participants that ranged from 2% to 23%. The studies that provided information about the setting were carried out in either primary care or outpatient clinics. The Roy-Byrne et al. (2010) study on the treatment of anxiety in primary care settings is the "parent" study that generated two other studies reporting subanalyses on Latinos (Barrios, 2011; Chavira et al., 2014). The Barrios (2011) study is an unpublished dissertation that examined differential effectiveness of the coordinated anxiety learning and management (CALM) intervention on moderator analyses. Both Latinos and Whites showed benefits from the intervention. However, strong associations between acculturation and greater symptom severity were reported. The Chavira et al.

(2014) study is a published version of some of the analyses conducted by Barrios. Thus, we treated these two studies as essentially the same. The Roy-Byrne et al. study was conducted at 17 primary care clinics in four cities and three states (Little Rock, Arkansas; Los Angeles and San Diego, California; and Seattle, Washington). The Hinton et al. (2011) study was conducted in Boston, Massachusetts. Other study sites included South Florida (Pérez Benítez et al., 2013) and Texas (Stanley et al., 2009). The remaining studies did not provide specific information about the setting. Another study with a lower percentage of Latinos that included PTSD (J. G. Beck & Coffey, 2005) reported group CBT to be less effective than individual CBT in reducing comorbid anxiety and depressive disorders.

CBT was found to be effective for generalized anxiety disorder (GAD) in English-speaking Latinos (Chavira et al., 2014). However, the parent project detailed major efforts by the investigators in translating instruments, training on cultural aspects of treatment, and making available a Spanish-speaking therapist (Roy-Byrne et al., 2010). Stanley et al. (2009) found no differences between CBT and enhanced usual care, whereas Roy-Byrne et al. (2010) showed that a group receiving CBT for GAD, social phobia, or PTSD had more improvements than usual care. This large multisite study thus demonstrated that CBT was superior to usual care in the treatment of these conditions. Using the same multisite study, Chavira et al. (2014) examined differences between Latinos and non-Latino Whites on measures of functioning and clinical improvement over time for multiple outcomes and found no differences between the two groups, suggesting that CBT is effective for the more acculturated and English-speaking Latinos. In addition, social anxiety disorder (SAD) was significantly mediated with CBT in a study by Boden et al. (2012), and positive outcomes were reported with a group CBT and mindfulness-based stress reduction (Goldin et al., 2016). Last, anxiety was also reduced when using relaxation training with imagery in pregnant women with anxiety (Bosic, 1981).

Cognitive Behavior Therapy Models and Manuals

In this section we discuss the primary CBT models and manuals used in the treatments identified in this review with Latinos. The models are presented according to the percentage of Latinos in the sample. As will be apparent, there is a great deal of cross-fertilization in the use of the basic cognitive and behavioral strategies originally developed by Albert Ellis (1962), Joseph Wolpe (1973), Aaron Beck (1979), and Michael Meichenbaum (1977).

Pérez Benítez et al. (2013) based their CBT model for treating PTSD on a manual developed by Marks, Lovell, Noshirvani, Livanou, and Thrasher

(1998) that entailed cognitive restructuring (i.e., teaching skills on how to identify negative thoughts and strategies to reinterpret emotions and beliefs). Through the use of diaries, patients could examine and record negative thoughts and reevaluate these cognitions by reasoning. Socratic questioning was used, and homework was monitored to help modify negative thoughts. Previously audiotaped sessions were used so patients could listen and refresh the strategies taught in therapy.

Hinton et al. (2011) conducted a careful cultural adaptation of the CBT protocol for PTSD. The authors adapted their manual to address key treatment challenges in minority and refugee populations—for example, poor English skills and minimal education were addressed by making sure the treatment was designed to be understood by people who have little formal education. Another thing they addressed was the high dropout rate when using exposure strategies. The authors recognized that minorities and refugees experience high levels of distress, and adapted their strategies in a unique approach that increased acceptability. The manual was based on an earlier study of CBT for PTSD with Vietnamese patients. The CBT was administered individually, focusing on providing psychoeducation for PTSD (Hinton et al., 2004), training on how trauma reminders may produce catastrophic thoughts that generate panic attacks, cognitive restructuring of fear networks (Foa & Rothbaum, 1998; Resick & Schnicke, 1993), conducting interoceptive exposure inclusive of reassociation of pleasant images (Falsetti & Resnick, 2000), and using an emotional cognitive processing protocol (Foa & Rothbaum, 2001; Rachman, 1980).

Olivares and García-López (2002) adapted a CBT guide designed by Bados (1991) to reduce anxiety about speaking in public. The intervention consisted of six weekly 2- to 3-hour sessions. The therapy involved training in public speaking, exposure training, training in self-instruction, and breathing exercises. They based their protocol for CBT on Wells's (2007) approach to metacognitive therapy for anxiety and social phobia. In all, 17 weekly CBT sessions were provided on the topics of psychoeducation, modification of core beliefs, exposure, and relapse prevention. Participants were also assigned homework and exercises to practice what was discussed in the treatment sessions. The Roy-Byrne et al. (2010) study developed the CALM intervention inspired by an earlier large-scale study of primary care for depression treatment (Unützer et al., 2002). CALM is a computer-assisted CBT treatment of 10 to 12 weekly sessions. These sessions included psychoeducation, self-monitoring, hierarchy development, breathing training, relapse prevention, cognitive restructuring, and exposure to stimuli. Two other substudies on moderator and mediator analyses to predict outcome (Chavira et al., 2014; Dour et al., 2014; Pérez Benítez et al., 2013) used the CALM intervention of the parent study.

Stanley et al. (2009) developed a manual for CBT to treat adults with GAD. They provided information on how the therapist should incorporate activities and homework for patients and take into consideration their backgrounds to establish a better rapport with them. The manual provides an outline for the sessions. Session 1 involves psychoeducation, motivation, and breathing skills; Session 2, progressive muscle relaxation; Sessions 3 to 4, changing thoughts; Session 5, problem solving; Session 6, changing behavior and sleep skills; Session 7, reviewing and practice of coping skills; and Session 8, review and finalization. The manual goes into detail about how to carry out the topics, activities, and techniques to guarantee proper administration of the CBT.

Boden et al. (2012) examined the role of core cognitions or maladaptive beliefs in the context of an RCT for SAD. The manual used was developed by Heimberg, Brozovich, and Rapee (2010). CBT entailed 16 one-hour sessions on a weekly basis, which included cognitive restructuring and exposure, using in-session and in vivo experiences to reduce both maladaptive core beliefs and symptoms of SAD.

Bosic (1981) examined the effects of relaxation training on the anxiety of pregnant women. Specifically, participants in the trial were taught the techniques of progressive relaxation training (Jacobson, 1938) in combination with imagery rehearsal and transcendental meditation, following many of the procedures originally suggested by Wolpe (1973).

Goldin et al. (2016) used the Heimberg and Becker (2002) protocol for their group CBT for SAD, which consisted of 12 sessions lasting 2.5 hours each. The treatment focused on psychoeducation, cognitive restructuring skills, graduated exposure to fear-inducing social situations, relapse prevention, and closure. Participants also used parts of a workbook (Hope, Heimberg, Juster, & Turk, 2006) to complement parts of the treatment. Patients used the workbook for SAD, which outlined each treatment session along with homework assignments. In addition, activities and homework for participants between their sessions were used as a supplement.

Finally, J. G. Beck et al. (2009) based her group CBT intervention for PTSD on Blanchard et al.'s (2003) individual CBT, adapting it to a group therapy format. The treatment consisted of 2-hour sessions lasting 14 weeks. The group CBT was organized in the following manner: Session 1 involved psychoeducation about PTSD; Sessions 2 to 14, exposure (imaginal and in vivo and mindfulness meditation training and practice); Sessions 4 to 7, muscle relaxation for stress management; Sessions 6 to 8, cognitive therapy interventions; Session 9 to 10, assertion training for anger and application of cognitive interventions; Sessions 11 to 12, behavior activation regarding social isolation and depression; and Sessions 13 to 14, relapse prevention training.

Measures and Instruments

The use of valid and reliable instruments that accurately measure the construct of interest is essential in treatment outcome research. In working with culturally and linguistically diverse populations, the use of instruments that have been adequately translated and validated is fundamental. However, the process of translation and adaptation represents an added burden on researchers because it is time-consuming and costly. An impressive literature on cross-cultural translation and validation of instruments (e.g., Alegría et al., 2004; Bravo, 2003; Brislin, 1976; Bullinger, Anderson, Cella, & Aaronson, 1993; Canino & Bravo, 1999; Geisinger, 1994; Leong, Leung, & Cheung, 2010; Sousa & Rojjanasrirat, 2011) is now available to researchers. A central question regarding the translation of instruments is whether the original instrument is equivalent to the translated one. Richard Brislin (1976) was one of the first to present a process for the translation, back translation, and review of the original version, translated version, and the back-translated version to the original language. This process determines the equivalence of the adapted instrument to the original one by a panel of experts. Brislin's (1976) original model has been used widely in cross-cultural research (Chávez & Canino, 2005; Jones, Lee, Phillips, Zhang, & Jaceldo, 2001; Kleinman, Eisenberg, & Good, 1978; van de Vijver & Leung, 1997), and there are now adaptations of his model with criteria to establish equivalence.

A practical and user-friendly toolkit available on the Web (Chávez & Canino, 2005) presents a 12-step process for translation and adaptation along with definitions of equivalence criteria. Chávez and Canino (2005) discussed five types of equivalence: (a) semantic, (b) content, (c) technical, (d) conceptual, and (e) criterion or metric. Briefly, *semantic equivalence* establishes that the meaning of each item is the same for both cultures. *Content equivalence* refers to the degree to which the content of the items is relevant to the cultural group of interest. *Technical equivalence* is established when the original and translated versions of the measures for different cultures show similar psychometric properties. *Criterion equivalence* is concerned with interpreting the results of an instrument when examined in terms of cultural norms. For example, is the cutoff score for a measure of anxiety the same in both cultures? Finally, *conceptual equivalence* is established when the same theoretical construct (e.g., components of anxiety) is studied in the target cultures. For example, are the theoretically proposed factors for anxiety in an English-language culture the same as those in a Spanish-language culture?

With the notable exception of the Hinton et al. (2011), Chavira et al. (2014), and Barrios (2011) studies, no other studies have used cultural equivalence criteria for the translation and adaptation of instruments for working with Latinos (Chávez & Canino, 2005). In Table 6.2 we present

TABLE 6.2

Psychometric Information for Instruments by Study Author, Language, Alpha for the Study, Alpha for Latino Subsample, Alpha From Other Studies, and Reporting of Metric Equivalence

Author	Instrument	Language	Alpha for non-Latino	Alpha Latino sample	Alpha from other study	Alpha for Latino from other study	Metric equivalence	Translation: equivalence criteria
Barrios (2011)	ASI	Spanish	.79–.90	.93	NA	.91	Yes	Technical
	BSI	Spanish	.74–.84	.81–.91	NA	.89	Yes	Technical
	GADSS	Spanish	NR	NR	.9	NA	NA	Not specified
	OASIS	Spanish	NR	NR	.86–.91	NA	NA	Not specified
J. G. Beck et al. (2009)	BAI	English	.90–.94	NR	NA	.82	Yes	No translation
	CAPS	English	NR	NR	.97	.84	NA	No translation
	IES-R Intrusion	English	.92	NR	.91–.95	NA	NA	No translation
	Avoidance		.88					
	Hyperarousal		.86					
Boden et al. (2012)	LSAS-SR	English	.91–.97	NR	.78–.92	NA	Yes	No translation
Bosic (1981)	OASIS	English	NR	NR	.86–.91	NA	NA	No translation
	STAI	English	NR	NR	.86–.95	.89	NA	No translation

Study	Measure	Language						Translation
Chavira et al. (2014)	ASI	Spanish by certified translator	NR	NR	.79–.90	.93	Yes	Technical
	BSI	Spanish by certified translator	NR	NR	.74–.84	.81–.91	Yes	Technical
Goldin et al. (2016)	LSAS-SR	English	.92	NR	.78–.92	NA	Yes	No translation
Hinton et al. (2011)	Nervios Scale	Spanish and validated	NR	NR	NA	NA	NA	Technical and content
	SCL-90-R	Spanish and validated	NR	.81	.79	.75	Yes	Technical
Olivares and García-López (2002)	SADS	Spanish	NR	NR	.94	.92	Yes	Technical
Pérez Benítez et al. (2013)	CAPS	English and Spanish	NR	NR	.97	.84	NA	Not specified
Rodríguez Biglieri et al. (2007)	STAI	Spanish	NR	NR	.86–.95	.89	NA	Not specified
Roy-Byrne et al. (2010)	BSI	English	NR	NR	.74–.84	.81–.91	Yes	No translation
Stanley et al. (2009)	PSWQ	Spanish	NR	NR	.9	.94	Yes (women)	Not specified

Note. ASI = Anxiety Sensitivity Index; BAI = Beck Anxiety Inventory; BSI = Brief Symptom Inventory; CAPS = Clinician-Administered PTSD Scale; GADSS = Generalized Anxiety Disorder Severity Scale; IES-R = Impact of Event Scale–Revised; LSAS-SR = Liebowitz Social Anxiety Scale–Self-Report; NA = not available or not found in literature searches; NR = information not reported by author(s); OASIS = Overall Anxiety Severity and Impairment Scale; PSWQ = Penn State Worry Questionnaire; SADS = Social Avoidance and Distress Scale; SCL-90-R = Symptom Checklist-90-Revised; STAI = State–Trait Anxiety Inventory.

information on the outcome measures, such as the availability of English- and Spanish-language versions and internal reliability coefficients (alpha) for the overall sample, the Latino subsample, and other studies used as a point of comparison or benchmark.

As Table 6.2 shows, 12 studies reported using English- and/or Spanish-language versions of the instruments to assess anxiety. Three of those studies (Chavira et al., 2014; Hinton et al., 2011; Pérez Benítez et al., 2013) reported using validated procedures or certified translations of the instruments. For the studies with 100% Latino participants, the internal reliability for the instruments used ranged from .81 to .93, which is relatively high. This range is comparable to that of alpha coefficients found for other studies with Latino samples for the same instruments (α = .74–.97; Daza, Novy, Stanley, & Averill, 2002; Martinez, Stillerman, & Waldo, 2005; Norton, 2007; Segura Camacho, Posada Gómez, Ospina, & Ospina Gómez, 2010). With regard to the use of translation equivalence for the instrument used, only the Hinton et al. (2011), Olivares and García-López (2002), Chavira et al. (2014), and Barrios (2011) studies reported having used technical and content equivalence as criteria for evaluating the Spanish-language versions.

Two studies (Barrios, 2011; Hinton et al., 2011) used instruments that reported proper procedures with the documentation on the measures used with Latino samples. For example, Barrios (2011) used instruments that were culturally tailored for Latinos, with an evaluation of the psychometric properties of the instruments used that provided a minimal test of how well the instruments work with a different population group under study. Hinton et al. (2011) used the Nervios Scale (Livanis & Tryon, 2010), which was designed specifically for a Latino sample, integrating an idiom that is native to the group. Unfortunately, not all studies provided adequate information on the psychometric properties of the instruments in their sample. The studies also lacked information on whether and to what extent the instruments were culturally adapted. Regardless of the instruments' reliability and validity, such information becomes less relevant if the instruments are not valid for the Latino samples under study.

As Table 6.2 shows, for the most part, the instruments used to evaluate anxiety have strong psychometric characteristics in terms of internal consistency and test–retest reliability. The table also presents studies on these measures that provide evidence of convergent validity with other measures of anxiety. We also identified studies that provided evidence of equivalence between the English- and Spanish-language instruments, such as with the Anxiety Sensitivity Index (Peterson & Heilbronner, 1987). Fewer studies were available on the translation and metric equivalence of the instruments.

CONCLUSION AND IMPLICATIONS

Our review of the research on CBT for anxiety with Latinos shows a growing literature that supports its efficacy and effectiveness. Progress has been made: There are now four studies on anxiety conditions that have a 100% Latino sample (Hinton et al., 2011; Olivares & García-López, 2002; Pérez Benítez et al., 2013; Rodríguez Biglieri et al., 2007). Although the sample sizes are relatively small, this finding alone represents progress, given that not a single study on anxiety with adult Latinos was reported in the review by Miranda et al. (2005).

The other eight studies we included in our review had less than 25% Latinos in the sample, ranging from a high of 23.2% to a low of 2%. It is not altogether clear what may be concluded from these studies with regard to efficacy for Latinos. One conclusion may be that CBT works as well for Latinos as for non-Latinos. That seemed to be the case in the large multisite study conducted by Roy-Byrne et al. (2010) that enrolled 1,004 patients with anxiety disorder in a trial of the CALM intervention versus usual care in 17 primary care clinics across four U.S. cities. In all, 194 Latinos participated in the trial. Those in the CALM condition showed significant improvements in anxiety compared with those in the comparison condition. The Barrios (2011) initial substudy was expanded by Chavira et al. (2014) in a careful comparison of Latinos versus non-Latino Whites that received CALM. In all, 85 patients randomized to CALM who selected CBT were Latinos and 285 were non-Latino Whites. The results showed equivalence for both groups, supporting the effectiveness of CBT for Latinos who were probably more acculturated and preferred English.

A question of interest is whether efficacy and effectiveness studies of CBT for anxiety with Latinos in English-language trials that do not attend to issues of diversity, such as language, culture, ethnicity, and discrimination, generalize to Latinos. In the Roy-Byrne et al. (2010) and Chavira et al. (2014) studies, the evidence suggests that CBT does generalize to Latinos. It may be the case that the same is true for the other studies in this review (J. G. Beck et al., 2009; Boden et al., 2012; Bosic, 1981; Goldin et al., 2016; Stanley et al., 2009), although subanalyses were not conducted to answer that question, and in some cases the sample sizes were simply too small to yield meaningful analyses. The caveat here, as Chavira et al. (2014) carefully pointed out, is that effectiveness is probably specific to a more acculturated group of Latinos who are fluent in or prefer English. Thus, in the absence of evidence to the contrary, using EBTs with Latinos for anxiety will likely be beneficial for English-speaking and acculturated Latinos. Although we simply do not know about the efficacy with Spanish-speaking Latinos, we believe that providing an EBT such as CBT is likely to be more beneficial than offering a treatment with no evidence in any population.

There are currently no CBTs that meet the Chambless and Hollon (1998) criteria for well-established treatments for Latinos who are primarily Spanish speaking. We added another criterion[3] that included at least one well-designed study with over 60% Latino participation in the sample. We determined the cutoff point on the basis of a larger set of treatment studies with Latinos in which we found a bimodal frequency distribution with a natural break at about 60% (Bernal et al., in press). No study was identified as well-established for Latinos with anxiety. However, CBT for PTSD was identified as a probably efficacious treatment, and CBT for OCD was identified as a treatment with limited empirical support. Additional studies will be needed to establish CBT as probably efficacious for PTSD and OCD and well-established for Spanish-speaking Latinos.

Cognitive Behavior Therapy Models With Latinos

Roy-Byrne et al. (2010) was the only study in our review reporting the treatment manual used: a computer-assisted treatment (CALM) inspired by an earlier large-scale project on the treatment of depression in primary care settings (Unutzer et al., 2002). CALM was also used by substudies (Chavira et al., 2014; Pérez Benítez et al., 2013) to the parent project. Other studies we examined used a variety of manuals, with two manuals used in the treatment of PTSD (requiring an extensive search of the literature to identify their authors). One was by Pérez Benítez et al. (2013) who based their CBT model for treating PTSD on a manual developed by Marks et al. (1998). The other was by Hinton et al. (2011) who devised a cultural adaptation of the CBT protocol for PTSD based on an earlier study with Vietnamese

---

[3]The criteria are based on those from the Task Force on the Promotion and Dissemination of Psychological Procedures of Division of Clinical Psychology of the American Psychological Association (Chambless, Babich, & Crits-Christoph, 1995), which helps determine whether a treatment may be classified as well-established, probably efficacious, or experimental without sufficient evidence for efficacy. Well-established treatments must have a minimum of two between-group design experiments demonstrating efficacy (statistical superiority over control or pill or psychological placebo or another treatment, equivalence to an established treatment with adequate sample size, or a large number of single case studies demonstrating efficacy). Other related criteria are that studies must be conducted with treatment manuals, the characteristics of the sample must be clearly described, and the effects must be demonstrated by different investigator teams. A probably efficacious treatment is determined by the results of two studies demonstrating statistical superiority to a wait-list control or one or more studies that meet the well-established treatment criteria or a small set of single case studies that meet the well-established treatment criteria.

patients (Hinton et al., 2004). Olivares and García-López (2002) also used and adapted a CBT manual designed by Bados (1991) for the reduction of anxiety about speaking in public. Another study that worked on reducing anxiety was by Rodríguez Biglieri et al. (2007), who based their protocol for CBT on Wells's (2007) approach to metacognitive therapy for anxiety and social phobia. Stanley et al. (2009) developed a CBT manual for use with adults with GAD.

Boden et al. (2012) examined the role of core cognitions or maladaptive beliefs in the context of an RCT for SAD. The manual used was developed by Heimberg et al. (2010). Bosic (1981) examined the effects of relaxation training on anxiety in pregnant women. Specifically, participants in the trial were taught the techniques of progressive relaxation training (Jacobson, 1938) in combination with imagery rehearsal and transcendental meditation following many of the procedures originally suggested by Wolpe (1973). Finally, two studies used group therapy with different manuals. Goldin et al. (2016) used the Heimberg and Becker (2002) protocol for their group CBT for SAD, and J. G. Beck and Coffey (2005) based their group CBT intervention for PTSD on Blanchard et al.'s (2003) individual CBT, adapting it to a group format.

In summary, we found a great deal of cross-fertilization in the use of cognitive and behavioral strategies based on the original behavioral and cognitive approaches (A. T. Beck, 1979; Ellis, 1962; Meichenbaum, 1977; Wolpe, 1973), with a high level of specification of the procedures used.

Measurement of Anxiety

There are at least a dozen different instruments to measure anxiety that have been used with Latinos; this is important progress that advances the science of clinical psychology with diverse populations. Also, for most of the instruments, there are Spanish-language translations with adequate psychometric data that justifies their use with Latinos. However, in eight of the 12 studies, no Spanish-language translations were available and no information was provided on the translation equivalence of the instruments. Also, the measurement models specified in English-language versions of outcome measures are too often not tested on the non–English-speaking population. If the measurement models are not the same, or a fit between models is not achieved, we may have a serious concern about the validity of an instrument because universality was incorrectly assumed. The same issue applies to working with diverse cultural groups that use the same language but have different cultural values and norms. Thus, further work is needed on the equivalence of measurement models for outcome measures of anxiety with diverse populations.

Concluding Comments

Progress has been made in the CBT treatment of anxiety for Latinos. Our review of the literature suggests that EBTs such as CBT are effective for Latinos in a variety of settings. There are now four studies with a 100% Latino sample and eight other studies with varying percentages of Latino participants. Furthermore, there are models of CBT available in individual and group formats, using a variety of cognitive and behavioral procedures, that include a range of procedures and strategies or modalities, such as meta-cognitive therapy, prolonged exposure, MBSR, meditation, relaxation, use of imagery, and so forth, for a wide range of anxiety disorders including personality disorders, GAD, PTSD, SAD, phobias, OCD, and so forth. Although the field has progressed, more work is required to adequately respond to the needs of Latinos given the population estimates for the near future. First, more studies are needed with immigrant Latinos who are primarily Spanish speaking. Such an endeavor would entail substantial work in the selection of instruments that have adequate psychometric properties, with tests of the validity of the measurement models of anxiety for Latino. Second, investigators who plan to include other diverse ethnic and racial populations such as Latinos have to take the necessary steps to carefully examine adequacy of the psychometric properties including tests of metric equivalence. With immigrant Latinos who prefer Spanish, certified Spanish-language translations and bilingual staff would be needed. Third, special efforts have to be made to engage Latinos in treatment. As noted earlier, Latinos are unlikely to obtain EBTs and remain in treatment. Research on engaging and retaining Latinos should be at the top of our agenda.

The degree to which cultural adaptations of CBT are beneficial in improving treatment engagement and outcome with Latinos is an important area of research. We found that four of the 12 studies used some form of cultural adaptation, yet these adaptations were conducted without the use of conceptual frameworks that can inform changes to a protocol while maintaining fidelity to the propositional and procedural models (Bernal & Domenech Rodríguez, 2012). Cultural adaptations of EBTs have growing support from several meta-analyses (Benish, Quintana, & Wampold, 2011; Smith, Rodríguez, & Bernal, 2011; Smith & Trimble, 2016; van Loon, van Schaik, Dekker, & Beekman, 2013).

To conclude, progress has been made in the CBT treatment of anxiety with Latinos. A growing, though modest, number of studies support the use of CBT with first-generation as well as more acculturated Latinos and with Latinos from countries such as Spain and Argentina. In the context of an increasingly multicultural society such as the United States, more work will be needed to further develop, test, and offer state-of-the-art-and-science treatments to Latinos. Adaptations of CBT to the Latino culture are critical to achieving engagement, retention, and beneficial outcomes. We look forward to research that can systematically personalize CBT to be optimally helpful to Latinos and other diverse populations.

REFERENCES

Albert Einstein College of Medicine. (2014). *Study of Hispanic/Latino health presents initial findings.* Retrieved from http://www.einstein.yu.edu/news/releases/980/study-of-hispanic-latino-health-presents-initial-findings/

Alegría, M., Mulvaney-Day, N., Torres, M., Polo, A., Cao, Z., & Canino, G. (2007). Prevalence of psychiatric disorders across Latino subgroups in the United States. *American Journal of Public Health, 97,* 68–75. http://dx.doi.org/10.2105/AJPH.2006.087205

Alegría, M., Vila, D., Woo, M., Canino, G., Takeuchi, D., Vera, M., . . . Shrout, P. (2004). Cultural relevance and equivalence in the NLAAS instrument: Integrating etic and emic in the development of cross-cultural measures for a psychiatric epidemiology and services study of Latinos. *International Journal of Methods in Psychiatric Research, 13,* 270–288. http://dx.doi.org/10.1002/mpr.181

Bados, A. (1991). Tratamiento conductual del miedo a hablar en público [Behavioral treatment of the fear of public speaking]. In G. Buela-Casa & V. Caballo (Eds.), *Manual de Psicología Clínica Aplicada* (pp. 323–343). Madrid, Spain: Siglo XXI.

Barrios, V. (2011). *Improving primary care outcomes for Hispanics with anxiety disorders: A randomized clinical trial evaluating the effectiveness of cognitive-behavioral therapy.* Ann Arbor, MI: ProQuest.

Beck, A. T. (1979). *Cognitive therapy of depression.* New York, NY: Guilford Press.

Beck, J. G., & Coffey, S. F. (2005). Group cognitive behavioral treatment for PTSD: Treatment of motor vehicle accident survivors. *Cognitive and Behavioral Practice, 12,* 267–277. http://dx.doi.org/10.1016/S1077-7229(05)80049-5

Beck, J. G., Coffey, S. F., Foy, D. W., Keane, T. M., & Blanchard, E. B. (2009). Group cognitive behavior therapy for chronic posttraumatic stress disorder: An initial randomized pilot study. *Behavior Therapy, 40,* 82–92. http://dx.doi.org/10.1016/j.beth.2008.01.003

Benish, S. G., Quintana, S., & Wampold, B. E. (2011). Culturally adapted psychotherapy and the legitimacy of myth: A direct-comparison meta-analysis. *Journal of Counseling Psychology, 58,* 279–289. http://dx.doi.org/10.1037/a0023626

Bernal, G., Adames, C., Rodriguez-Quintana, N., Almonte, M., Yusif, N., & Delgado, J. (in press). State of the science on the psychological treatment of adult Latinos with depression: A systematic review of the literature. In F. T. L. Leong, G. Bernal, & N. T. Buchanan (Eds.), *Clinical psychology of diverse racial and ethnocultural groups.* Washington, DC: American Psychological Association.

Bernal, G., Bonilla, J., & Bellido, C. (1995). Ecological validity and cultural sensitivity for outcome research: Issues for the cultural adaptation and development of psychosocial treatments with Hispanics. *Journal of Abnormal Child Psychology, 23*, 67–82. http://dx.doi.org/10.1007/BF01447045

Bernal, G., & Domenech Rodríguez, M. M. (Eds.). (2012). *Cultural adaptations: Tools for evidence-based practice with diverse populations.* Washington, DC: American Psychological Association. http://dx.doi.org/10.1037/13752-000

Bernal, G., Jiménez-Chafey, M. I., & Domenech Rodríguez, M. M. (2009). Cultural adaptation of treatments: A resource for considering culture in evidence-based practice. *Professional Psychology: Research and Practice, 40*, 361–368. http://dx.doi.org/10.1037/a0016401

Bernal, G., & Scharró-del-Río, M. R. (2001). Are empirically supported treatments valid for ethnic minorities? Toward an alternative approach for treatment research. *Cultural Diversity and Ethnic Minority Psychology, 7*, 328–342. http://dx.doi.org/10.1037/1099-9809.7.4.328

Blanchard, E. B., Hickling, E. J., Devineni, T., Veazey, C. H., Galovski, T. E., Mundy, E., . . . Buckley, T. C. (2003). A controlled evaluation of cognitive behavioral therapy for posttraumatic stress in motor vehicle accident survivors. *Behaviour Research and Therapy, 41*, 79–96.

Boden, M. T., John, O. P., Goldin, P. R., Werner, K., Heimberg, R. G., & Gross, J. J. (2012). The role of maladaptive beliefs in cognitive-behavioral therapy: Evidence from social anxiety disorder. *Behaviour Research and Therapy, 50*, 287–291. http://dx.doi.org/10.1016/j.brat.2012.02.007

Bosic, D. J. (1981). *Effect of relaxation training on anxiety manifestations displayed by pregnant women* (Doctoral dissertation). Available from ProQuest Dissertations and Theses database. (UMI No. 8114735)

Bravo, M. (2003). Instrument development: Cultural adaptations for ethnic minority research. In G. Bernal, J. E. Trimble, A. K. Burlew, & F. T. L. Leong (Eds.), *Handbook of racial and ethnic minority psychology* (pp. 220–236). Thousand Oaks, CA: Sage. http://dx.doi.org/10.4135/9781412976008.n12

Brislin, R. W. (1976). Comparative research methodology: Cross-cultural studies. *International Journal of Psychology, 11*, 215–229. http://dx.doi.org/10.1080/00207597608247359

Bullinger, M., Anderson, R., Cella, D., & Aaronson, N. (1993). Developing and evaluating cross-cultural instruments from minimum requirements to optimal models. *Quality of Life Research, 2*, 451–459. http://dx.doi.org/10.1007/BF00422219

Canino, G., & Bravo, M. (1999). The translation and adaptation of diagnostic instruments for cross-cultural use. In D. Shaffer, C. P. Lucas, & J. E. Richters (Eds.), *Diagnostic assessment in child and adolescent psychopathology* (pp. 285–298). New York, NY: Guilford Press.

Chambless, D. L., Babich, K., & Crits-Christoph, P. (1995). Training in and dissemination of empirically-validated psychological treatments: Report and recommendations. *Clinical Psychologist, 48*, 3–24.

Chambless, D. L., & Hollon, S. D. (1998). Defining empirically supported therapies. *Journal of Consulting and Clinical Psychology, 66*, 7–18. http://dx.doi.org/
10.1037/0022-006X.66.1.7

Chávez, L. M., & Canino, G. (2005). *Toolkit on translating and adapting instruments*. Retrieved from https://www.hsri.org/files/uploads/publications/PN54_
Translating_and_Adapting.pdf

Chavira, D. A., Golinelli, D., Sherbourne, C., Stein, M. B., Sullivan, G., Bystritsky,
A., . . . Craske, M. (2014). Treatment engagement and response to CBT among
Latinos with anxiety disorders in primary care. *Journal of Consulting and Clinical
Psychology, 82*, 392–403. http://dx.doi.org/10.1037/a0036365

Cohen, R. A., & Martinez, M. E. (2012). *Health insurance coverage: Early release
of estimates from the National Health Interview Survey, January–March 2012*.
Atlanta, GA: Centers for Disease Control and Prevention.

Comas-Díaz, L. (2012). *Multicultural care: A clinician's guide to cultural competence*.
Washington, DC: American Psychological Association. http://dx.doi.org/
10.1037/13491-000

Daza, P., Novy, D. M., Stanley, M. A., & Averill, P. (2002). The Depression Anxiety
Stress Scale–21: Spanish translation and validation with a Hispanic sample.
Journal of Psychopathology and Behavioral Assessment, 24, 195–205.

Dour, H. J., Wiley, J. F., Roy-Byrne, P., Stein, M. B., Sullivan, G., Sherbourne,
C. D., . . . Craske, M. G. (2014). Perceived social support mediates anxiety
and depressive symptom changes following primary care intervention. *Depression and Anxiety, 31*, 436–442. http://dx.doi.org/10.1002/da.22216

Ellis, A. (1962). *Reason and emotion in psychotherapy*. Oxford, England: Lyle Stuart.

Falsetti, S. A., & Resnick, H. S. (2000). Treatment of PTSD using cognitive and
cognitive behavioral therapies. *Journal of Cognitive Psychotherapy, 14*, 261–285.

Foa, E. B., & Rothbaum, B. O. (1998). *Treating the trauma of rape: Cognitive-behavioral
therapy for PTSD*. New York, NY: Guilford Press.

Foa, E. B., & Rothbaum, B. O. (2001). *Treating the trauma of rape: Cognitive-behavioral
therapy for PTSD*. New York, NY: Guilford Press.

Geisinger, K. F. (1994). Cross-cultural normative assessment: Translation and
adaptation issues influencing the normative interpretation of assessment
instruments. *Psychological Assessment, 6*, 304–312. http://dx.doi.org/10.1037/
1040-3590.6.4.304

Goldin, P. R., Morrison, A., Jazaieri, H., Brozovich, F., Heimberg, R., & Gross, J. J.
(2016). Group CBT versus MBSR for social anxiety disorder: A randomized
controlled trial. *Journal of Consulting and Clinical Psychology, 84*, 427–437. http://
dx.doi.org/10.1037/ccp0000092

Hall, G. C. N. (2001). Psychotherapy research with ethnic minorities: Empirical,
ethical, and conceptual issues. *Journal of Consulting and Clinical Psychology, 69*,
502–510. http://dx.doi.org/10.1037/0022-006X.69.3.502

Heimberg, R. G., & Becker, R. E. (2002). *Cognitive-behavioral group therapy for social
phobia: Basic mechanisms and clinical strategies*. New York, NY: Guilford Press.

Heimberg, R. G., Brozovich, F. A., & Rapee, R. M. (2010). A cognitive-behavioral model of social anxiety disorder: Update and extension. *Social anxiety: Clinical, developmental, and social perspectives, 2*, 395–422.

Hinton, D. E., Hofmann, S. G., Rivera, E., Otto, M. W., & Pollack, M. H. (2011). Culturally adapted CBT (CA-CBT) for Latino women with treatment-resistant PTSD: A pilot study comparing CA-CBT to applied muscle relaxation. *Behaviour Research and Therapy, 49*, 275–280. http://dx.doi.org/10.1016/j.brat.2011.01.005

Hinton, D. E., Pham, T., Tran, M., Safren, S. A., Otto, M. W., & Pollack, M. H. (2004). CBT for Vietnamese refugees with treatment-resistant PTSD and panic attacks: A pilot study. *Journal of Traumatic Stress, 17*, 429–433. http://dx.doi.org/10.1023/B:JOTS.0000048956.03529.fa

Hofmann, S. G., & Smits, J. A. (2008). Cognitive-behavioral therapy for adult anxiety disorders: A meta-analysis of randomized placebo-controlled trials. *The Journal of Clinical Psychiatry, 69*, 621–632. http://dx.doi.org/10.4088/JCP.v69n0415

Hope, D. A., Heimberg, R. G., Juster, H. R., & Turk, C. L. (2006). *Managing social anxiety: A cognitive-behavioral therapy approach: Therapist guide.* New York, NY: Oxford University Press.

Jacobson, E. (1938). *Progressive relaxation.* Chicago, IL: University of Chicago Press.

Jones, P. S., Lee, J. W., Phillips, L. R., Zhang, X. E., & Jaceldo, K. B. (2001). An adaptation of Brislin's translation model for cross-cultural research. *Nursing Research, 50*, 300–304. http://dx.doi.org/10.1097/00006199-200109000-00008

Kleinman, A., Eisenberg, L., & Good, B. (1978). Culture, illness, and care: Clinical lessons from anthropologic and cross-cultural research. *Annals of Internal Medicine, 88*, 251–258. http://dx.doi.org/10.7326/0003-4819-88-2-251

La Roche, M. J. (2012). *Cultural psychotherapy: Theory, methods, and practice.* Thousand Oaks, CA: Sage.

Lau, A. S., Chang, D. F., Okazaki, S., & Bernal, G. (2016). Psychotherapy research with ethnic minorities: What is the research agenda? In N. W. S. Zane, G. Bernal, & F. T. L. Leong (Eds.), *Evidence-based psychological practice with ethnic minorities: Culturally informed research and clinical strategies* (pp. 31–53). Washington, DC: American Psychological Association.

Leong, F. T. L., Leung, K., & Cheung, F. M. (2010). Integrating cross-cultural psychology research methods into ethnic minority psychology. *Cultural Diversity and Ethnic Minority Psychology, 16*, 590–597. http://dx.doi.org/10.1037/a0020127

Livanis, A., & Tryon, G. S. (2010). The development of the Adolescent Nervios Scale: Preliminary findings. *Cultural Diversity and Ethnic Minority Psychology, 16*, 9–15. http://dx.doi.org/10.1037/a0014905

Mak, W. W., Law, R. W., Alvidrez, J., & Pérez-Stable, E. J. (2007). Gender and ethnic diversity in NIMH-funded clinical trials: Review of a decade of published research. *Administration and Policy in Mental Health and Mental Health Services Research, 34*, 497–503. http://dx.doi.org/10.1007/s10488-007-0133-z

Marks, I., Lovell, K., Noshirvani, H., Livanou, M., & Thrasher, S. (1998). Treatment of posttraumatic stress disorder by exposure and/or cognitive restructuring: A controlled study. *Archives of General Psychiatry, 55*, 317–325. http://dx.doi.org/10.1001/archpsyc.55.4.317

Martinez, S., Stillerman, L., & Waldo, M. (2005). Reliability and validity of the SCL-90-R with Hispanic college students. *Hispanic Journal of Behavioral Sciences, 27*, 254–264. http://dx.doi.org/10.1177/0739986305274911

Meichenbaum, D. (1977). Cognitive behaviour modification. *Cognitive Behaviour Therapy, 6*, 185–192.

Miranda, J., Bernal, G., Lau, A., Kohn, L., Hwang, W. C., & LaFromboise, T. (2005). State of the science on psychosocial interventions for ethnic minorities. *Annual Review of Clinical Psychology, 1*, 113–142. http://dx.doi.org/10.1146/annurev.clinpsy.1.102803.143822

Norton, P. J. (2007). Depression Anxiety and Stress Scales (DASS-21): Psychometric analysis across four racial groups. *Anxiety, stress, and coping, 20*, 253–265. http://dx.doi.org/10.1080/10615800701309279

Office of the Surgeon General, Center for Mental Health Services, & National Institute of Mental Health. (2001). *Mental health: Culture, race, and ethnicity: A supplement to* Mental Health: A Report of the Surgeon General. Retrieved from http://www.ncbi.nlm.nih.gov/books/NBK44243/

Olatunji, B. O., Cisler, J. M., & Deacon, B. J. (2010). Efficacy of cognitive behavioral therapy for anxiety disorders: A review of meta-analytic findings. *Psychiatric Clinics of North America, 33*, 557–577. http://dx.doi.org/10.1016/j.psc.2010.04.002

Olivares, J., & García-López, L. J. (2002). Resultados a largo plazo de un tratamiento en grupo para el miedo a hablar en público [Long-term follow-up of group treatment of fear of speaking in public]. *Psicothema, 14*, 405–409.

Pérez Benítez, C. I., Zlotnick, C., Gomez, J., Rendón, M. J., & Swanson, A. (2013). Cognitive behavioral therapy for PTSD and somatization: An open trial. *Behaviour Research and Therapy, 51*, 284–289. http://dx.doi.org/10.1016/j.brat.2013.02.005

Peterson, R. A., & Heilbronner, R. L. (1987). The Anxiety Sensitivity Index: Construct validity and factor analytic structure. *Journal of Anxiety Disorders, 1*, 117–121. http://dx.doi.org/10.1016/0887-6185(87)90002-8

Rachman, S. (1980). Emotional processing. *Behaviour Research and Therapy, 24*, 685–688.

Resick, P. A., & Schnicke, M. (1993). *Cognitive processing therapy for rape victims: A treatment manual* (Vol. 4). Thousand Oaks, CA: Sage.

Rodríguez Biglieri, R., Vetere, G., & Keegan, E. (2007). Resultados del seguimiento de pacientes con Trastorno Obsesivo Compulsivo tratados con dos variantes de Terapia Cognitiva [Follow-up of patients with obsessive compulsive disorder treated with two variants of cognitive therapy]. *Anuario de investigaciones, 14*. Retrieved from http://www.scielo.org.ar/scielo.php?script=sci_arttext&pid=S1851-16862007000100003&nrm=iso

Roy-Byrne, P., Craske, M. G., Sullivan, G., Rose, R. D., Edlund, M. J., Lang, A. J., . . . Stein, M. B. (2010, May 19). Delivery of evidence-based treatment for multiple anxiety disorders in primary care: A randomized controlled trial. *JAMA*, *303*(19), 1921–1928. http://dx.doi.org/10.1001/jama.2010.608

Ryan, R., Hill, S., Prictor, M., & McKenzie, J. (2013). *Cochrane Consumers and Communication Review Group study quality guide: Guide for review authors on assessing study quality*. Retrieved from https://cccrg.cochrane.org/sites/cccrg.cochrane.org/files/public/uploads/StudyQualityGuide_May%202013.pdf

Segura Camacho, S., Posada Gómez, S., Ospina, M. L., & Ospina Gómez, H. A. (2010). Estandarización del Inventario CDI en niños y adolescente entre 12 y 17 años de edad, del Municipio de Sabaneta del Departamento de Antioquia-Colombia [Inventory Standardization of Children Depression scale for adolescents aged 12 and 17 years of age, the Municipality of Sabaneta, Department Antioquia, Colombia]. *International Journal of Psychological Research*, *3*, 63–73.

Smith, T. B., Rodríguez, M. D., & Bernal, G. (2011). Culture. *Journal of Clinical Psychology*, *67*, 166–175. http://dx.doi.org/10.1002/jclp.20757

Smith, T. B., & Trimble, J. E. (2016). Culturally adapted mental health services: An updated meta-analysis of client outcomes. In T. B. Smith & J. E. Trimble (Eds.), *Foundations of multicultural psychology: Research to inform effective practice* (pp. 129–144). Washington, DC: American Psychological Association. http://dx.doi.org/10.1037/14733-007

Sousa, V. D., & Rojjanasrirat, W. (2011). Translation, adaptation and validation of instruments or scales for use in cross-cultural health care research: A clear and user-friendly guideline. *Journal of Evaluation in Clinical Practice*, *17*, 268–274. http://dx.doi.org/10.1111/j.1365-2753.2010.01434.x

Stanley, M. A., Wilson, N. L., Novy, D. M., Rhoades, H. M., Wagener, P. D., Greisinger, A. J., . . . Kunik, M. E. (2009, April 8). Cognitive behavior therapy for generalized anxiety disorder among older adults in primary care: A randomized clinical trial. *JAMA*, *301*, 1460–1467. http://dx.doi.org/10.1001/jama.2009.458

Stewart, R. E., & Chambless, D. L. (2009). Cognitive-behavioral therapy for adult anxiety disorders in clinical practice: A meta-analysis of effectiveness studies. *Journal of Consulting and Clinical Psychology*, *77*, 595–606. http://dx.doi.org/10.1037/a0016032

Sue, S. (1999). Science, ethnicity, and bias: Where have we gone wrong? *American Psychologist*, *54*, 1070–1077. http://dx.doi.org/10.1037/0003-066X.54.12.1070

Unützer, J., Katon, W., Callahan, C. M., Williams, J. W., Jr., Hunkeler, E., Harpole, L., . . . Langston, C. (2002, December 11). Collaborative care management of late-life depression in the primary care setting: A randomized controlled trial. *JAMA*, *288*, 2836–2845. http://dx.doi.org/10.1001/jama.288.22.2836

van de Vijver, F. J., & Leung, K. (1997). *Methods and data analysis for cross-cultural research* (Vol. 1). Thousand Oaks, CA: Sage.

van Loon, A., van Schaik, A., Dekker, J., & Beekman, A. (2013). Bridging the gap for ethnic minority adult outpatients with depression and anxiety disorders by culturally adapted treatments. *Journal of Affective Disorders, 147*, 9–16. http://dx.doi.org/10.1016/j.jad.2012.12.014

van Tulder, M., Furlan, A., Bombardier, C., & Bouter, L. (2003). Updated method guidelines for systematic reviews in the Cochrane Collaboration Back Review Group. *Spine, 28*, 1290–1299. http://dx.doi.org/10.1097/01.BRS.0000065484.95996.AF

Ward, B. W., Schiller, J., Freeman, G., & Peregoy, J. (2013). *Early release of selected estimates based on data from the 2012 National Health Interview Survey.* National Center for Health Statistics. Retrieved from https://www.cdc.gov/nchs/nhis/index.htm

Wassertheil-Smoller, S., Arredondo, E. M., Cai, J., Castaneda, S. F., Choca, J. P., Gallo, L. C., . . . Zee, P. C. (2014). Depression, anxiety, antidepressant use, and cardiovascular disease among Hispanic men and women of different national backgrounds: Results from the Hispanic Community Health Study/Study of Latinos. *Annals of Epidemiology, 24*, 822–830. http://dx.doi.org/10.1016/j.annepidem.2014.09.003

Weisz, J. R., Doss, A. J., & Hawley, K. M. (2005). Youth psychotherapy outcome research: A review and critique of the evidence base. *Annual Review of Psychology, 56*, 337–363. http://dx.doi.org/10.1146/annurev.psych.55.090902.141449

Weisz, J. R., & Hawley, K. M. (1998). Finding, evaluating, refining, and applying empirically supported treatments for children and adolescents. *Journal of Clinical Child Psychology, 27*, 206–216. http://dx.doi.org/10.1207/s15374424jccp2702_7

Wells, A. (2007). Cognition about cognition: Metacognitive therapy and change in generalized anxiety disorder and social phobia. *Cognitive and Behavioral Practice, 14*, 18–25. http://dx.doi.org/10.1016/j.cbpra.2006.01.005

Wolpe, J. (1973). *The practice of behavior therapy.* Oxford, England: Pergamon.

Woodward, A. T., Taylor, R. J., Bullard, K. M., Aranda, M. P., Lincoln, K. D., & Chatters, L. M. (2012). Prevalence of lifetime *DSM–IV* affective disorders among older African Americans, Black Caribbeans, Latinos, Asians and non-Hispanic White people. *International Journal of Geriatric Psychiatry, 27*, 816–827. http://dx.doi.org/10.1002/gps.2790

7

COGNITIVE BEHAVIORAL MODELS, MEASURES, AND TREATMENTS FOR ANXIETY DISORDERS IN AFRICAN AMERICANS

MICHELE M. CARTER AND TRACY SBROCCO

There is a substantial history of cognitive behavioral theory about and therapy for anxiety. A basic cognitive model has established the role of cognitive processes in the genesis, exacerbation, and treatment of anxiety disorders. Although there can be no doubt about the significance of cognitive processes in anxiety and related conditions, the literature, in large part, has not extended to African Americans with anxiety disorders. The underlying assumption has been that work establishing cognitive behavioral frameworks as central to the anxiety disorders would be uniformly applicable across cultures. However, in the last decade, there has been mounting evidence that the study of anxiety among African Americans may necessitate modification with respect to measurement and treatment. Several recent studies have found that common measures of anxiety developed from a cognitive framework and validated among non-Hispanic Caucasians are not culturally equivalent psychometrically in the measurement of anxiety among African Americans.

http://dx.doi.org/10.1037/0000091-008
Treating Depression, Anxiety, and Stress in Ethnic and Racial Groups: Cognitive Behavioral Approaches, E. C. Chang, C. A. Downey, J. K. Hirsch, and E. A. Yu (Editors)
Copyright © 2018 by the American Psychological Association. All rights reserved.

There is also a body of literature indicating that efficacy of treatment may be different between African Americans and non-Hispanic Caucasians. It has been posited that part of the difficulty that exists in measuring and treating African Americans is that cultural factors in the conceptualization of anxiety have traditionally been ignored. Specifically, research has often ignored the influence of ethnic identity and culture on the measurement of anxiety, as well as the role of cultural sensitivity in the treatment of African Americans. This has led several researchers to posit cognitively based theoretical models that allow one to explore and predict where differences might be expected among African Americans with anxiety disorders.

In this chapter, we begin with a basic cognitive model of anxiety and then present models that were developed specifically for African Americans with anxiety disorders. We then review the extant literature addressing the measurement of anxiety and discuss the implications of cultural equivalence at the level of symptom and syndromal measurement, as well as at the level of psychological constructs. We also review the scant treatment literature and discuss outcomes from standard cognitive behavioral treatments, as well as novel, more culturally specific approaches to treatment. Finally, we discuss the directions we believe are most important to continue to push forward in evaluating, measuring, and treating anxiety disorders among African Americans.

ANXIETY AND ANXIETY DISORDERS

From a cognitive perspective, anxiety consists of three core components. First is the physical symptoms experienced. Typically, these are symptoms of autonomic hyperarousal and may include heart racing, sweating, shortness of breath, and trembling. The second component is negative cognitions. Cognitive symptoms may include thoughts of impending doom—for example, "I might have a heart attack" or "Others will think I am stupid." The third component is behavioral and prototypically involves either escape or avoidance of situations associated with the anxiety.

The *Diagnostic and Statistical Manual of Mental Disorders* (DSM; fifth ed., American Psychiatric Association, 2013) classifies disorders that share the overarching features of excessive fear, anxiety, and behavioral manifestations (e.g., avoidance) as anxiety disorders. In general, the anxiety experienced is substantially more intense than anxiety experienced by non-anxiety disordered individuals. Studies have found differences in the prevalence rates of anxiety disorders among African Americans (Asnaani, Richey, Dimaite, Hinton, & Hofmann, 2010; Himle, Baser, Taylor, Campbell, & Jackson, 2009). Asnaani and colleagues (2010) found that African Americans more often met diagnostic criteria for posttraumatic stress disorder (PTSD; no longer listed as an anxiety disorder in *DSM–5*) and less often met criteria for generalized anxiety disorder (GAD), panic disorder, and social anxiety disorder compared with their non-Hispanic Caucasian counterparts. Himle and colleagues (2009) also found that African Americans more often met criteria for PTSD than either non-Hispanic Caucasians or Caribbean Blacks. They also noted that when African Americans and Caribbean Blacks met criteria for an anxiety disorder, they reported higher illness severity and functional impairment than non-Hispanic Caucasians. Although there are several theories put forth to account for the development of the anxiety disorders, few have garnered the empirical support the cognitive behavioral model has.

COGNITIVE BEHAVIORAL MODEL OF ANXIETY

Several theorists have put forth cognitive behavioral models for the development of anxiety disorders (Barlow, 2002; Beck, 1970; Beck & Clark, 1997; Carter, Forys, & Oswald, 2008). Although the specifics of each model vary somewhat, the basic tenet is consistent across theorists and emphasizes the role cognitions play in the genesis of anxiety. A basic cognitive behavioral model holds that one's thoughts serve as a mediator between a person and their reaction to external situations. Consider the example of a socially anxious individual, as depicted in Figure 7.1. In this case, the person would have an underlying tendency to view the world (in general) and social interactions (in particular) as threatening. The vulnerable person then experiences an activating event (e.g., a mildly negative comment about his or her appearance)—for example, a colleague who comments, "I don't think I would have picked that color for you" in response to a new piece of clothing the vulnerable person is wearing. The anxiety-prone person may then have an initial negative thought that produces heightened physiological reactivity. Recognition of those symptoms may serve as evidence something is wrong with their appearance and produce catastrophic thoughts such as "I look like a fool" or "Everyone is going to reject me." The consequence of these thoughts would be to escape the situation, if possible, or change behaviors (e.g., avoiding coworkers at lunch, carefully controlling attire). The key in this model is the negative interpretation the person initially makes and the subsequent catastrophic thoughts that occur. In the absence of such problematic thoughts, the cognitive behavioral model posits that any anxiety experienced would have been greatly attenuated or eliminated altogether. Although there is ample evidence supporting the role of cognitions in anxiety disorders, only recently have researchers explored the utility of this model in reference to African Americans.

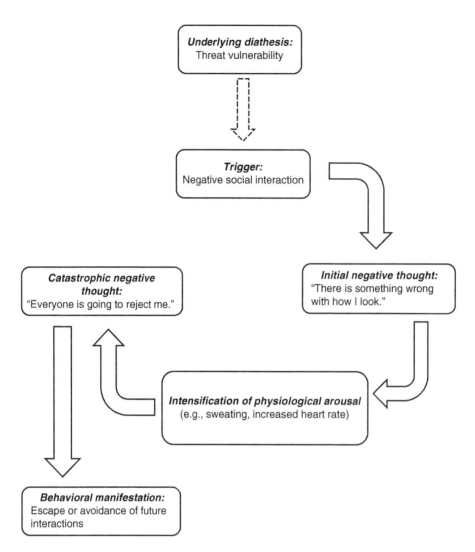

Figure 7.1. Basic cognitive model.

Ethnic-Specific Model of Anxiety

There have been attempts to expand on the basic cognitive model to include the influence of culture in the expression of anxiety. One put forth by Carter, Sbrocco, and Carter (1996) proposed that the slow and inconsistent findings addressing African American anxiety research and treatment were partly based on the absence of an ethnic-specific theoretical framework. Building on the work of Neal and Turner (1991), the authors proposed that there was mounting evidence that African Americans may present with different anxiety symptoms than non-Hispanic Caucasians. They proposed that this is partly due to diagnostic constructs being misapplied or being in-appropriate for African Americans. The authors pointed to the occurrence of isolated sleep paralysis (ISP) as an example. ISP is a condition characterized by a brief period of paralysis either before falling asleep or awakening. Although ISP occurs in both African Americans and non-Hispanic Caucasians, it has been found to occur more frequently among African Americans who experience anxiety disorders, most notably panic disorder (Bell, Dixie-Bell, & Thompson, 1986; Paradis, Friedman, & Hatch, 1997). Carter and colleagues (1996) also suggested that an incomplete cultural conceptualization of anxiety would contribute to the differential attrition and treatment response noted between African Americans and non-Hispanic Caucasians.

Carter et al. (1996) asserted that most research addressed anxiety among African Americans with a static, nondynamic definition of ethnicity. They proposed that ethnicity is a multifaceted variable that consists of ethnic identification and acculturation, each considered quasiorthogonal from the other. They posited that ethnic identity would affect the presentation of symptoms, beliefs about the meaning of those symptoms, and expectations about the best method to address problematic anxiety symptoms. For example, a person with a strong ethnic identity may tend to believe anxious symptoms result from coexisting medical conditions because it is common in African American culture to attribute symptoms to physiological causes. In this case, one may be more likely to believe that anxious symptoms represent an underlying physiological problem and think, "My father had heart problems, so I might too." This belief would then influence the reporting of those symptoms (perhaps not recognizing they are a product of anxiety), as well as the management of them (e.g., do nothing, consult one's physician). Ethnic identity is also thought to influence treatment seeking. If one strongly identifies with African American culture, one may have less trust in Western treatment approaches and, consequently, be more likely to seek alternative sources or to drop out of treatment altogether. Acculturation is considered a moderator variable that may attenuate or exacerbate the influence of racial identity.

Hunter and Schmidt (2010) put forth a related model. In their sociocultural approach, the authors specified variables that could influence the expression of anxiety symptoms among African Americans. Although the overarching cognitive model of anxiety is likely accurate, contextual factors can have a strong influence in distinguishing the specific perceptions of threat that give rise to anxiety. That is, the authors postulated that what one learns to fear, how one interprets symptoms, and where he or she seeks treatment are inextricably linked to the concept of ethnicity, particularly as outlined by Carter and colleagues (1996). In other words, ethnicity matters. Three specific variables were highlighted as being most influential. One is awareness of racism. Hunter and Schmidt noted that most African Americans are aware of the poignant history of African Americans in the United States, which creates negative emotional and psychological consequences in their daily lives (e.g., racial stress) and engenders mistrust in science in general. Although this awareness is considered adaptive in some circumstances, it affects where one seeks treatment for anxiety-related issues. Awareness of racism can be conceptualized as a proximal variable related to ethnic and racial identity (Carter et al., 1996).

The second variable is salience of physical symptoms. In the African American community, it is commonly known that there are health problems particular to African Americans (e.g., Type 2 diabetes mellitus, hypertension, cardiovascular disease). Hunter and Schmidt (2010) proposed that the tendency to attribute somatic sensations (perhaps from anxiety) to physical causes has the potential to contribute to misdiagnoses and the tendency to report to their primary care physician rather than to a mental health care provider. Because the symptoms of anxiety common to African Americans overlap with the symptoms of physical disorders, it is reasonable to expect some misinterpretation about the meaning of the symptoms. Further, it is noted in this model that the salience of physical symptoms could contribute to the catastrophic misinterpretation of symptoms that a cognitive model of anxiety would consider central to the genesis of anxiety.

The third component is the stigma associated with mental illness. Although stigma is not uncommon for many groups, it may be particularly problematic for African Americans given the mistrust issue discussed earlier. Stigma may have a direct effect on self-disclosure, treatment seeking, or attrition. Hunter and Schmidt (2010) further stated that specific disorders such as social and generalized anxiety might be particularly problematic because these concerns may be related to the daily threat of living as a member of a minority group. It is important to note that this model (like the Carter et al., 1996, model) emphasizes the important role that racial stress and protective factors such as extended family support can have on the expression of anxiety.

It should be noted that the concepts of family and family support have been depicted as particularly important for African Americans (Sue & Sue, 2013). Typically, the family structure is characterized as headed by single parents. Nonetheless, the support from the family comes not only from the parents but also from extended kinship relationships. In addition, the African American family has been described as consisting of warmth and emphasizing discipline. Although strict and protective parenting has typically been associated with elevated anxiety among non-Hispanic Caucasians, it has been found to negatively correlate with anxiety and depression among African Americans (Carter, Sbrocco, Lewis, & Friedman, 2001).

Although the models put forth by Carter et al. (1996) and Hunter and Schmidt (2010) hold explanatory value with respect to anxiety among

African Americans, neither is conceptualized as inconsistent with a cognitive model of anxiety. The types of negative thoughts believed to be causal in the genesis of anxiety are likely still influential for African Americans. These models are simply specifying the ethnic and sociocultural factors that influence the interpretation of anxiety. In this light, they both serve to extend the cognitive model by incorporating variables thought to moderate the interpretive bias commonly found among those who have anxiety disorders. As shown in Figure 7.2 (it should be noted that the dotted lines indicate where cultural

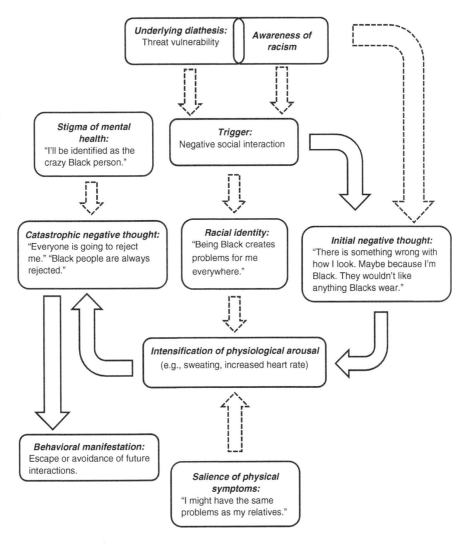

Figure 7.2. Cognitive model adjusted for African Americans.

variables can modify the traditional cognitive model), one can conceive of racial awareness serving as both an underlying diathesis that has the potential to influence the interpretation of any given social situation and as a direct cause of initial negative thoughts. An example of the threat vulnerability may be related to an ethnic-specific variable such as stereotype threat (Steele & Aronson, 1995). African Americans may be at risk of confirming the negative beliefs espoused in the larger society and, consequently, be primed to trigger a negative social interaction, for example. In this case the original negative thought might also be accompanied by additional thoughts such as, "This might be because I'm Black." This will consequently further increase the anxiety, including physiological arousal, an African American may feel in that situation beyond that experienced by non-Hispanic Caucasians. For some African Americans, a strong racial identity (also depicted in Figure 7.2) also affects the meaning of the interpretation of physical symptoms. For some, increased nervousness regarding the social situation is heightened when combined with the expected deleterious effects of unexplained physiological arousal. This further intensifies the anxiety experience. Finally, the additional stigma of experiencing psychological issues is likely to enhance catastrophic negative thoughts in African Americans.

As can be seen in Figure 7.2, the overall cognitive model remains intact and is still quite viable for Africans Americans but may simply require further specification. Combining the Carter et al. (1996) and Hunter and Schmidt (2010) models with a cognitive model has the potential to accomplish a few major goals. One is that it explains how a cognitive behavioral framework may still be relevant with African Americans. Second, the addition of cultural variables may help explain some inconsistent findings in the treatment outcome literature (discussed next). It seems reasonable to presume that ignoring the role of sociocultural factors in the expression of anxiety in typical treatment outcome studies would result in lower treatment efficacy. Third, the inclusion of African American cultural variables in the cognitive understanding of anxiety disorders may also explain why some common measures of anxiety have been found not to be culturally equivalent with African Americans. Because researchers have not typically taken these issues into account in scale development, it cannot be surprising that some scales do not accurately capture anxiety among African Americans.

MEASURING ANXIETY IN AFRICAN AMERICANS

The psychometric properties of several of the more common measures of anxiety have been examined with African Americans. The measurement devices can be largely grouped into general measures and disorder-specific measures. The former are measures that assess anxiety generally, whereas the latter are measures that have been linked to a specific variant of one of the anxiety disorders.

General Anxiety Measures

The Positive and Negative Affect Schedule–Expanded Form (PANAS-X) is a widely used measure of general distress and has been used to assess general anxiety with African Americans. Petrie, Chapman, and Vines (2013) administered the PANAS-X to a community sample of African American females. The results from their receiver operating characteristic analysis indicated that both positive and negative affect accurately predicted social anxiety disorder when compared with diagnoses assigned through a structured clinical interview. The authors noted that the PANAS-X might be a sound screening device for anxiety disorders among African American females.

Chapman, Williams, Mast, and Woodruff-Borden (2009) investigated the psychometric properties of the Beck Anxiety Inventory (BAI; Beck, Epstein, Brown, & Steer, 1988) among a sample of African Americans and non-Hispanic Caucasians. The authors reported that a confirmatory factor analysis (CFA) indicated that the original two-factor (somatic and subjective anxiety) solution was not a good fit for either population. Follow-up factor analyses indicated that a revised scale consisting of 19 rather than 21 items (with additional item changes) produced the best fit for the data from both groups. It was also reported that both groups tended to report anxiety with more somatic than cognitive complaints. This study suggests ethnic equivalence for this particular scale and indicates that the BAI may also be a useful screening tool for anxiety among African Americans.

Disorder-Specific Measures

Although there are a number of measures designed to assess a particular type of anxiety disorder, comparatively few have been evaluated with an African American population or guided by theory relevant for African Americans. Currently, measures assessing the concept of worry, social anxiety, panic, and specific phobia have been evaluated for cultural equivalence with African Americans.

Worry

Worry, a central feature of GAD, is most commonly assessed using the Penn State Worry Questionnaire (PSWQ; Meyer, Miller, Metzger, & Borkovec, 1990). In evaluating the original version of this scale, Carter and colleagues (2005) conducted a multigroup CFA between African American and non-Hispanic Caucasian college students. The authors found evidence consistent with previous studies that the affirmative items of the PSWQ all loaded onto a single factor for both groups. A discrepancy was noted, however, in the factor structure of the negatively worded items. For African Americans, there was evidence of two factors (compared with one factor for non-Hispanic Caucasians). Furthermore, African Americans scored significantly lower on the PSWQ than non-Hispanic Caucasians. Similarly, DeLapp, Chapman, and Williams (2016) evaluated a shortened version of the PSWQ that contains only the affirmative items and reported invariance between African Americans and European Americans. The data from these two investigations suggest the concept of worry, though perhaps not worry absence or dismissal, is adequately captured in the PSWQ. It should be noted, however, that Hambrick et al. (2010) found evidence that the PSWQ might fail to detect differences in worry in nonclinical samples of African Americans.

Social Anxiety

Evidence regarding measures designed to assess the construct of social anxiety is less consistent. For example, Hambrick and colleagues (2010) examined the ethnic equivalence of the Social Interaction Anxiety Scale (SIAS; Mattick & Clarke, 1998) among African Americans and non-Hispanic Caucasians. The authors reported the overall factor structure to be comparable across groups. Further analysis, however, indicated that three items less effectively differentiated between African American and non-Hispanic Caucasian respondents. In addition, they noted that African Americans were more likely to report greater pathology than their non-Hispanic counterparts. The authors concluded that use of the SIAS could lead to biased conclusions in interethnic comparisons.

Relatedly, Carter, Sbrocco, Tang, Rekrut, and Condit (2014) conducted a CFA followed by an exploratory factor analysis within a confirmatory framework, of the SIAS and Social Phobia Scale (SPS; Mattick & Clarke, 1998). Overall, after model respecification, the data from African Americans seemed to be consistent with that from non-Hispanic Caucasians in that two factors (Interaction and Performance Anxiety) were extracted. Importantly, each factor contained a mixture of both types of items for African Americans. That is, it was difficult to discern the interaction from the performance scales of these two measures. It was argued that certain items (e.g., "Disagreeing with another's view") might represent a performance concern (or how they appear) rather than an interaction concern. It was further posited that what appears to be social anxiety may be based on the belief that others are paying attention to African Americans because of their ethnicity and not because of inadequacy on their part. The authors concluded that although the use of the combined scales is warranted with African Americans, interpretations attempting to separate interaction from performance anxiety should be made with caution for African Americans.

Melka, Lancaster, Adams, Howarth, and Rodriguez (2010) conducted a CFA of the Fear of Negative Evaluation (FNE) and Social Avoidance and Distress (SAD) scales in samples of African American and Caucasian undergraduate students. Multiple group analyses indicated that the original factor structure did not fit the data for the Caucasians or African Americans. For Caucasians one item was removed, whereas for African Americans, five items were removed from the FNE ("I am unconcerned even if I know people are forming an unfavorable impression of me," "The opinions that important people have of me cause me little concern," "I react very little when other people disapprove of me," "I am often indifferent to the opinions others have of me," "I am usually confident that others will have a favorable impression of me") to adequately improve the fit characteristics of the FNE. With respect to the SAD among African Americans, two items ("I often find social occasions upsetting," "I am seldom at ease in a large group of people") did not fit the typical response pattern of participants. The authors noted that the removed items for the African American sample suggested that those items are irrelevant or represent a separate construct.

Beard, Rodriguez, Moitra, et al. (2011) conducted the one study that found ethnic equivalence in the measurement of social anxiety. These authors reported on the psychometric properties of the Liebowitz Social Anxiety Scale (LSAS; Liebowitz, 1987) among African American participants diagnosed with a variety of anxiety disorders. The authors found that scores on the fear and avoidance subscales were redundant. They further noted that the commonly found two-, four-, and five-factor models were poor fits with the data, although the four-factor model was the best fit of those tested. The authors concluded that the LSAS performed similarly between African Americans and non-Hispanic Caucasians, although they suggested the use of an exploratory factor analysis to determine whether a better factor structure may exist for African Americans. This study is somewhat difficult to interpret, however, given the small sample size and the diagnostic heterogeneity of the sample.

Anxiety Sensitivity

The results are somewhat mixed with respect to the measurement of anxiety sensitivity (a trait cognitive vulnerability factor that has been found to predict fearful response from a number of challenge procedures). Carter, Miller, Sbrocco, Suchday, and Lewis (1999) conducted one of the first studies examining the factor structure of the Anxiety Sensitivity Index (ASI) among

African Americans. Through CFA they found evidence that the typical factor structure found for non-Hispanic Caucasians did not fit the data for African Americans. It was noted that the Physical Concerns subscale was divided into Unsteady and Cardiovascular Concerns factors. For example, they found evidence that items typically associated with social anxiety were more associated with emotional controllability. Similarly, Hunter, Keough, Timpano, and Schmidt (2012) found evidence of a four-factor solution for the ASI among African Americans. In addition to finding two physical concerns subscales, they noted that each of these scales appeared to operate orthogonally.

Conversely, Arnau, Broman-Fulks, Green, and Berman (2009) examined the factor structure of the revised ASI in African American and non-Hispanic Caucasian participants and found that the number of factors, first-order factor pattern, and second-order factor patterns were invariant across both groups. It should be noted that this study examined the 36- and 21-item revisions of the ASI and found that the 36-item ASI was a stronger device and was invariant across cultural groups.

Specific Phobia

Chapman, Kertz, Zurlage, and Woodruff-Borden (2008) evaluated the psychometric properties of the second edition Fear Survey Schedule (FSS-II) in a sample of African Americans and non-Hispanic Caucasians. They found that the African American sample reported greater animal fears than the non-Hispanic Caucasians, whereas the non-Hispanic Caucasians reported greater social and blood-injection-injury (BII) fears than the African Americans. Furthermore, CFAs indicated that BII and situational factors did not load for the Africans Americans, whereas the BII and natural environment factors did not load among Caucasians. Finally, the content of the social anxiety factors of the FSS-II differed between groups. For non-Hispanic Caucasians, social anxiety consisted of self-consciousness and fears of being criticized and looking foolish, whereas among African Americans, social anxiety also included fear of not being successful. In a follow-up study of the FSS-II, Chapman, Vines, and Petrie (2011) found that their community sample did not endorse natural environment fears and that there was extensive similarity between community and college samples of African Americans in the animal and social factors of the FSS-II.

In summary, there is ample evidence from the literature evaluating the measurement of anxiety among African Americans to indicate that there are some differences between African American and non-Hispanic Caucasians in how anxiety-related constructs are measured. It is difficult to determine whether the noted differences are due to problems in the measurement of the constructs or to true cultural differences between the groups. It is also unknown whether there are any significant differences between African Americans and other minority groups. What does seem clear is that many of the current measurement devices have to be interpreted with caution for African Americans.

Taken together, the results from the few studies using general anxiety measures suggest that in their current form they may be of use to screen for anxiety. However, there is a relatively consistent finding that disorder-specific measures (with perhaps the exception of the PSWQ because it appears to be largely ethnically invariant) are not capturing the respective constructs among African Americans. It seems likely that measures of general distress work well simply because they are designed to indicate the presence of a general disturbance. At this symptom level of measurement, the report of distress may not be influenced by cultural factors. In this case, it would be akin to asking the question "Do you feel nervous?" An affirmative response would indicate that something is wrong but could not specify where the problem lies. When we examine the measures designed to answer the question of what specifically is a problem, we can expect the influence of culture to interact. In other words, the assessment of the cognitive and physiological symptoms of anxiety that allow us to separate one variant of anxiety from the others is likely influenced by culture.

As indicated in Figure 7.2, variables such as "awareness of racism," "racial identity," and "salience of physical symptoms" can influence the experience and, consequently, the reporting of symptoms. Consider social anxiety. General measures of anxiety indicate the presence of nervousness. The more specific measures of social anxiety, however, may fail to capture the entire construct because the thoughts (e.g., being socially anxious because of the constant negative social evaluation for being African American) and the meaning of the symptoms (e.g., this is a blight on all African Americans) captured in typical scales of social anxiety have been developed without consideration of the influence of culturally based (e.g., symptom manifestation) or discriminatory factors (e.g., racism). If the modified cognitive model is correct, it should not be surprising that existing measures would fall short of an accurate assessment of anxiety for African Americans. This explains why ethnic differences appear in the measurement of disorder-specific constructs and not among more general measures. The same cultural variables may be influencing treatment outcome results as well.

TREATMENT OUTCOME STUDIES

Sibrava et al. (2013) conducted a prospective study that followed patients treated in a larger treatment outcome study. Reporting only on the African American sample, the authors found that GAD, social anxiety disorder, and panic disorder are chronic conditions among African Americans. In this study, the authors evaluated the course of the aforementioned disorders across a 2-year period. They reported that recovery rates were low for GAD (.23), social anxiety disorder (.07), and panic disorder (.00) over the 2 years and concluded that anxiety disorders have a more chronic course among African Americans. Despite such findings, there is evidence that the inclusion of minorities in randomized clinical trials is lacking. For example, Mendoza, Williams, Chapman, and Powers (2012) conducted a search for randomized clinical trials of panic disorder, finding that less than half the studies reported ethnic data. Of those that did report participant ethnicity, only 4.9% of the sample was African American. Clearly, there is a need to continue efforts to recruit minorities in treatment outcome studies and a need for efforts on the part of researchers to evaluate their data by ethnicity. Furthermore, the results from the relatively few studies that directly addressed the treatment efficacy of cognitive behavior therapy for African Americans with anxiety disorders have been mixed.

Panic Disorder

Friedman and Paradis (1991) compared the symptom severity and treatment response in a small sample ($n = 15$ in each group) of African American and non-Hispanic Caucasian patients with panic disorder. There were no differences between groups at the start of treatment (consisting of in vivo exposure and tricyclic antidepressants) in terms of age of onset or symptom severity. At posttreatment, 84% of non-Hispanic Caucasians were moderately or significantly improved, whereas only 33% of the African Americans received the same rating. Conversely, 16% of non-Hispanic Caucasians were rated as slightly improved or were early dropouts compared with 66% of the African American sample. Although the specific reason for the poorer response of African Americans (e.g., use of medication among African Americans, lack of cultural sensitivity of therapists) could not be determined, this study served as the starting point for subsequent investigations in this area.

Chambless and Williams (1995) provided 10 to 20 sessions of therapist-assisted in vivo exposure to a sample of 18 African American and 57 non-Hispanic Caucasian patients with panic disorder. Suggesting comparable treatment efficacy, the authors reported invariance on fear of fear, panic frequency, and depression at posttreatment. Although both groups evidenced significant improvement in these measures, the African Americans did not improve in panic frequency. Furthermore, comparisons between groups indicated that African Americans continued to be more severe in their primary phobia, anxiety, and avoidance. These differences continued at the 6-month follow-up assessment. The reason for the comparatively poorer performance of African Americans in behavior therapy was posited to be related to severity of illness, the addition of racial stress, low socioeconomic status (SES; possibly resulting in difficulty attending sessions), or the therapeutic approach itself. It has been further suggested that a standard behavioral treatment does not allow for the systematic management of cultural variables in the course of treatment.

Carter, Sbrocco, Gore, Marin, and Lewis (2003) conducted one of the only randomized controlled trials of the treatment of African Americans with panic disorder. In this investigation, the authors randomly assigned panic patients to either 11 sessions of cognitive behavior therapy (CBT) or a wait-list condition. It was found that the treatment was associated with significant reductions in panic frequency, avoidance behavior, state and trait anxiety, and anxiety sensitivity and a trend toward a significant decrease in depressive symptoms. No changes were noted in the wait-list condition. The authors reported 54% of the sample was classified as recovered and 17% classified as improved but not recovered, and there was a strong overall effect size of .93. Comparatively, 95% of participants in the wait-list condition remained unimproved. It should be noted, however, that the percentage of high endstate functioners (those who scored within normal limits on all measures at the end of treatment) was considerably lower than the percentage reported in studies with predominantly non-Hispanic Caucasians. The authors noted that the results might have been due, in part, to the use of African American therapists or to the fact that the sample was of middle- to upper SES and well-educated. The results are more likely due to the open discussion of cultural issues (e.g., anxiety about being African American in a non-Hispanic Caucasian workplace) that were systematically incorporated into treatment.

Friedman, Braunstein, and Halpern (2006) compared the efficacy of CBT in treating panic disorder in a sample of 24 African American and 16 non-Hispanic Caucasian patients in an urban setting. Treatment consisted of approximately 16 individual sessions of standard CBT. The authors noted that treatment was associated with significant reductions in avoidance and panic symptomatology and found no significant ethnic differences between groups at posttreatment on anxiety-related measures. They noted that treatment clinicians had considerable experience in treating anxiety among a variety of ethnic groups, indicating some level of cultural sensitivity. It seems likely that discussions of cultural issues occurred and were managed over the course of treatment. Specifically, Friedman and colleagues (2006) reported that they commonly extended the psychoeducation phase of treatment and were aware that many African American patients might have a greater fear of mental illness. These and related nonsystematic changes may have altered the outcome and produced findings similar to Carter et al. (2003).

Social Anxiety

With respect to social anxiety disorder, Fink, Turner, and Beidel (1996) reported that social effectiveness treatment was effective in the treatment of an African American woman with social anxiety disorder. This particular treatment included 12 weekly sessions of imaginal and in vivo exposure to fearful social situations. Each session was terminated following a 50% reduction in within-session reactivity (assessed through subjective units of discomfort and physiological monitoring). Importantly, the exposure program included exposure to racially relevant cues, such as the patient introducing herself to unfamiliar non-Hispanic Caucasian medical professionals. The authors reported a significant improvement in symptoms that was maintained at a 4-month follow-up period. Therefore, there is evidence that including cultural factors in treatment is effective for the single case of an African American woman with social phobia.

Other Disorders

Markell and colleagues (2014) compared African American and non-Hispanic Caucasian patients with GAD who were treated with venlafaxine and offered an adjunct of CBT. They noted invariance between the two ethnic groups. Although promising, treatment included medication and, therefore, cannot directly speak to the benefit of CBT alone. It should be noted that although PTSD and obsessive–compulsive disorder are no longer listed as anxiety disorders in the *DSM*, there is evidence of the efficacy of CBT approaches for both disorders (Lester, Artz, Resick, & Young-Xu, 2010; Rosenheck, Fontana, & Cottrol, 1995; Zoellner, Feeny, Fitzgibbons, & Foa, 1999), including with African Americans with obsessive–compulsive disorder (Friedman et al., 2003; Hatch, Friedman, & Paradis, 1996; Williams, Chambless, & Steketee, 1998).

Taken together, there is evidence of the efficacy of CBT with African Americans with certain anxiety disorders, although which components of these treatment packages are more or less effective awaits future research (Carter, Mitchell, & Sbrocco, 2012). It must be noted that each of these studies implemented changes that rendered the overall approach more culturally appropriate. These changes have to be made more systematically and evaluated for their efficacy. There has also yet to be an investigation that has relied entirely on a standard treatment protocol. And because there have been no studies that compare a standard treatment package with one that has been modified to be more culturally sensitive, it is impossible to establish the efficacy of either modality in the treatment of anxiety with African Americans.

The scant treatment outcome literature may reflect an underlying assumption that all people should respond similarly to all treatment approaches. It may also be that treatment outcome studies with African Americans may be more difficult to conduct because of the problems in measurement noted earlier and perhaps because of the additional barriers to seeking treatment, such as inadequate finances and racial stress (Davis, Ressler, Schwartz, Stephens, & Bradley, 2008). It is also possible that the field of psychology has done a poor job disseminating information about anxiety and its treatment to African Americans. Coles, Schubert, Heimberg, and Weiss (2014) noted that when presented with vignettes, African Americans and non-Hispanic Caucasian participants were equally poor at correctly recognizing anxiety disorders. In a follow-up study, it was found that participants would more commonly seek help from a primary care physician and that African Americans were more likely than non-Hispanic Caucasians to recommend seeking help for GAD (Schubert, Coles, Heimberg, & Weiss, 2014).

In Figure 7.1, a cognitive behavioral model would suggest that intervention be aimed at the initial negative thoughts and the catastrophic thoughts that follow. In the treatment of African Americans with anxiety, we suggest that attention be paid to the additional variables depicted in Figure 7.2—that is, to focus on variables such as awareness of racism, salience of physical symptoms, racial identity, and stigma. A focus on these variables should produce more effective treatment because treatment would incorporate the ethnic-specific variables that serve to drive or exacerbate the anxiety. Although many of the studies that have demonstrated beneficial treatment outcomes have incorporated this type of cultural sensitivity, it should occur more systematically in the treatment of African Americans. This would allow for the development and evaluation of more culturally specific approaches that would lead to more refined treatment approaches. This type of adjustment would still be consistent with an overall cognitive model and, in our estimation, is required to improve the outcome of an overall cognitive treatment model.

An alternative to the type of model respecification we are advocating is to develop approaches that are more consistent with African American culture. Neal-Barnett et al. (2011) put forth one ethnocentric option to standard treatment packages. These researchers led a focus group to examine the possible utility of "sister circles" in the treatment of panic-related issues. Sister circles are support groups that originated in African American churches and are designed to provide a safe, culturally appropriate strategy for addressing a variety of issues (e.g., physical health). Although these groups are largely educational, Neal-Barnett and colleagues found African American women willing to use them as a potential mechanism to learn about anxiety and to receive empirically supported strategies for managing anxiety. This approach would aid in solving the problem of dissemination noted earlier. Participants specifically reported that a sister circle would help reduce the stigma associated with standard mental health services (noted as a key variable in Figure 7.2) and that it was consistent with African American culture. Potential problems noted included use of homework and confidentiality.

This approach is akin to an overall community-based participatory research (CBPR) strategy. In CBPR, one unique strategy might be first to conduct a focus group session in which basic psychoeducation is provided about what anxiety is, as well as how ethnic-specific variations of anxiety may be important to focus on. One could then offer several treatment options and formats consistent with a cognitive perspective. For example, one could offer in vivo or interoceptive exposure, cognitive restructuring, or role-playing individually or in groups and then allow the community to select the approach they feel is most consistent with members of the community. This would also serve to help reduce the stigma believed to be problematic for African Americans. This type of approach could be attempted at accessible public locales, such as community centers or neighborhood churches. The advantage of these locations would be increased comfort for participants, fewer travel restrictions, and an increased chance at group cohesiveness, all of which might decrease attrition and increase treatment adherence.

CONCLUSION

We have reviewed the current literature on the issues of measurement and treatment for African American adults with anxiety disorders. In our review, we highlighted numerous important considerations. Principally, ethnic differences exist when comparing either the psychometric properties of common measures of anxiety or treatment response. We cited several lines of research that have demonstrated that the construct equivalence of measures of anxiety should be questioned. Although there is evidence of the efficacy of treatment of anxiety for African Americans from a cognitive perspective, most studies have made cultural changes that likely affected that outcome. Unfortunately, no one has undertaken the challenge of systematically incorporating or assessing the effect of cultural variables in the treatment of African Americans with anxiety. Until this is accomplished, it is difficult to determine whether culturally specific changes in treatment work better than simply applying the standard protocol, although we suspect that this pattern would occur.

A larger issue is trying to understand why those differences exist. We contend that part of the issue in measurement and treatment research of African Americans with anxiety is that the general cognitive model has not been expanded to be more specific for African Americans. As we discussed earlier, consideration of specific contextual factors can explain many of the inconsistent findings in the literature. Like the development of the cognitive behavioral perspective, it is necessary to develop, test, and proceed from models that are specific for African Americans. The development of such models will allow one to refine measurement and treatment in a systematic manner. Until that happens, the movement toward understanding the disparate findings in this area will be slowed and disjointed. Although the field has amassed an impressive amount of evidence for a cognitive perspective of anxiety, it has also seemed collectively unwilling or uninterested in evaluating the role that being African American plays in altering that perspective.

In the future, there should be an open examination of African American culture in relation to the genesis, interpretation, exacerbation, and modification of both subclinical and pathological anxiety. That requires us to examine specific cultural factors. For example, there is ample evidence that stress plays an important role in the development and expression of anxiety symptoms, but we largely ignore a major source of stress: being African American. African Americans experience race-related stress that directly affects their expression of anxious pathology (Soto, Dawson-Andoh, & BeLue, 2011). Simply living under the constant scrutiny of being African American, directly (e.g., being followed in stores or asked to teach the course on minority issues) and indirectly (e.g., via microaggressions concerning the inherent athletic ability or rhythm of African Americans), has the capability of influencing one's anxiety and deserves attention theoretically and in research and clinical work. Also underresearched is the concept of ethnic identity. Among African Americans, there is evidence that ethnic identity is related to a reduction in anxiety symptoms (Williams, Chapman, Wong, & Turkheimer, 2012), and it will be imperative to include this variable in future investigations. Thus, finally, although there is evidence of the preliminary exploration of ethnic variance in a number of areas of anxiety research, it is necessary to continue to investigate the influence of African American culture on all aspects of anxiety, including theoretical models, development and adaptation of measures, and treatment.

REFERENCES

American Psychiatric Association. (2013). *Diagnostic and statistical manual of mental disorders* (5th ed.). Arlington, VA: Author.

Arnau, R. C., Broman-Fulks, J. J., Green, B. A., & Berman, M. E. (2009). The Anxiety Sensitivity Index–Revised: Confirmatory factor analyses, structural invariance in Caucasian and African American samples, and score reliability and validity. *Assessment, 16,* 165–180. http://dx.doi.org/10.1177/1073191108328809

Asnaani, A., Richey, J. A., Dimaite, R., Hinton, D. E., & Hofmann, S. G. (2010). A cross-ethnic comparison of lifetime prevalence rates of anxiety disorders.

Journal of Nervous and Mental Disease, 198, 551–555. http://dx.doi.org/10.1097/NMD.0b013e3181ea169f

Barlow, D. H. (2002). *Anxiety and its disorders: The nature and treatment of anxiety and panic* (2nd ed.). New York, NY: Guilford Press.

Beard, C., Rodriguez, B. F., Moitra, E., Sibrava, N. J., Bjornsson, A., Weisberg, R. B., & Keller, M. B. (2011). Psychometric properties of the Liebowitz Social Anxiety Scale (LSAS) in a longitudinal study of African Americans with anxiety disorders. *Journal of Anxiety Disorders, 25*, 722–726. http://dx.doi.org/10.1016/j.janxdis.2011.03.009

Beck, A. T. (1970). Cognitive therapy: Nature and relation to behavior therapy. *Behavior Therapy, 1*, 184–200. http://dx.doi.org/10.1016/S0005-7894(70)80030-2

Beck, A. T., & Clark, D. A. (1997). An information processing model of anxiety: Automatic and strategic processes. *Behaviour Research and Therapy, 35*, 49–58. http://dx.doi.org/10.1016/S0005-7967(96)00069-1

Beck, A. T., Epstein, N., Brown, G., & Steer, R. A. (1988). An inventory for measuring clinical anxiety: Psychometric properties. *Journal of Consulting and Clinical Psychology, 56*, 893–897. http://dx.doi.org/10.1037/0022-006X.56.6.893

Bell, C. C., Dixie-Bell, D. D., & Thompson, B. (1986). Further studies on the prevalence of isolated sleep paralysis in black subjects. *Journal of the National Medical Association, 78*, 649–659.

Carter, M. M., Forys, K. L., & Oswald, J. C. (2008). The cognitive behavioral model. In M. Hersen & A. M. Gross (Eds.), *Handbook of clinical psychology* (Vol. 1, pp. 171–201). Hoboken, NJ: Wiley.

Carter, M. M., Miller, O., Sbrocco, T., Suchday, S., & Lewis, E. L. (1999). Factor structure of the Anxiety Sensitivity Index among African American college students. *Psychological Assessment, 11*, 525–533. http://dx.doi.org/10.1037/1040-3590.11.4.525

Carter, M. M., Mitchell, F. E., & Sbrocco, T. (2012). Treating ethnic minority adults with anxiety disorders: Current status and future recommendations. *Journal of Anxiety Disorders, 26*, 488–501. http://dx.doi.org/10.1016/j.janxdis.2012.02.002

Carter, M. M., Sbrocco, T., & Carter, C. (1996). African Americans and anxiety disorders research: Development of a testable theoretical framework. *Psychotherapy: Theory, Research, Practice, Training, 33*, 449–463. http://dx.doi.org/10.1037/0033-3204.33.3.449

Carter, M. M., Sbrocco, T., Gore, K. L., Marin, N. W., & Lewis, E. L. (2003). Cognitive-behavioral group therapy versus a wait-list control in the treatment of African American women with panic disorder. *Cognitive Therapy and Research, 27*, 505–518. http://dx.doi.org/10.1023/A:1026350903639

Carter, M. M., Sbrocco, T., Lewis, E. L., & Friedman, E. K. (2001). Parental bonding and anxiety: Differences between African American and European American college students. *Journal of Anxiety Disorders, 15*, 555–569. http://dx.doi.org/10.1016/S0887-6185(01)00081-0

Carter, M. M., Sbrocco, T., Miller, O., Jr., Suchday, S., Lewis, E. L., & Freedman, R. E. K. (2005). Factor structure, reliability, and validity of the Penn State Worry Questionnaire: Differences between African-American and White-American college students. *Journal of Anxiety Disorders, 19*, 827–843. http://dx.doi.org/10.1016/j.janxdis.2004.11.001

Carter, M. M., Sbrocco, T., Tang, D., Rekrut, F. M., & Condit, C. (2014). Psychometric properties of the social phobia and social interaction anxiety scales: Evidence of construct equivalence in an African American sample. *Journal of Anxiety Disorders, 28*, 633–643. http://dx.doi.org/10.1016/j.janxdis.2014.07.003

Chambless, D. L., & Williams, K. E. (1995). A preliminary study of African Americans with agoraphobia: Symptom severity and outcome of treatment with in vivo exposure. *Behavior Therapy, 26*, 501–515. http://dx.doi.org/10.1016/S0005-7894(05)80097-8

Chapman, L. K., Kertz, S. J., Zurlage, M. M., & Woodruff-Borden, J. (2008). A confirmatory factor analysis of specific phobia domains in African American and Caucasian American young adults. *Journal of Anxiety Disorders, 22*, 763–771. http://dx.doi.org/10.1016/j.janxdis.2007.08.003

Chapman, L. K., Vines, L., & Petrie, J. (2011). Fear factors: Cross validation of specific phobia domains in a community-based sample of African American adults. *Journal of Anxiety Disorders, 25*, 539–544. http://dx.doi.org/10.1016/j.janxdis.2010.12.009

Chapman, L. K., Williams, S. R., Mast, B. T., & Woodruff-Borden, J. (2009). A confirmatory analysis of the Beck Anxiety Inventory in African American and European American young adults. *Journal of Anxiety Disorders, 23*, 387–392. http://dx.doi.org/10.1016/j.janxdis.2008.12.003

Coles, M. E., Schubert, J. R., Heimberg, R. G., & Weiss, B. D. (2014). Disseminating treatment for anxiety disorders: Step 1. Recognizing the problem as a precursor to seeking help. *Journal of Anxiety Disorders, 28*, 737–740. http://dx.doi.org/10.1016/j.janxdis.2014.07.011

Davis, R. G., Ressler, K. J., Schwartz, A. C., Stephens, K. J., & Bradley, R. G. (2008). Treatment barriers for low-income, urban African Americans with undiagnosed posttraumatic stress disorder. *Journal of Traumatic Stress, 21*, 218–222. http://dx.doi.org/10.1002/jts.20313

DeLapp, R. C. T., Chapman, L. K., & Williams, M. T. (2016). Psychometric properties of a brief version of the Penn State Worry Questionnaire in African Americans and European Americans. *Psychological Assessment, 28*, 499–508. http://dx.doi.org/10.1037/pas0000208

Fink, C. M., Turner, S. M., & Beidel, D. C. (1996). Culturally relevant factors in the behavioral treatment of social phobia: A case study. *Journal of Anxiety Disorders, 10*, 201–209. http://dx.doi.org/10.1016/0887-6185(96)00005-9

Friedman, S., Braunstein, J. W., & Halpern, B. (2006). Cognitive behavioral treatment of panic disorder and agoraphobia in a multiethnic urban outpatient clinic: Initial presentation and treatment outcome. *Cognitive and Behavioral Practice*, *13*, 282–292. http://dx.doi.org/10.1016/j.cbpra.2006.04.009

Friedman, S., & Paradis, C. (1991). African American patients with panic disorder and agoraphobia. *Journal of Anxiety Disorders*, *5*, 35–41. http://dx.doi.org/10.1016/0887-6185(91)90015-L

Friedman, S., Smith, L. C., Halpern, B., Levine, C., Paradis, C., Viswanathan, R., . . . Ackerman, R. (2003). Obsessive-compulsive disorder in a multi-ethnic urban outpatient clinic: Initial presentation and treatment outcome with exposure and ritual prevention. *Behavior Therapy*, *34*, 397–410. http://dx.doi.org/10.1016/S0005-7894(03)80008-4

Hambrick, J. P., Rodebaugh, T. L., Balsis, S., Woods, C. M., Mendez, J. L., & Heimberg, R. G. (2010). Cross-ethnic measurement equivalence of measures of depression, social anxiety, and worry. *Assessment*, *17*, 155–171. http://dx.doi.org/10.1177/1073191109350158

Hatch, M. L., Friedman, S., & Paradis, C. M. (1996). Behavioral treatment of obsessive-compulsive disorder in African Americans. *Cognitive and Behavioral Practice*, *3*, 303–315. http://dx.doi.org/10.1016/S1077-7229(96)80020-4

Himle, J. A., Baser, R. E., Taylor, R. J., Campbell, R. D., & Jackson, J. S. (2009). Anxiety disorders among African Americans, Blacks of Caribbean descent, and non-Hispanic Whites in the United States. *Journal of Anxiety Disorders*, *23*, 578–590. http://dx.doi.org/10.1016/j.janxdis.2009.01.002

Hunter, L. R., Keough, M. E., Timpano, K. R., & Schmidt, N. B. (2012). Ethnoracial differences in anxiety sensitivity: Examining the validity of competing anxiety sensitivity index subscales. *Journal of Anxiety Disorders*, *26*, 511–516. http://dx.doi.org/10.1016/j.janxdis.2012.02.004

Hunter, L. R., & Schmidt, N. B. (2010). Anxiety psychopathology in African American adults: Literature review and development of an empirically informed sociocultural model. *Psychological Bulletin*, *136*, 211–235. http://dx.doi.org/10.1037/a0018133

Lester, K., Artz, C., Resick, P. A., & Young-Xu, Y. (2010). Impact of race on early treatment termination and outcomes in posttraumatic stress disorder treatment. *Journal of Consulting and Clinical Psychology*, *78*, 480–489. http://dx.doi.org/10.1037/a0019551

Liebowitz, M. R. (1987). Social phobia. *Modern Problems of Pharmacopsychiatry*, *22*, 141–173. http://dx.doi.org/10.1159/000414022

Markell, H. M., Newman, M. G., Gallop, R., Gibbons, M. B., Rickels, K., & Crits-Christoph, P. (2014). Combined medication and CBT for generalized anxiety disorder with African American participants: Reliability and validity of assessments and preliminary outcomes. *Behavior Therapy*, *45*, 495–506. http://dx.doi.org/10.1016/j.beth.2014.02.008

Mattick, R. P., & Clarke, J. C. (1998). Development and validation of measures of social phobia scrutiny fear and social interaction anxiety. *Behaviour Research and Therapy*, *36*, 455–470. http://dx.doi.org/10.1016/S0005-7967(97)10031-6

Melka, S. E., Lancaster, S. L., Adams, L. J., Howarth, E. A., & Rodriguez, B. F. (2010). Social anxiety across ethnicity: A confirmatory factor analysis of the FNE and SAD. *Journal of Anxiety Disorders*, 24, 680–685. http://dx.doi.org/10.1016/j.janxdis.2010.04.011

Mendoza, D. B., Williams, M. T., Chapman, L. K., & Powers, M. (2012). Minority inclusion in randomized clinical trials of panic disorder. *Journal of Anxiety Disorders*, 26, 574–582. http://dx.doi.org/10.1016/j.janxdis.2012.02.011

Meyer, T. J., Miller, M. L., Metzger, R. L., & Borkovec, T. D. (1990). Development and validation of the Penn State Worry Questionnaire. *Behaviour Research and Therapy*, 28, 487–495. http://dx.doi.org/10.1016/0005-7967(90)90135-6

Neal, A. M., & Turner, S. M. (1991). Anxiety disorders research with African Americans: Current status. *Psychological Bulletin*, 109, 400–410. http://dx.doi.org/10.1037/0033-2909.109.3.400

Neal-Barnett, A. M., Stadulis, R., Payne, M. R., Crosby, L., Mitchell, M., Williams, L., & Williams-Costa, C. (2011). In the company of my sisters: Sister circles as an anxiety intervention for professional African American women. *Journal of Affective Disorders*, 129, 213–218. http://dx.doi.org/10.1016/j.jad.2010.08.024

Paradis, C. M., Friedman, S., & Hatch, M. (1997). Isolated sleep paralysis in African Americans with panic disorder. *Cultural Diversity and Mental Health*, 3, 69–76. http://dx.doi.org/10.1037/1099-9809.3.1.69

Petrie, J. M., Chapman, L. K., & Vines, L. M. (2013). Utility of the PANAS-X in predicting social phobia in African American females. *Journal of Black Psychology*, 39, 131–155. http://dx.doi.org/10.1177/0095798412454677

Rosenheck, R., Fontana, A., & Cottrol, C. (Eds.). (1995). Effect of clinician–veteran racial pairing in the treatment of posttraumatic stress disorder. *The American Journal of Psychiatry*, 152, 555–563. http://dx.doi.org/10.1176/ajp.152.4.555

Schubert, J. R., Coles, M. E., Heimberg, R. G., & Weiss, B. D. (2014). Disseminating treatment for anxiety disorders step 2: Peer recommendations to seek help. *Journal of Anxiety Disorders*, 28, 712–716. http://dx.doi.org/10.1016/j.janxdis.2014.07.010

Sibrava, N. J., Beard, C., Bjornsson, A. S., Moitra, E., Weisberg, R. B., & Keller, M. B. (2013). Two-year course of generalized anxiety disorder, social anxiety disorder, and panic disorder in a longitudinal sample of African American adults. *Journal of Consulting and Clinical Psychology*, 81, 1052–1062. http://dx.doi.org/10.1037/a0034382

Soto, J. A., Dawson-Andoh, N. A., & BeLue, R. (2011). The relationship between perceived discrimination and Generalized Anxiety Disorder among African Americans, Afro Caribbeans, and non-Hispanic Whites. *Journal of Anxiety Disorders*, 25, 258–265. http://dx.doi.org/10.1016/j.janxdis.2010.09.011

Steele, C. M., & Aronson, J. (1995). Stereotype threat and the intellectual test performance of African Americans. *Journal of Personality and Social Psychology*, 69, 797–811. http://dx.doi.org/10.1037/0022-3514.69.5.797

Sue, D. W., & Sue, D. (2013). *Counseling the culturally diverse: Theory and practice.* Hoboken, NY: Wiley.

Williams, K. E., Chambless, D. L., & Steketee, G. (1998). Behavioral treatment of obsessive-compulsive disorder in African Americans: Clinical issues. *Journal of Behavior Therapy and Experimental Psychiatry, 29,* 163–170. http://dx.doi.org/10.1016/S0005-7916(98)00004-4

Williams, M. T., Chapman, L. K., Wong, J., & Turkheimer, E. (2012). The role of ethnic identity in symptoms of anxiety and depression in African Americans. *Psychiatry Research, 199,* 31–36. http://dx.doi.org/10.1016/j.psychres.2012.03.049

Zoellner, L. A., Feeny, N., Fitzgibbons, L. A., & Foa, E. B. (1999). Response of African American and European American women in cognitive behavioral therapy for PTSD. *Behavior Therapy, 30,* 581–595.

8

COGNITIVE BEHAVIORAL MODELS, MEASURES, AND TREATMENTS FOR ANXIETY DISORDERS IN AMERICAN INDIANS AND ALASKA NATIVES

JOHN McCULLAGH AND JACQUELINE S. GRAY

Anxiety disorders experienced by American Indians and Alaska Natives (AI/AN), and the various factors that contribute to these disorders among AI/ANs, cannot be fully understood without also understanding the broader historical context of AI/ANs. Many of the current social, economic, and mental health-related issues experienced by AI/ANs are legacies of a historical narrative characterized by decimation through disease, warfare, famine, and relocation. Through forced acculturation, AI/ANs have also been subjected to the systematic and government-sanctioned elimination of AI/AN languages, religious and spiritual beliefs, customs, and traditional practices (Duran & Duran, 1995; Garrett & Pichette, 2000). This policy of forced indoctrination has had a lasting effect on contemporary AI/AN life. The trauma and pain caused by this legacy of historical oppression are believed to have created an indelible impact on AI/AN worldviews, which influences how AI/ANs view themselves and their cultural heritage. In turn, these damaged views

http://dx.doi.org/10.1037/0000091-009
Treating Depression, Anxiety, and Stress in Ethnic and Racial Groups: Cognitive Behavioral Approaches,
E. C. Chang, C. A. Downey, J. K. Hirsch, and E. A. Yu (Editors)

of the world and self have affected the way in which AI/ANs perceive and navigate their relationships, communities, and U.S. society as a whole (Evans-Campbell, 2008). The decimation of the AI/AN people and the severing of cultural traditions and practices thousands of years old are believed to have contributed to increased stress, hopelessness, and disenfranchisement among AI/ANs. The negative psychological impact of these collective experiences across generations of AI/ANs has been called *historical trauma* or *intergenerational trauma* and has also been referred to as a *soul wounding* (Brave Heart, 2003; Brave Heart & DeBruyn, 1998). This historical trauma is believed to place a high psychological and emotional burden on AI/ANs, which affects the ways in which AI/ANs view and navigate their current struggles and experiences with oppression and marginalization.

In many ways, the contemporary issues of poverty with AI/ANs are an extension of this historical oppression, and American Indian reservations are some of the most impoverished communities in the United States. These disparities highlight the great need for accessible mental health treatment in AI/AN communities. Unfortunately, even when mental health services are available, many AI/ANs choose not to use mental health care because of the stigma associated with mental illness (Grandbois, 2005). A number of factors contribute to this stigma and resistance toward mental health care use. Experiences of discrimination, lack of culturally competent treatment providers, absence of culturally adapted treatments, and a general mistrust in a treatment system that operates from a Western medical model framework can all increase the stigma associated with seeking mental health services (Gary, 2005; Grandbois, 2005). Gary (2005) characterized this intersection between racial minority group characteristics and mental health stigma as a "double stigma" that further increases disparities in mental health. The multitude of challenges that perpetuate mental health issues in AI/ANs, as well the many barriers to mental health care access, highlight the need to better understand and treat mental health issues in AI/AN populations. In this chapter, we review the literature on anxiety treatments for AI/ANs and provide recommendations for adapting treatments for these clients.

ANXIETY DISORDERS AMONG AMERICAN INDIANS AND ALASKA NATIVES

Anxiety disorders are some of the most prevalent mental health disorders globally and impose a heavy burden on individuals, families, and society (Kessler, Berglund, Demler, Jin, Merikangas, & Walters, 2005; Kessler, Chiu, Demler, & Walters, 2005). Greater levels of anxiety are associated with decreased physical health, greater levels of stress, increased substance use, and lower quality of life (Olatunji, Cisler, & Tolin, 2007; Smith et al., 2006; Strine, Chapman, Kobau, Balluz, & Mokdad, 2004). As stated previously, AI/ANs are faced with glaring mental health disparities compared with the general population. However, despite several studies examining the prevalence of mental health disorders among AI/ANs, the scope and nature of anxiety in AI/AN populations remain unclear, and investigations have yielded seemingly contradictory results. For example, in a large-scale epidemiological study examining the prevalence rates of mental health disorders between Whites, Blacks, Asians, Hispanics, and American Indians (AIs), Smith et al. (2006) found that AIs reported having the highest levels of anxiety compared with every other racial group. Twelve-month prevalence rates for anxiety disorders were approximately 15% for AIs, whereas Whites, Blacks, Hispanics, and Asians had 12-month prevalence rates of 12%, 10%, 9%, and 7%, respectively. However, in their study comparing samples from two geographically distinct reservation populations (1,446 Southwest AIs and 1,638 Northern Plains AIs), Beals, Manson, et al. (2005) reported significantly lower rates of anxiety for AIs. Twelve-month prevalence rates for anxiety disorders in the Southwest AI sample was approximately 7.5% and for Northern Plains AIs was 7%. Of the different anxiety and stress-related disorders presented in the Beals et al. study, the one disorder that stood out was posttraumatic stress disorder (PTSD). Women had especially high rates of PTSD, with prevalence rates of 19.5% and 19.2% for the Southwest tribe and Northern Plains tribe, respectively.

The large-scale studies by Smith et al. (2006) and Beals, Manson, et al. (2005) both used trained professionals to conduct interviews. However, the authors reported very different results for prevalence of anxiety in their samples. Smaller scale studies have also provided mixed results on the scope of anxiety disorders among AI/ANs. For example, in a community sample of 147 Northern Plains AIs, De Coteau, Hope, and Anderson (2003) found that reported levels of anxiety were comparatively lower than those of the general population. McDonald, Jackson, and McDonald (1991) reported that in a sample of AI/AN college students, greater levels of anxiety were present among AI/AN college students than among their White counterparts. Finally, in a study by Zvolensky, McNeil, Porter, and Stewart (2001), AI/AN students reported experiencing greater levels of anxiety sensitivity than did White students. With the exception of PTSD, it is unclear whether AI/ANs experience greater or fewer anxiety disorders than the general population. The conflicting results reported in the various studies paint a complex picture of anxiety among AI/ANs, leading to more questions regarding how prevalent anxiety disorders truly are among AI/AN populations.

IMPACT OF ACCULTURATION ON THE ASSESSMENT AND TREATMENT OF ANXIETY DISORDERS AMONG AMERICAN INDIANS AND ALASKA NATIVES

One major factor that can further complicate both the assessment and treatment of anxiety among AI/ANs is level of acculturation. *Acculturation* refers to the extent to which an AI/AN individual can adapt to the norms, conventions, and expectations of different social and cultural groups. For AI/ANs, this would be the culture of their AI/AN family and community and that of the mainstream White culture. Acculturation affects AI/AN perspectives and worldviews, as well as how AI/ANs navigate the world around them, including the mental health care system. Of note, acculturation affects perspectives on healing and attitudes toward mental health treatment and engagement in treatment. Clearly, there are significant clinical implications for the level of acculturation among AI/ANs in the treatment of anxiety disorders. For example, AI/ANs who adhere to more traditional backgrounds and belief systems may be more likely to be wary of Western models of mental health treatment and assessment and may also be more likely to use more traditional AI/AN practices (e.g., smudging, sweat lodge ceremonies, herbal medicine, pipe ceremonies) to address mental health concerns, whereas AI/ANs who are more acculturated to the general population may be more open to Western approaches to mental health treatment, including traditional psychotherapy, psychological assessment, and use of psychotropic medication (Jackson, Schmutzer, Wenzel, & Tyler, 2006). Acculturation is inherently related to clients' worldviews, as well as to their perspective on mental health treatment. It is thus imperative that clinicians consider level of acculturation when working with AI/AN clients (Duran, 2006).

COGNITIVE BEHAVIORAL MODELS FOR UNDERSTANDING ANXIETY DISORDERS IN AMERICAN INDIANS AND ALASKA NATIVES

Mental health therapy and the field of mental health care as a whole are often seen by AI/ANs as an extension of White majority culture; thus, AI/AN attitudes toward Western models of mental health treatment and psychotherapy are often negative (Gone, 2004). The mental health field, in turn, often reinforces this perception through the lack of culturally appropriate treatment practices and the lack of culturally competent providers (Gone, 2004; Gone & Trimble, 2012). This makes it even more imperative that clinicians use models of healing that are culturally congruent with AI/AN worldviews.

There are several aspects of the cognitive behavior therapy (CBT) model that may not be congruent with AI/AN models of wellness and healing. Many AI/ANs see CBT's focus on specific symptom reduction, the conceptualization of mental health disorders through a disease model framework, linear perspectives on cause and effect in psychopathology and treatment, and the strong emphasis on the individual (as opposed to the family or community) as incompatible with their own conceptualization of health, well-being, and the healing process (Grandbois, 2005; Hodge, Limb, & Cross, 2009). This incongruence between AI/AN models of wellness and prevailing Western mental health treatment paradigms can have a significant impact on the effectiveness of current mental health treatment approaches when used with AI/ANs.

There are major clinical implications stemming from the difference in worldviews between mental health clinicians and AI/AN clients, particularly as it relates to conceptual differences of wellness and healing. If a clinician who is trained through a Western therapeutic framework appears to be imposing a wholly foreign or unfamiliar treatment approach onto an AI/AN client, the client may not agree with nor fully accept the treatment approach. Understandably, this lack of collaboration and goal consensus is likely to negatively affect treatment. Likewise, the client may perceive the clinician as unwilling or unable to comprehend and empathize with the client's struggles and the sociocultural context in which these issues have occurred. CBT, as a model that was developed through a Western majority culture framework, must be adapted and tailored to the different cultural populations to which it is applied. To increase the effectiveness of CBT with AI/AN populations, it is necessary to alter aspects of CBT to present this treatment approach in more culturally congruent ways.

To effectively adapt CBT to AI/ANs, it is important to examine how AI/ANs perceive the fundamental components of CBT, as well as how these components fit with AI/AN conceptualizations of the healing process. Although there is only minimal research exploring this question, a study by Jackson et al. (2006) examining the cross-cultural applicability of cognitive behavioral treatments with AIs highlights how some AI/ANs may perceive CBT. In addition, this unique study indicated how CBT might be altered to make it more compatible with AI/AN worldviews.

Jackson and her colleagues (2006) selected a sample of White and AI participants and compared their ratings on the Cognitive Behavior Therapy Applicability Scale (CBT-AS; Jackson, Schmutzer, & Wenzel, 2002). The CBT-AS is a self-report measure that examines a person's preferences and attitudes toward major components of CBT. It is composed of three major subscales: (a) Focused In-Session Behavior, which examines the degree to which individuals believe that therapy should include a linear examination of the connection between cognition and emotional reaction; (b) Active Stance, which explores the degree to which the individual believes that therapy should include a proactive stance by both the therapist and the client toward engaging in therapy or therapeutic work inside and outside of session; and (c) Structured Therapeutic Relationship, which examines the degree to which individuals believe that the therapeutic relationship is a clearly defined and time-limited professional relationship between the therapist and the client in which the client has the ultimate responsibility as their own agent of change.

Important differences emerged between these two groups: AI participants had significantly lower scores on the Focused In-Session Behavior subscale and Structured Therapeutic Relationship subscale, indicating that they were less likely to endorse a preference toward these aspects of CBT than were White participants. However, AI participants had similar scores to White participants on the Active Stance subscale. These findings have some important implications for altering CBT to treat anxiety in AI/ANs more effectively. Jackson et al. (2006) noted that the linear nature of connecting cognition to emotional reaction might not fit with AI/AN conceptualizations that are more focused on harmony, both within oneself and with that person's environment. Similarly, the inflexibility of the structured professional relationship may be incongruent with how AI/ANs view the role of those professionals they go to for support, guidance, and healing, which often include tribal elders, mentors, extended family members, and traditional healers (Garrett & Herring, 2001; Portman & Garrett, 2006). The boundaries of these relationships are less clearly defined and more flexible than the distinct professional boundaries that often typify the relationship between client and therapist in the Western mental health paradigm. Though this study does not explicitly answer the question of whether CBT is more or less effective with AI/ANs, there are significant clinical implications that therapeutic outcomes are, at least in part, determined by client preference. For therapeutic interventions to be most effective, the client and clinician should mutually agree on the treatment approach and collaboratively work toward these same goals (Messer & Wampold, 2002).

CULTURALLY CONGRUENT AMERICAN INDIAN AND ALASKA NATIVE MODELS OF TREATMENT AND HEALING

The research by Jackson et al. (2006) highlights the importance of shifting the way CBT is conceptualized and conducted with AI/AN clients. One way in which many AI/ANs conceptualize health and personal wellness can be represented through the concept of the *medicine wheel* (BigFoot &

Schmidt, 2010; Dapice, 2006; Hodge et al., 2009). At its most basic level, the concept of the AI/AN medicine wheel posits that each individual has an emotional, intellectual, spiritual, and physical self. These aspects of the self are represented as four quadrants of the medicine wheel. It is believed that imbalance between these four areas of one's life creates disharmony and stress and leads to a lower quality of life. The set of symbols represented in the medicine wheel signifies a culturally congruent framework through which cognitive behavioral interventions can be more effectively provided. Because many AI/ANs conceptualize problems with stress and anxiety as an imbalance in how they may be living their lives, a more holistic framework that takes into account the physical, emotional, mental and intellectual, and spiritual needs of the client may be what is needed to facilitate greater understanding and acceptance of psychological treatment by AI/ANs.

The Native model of wellness (Hodge et al., 2009) represents a culturally congruent framework through which cognitive behavioral interventions can be tailored and more effectively applied to AI/AN clients. Hodge et al. (2009) stated that in their model, wellness is achieved through harmony and balance between one's spirit, body, mind (emotions and thoughts), and the context in which one lives. The ideas of balance and harmony are key concepts within this model. Hodge et al. described the concept of *balance* as "a natural state that results from the normal processes of stimuli and response, drive and drive satisfaction, and complex system interactions" (p. 215). Accordingly, human beings are constantly moving toward balance, and we respond and adapt to both internal and external stimuli to either maintain or reestablish balance. The (often) maladaptive coping mechanism of avoidance serves as an example of how an individual struggling with anxiety may cope with their issues to maintain a sense of balance. According to Hodge et al., this may allow the individual to continue functioning, though not necessarily in the healthiest or most ideal fashion. Hodge et al. also stated that when there is greater balance between one's spirit, mind, body, and context or environment, one is more likely to experience greater wellness.

Harmony is a second major key concept of the model. As opposed to balance, which is conceptualized as a more natural resting state, harmony comes from the active search for greater or healthier balance in one's life. This active pursuit of healthier balance can be worked toward in a multitude of ways. Engaging in physical exercise, developing strong relationships with others, using prayer and ritual, and developing and practicing healthy coping skills are all ways in which one may work toward greater harmony. When major aspects of one's life (mind, body, spirit, and context or environment) are in harmony with one another, one is much more likely to prosper, increase resiliency, and improve physical and mental health.

In addition to recognizing the importance of cognitive and emotional processes in maintaining or working toward wellness, the Native model of wellness also conceptualizes the self as a spiritual being and acknowledges that for many AI/ANs, spirituality, religious community, and religious practices and rituals are of great importance in that these play a major role in maintaining positive health and well-being. The model also emphasizes the context and environment in which the person lives. The family unit, the tribe, and the community, as well as cultural traditions and practices, are seen as integral aspects of wellness within this model. Implicit in the model is the context of oppression, discrimination, and marginalization that AI/ANs have experienced both historically and currently. The recognition that the life, culture, and experiences of many AI/ANs are vastly different from the majority culture is an incredibly important contribution of this model in that it does not examine wellness in isolation from the current social, economic, and geopolitical realities of the world through which AI/ANs must navigate.

The Native model of wellness is congruent with many of the key tenets of CBT and may serve as a powerful framework through which CBT interventions can be integrated into mental health treatment with AI/AN clients. Both models recognize the importance of the interrelated connections between thoughts, emotions, and behaviors. In addition, many CBT interventions for anxiety can be accessed through the holistic lens outlined in the Native model of wellness. Understanding how negative thought patterns and unhealthy behaviors (e.g., catastrophic thinking and avoidance behaviors) represent both imbalance and the maladaptive attempt to restore balance are examples of how CBT concepts can be used through the framework of balance. The concept of harmony, which is conceptualized as a more active and intentional pursuit of healthier balance, may include interventions that focus on improving physical health through exercise, exploring ways to enhance social connections (e.g., with friends, family, community), intentionally working to improve emotional awareness and acceptance, and increasing recognition of unhealthy thought patterns through journaling. These represent only a few CBT-based interventions that can be used in the harmony framework.

Another AI/AN treatment model that deserves mention is Honoring Children, Mending the Circle (HC-MC; BigFoot & Schmidt, 2010), which is a trauma-focused CBT designed for use with AI/AN children. This treatment approach has great overlap with the Native model of wellness in that it also uses the medicine wheel framework to understand wellness as a balance and harmony between one's thoughts, emotions, physical body, spirit, and the environmental context in which one lives. This treatment model explicitly integrates CBT interventions such as affect management, relaxation training, and gradual exposure to reduce physiological symptoms of

PTSD, reduce maladaptive behavioral responses to trauma, and change maladaptive trauma-related beliefs. According to BigFoot and Schmidt (2010), one of the key components of this model is gradual exposure through a *trauma narrative*. The clinician, child, and family collaboratively identify the means through which the traumatic story is gradually told and retold. Congruent with AI/AN communication, this can occur through story, traditional dance, and "journey stick" (the journey stick represents a method of recording a journey by collecting objects that have meaning to the individual and tying these objects to a stick in chronological order to present a personal narrative or story). The treatment program also places great emphasis on the importance of family and spirituality, and these components are infused throughout the treatment process. HC-MC serves as an archetype for a more structured CBT treatment model that has been adapted and tailored to meet the unique needs, worldviews, and culture of AI/ANs.

ASSESSMENT OF ANXIETY DISORDERS IN AMERICAN INDIANS AND ALASKA NATIVES

There exist major challenges in the accurate assessment of anxiety symptoms in AI/AN populations. The most widely used assessment and screening instruments for anxiety have largely been normed using mainstream White samples. There are few studies that have explored the cross-cultural applicability of anxiety assessment instruments, and because of this, the validity of these measures as applied to AI/AN populations remains largely unknown. Complicating the understanding of the validity of anxiety assessment instruments is the sheer diversity of AI/AN populations, which makes accurate assessment difficult because an instrument may be valid with one community of AI/ANs but not another.

The Anxiety Sensitivity Index (ASI; Reiss, Peterson, Gursky, & McNally, 1986), a measure that examines the degree to which an individual has fears regarding anxiety symptoms, represents one of the few anxiety-related measures that has been examined with AI/AN populations. In a sample of 282 AI/AN college students, Zvolensky et al. (2001) found that the ASI had a high level of internal consistency (Cronbach alpha = .81) and three lower order factors consisting of physical, psychological, and social concerns. These three factors loaded on a single higher order factor that the authors called the Global Anxiety Sensitivity factor. The results of this study were consistent with previous research and lent significant support to the validity of the ASI with AI/AN populations.

Norton, De Coteau, Hope, and Anderson (2004) examined the ASI using a more homogenous sample consisting specifically of Northern Plains

AIs. Norton et al. tested the factor structure previously found by Zvolensky et al. (2001), with results failing to support the three-factor model found in Zvolensky's study. Rather, Norton and his colleagues found that a single global factor of anxiety sensitivity yielded the best fit to their data. On the basis of the results of their study Norton et al. recommended that research with AI/ANs focus on specific AI/AN populations because there may be unique differences between discrete populations that would not be captured if more heterogeneous samples (such as the one in the Zvolensky et al., 2001, study) are used to explore the validity of assessment instruments.

There also exist a few studies examining the cross-cultural validity of the Beck Anxiety Inventory (BAI; Beck, Epstein, Brown, & Steer, 1988) with AI/ANs. These studies lend some support to the utility of the BAI in screening for anxiety in AI/ANs, while also highlighting the need for additional research. De Coteau et al. (2003) used the BAI in their study that explored the relationship between anxiety and health outcomes in a population of 147 Northern Plains AI adults. Consistent with studies of the general population, De Coteau et al. found that greater levels of self-reported stress and health problems were related to increased levels of anxiety. De Coteau and her colleagues also found that the BAI demonstrated a high level of internal consistency (Cronbach alpha = .93).

In a more in-depth exploration of the cross-cultural validity of the BAI, Gray, McCullagh, and Petros (2016) compared a clinical sample of Northern Plains AIs recruited from mental health treatment settings with a community sample of AIs. Gray and her colleagues found significant support for the use of the BAI with AI/ANs. The BAI demonstrated strong internal consistency (Cronbach alpha = .95) and was highly correlated with other measures of anxiety, such as the anxiety subscale of the Symptom Checklist-90 (SCL-90; Derogatis & Unger, 2010). Further, higher scores were reported by the clinical sample, compared with the community sample. The study by Gray et al. also raised some important questions regarding the cross-cultural validity of the BAI. Gray et al. examined the factor structure of the BAI through an exploratory factor analysis (EFA). Their EFA yielded three primary factors they labeled as *Fear*, *Cardiorespiratory*, and *Body Instability* symptoms. The factor structure of the BAI that was found in the Gray et al. study was different from the two-factor structure originally established by Beck et al. (1988) and raises questions regarding the validity of the BAI with AI/AN populations. Although speculative, the different factor structure found across studies may indicate that BAI items are interpreted differently by AI/ANs or that anxiety may be conceptualized differently among AI/ANs.

In addition to questions regarding the cross-cultural validity of anxiety screening instruments, there exist major challenges regarding how mental health screenings and clinical interviews are conducted with AI/ANs.

Although structured interviews and specific symptom-focused screening instruments may be effective in assessing anxiety among the mainstream population, this method of anxiety assessment may be incongruent with how some AI/ANs conceptualize and communicate their mental health concerns. For many AI/ANs, communicating mental health struggles through story, dance, song, or prayer may feel more comfortable than doing so through symptom-screening instruments (De Coteau, Anderson, & Hope, 2006).

COGNITIVE BEHAVIORAL TREATMENTS FOR ANXIETY DISORDERS IN AMERICAN INDIANS AND ALASKA NATIVES

Despite the growing interest in understanding and treating psychological disorders in AI/ANs, empirical research examining the efficacy of psychological treatments for anxiety among AI/AN populations remains largely nonexistent. Currently, no studies have examined the effectiveness of CBT treatments for anxiety specifically with AI/ANs, and the published literature that exists on the subject is largely conceptual or qualitative. The only published work that provides guidelines specifically for adapting manualized mental health treatments for anxiety with AI/ANs is an article by De Coteau et al. (2006). Though representing an important step in understanding and treating anxiety among AI/ANs, the generalizability of the recommendations is limited, and the authors themselves acknowledged that their article largely reflects the primary author's personal clinical experiences working on rural reservations in the Midwest. In the following section, we review the limited literature on treating anxiety and general mental health issues in AI/AN clients. In addition, we provide basic recommendations and a general framework through which CBT can be tailored to enhance the effectiveness of anxiety treatment with AI/ANs.

Using Cognitive Behavior Therapy Conceptualizations and Interventions Through an American Indian and Alaska Native Framework

A great multitude of interventions for anxiety are available to practitioners of CBT. These include relaxation training, exposure and systematic desensitization, cognitive restructuring, and behavioral activation, as well as exercise and nutritional interventions. In terms of addressing anxiety, the ultimate goal of these forms of interventions is to reduce physiological reactivity in the face of stressors (both internal and external), eliminate or reduce maladaptive behaviors (such as avoidance) that perpetuate anxiety, and change cognitions (negative self-talk) that create and perpetuate states of constant worry (Craske, 1999). On the surface, these interventions are not necessarily incongruent with an AI/AN worldview or AI/AN perspectives on what may help to overcome anxiety. Preliminary research has indicated that AI/AN clients may appreciate learning skills, developing concrete strategies for addressing anxiety, and proactively working toward their treatment goals both in and outside of counseling (Bennett & BigFoot-Sipes, 1991; Jackson et al., 2006; Lokken & Twohey, 2004; Stewart, Swift, Freitas-Murrell, & Whipple, 2013). Incompatibility with CBT may not necessarily lay in many of the specific interventions themselves but, rather, in how wellness is framed and communicated with AI/AN clients, the manner in which interventions are used, and the different expectations regarding the healing process and the relationship between client and clinician (Duran, 2006; Hodge et al., 2009; Jackson et al., 2006).

It is important to recognize that the major principle of CBT—that one's environment, cognitions, emotions, and behaviors are inherently connected—is also not necessarily incongruent with AI/AN perspectives of wellness (Bigfoot & Schmidt, 2010). As stated previously, AI/ANs are more likely to conceptualize wellness in a holistic sense and are likely to view the healing process as a proactive journey toward achieving balance and harmony in their lives (Hodge et al., 2009). AI/ANs believe this balance and harmony is achieved through the interplay between thoughts, emotions, spirituality, body, and environment. One can clearly recognize that there is significant overlap between traditional AI/AN models of wellness and the CBT treatment model. However, there remain important distinctions between these models with significant clinical implications.

One of the most salient illustrations of the discrepancy between CBT and traditional AI/AN models of wellness can be seen in how AI/ANs perceive one of the core aspects of CBT—conceptualizing problems in cognitive terms and linking these cognitions to emotions and behaviors. The strong focus of traditional CBT conceptualizations on how cognition is causally related to emotion and behavior may appear overly linear for AI/AN clients (Hodge et al., 2009; Jackson et al., 2006; Limb, Hodge, & Panos, 2008). In this context, a more effective way to integrate the relationship between thoughts, feelings, and behaviors may be through an approach that is in line with the more holistic framework to which many AI/ANs subscribe. Conceptualizing and communicating to AI/AN clients that maladaptive cognitions are a byproduct of imbalance and disharmony in a person's life and exploring how these cognitions are related to other major aspects of the client's life (i.e., spiritual, physical, emotional, and environmental context) may be a more culturally congruent and effective way of reframing the client's presenting issues.

Establishing the Relationship and Developing Rapport

Arguably, the most important aspect of therapy is the therapeutic relationship between the client and the mental health care provider. This relationship serves as the foundation on which therapeutic change occurs. Many of the factors that strengthen the therapeutic relationship among clients in general also apply to AI/AN clients. A qualitative study by Lokken and Twohey (2004) supports this premise, while also providing some insight as to how clinicians can modify their behavior to more effectively connect with AI/AN clients. Using a sample of 13 AI/AN participants who had previously engaged in counseling with White clinicians, Lokken and Twohey found that the clinician factors that were most salient for the participants were therapist authenticity, expression of concern for the client, therapist self-disclosure, expression of empathy, and the purposeful slowing down of the pace of counseling when identifying the problem of concern. Lokken and Twohey recommended that when working with AI/AN clients, it might be important to increase the use of self-disclosure and slow the pace before transitioning into problem identification because these may be uniquely beneficial in developing trust and rapport with AI/AN clients.

The great diversity among AI/AN tribes makes it difficult to provide strict guidelines regarding ways to interact interpersonally with AI/AN clients in a manner that is sensitive to customs, communication styles, and acculturation levels. Nevertheless, several scholars have provided some basic information on ways to interact interpersonally with AI/AN clients (De Coteau et al., 2006; Garrett & Herring, 2001; Garrett & Wilbur, 1999). These guidelines provide additional information and recommendations regarding how to use silence, eye contact, humility, and culturally appropriate greetings such as handshaking with AI/ANs. Although these guidelines can be a helpful resource when working with AI/AN clients, our recommendation is to follow the recommendation by Limb et al. (2008), who stated that the best course might be to follow clients' leads and subtly match them in terms of their verbal and nonverbal communication style.

A final key aspect of the therapeutic relationship involves expectations regarding the nature and boundaries of the relationship itself. The structured approach and clearly defined professional boundaries that characterize Western models of CBT may not be congruent with AI/AN conceptualizations of healing and the healing relationship (Jackson et al., 2006). As stated previously, many healing relationships with AI/ANs have traditionally been through elders, mentors, and medicine men, often part of the family or extended family, with personal and professional boundaries often less clearly defined. In accordance with the more informal nature of traditional healing relationships, it is recommended that clinicians consider exercising greater latitude with openness and self-disclosure when working with AI/AN clients. Clinicians who work with AI/ANs are also encouraged to be creative with treatment and exercise greater flexibility with session lengths, frequency of sessions, and the location in which therapy occurs. This greater flexibility is more congruent with AI/AN perspectives on healing relationships and may be more effective than a strict adherence to session limits and professional boundaries (De Coteau et al., 2006; Jackson et al., 2006).

It is important to remember that the initial interactions with AI/AN clients represent a critical juncture in that AI/AN clients' attitudes toward treatment and level of trust in the therapeutic process can be strongly influenced in the first few minutes of contact. It is crucial that clinicians make an active effort to be sensitive to issues of comfort, trust, and safety with AI/AN clients, particularly at the earliest stages of treatment. Like the general population, AI/AN clients are more likely to connect with clinicians who can better understand and empathize with their experience (Bennett & BigFoot-Sipes, 1991). In this capacity, clinicians should be sensitive to client attitudes and beliefs and should exercise caution so as not to invalidate the client's worldviews. In addition, it is recommended that clinicians work purposefully toward adapting the way in which they communicate with clients to engage clients in a manner congruent with their communication style.

Integrating Family Into Treatment

It is important for clinicians working with AI/AN clients to understand the role of family and community in both the expression and treatment of anxiety issues among AI/ANs. In this regard, families can be a source of stress as well as a source of great support for AI/ANs. As previously noted, issues such as poverty and high rates of substance use and intrafamilial violence are endemic to many AI/AN communities (Oetzel & Duran, 2004; Smith et al., 2006). This has significant implications for how and to whom AI/ANs reach out for support when they are struggling with mental health issues.

AI/ANs are believed to have a communal orientation and to espouse values that emphasize the importance of family, tribe, and community. For many AI/ANs, familial connections extend far beyond that of the Western concept of the nuclear family. Among certain tribes, the term *family* references the immediate and extended family, as well as the other members of the tribe or community (Limb et al., 2008). Research with AI/ANs has shown that greater connectedness to one's family and community is associated with several factors that increase resiliency, including greater self-esteem, higher academic achievement, and decreased alcohol abuse (King, Beals, Manson, & Trimble, 1992; LaFromboise, Hoyt, Oliver, & Whitbeck, 2006; Whitbeck, Chen, Hoyt,

& Adams, 2004). In addition, it is often through family members, particularly elder family members, that the cultural norms and values are transmitted to younger generations, which affirms identity, fosters connection to the larger community, and builds greater resiliency (LaFromboise et al., 2006).

As a major factor contributing to resiliency among AI/ANs, one of the crucial aspects of adapting treatment for anxiety with AI/AN clients involves the integration of family and extended family into the treatment process (De Coteau et al., 2006). Clinicians working with AI/AN clients can inquire about the family members and support networks that are especially important to the client. These family members and supports may then be invited to attend therapy sessions if clients believe this will be beneficial to their treatment. For many AI/ANs, because of the connectedness to family, this mode of counseling may be more comfortable than individual sessions and may ultimately be a more effective modality of treatment (Brucker & Perry, 1998; LaFromboise, Trimble, & Mohatt, 1990). In the context of integrating AI/AN family members and supports into treatment, clinicians working with AI/AN clients should pay attention to their own biases, values, and perspectives regarding family. A clinician with a very different perspective on family may be more likely to view interaction patterns among family members as manifestations of unhealthy enmeshment, as opposed to evidence of deep connectedness and respect among family members.

Integrating Spirituality and Traditional Healing Practices Into Treatment

As previously mentioned, AI/AN models of healing and wellness often focus on harmony between the mind, body, community, and spirituality (Portman & Garrett, 2006). When discussing the physiological, cognitive, and behavioral aspects of anxiety with AI/ANs, integrating spirituality as a fourth dimension may be of great importance (De Coteau et al., 2006). This is especially true for AI/ANs who believe that spiritual wellness is related to their physical and mental health.

Clinicians should work to be especially sensitive to the religious and spiritual identity of AI/AN clients and to be aware of how prayer, ceremony, and religious community supports can be integrated into the client's movement toward increased wellness. Clinicians can facilitate the integration of spirituality into treatment by inviting AI/AN clients to open a conversation about their religious and spiritual beliefs. Clinicians are also encouraged to invite AI/AN clients to explore the role that spirituality plays in how they can work toward greater wellness. For AI/ANs, prayers, ceremonies, and healing practices are often inherently connected to spirituality. Across different tribal groups there exists a multitude of different ceremonies and rituals that are used for healing, cleansing, empowering, celebrating, and expressing appreciation or gratitude (Portman & Garrett, 2006). Examples of such ceremonies and traditional practices include smudging, sweat lodge ceremonies, vision quests, powwows, and pipe ceremonies (Rybak & Decker-Fitts, 2009). Song, dance, and storytelling often play an integral role in many of these traditional practices (Portman & Garrett, 2006; Rybak & Decker-Fitts, 2009).

The integration of spirituality and traditional healing practices into therapy serves several functions. This integration can foster community and greater social interaction. It can also strengthen cultural and ethnic identity. These important components are associated with increased wellness and resiliency (LaFromboise et al., 2006). Clinicians who are intentional about the integration of spirituality and traditional healing practices into treatment demonstrate to AI/AN clients that their worldviews and cultural practices are seen as a valued part of the treatment process.

Active Stance as an Effective Component of Cognitive Behavior Therapy With American Indians and Alaska Natives

According to research by Jackson et al. (2006), AI/ANs may have a similar level of preference toward the active stance component of CBT as the general population. There are important implications for cognitive behavioral treatments for anxiety that may be taken from this unique finding. This finding indicates that both the therapist and client can benefit from taking an active role in the treatment process. That is, it is the role of the therapist to empower the client, provide support, teach anxiety and stress management skills, and provide "homework" the client can do outside the session. Likewise, it is the role of the client to complete homework assignments, practice stress and anxiety reduction techniques, and engage in behaviors and practices that decrease anxiety. One potential way to increase the effectiveness of this active stance approach is to frame anxiety reduction interventions as a way clients can actively work toward greater harmony and balance in their lives. Using the medicine wheel framework, as in the Native model of wellness, while also taking an active stance approach to treatment may empower clients and help them develop agency in a way that is congruent with their worldview.

The qualitative study by Lokken and Twohey (2004) on AI/AN perspectives of counseling supports the premise that an active approach in therapy is effective with AI/AN clients. The authors of the study reported that their sample of 13 AI/AN clients who participated in counseling reported a stronger preference toward therapists who were both active and open about explaining the process of counseling. The AI/AN participants also indicated that although they appreciated the active approach, they viewed themselves as the ultimate decider in the determination of the direction of counseling. Clinicians may thereby increase the effectiveness of their work with AI/AN clients by being more open about the therapeutic process and choice of interventions while also providing clients with greater autonomy in terms of determining the treatment approach and interventions they feel could be most beneficial.

THE FUTURE OF COGNITIVE BEHAVIORAL MODELS, METHODS, AND TREATMENTS FOR ANXIETY DISORDERS IN AMERICAN INDIANS AND ALASKA NATIVES

It is our sincere hope that this chapter has illuminated the great need for additional research on anxiety in AI/ANs. The lack of empirical examination into the efficacy of mental health assessment and treatment interventions for anxiety in AI/ANs is disheartening, especially given the multiple mental health disparities that exist for AI/ANs.

It is important to note that for us, the authors of this chapter, the concept of adapting CBT models of treatment for AI/ANs does not simply signify the addition of specific components (i.e., increased focus on family, spirituality, traditional practices) into the treatment process. Rather, the reverse is more accurate: CBT techniques, interventions, and perspectives are added to existing AI/AN models and conceptualizations of healing and wellness. We believe that what makes treatment more effective for AI/ANs is that there is a paradigm shift in how the CBT framework is conceptualized and used with AI/AN clients. Through culturally adapted therapies and culturally competent treatment providers, we believe CBT can be reframed and used in ways that are culturally congruent with AI/AN worldviews, practices, and attitudes. AI/AN healing practices and traditions are not simply conceptualized as behaviors and cognitive processes that promote better mental health but are also seen as fundamentally connected to AI/AN culture and identity. Therefore, we assert that the most effective treatments for anxiety disorders among AI/ANs will occur through the integration of Western and AI/AN healing traditions; however, whether this is truly the case remains to be seen. As has been underscored throughout this chapter, there are few treatments for anxiety that have been culturally adapted for use with AI/ANs. The few treatments that have undergone cultural adaptation, such as the PTSD-focused HC-MC program created by BigFoot and Schmidt (2010), have not been evaluated through rigorous outcomes research. Next steps in future research include creating new CBT-based intervention programs for other anxiety disorders (i.e., generalized anxiety disorder, panic disorder, specific phobias) and adapting treatments to the unique needs and perspectives of AI/AN clients. These interventions also require a formal and rigorous examination of outcomes to determine their effectiveness. At present, it remains largely unknown whether even the culturally adapted mental health treatments for anxiety among AI/ANs are truly effective.

In addition to highlighting the need for culturally adapted therapies, the goals of this chapter were to highlight the need for more culturally competent mental health clinicians and to provide mental health clinicians with additional information to increase their competence as it relates to using CBT for anxiety with AI/AN clients. It is our sincere hope that empirically based treatments will not only be created but will also be effectively disseminated to clinicians. However, we also recognize that the ability to conduct effective therapy within AI/AN communities and with AI/AN clients cannot occur solely through reading articles, treatment manuals, and book chapters. Future intervention and education efforts should focus on how effective, culturally adapted treatments are taught to clinicians. Given the diversity of tribal groups, unique worldviews, and healing traditions, this prospect can seem exceedingly challenging. Nonetheless, this is necessary because the creation of effective treatment programs is inadequate if clinicians, on a broader scale, cannot be trained to use these treatment approaches and interventions effectively.

One final point to emphasize is the important question of how CBT-based interventions can be most effectively used, given the stigma, issues of poverty, and other social problems within AI/AN communities. An important future direction for research and practice may be to focus on how mental health treatments for anxiety can be more effectively used on a broader level to increase treatment accessibility and service use—major problems among AI/ANs. This form of engagement would necessitate partnered collaboration between multiple institutions and parties within AI/AN communities. The importance of a stronger and more comprehensive community mental health approach cannot be understated. Even if culturally competent providers and empirically supported treatments for anxiety issues among AI/ANs did exist, problems related to accessibility and use would continue to represent major barriers to treatment for many AI/ANs. Given the importance of family, extended family, and community, an important direction for research is how to adapt and integrate mental health treatment in ways that are in line with this communal orientation. Substance abuse issues and adolescent suicide are two major problems faced by many AI/AN communities. Treatment programs and initiatives for these issues have benefited from partnered collaborations between multiple agencies and parties dedicated to increasing health and wellness among AI/ANs (e.g., LaFromboise & Lewis, 2008; Mohatt, Fok, Henry, & Allen, 2014). Treatments for anxiety disorders can also benefit from collaborations between schools, tribal government, the greater health system, and other agencies dedicated to increased wellness among AI/ANs.

CONCLUSION

The goal of our chapter was to synthesize the literature on anxiety treatments for AI/ANs and provide recommendations that may enable clinicians to adapt treatment to the unique needs and perspectives of AI/AN clients. It is important to recognize that what was covered in this chapter was specific to AI/AN anxiety and does not fully capture the depth or breadth of the social problems that affect AI/AN communities. These issues certainly influence AI/AN anxiety and help-seeking behavior. Similarly, it is just as important to recognize the great resiliency displayed by AI/AN individuals and communities in the face of massive historical and contemporary oppression. The traditions, perspectives, and healing practices that are unique to AI/ANs have been integral to building and promoting resiliency among AI/ANs. As such, these beliefs and practices, when integrated with Western models of treatment, are key factors in creating culturally congruent mental health treatment approaches.

REFERENCES

Beals, J., Manson, S. M., Whitesell, N. R., Spicer, P., Novins, D. K., & Mitchell, C. M. (2005). Prevalence of *DSM–IV* disorders and attendant help-seeking in 2 American Indian reservation populations. *Archives of General Psychiatry, 62,* 99–108. http://dx.doi.org/10.1001/archpsyc.62.1.99

Beck, A. T., Epstein, N., Brown, G., & Steer, R. A. (1988). An inventory for measuring clinical anxiety: Psychometric properties. *Journal of Consulting and Clinical Psychology, 56,* 893–897. http://dx.doi.org/10.1037/0022-006X.56.6.893

Bennett, S. K., & BigFoot-Sipes, D. S. (1991). American Indian and White college student preferences for counsellor characteristics. *Journal of Counseling Psychology, 38,* 440–445. http://dx.doi.org/10.1037/0022-0167.38.4.440

BigFoot, D. S., & Schmidt, S. R. (2010). Honoring children, mending the circle: Cultural adaptation of trauma-focused cognitive-behavioral therapy for American Indian and Alaska Native children. *Journal of Clinical Psychology, 66,* 847–856. http://dx.doi.org/10.1002/jclp.20707

Brave Heart, M. Y. H. (2003). The historical trauma response among natives and its relationship with substance abuse: A Lakota illustration. *Journal of Psychoactive Drugs, 35,* 7–13. http://dx.doi.org/10.1080/02791072.2003.10399988

Brave Heart, M. Y. H., & DeBruyn, L. M. (1998). The American Indian Holocaust: Healing historical unresolved grief. *American Indian and Alaska Native Mental Health Research, 8,* 56–78.

Brucker, P. S., & Perry, B. J. (1998). American Indians: Presenting concerns and considerations for family therapists. *American Journal of Family Therapy, 26,* 307–319. http://dx.doi.org/10.1080/01926189808251109

Craske, M. G. (1999). *Anxiety disorders: Psychological approaches to theory and treatment.* Boulder, CO: Westview Press.

Dapice, A. N. (2006). The medicine wheel. *Journal of Transcultural Nursing, 17,* 251–260. http://dx.doi.org/10.1177/1043659606288383

De Coteau, T., Anderson, J., & Hope, D. (2006). Adapting manualized treatments: Treating anxiety disorders among Native Americans. *Cognitive and Behavioral Practice, 13,* 304–309. http://dx.doi.org/10.1016/j.cbpra.2006.04.012

De Coteau, T. J., Hope, D. A., & Anderson, J. (2003). Anxiety, stress, and health in northern plains Native Americans. *Behavior Therapy, 34,* 365–380. http://dx.doi.org/10.1016/S0005-7894(03)80006-0

Derogatis, L. R., & Unger, R. (2010). Symptom Checklist-90–Revised. In I. B. Weiner & W. E. Craighead (Eds.), *The Corsini encyclopedia of psychology* (pp. 81–84). New York, NY: Wiley.

Duran, E. (2006). *Healing the soul wound: Counseling with American Indians and other Native peoples.* New York, NY: Teacher's College.

Duran, E., & Duran, B. (1995). *Native American postcolonial psychology.* Albany: SUNY Press.

Evans-Campbell, T. (2008). Historical trauma in American Indian/Native Alaska communities: A multilevel framework for exploring impacts on individuals, families, and communities. *Journal of Interpersonal Violence, 23,* 316–338. http://dx.doi.org/10.1177/0886260507312290

Garrett, M. T., & Herring, R. D. (2001). Honoring the power of relation: Counseling Native adults. *The Journal of Humanistic Counseling, Education and Development, 40,* 139–160. http://dx.doi.org/10.1002/j.2164-490X.2001.tb00113.x

Garrett, M. T., & Pichette, E. F. (2000). Red as an apple: Native American acculturation and counseling with or without reservation. *Journal of Counseling & Development, 78,* 3–13. http://dx.doi.org/10.1002/j.1556-6676.2000.tb02554.x

Garrett, M. T., & Wilbur, M. P. (1999). Does the worm live in the ground? Reflections on Native American spirituality. *Journal of Multicultural Counseling and Development, 27,* 193–206. http://dx.doi.org/10.1002/j.2161-1912.1999.tb00335.x

Gary, F. A. (2005). Stigma: Barrier to mental health care among ethnic minorities. *Issues in Mental Health Nursing, 26,* 979–999. http://dx.doi.org/10.1080/01612840500280638

Gone, J. P. (2004). Mental health services for Native Americans in the 21st century United States. *Professional Psychology: Research and Practice, 35,* 10–18. http://dx.doi.org/10.1037/0735-7028.35.1.10

Gone, J. P., & Trimble, J. E. (2012). American Indian and Alaska Native mental health: Diverse perspectives on enduring disparities. *Annual Review of Clinical Psychology, 8*, 131–160. http://dx.doi.org/10.1146/annurev-clinpsy-032511-143127

Grandbois, D. (2005). Stigma of mental illness among American Indian and Alaska Native nations: Historical and contemporary perspectives. *Issues in Mental Health Nursing, 26*, 1001–1024. http://dx.doi.org/10.1080/01612840500280661

Gray, J. S., McCullagh, J. A., & Petros, T. (2016). Assessment of anxiety among Northern Plains Indians. *American Journal of Orthopsychiatry, 86*, 186–193. http://dx.doi.org/10.1037/ort0000103

Hodge, D. R., Limb, G. E., & Cross, T. L. (2009). Moving from colonization toward balance and harmony: A Native American perspective on wellness. *Social Work, 54*, 211–219. http://dx.doi.org/10.1093/sw/54.3.211

Jackson, L. C., Schmutzer, P. A., & Wenzel, A. (2002, November). *Construction and validation of the Cognitive Behavior Therapy Applicability Scale (CBT-AS)*. Poster session presented at the meeting of the Association for the Advancement of Behavior Therapy, Reno, NV.

Jackson, L. C., Schmutzer, P. A., Wenzel, A., & Tyler, J. D. (2006). Applicability of cognitive-behavior therapy with American Indian individuals. *Psychotherapy: Theory, Research, Practice, Training, 43*, 506–517. http://dx.doi.org/10.1037/0033-3204.43.4.506

Kessler, R. C., Berglund, P., Demler, O., Jin, R., Merikangas, K. R., & Walters, E. E. (2005). Lifetime prevalence and age-of-onset distributions of DSM–IV disorders in the National Comorbidity Survey Replication. *Archives of General Psychiatry, 62*, 593–602. http://dx.doi.org/10.1001/archpsyc.62.6.593

Kessler, R. C., Chiu, W. T., Demler, O., & Walters, E. E. (2005). Prevalence, severity, and comorbidity of 12-month DSM–IV disorders in the National Comorbidity Survey Replication. *Archives of General Psychiatry, 62*, 617–627. http://dx.doi.org/10.1001/archpsyc.62.6.617

King, J., Beals, J., Manson, S. M., & Trimble, J. E. (1992). A structural equation model of factors related to substance use among American Indian adolescents. *Drugs & Society, 6*, 253–268. http://dx.doi.org/10.1300/J023v06n03_04

LaFromboise, T. D., Hoyt, D. R., Oliver, L., & Whitbeck, L. B. (2006). Family, community, and school influences on resilience among American Indian adolescents in the upper Midwest. *Journal of Community Psychology, 34*, 193–209. http://dx.doi.org/10.1002/jcop.20090

LaFromboise, T. D., & Lewis, H. A. (2008). The Zuni Life Skills Development Program: A school/community-based suicide prevention intervention. *Suicide and Life-Threatening Behavior, 38*, 343–353. http://dx.doi.org/10.1521/suli.2008.38.3.343

LaFromboise, T. D., Trimble, J. E., & Mohatt, G. V. (1990). Counseling intervention and American Indian tradition: An integrative approach. *The Counseling Psychologist, 18*, 628–654. http://dx.doi.org/10.1177/0011000090184006

Limb, G. E., Hodge, D. R., & Panos, P. (2008). Social work with native people: Orienting child welfare workers to the beliefs, values, and practices of Native American families and children. *Journal of Public Child Welfare, 2*, 383–397. http://dx.doi.org/10.1080/15548730802463595

Lokken, J. M., & Twohey, D. (2004). American Indian perspectives of Euro-American counseling behavior. *Journal of Multicultural Counseling and Development, 32*, 320–331.

McDonald, J. D., Jackson, T. L., & McDonald, A. L. (1991). Perceived anxiety differences among reservation and non-reservation Native American and majority culture college students. *Journal of Indigenous Studies, 2*, 71–79.

Messer, S. B., & Wampold, B. E. (2002). Let's face facts: Common factors are more potent than specific therapy ingredients. *Clinical Psychology: Science and Practice, 9*, 21–25. http://dx.doi.org/10.1093/clipsy.9.1.21

Mohatt, G. V., Fok, C. C. T., Henry, D., & Allen, J. (2014). Feasibility of a community intervention for the prevention of suicide and alcohol abuse with Yup'ik Alaska Native youth: The Elluam Tungiinun and Yupiucimta Asvairtuumallerkaa studies. *American Journal of Community Psychology, 54*, 153–169. http://dx.doi.org/10.1007/s10464-014-9646-2

Norton, P. J., De Coteau, T. J., Hope, D. A., & Anderson, J. (2004). The factor structure of the Anxiety Sensitivity Index among Northern Plains Native Americans. *Behaviour Research and Therapy, 42*, 241–247. http://dx.doi.org/10.1016/j.brat.2003.10.002

Oetzel, J., & Duran, B. (2004). Intimate partner violence in American Indian and/or Alaska Native communities: A social ecological framework of determinants and interventions. *American Indian and Alaska Native Mental Health Research, 11*, 49–68. http://dx.doi.org/10.5820/aian.1103.2004.49

Olatunji, B. O., Cisler, J. M., & Tolin, D. F. (2007). Quality of life in the anxiety disorders: A meta-analytic review. *Clinical Psychology Review, 27*, 572–581. http://dx.doi.org/10.1016/j.cpr.2007.01.015

Portman, T. A. A., & Garrett, M. T. (2006). Native American healing traditions. *International Journal of Disability Development and Education, 53*, 453–469. http://dx.doi.org/10.1080/10349120601008647

Reiss, S., Peterson, R. A., Gursky, D. M., & McNally, R. J. (1986). Anxiety sensitivity, anxiety frequency and the prediction of fearfulness. *Behaviour Research and Therapy, 24*, 1–8. http://dx.doi.org/10.1016/0005-7967(86)90143-9

Rybak, C., & Decker-Fitts, A. (2009). Understanding Native American healing practices. *Counselling Psychology Quarterly, 22*, 333–342. http://dx.doi.org/10.1080/09515070903270900

Smith, S. M., Stinson, F. S., Dawson, D. A., Goldstein, R., Huang, B., & Grant, B. F. (2006). Race/ethnic differences in the prevalence and co-occurrence of substance use disorders and independent mood and anxiety disorders: Results from the National Epidemiologic Survey on Alcohol and Related Conditions. *Psychological Medicine, 36,* 987–998. http://dx.doi.org/10.1017/S0033291706007690

Stewart, T. J., Swift, J. K., Freitas-Murrell, B. N., & Whipple, J. L. (2013). Preferences for mental health treatment options among Alaska Native college students. *American Indian and Alaska Native Mental Health Research, 20,* 59–78. http://dx.doi.org/10.5820/aian.2003.2013.59

Strine, T. W., Chapman, D. P., Kobau, R., Balluz, L., & Mokdad, A. H. (2004). Depression, anxiety, and physical impairments and quality of life in the U.S. noninstitutionalized population. *Psychiatric Services, 55,* 1408–1413. http://dx.doi.org/10.1176/appi.ps.55.12.1408

Whitbeck, B. L., Chen, X., Hoyt, D. R., & Adams, G. W. (2004). Discrimination, historical loss and enculturation: Culturally specific risk and resiliency factors for alcohol abuse among American Indians. *Journal of Studies on Alcohol, 65,* 409–418. http://dx.doi.org/10.15288/jsa.2004.65.409

Zvolensky, M. J., McNeil, D. W., Porter, C. A., & Stewart, S. H. (2001). Assessment of anxiety sensitivity in young American Indians and Alaska Natives. *Behaviour Research and Therapy, 39,* 477–493. http://dx.doi.org/10.1016/S0005-7967(00)00010-3

III

COGNITIVE BEHAVIORAL MODELS, MEASURES, AND TREATMENTS FOR STRESS DISORDERS

9

COGNITIVE BEHAVIORAL MODELS, MEASURES, AND TREATMENTS FOR STRESS DISORDERS IN ASIAN AMERICANS

JOYCE CHU, HOLLY BATCHELDER, AND GABRIELLE POON

Stress is widely understood as both the emotional and physical response to threatening events, with the subjective experience and approaches to measurement of stress differing across person and context (Amirkhan, Urizar, & Clark, 2015; Wenzel, Glanz, & Lerman, 2002). Biological indicators of stress have been measured through cortisol levels and physiological responses such as muscle tension, sweating, and pulse rate (Adam & Kumari, 2009), whereas psychological measures of stress have included life events checklists, perceived stress interviews, and specific characteristics such as socioeconomic status (Amirkhan et al., 2015). Although there are many individual experiences of stress, research to date strongly indicates psychosocial stress as a risk factor for a wide array of negative physical, cognitive, and emotional outcomes, which may lead to impairment in daily functioning and chronic mental health issues (Hammen, 2015).

http://dx.doi.org/10.1037/0000091-010

Treating Depression, Anxiety, and Stress in Ethnic and Racial Groups: Cognitive Behavioral Approaches, E. C. Chang, C. A. Downey, J. K. Hirsch, and E. A. Yu (Editors)

Asian Americans, in particular, have been underresearched in understanding the effects and treatments of stress. Though Asian Americans have been found to respond to stress in different ways than Caucasian populations (e.g., somatization; H. Lee & Mason, 2014), many of the existing research and treatments for stress have implemented a one-size-fits-all approach, leaving out key cultural elements for evaluation and treatment. Modifications for existing evidence-based treatments have been created for Asian American populations (Chu, Huynh, & Areán, 2012; Hwang, Wood, Lin, & Cheung, 2006), but such culturally modified treatments are not widely available, and Asian Americans remain more likely than the general population to underuse services and terminate treatment prematurely (S. Sue, Cheng, Saad, & Chu, 2012). In addition, many of these approaches address only select Asian American subgroups, with fewer interventions addressing specific within-group differences among various Asian American subgroups and few interventions tested with non-Chinese Asian American subgroups (Chu et al., 2012; Hwang, 2009; Kim, Yang, Atkinson, Wolfe, & Hong, 2001; Pan, Huey, & Hernandez, 2011). The 2010 U.S. Census revealed that at least 25 different Asian cultural groups exist in the United States, including ethnic subgroups such as Asian Indian, Burmese, Chinese, Hmong, Korean, Malaysian, Pakistani, and others (Hoeffel, Rastogi, Kim, & Shahid, 2012). Kim and colleagues (2001) examined differences in traditional Asian values between four Asian American ethnic groups: Chinese American, Filipino American, Japanese American, and Korean American. This examination revealed significant differences in adherence to traditional values. For example, Filipino Americans demonstrated lesser adherence to the filial piety factor than the other ethnic groups, Japanese Americans had greater adherence to conformity to norms than Chinese Americans, and Korean Americans exhibited a firmer adherence to family recognition through achievement compared with Chinese Americans. The results of this study underscore the importance of awareness of diversity within the Asian American population (Kim et al., 2001).

In this chapter, we present a comprehensive analysis of how cultural factors and variations affect the stress response and coping process among Asian Americans, focusing on theoretical considerations, culturally specific stressors, expressions of stress, and coping responses. In light of these cultural variations in stress, we review the applicability of current and predominant approaches to assessment and cognitive behavioral treatment to stress among the diverse Asian American groups and discuss proposed cognitive behavioral adaptations to ensure a culturally competent and individualized approach with this underserved population.

STRESS THEORIES AND THE INFLUENCE OF CULTURE

Predominant theories of stress and coping allude to mechanisms of cultural influence in their emphasis on the interaction between individuals and their environment. Lazarus and Folkman's (1984) transactional model of stress posits that one's coping response and emotional and physical experience of stress are determined by the interaction of a person's cognitive appraisals of an event and elements of the environment (Folkman & Lazarus, 1988). Primary appraisal (personal interpretation of an event) is followed by secondary appraisal, or how the event is understood and whether the outcome can be controlled by the individual.

Subsequently, specific appraisals or judgments of stressful events yield problem-focused and emotion-focused coping strategies (Lazarus & Folkman, 1984; Roubinov, Turner, & Williams, 2015). The selection of the types of coping depends on how an event is appraised (Folkman & Moskowitz, 2004). Lazarus and Folkman (1984) identified problem-focused coping as a form of coping based on changing the fundamental cause of a stressor. This strategy has been found to be effective if the stress is modifiable but ineffective when the stressor is unchangeable (Conway & Terry, 1992). Emotion-focused coping involves self-reflection and controlling one's emotions through the cognitive reappraisal process (Carver, 2011). Emotion-focused coping techniques have been found to be effective when paired with unchangeable stressors (DeGraff & Schaffer, 2008).

Given that changeability of a stressor is largely influenced by cultural aspects of one's environment, Lazarus and Folkman's (1984) transactional model of stress implicitly alludes to the importance of culture. For example, if a traditional Korean family's disapproval of interracial marriage is unlikely to change because of cultural traditions and beliefs, the environmental stressor may not change, and emotion-focused or avoidance rather than problem-focused or approach coping may be indicated. Overall, however, the transactional model of stress does not directly or explicitly integrate cultural factors into its theoretical explanations.

Epstein's (1990) cognitive-experiential self-theory (CEST) also provides an opening to understanding the influence of culture on stress and coping without directly positing a mechanism of effect. The CEST is a model of coping that describes how people relate to their external environment through past experiences, with constructive and destructive thought patterns measured by the Constructive Thinking Inventory (CTI; Epstein & Meier, 1989). Hypothetically, if Asian Americans experience their cultural world differently, they might react to their external environment differently, as measured by the CTI.

Social problem solving according to D'Zurilla (1986) refers to the cognitive, affective, and behavioral process by which a person attempts to cope in the real world. This theory's emphasis on coping processes in interaction with real-world problems suggests that environmental systems and cultural influences would affect one's choice and use of coping strategies, though such cultural factors are not directly addressed.

INTEGRATION OF CULTURAL INFLUENCES WITH STRESS THEORIES

Though existing theories of stress provide a platform for the influence of culture and ethnicity within their integration of environmental influences in the coping process, they stop short of directly or explicitly addressing cultural factors in their conceptualization of stress. To obtain an accurate understanding of stress among Asian Americans, cultural factors must be identified and incorporated into our theoretical understandings. Three theories in particular—Bronfenbrenner's (1979) ecological model; Chu, Goldblum, Floyd, and Bongar's (2010) cultural theory and model of suicide; and Meyer's (1995) minority stress model—demonstrate that stress in cultural minorities such as Asian Americans should be understood from models that are broader in context and account for culturally specific risk factors, coping styles, and idioms of distress.

First, Bronfenbrenner's (1979) ecological model demonstrates how environmental factors such as social and cultural elements affect human development in terms of how an individual perceives, experiences, and interacts with his or her environment—including the development of stress. Bronfenbrenner proposed that essential to understanding human development and stress is the examination of cultural differences at four main levels of an ecological system: the *microsystem* (one's immediate environment), *mesosystem* (the interactions between one's multiple microsystems), *exosystem* (influential environmental settings not directly contacted by an individual such as local government activities), and *macrosystem* (attitudes and ideologies of the culture). Bronfenbrenner's ecological theory maintains that cultural influence on stress should be understood within a broader context of environmental influence within a multilayered system.

Second, cultural theories addressing mental health constructs related to stress might inform the integration of cultural influences into theoretical understandings of stress. The cultural theory and model of suicide (Chu et al., 2010) serves as an example of the full integration of cultural factors into a conceptualization of developmental pathways to suicidal behaviors (a potential manifestation of stress). The three main theoretical principles of the cultural theory and model of suicide yield important information for translation to a similar cultural model for the developmental pathway of stress. The first principle of the cultural theory and model of suicide states that culture influences the types of stressors or life events—namely, minority stress, social discord, and shame events—that precipitate suicidal distress. The second theoretical principle states that culture affects the manner and language by which suicidal distress is expressed and experienced. The third principle contends that the cultural meanings ascribed to stressors or the experience of suicidal distress affect the development of distress.

Third, Meyer's (1995) minority stress model, which was derived from a number of social and psychological approaches, integrates smoothly with the cultural theory and model of suicide. Meyer's model highlights stress related to stigmatization and minority status of cultural minority groups and the cumulative impact on distress. For example, among gay men, stress related to internalized homophobia, perceived stigma, discrimination, and violence contributes directly to the experience of minority stress, which predicts poorer health outcomes. The aggregate minority stress experience was found to increase the risk of high levels of psychological distress two- to threefold (Meyer, 1995). This increased exposure to minority stress and the resulting increase in psychological distress also reduces the availability of coping resources (Meyer, Schwartz, & Frost, 2008). These coping resources include lesser social resources—specifically, a smaller social network from which individuals can draw support, such as assistance with household responsibilities, companionship, and the ability to borrow money, and a reduced sense of mastery, including helplessness and feelings of loss of control (Meyer et al., 2008). Our review of the literature regarding Asian American mental health shows that the theoretical principles of the cultural theory and model of suicide and the minority stress model also apply to the ways in which culture influences the development and experience of psychological stress.

As indicated by cultural models and theories, when understanding the development of stress, coping responses to stress, and ultimately how to treat stress, cultural factors are influential at several major junctures. In the following sections, we discuss three major cultural factors that influence the developmental pathway of stress: (a) culturally specific stressors (many of which take place at different levels of one's ecological system) that uniquely affect Asian American individuals, (b) cultural expressions or idioms of stress reactions among Asian Americans, and (c) cultural differences among Asian Americans in coping responses to stress (as influenced by the cultural meanings ascribed to the use of different coping strategies). These three categories of cultural influence mirror those delineated in the cultural theory and model of suicide (Chu et al., 2010) and the minority stress theory (Meyer, 1995), and are represented within multiple levels of the ecological system (Bronfenbrenner, 1979).

CULTURALLY SPECIFIC STRESSORS

Cultural theories depicting developmental psychopathology have identified culturally specific life events and stressors as triggers of mental health symptoms and stress. The majority of these life events and stressors reside within the micro-, meso-, macro-, and exosystem levels of the ecological environment. In this section, we discuss several culturally specific stressors salient for Asian American communities, presented in order of occurrence in the micro to macro levels of the ecological system: perfectionism, loss of face, family and intergenerational conflict, stress related to minority status, acculturative stress, and stigma and shame. These culturally specific stressors are important to identify, understand, and incorporate into cognitive and behavioral treatment approaches to stress among Asian Americans.

Perfectionism

Perfectionism is the critical evaluation of one's self while striving for extremely high and unrealistic standards, with maladaptive perfectionism occurring in the presence of a discrepancy between expectations and performance (Stoeber & Otto, 2006). Those with maladaptive perfectionism are likely to equate flawless performance with self-worth, increasing the internalization of personal failure. In addition, self-critical perfectionism can be a vulnerability factor for stress and depressive disorders.

Maladaptive perfectionism may have unique relevance to Asian Americans originating from South Korea, China, and India, for whom the individual perfectionism construct may stem from microsystem influences of greater parental criticism and higher parental expectations than non-Hispanic whites (Rowell, Mechlin, Ji, Addamo, & Girdler, 2011). Indeed, studies have found that maladaptive perfectionism is highly related to depression in East Asian international students (Hamamura & Laird, 2014). Acculturative stress, in particular, has been found to increase the negative effects of perfectionism on Asian American international students, including individuals identifying with Chinese, Filipino, Japanese, Korean, Laotian, multiethnic Asian, Taiwanese, and Vietnamese heritage (Wei et al., 2007).

Family and Intergenerational Conflict

Conflict at the microsystem level within the family system can be a culturally salient predictor of stress among Asian Americans. Value and acculturation discrepancies (e.g., in the areas of familial obligations and cultural traditions) are main sources of family conflict among both immigrant and U.S.-born Asian Americans (Ma, Desai, George, San Filippo,

& Varon, 2014; Phinney, Ong, & Madden, 2000; Tsai-Chae & Nagata, 2008). For example, Asian American adults (i.e., Asian Indian, Taiwanese, Chinese, Japanese, and Filipino) who select career paths that differ from familial expectations and obligations also experience stress related to familial disapproval or misunderstanding as a result of differing cultural values and the underlying roots of filial piety (Ma et al., 2014). Among Korean women, child care and household burdens combined with the absence of the husband and along with conflicting identities of wife, mother, and daughter-in-law can result in marital discord and conflict with in-laws, causing significant stress (J. K. Lee & Park, 2001). Generational status in the United States also affects the perception of conflict. For example, first-generation Asian Americans may perceive greater reciprocity and less conflict in familial interactions compared with second-generation Asian Americans (Costigan, Bardina, Cauce, Kim, & Latendresse, 2006). The severity of the family conflict affects the stress experience via positive affect, negative affect, and somatic symptoms and has been found to be a highly relevant issue, particularly among Asian American children and young adults (R. M. Lee, Su, & Yoshida, 2005).

Stress Related to Minority Status

Stressors related to minority status can occur across the ecological system at the micro-, meso-, macro-, and exosystem levels. Minority stress involves stressors related to minority status such as prejudice or discrimination in the form of microaggressions, obvious discrimination, and social disadvantages due to one's minority status (Chu et al., 2010). Racial microaggressions directed at Asian Americans commonly include the assumption that all Asian Americans are foreigners, ascription of intelligence, dismissal of Asian Americans' experience of racism or discrimination, exoticization of Asian American women (including beliefs and interpretations that Asian American women are subservient in caring for the needs of men), dismissal of interethnic differences among Asian subgroups, penalization or pathologization of cultural values and communication styles, and experience of being overlooked or invisible (D. W. Sue, Bucceri, Lin, Nadal, & Torino, 2009). These microaggressions and perceived discrimination have a significant negative impact on stress and well-being among South Asians (e.g., individuals originating from Pakistan, India, Bangladesh; Kaduvettoor-Davidson & Inman, 2013). For example, in a study evaluating the impact of these microaggressions, over three quarters of participants experienced at least one microaggression within a 2-week period, and those who experienced more microaggressions also reported higher levels of negative affect and more somatic symptoms (Ong, Burrow, Fuller-Rowell, Ja, & Sue, 2013).

Asian Americans experience varied modes of discrimination including being subjected to racial slurs such as name-calling and pretending to speak in or mocking an Asian language; being considered as "eternal others," thus invalidating their American identities; and being unfairly treated in academic and/or professional settings because of the model minority image and stereotypes (Jun, 2012). High levels of discrimination are related to low perceptions of well-being among South Asian Americans (Kaduvettoor-Davidson & Inman, 2013). Minority stress also encompasses social disadvantages due to minority status. A study by Spencer-Rodgers and Peng (2014) revealed disadvantages among Asian Americans to include various experiences, such as being excluded socially, experiencing disadvantages due to linguistic and cultural differences, not being selected for athletic teams, experiencing disadvantages due to competition with other identified Asians, and experiencing incidents involving professionals, clerks, or officials. Financial disadvantages also exist, with Asian Americans born and educated outside the United States (i.e., Chinese, Filipino, Japanese, Asian Indian, Southeast Asian) earning approximately 16% less than American-born and educated Caucasians and Asians (Zeng & Xie, 2004). In addition, the rate of working poverty among Asian immigrant females is approximately 3 times that of American-born females, and the rate of job mismatch is approximately 1.5 times that of American-born females (De Jong & Madamba, 2001).

Acculturative Stress

At the mesosystem level, the process of migration and *acculturation*—the change and adjustment that takes place amidst contact with a different cultural group—can serve as stressful experiences for both immigrant Asian and Asian American individuals (Berry, 2005). Acculturating individuals of Chinese, Vietnamese, Japanese, Taiwanese, and Korean ethnic groups struggling to adapt to the mainstream culture experience greater distress, which significantly affects psychological well-being (Hwang & Ting, 2008). Stress reactions that occur in response to problems related to the process of acculturation and adjustment to American culture are termed *acculturative stress* (Berry, 2005). Among Asian Americans (i.e., Chinese, Filipino, Vietnamese, and other Asian ethnic groups), acculturative stress reactions are commonly precipitated by problems related to English-language proficiency, discrimination, family cohesion, and context of the migration from one's home country (Lueck & Wilson, 2010). In addition, stress related to other domains of acculturation, such as identification or ties with the country of origin and the experience of social distance from family, friends, and community, is a common experience for Asian American immigrants (D. S. Lee & Padilla, 2014).

As much as 70% of Asian immigrants report experiencing acculturative stress (Lueck & Wilson, 2010), though such figures may represent underestimations because of the cultural norm of underreporting stress among immigrant Asian Americans (Uppaluri, Schumm, & Lauderdale, 2001). Among acculturating individuals, particularly the elderly (i.e., Chinese, Filipino, Indian, Japanese, Korean, and Japanese), high rates of depression are attributed to acculturative stress (Mui & Kang, 2006). This pattern has also been demonstrated among Asian college students (i.e., Chinese, Vietnamese, Japanese, Taiwanese, and Korean), with each incremental increase in perceived acculturative stress increasing odds for depression by 1.37 times (Hwang & Ting, 2008). In an examination of patterns of acculturative stress, research has shown that although individuals experience these stressors from the time of arrival in the host country, the stress level is lower immediately following immigration and increases with each passing year in the United States (Uppaluri et al., 2001).

Stigma and Shame

In the exo- and macrosystem levels of many collectivist cultures, having a mental illness is considered to be shameful and highly stigmatizing (B. C. Kuo, 2011). The fear of shame is also related to preserving one's family name by "saving face." Shame itself may serve as a stressor because individuals blame themselves when they experience significant levels of distress (Leong & Lau, 2001). Asian Americans may fear being perceived as "weak" or "crazy," leading to underreporting and low treatment-seeking behavior (Gee, Spencer, Chen, Yip, & Takeuchi, 2007). Therefore, the fear of being stigmatized, avoidance of treatment and support, and shame of expressing mental health symptoms are precipitates of stress. Contrary to belief, greater levels of acculturation may not necessarily yield decreased stigma about mental illness. For example, S. Y. Lin (2013) found that the social stigma associated with mental disorders was at the same levels among Chinese American acculturated immigrants as new Chinese immigrants.

CULTURALLY VARIANT EXPRESSIONS AND EXPERIENCES OF STRESS AMONG ASIAN AMERICANS

Regardless of the specific stressor or event that precipitates a stress response, research has indicated that Asian Americans experience culturally variant expressions or idioms of stress. In the cognitive, affective, somatic, and behavioral realms, Asian Americans may be less likely to express psychological stress in the affective domain.

Somatization

The mind–body experience of Asian Americans has been shown to be notably different from Western conceptualizations. In many Asian American cultures, mind and body are equally important, such as in traditional Chinese medicine. These cultural and social forces shape how distress is expressed through physical symptoms, which may help decrease stigmatization related to mental health. This "somatization" may be reinforced through the mind–body integration prominent in Asian culture (e.g., Singaporean individuals), making clients feel more comfortable reporting somatic symptoms rather than emotional distress (B. Lee, 2013). Indeed, research has suggested that psychologization of distress is more common in Western cultures, with somatization an idiom of distress worldwide, including among Chinese Americans (Ryder et al., 2008).

Stoicism

Stoicism has been valued as a way of coping in Eastern Asian philosophy (Sun, 2016; Uba, 2002). The act of stoicism has been directly related to the cultural value of maintaining self-conduct. In traditional Asian cultures, preserving harmony among others is important, especially when one may be experiencing pain. Asian clients may exemplify stoicism in the face of extreme pain to maintain dignity and respect within their cultural context and to avoid drawing attention to themselves. Asian clients (i.e., Southeast Asian refugees) may also avoid complaining about emotional pain to a doctor, nurse, or other authority figure because the social status of a health professional may be superior to their own (Pityaratstian et al., 2015). Therefore, an individual may be experiencing intense sadness but has been socialized to maintain this strong cultural value of self-conduct and respect (Sun, 2016).

COGNITIVE AND BEHAVIORAL DIFFERENCES IN COPING RESPONSE TO STRESS

Not only do Asian Americans experience culturally specific stressors and events that precipitate a uniquely expressed psychological stress response, but further down the pathway of the stress response, Asian Americans also choose and use different coping strategies. Though the specific reasons for these differences in coping strategies still require further study, research and theory have indicated that cultural meanings ascribed to the use of different coping strategies may selectively reinforce some coping strategies as more acceptable and sanctioned than others. Research has suggested several cognitive and behavioral differences in the coping response to stress among Asian Americans.

One prominent example of ethnic variations in coping among Asian Americans is related to the cultural value and practice of emotional control. Emotional control has been highly emphasized in East Asian cultures, resulting in diminished emotional responding (Eid & Diener, 2001; Tsai & Levenson, 1997). Similarly, people experiencing depressive symptoms also demonstrate diminished reactivity to various emotional cues (Rottenberg, Kasch, Gross, & Gotlib, 2002). Given this understanding, one might expect Asian Americans with depression to also demonstrate the same diminished responding. Contrary to these expectations, Chentsova-Dutton and colleagues (2007) found that although nondepressed Asian Americans demonstrated emotional inhibitions, depressed Asian Americans demonstrated greater expressions of sadness (indicated by crying) in response to a sad film compared with European Americans. These results suggest that ethnic and cultural factors can yield a contradiction in norms of symptom presentation and that deviations in symptom expression from cultural norms may increase one's risk of negative symptoms or stressful experiences. Though Asian Americans typically practice control of their emotional expression, at more severe levels of stress (i.e., clinical levels of depression), coping strategies of emotion suppression or emotional control are replaced by a coping strategy that differs from cultural norms—one of increased expression.

Other research has also pointed to significant ethnic variations in coping strategies among Asian Americans. E. C. Chang (2001), for example, found ethnic differences in disengagement-oriented coping efforts, with Asian Americans reporting higher scores on problem avoidance and social withdrawal (i.e., distancing oneself from others and the problem that may help with the problem) than their Caucasian counterparts. In addition, on a measure that assesses coping at more of a trait level (the CTI), E. C. Chang found that Asian Americans reported less global constructive thinking (greater constructive thinking ability) and emotional coping (e.g., the tendency to not worry, to not be sensitive to disapproval) than Caucasian Americans. Moreover, Asian Americans reported higher superstitious thinking, esoteric thinking, categorical thinking, and naive optimism. Finally, on the Social Problem-Solving Inventory–Revised (D'Zurilla, Nezu, & Maydeu-Olivares, 2018), E. C. Chang found that Asian Americans endorsed higher impulsivity and carelessness style scores compared with Caucasian Americans.

Other research has demonstrated that Chinese individuals and families experience stress simultaneously through important social entities, such as their family and workplace, suggesting a multilayered coping process (Phillips & Pearson, 1987). In addition to contextual differences, H. Lee and Mason (2014) found that Korean Americans had higher scores on emotion-focused coping strategies and avoidant coping strategies than Caucasian Americans. Gender may also contribute to different coping strategies among Asian Americans; Korean older women scored higher on religious coping and denial, whereas Korean older men were more likely to use instrumental support and substance abuse, demonstrating the importance of access to resources (H. Lee & Mason, 2014).

ASSESSING STRESS

Valid and reliable tools for establishing stress levels are essential to determine treatment approaches and track outcomes. Assessments that measure stress have ranged from physical (e.g., cortisol, physiological reactions) to self-report (e.g., perceived levels, types of stressful events). Various measures assessing different domains of stress exist and are well researched. However, few of these assessments have been normed for Asian Americans, who, as previously described, may experience and exhibit symptoms of stress differently from the general population and who also experience different types of events as more stressful (e.g., loss of face).

Generic Measures of Stress

In this section, we review general measures for stress and measures tailored to culturally based stressors and expressions of stress among Asian Americans.

Depression Anxiety Stress Scales

The Depression Anxiety Stress Scales 21 (DASS-21) has been shown to hold sufficient construct validity and is highly regarded for nonclinical populations (Henry & Crawford, 2005). The DASS-21 is a short form of Lovibond and Lovibond's (1995) 42-item self-report measure of depression, anxiety, and stress. The 21 items using a 3-point rating scale include statements such as "I found it hard to wind down" and "I was intolerant of anything that kept me from getting on with what I was doing." The stress scale is characterized by statements about being overaroused and irritable and feeling nervy, jumpy, easily startled, fidgety, and unable to relax.

Each scale produced high reliabilities (internal consistencies) of .88 (95% CI [.87, .89]; Henry & Crawford, 2005). The reliability of the Stress scale was .93 (95% CI [93, .94]). Finally, convergent (.78) and discriminant validity (.72) of the DASS-21 was high, as indicated by the Personal Disturbance Scale (Bedford & Foulds, 1978) and the Hospital Anxiety and Depression Scale (Zigmond & Snaith, 1983). After testing four major ethnicities, including Asian Americans, Norton (2007) found that convergent and divergent validity and internal consistency were similar across racial groups.

Perceived Stress Scale

The Perceived Stress Scale (PSS; Cohen, Kamarck, & Mermelstein, 1983) is a self-report questionnaire consisting of three versions measuring "the degree to which individuals appraise situations in their lives as stressful" in the past month (Cohen et al., 1983, p. 385) and the degree to which individuals perceive their lives to be uncontrollable, unpredictable, and overloaded. The original, second, and third versions contain 14, 10, and four items, respectively (PSS-14, PSS-10, PSS-4). The PSS has been widely used and has been translated into 25 other languages from English. In addition, the PSS has been studied among Chinese, Thai, and Japanese populations (Leung, Lam, & Chan, 2010; Mimura & Griffiths, 2004; Wongpakaran & Wongpakaran, 2010) and among workers and college students (E. H. Lee, 2012).

E. H. Lee (2012) evaluated the psychometric properties of the PSS by studying the 19 articles that reported these properties. E. H. Lee found that factorial validity, internal consistency reliability, and hypothesis validity of the PSS were well reported in these studies. However, the criterion validity and test–retest reliability were rarely evaluated. Overall, the 10-item PSS (PSS-10) was found to be superior to the PSS-14, whereas the four-item scale was least psychometrically sound. E. H. Lee concluded that the PSS is an easy-to-use questionnaire with established acceptable psychometric properties. Future studies should evaluate these psychometric properties in greater depth and validate the scale using diverse populations.

Culturally Specific Measures of Stress

Culturally specific types of stress, such as stress related to acculturation, discrimination, and perfectionism, are described in this section.

Acculturative Stress

Measures of acculturative stress have evolved over the years to result in the now numerous measures and translated versions for diverse individuals who may experience this type of stress (Rudmin, 2009). An example of this is the East Asian Acculturation Measure–Chinese Version, which was translated into Chinese (S. F. Kuo, Chang, Chang, Chou, & Chen, 2013). This measure evaluates acculturation based on separation, integration, assimilation, and marginalization. Following translation, this previously validated measure was assessed to still have acceptable reliability and validity for use with Chinese speakers (S. F. Kuo et al., 2013).

Asian American Racism-Related Stress Inventory

The Asian American Racism-Related Stress Inventory (AARRSI) was developed by Liang, Li, and Kim (2004) to assess the degree to which Asian Americans are bothered or stressed by general and specific experiences of racism that are unique to the population. The self-report measure consists of 29 items and includes Socio-Historical Racism, General Racism, and Perpetual Foreigner Racism subscales. The Socio-Historical Racism subscale contains 14 items that reflect vicarious and transgenerational experiences with cultural or institutional racism. The General Racism subscale consists of eight items that reflect direct day-to-day incidents that Asian Americans experience. The third subscale, Perpetual Foreigner Racism, includes seven items that assess a specific form of racism unique to Asian Americans. Higher subscales scores are related to higher racism-related stress levels. The AARRSI was measured and normed among a wide variety of Asian American subgroups, including Korean, Chinese, Asian Indians, Filipinos, Vietnamese, Taiwanese, Japanese, Cambodian, Pakistani, and multiethnic Asian groups.

In regard to the AARRSI's concurrent and discriminant validity, Liang et al. (2004) found positive correlations with the Minority Status Stress scale (Smedley, Myers, & Harrell, 1993), Perceived Racism Scale (McNeilly et al., 1996), Schedule of Racist Events (Landrine & Klonoff, 1996), and the Cultural Mistrust Inventory (Terrell & Terrell, 1981).

Liang et al. (2004) found the coefficient alphas were .90 for the total scale and between .75 and .84 for the subscales. Further, 2-week test–retest reliability coefficients for the AARRSI and the Socio-Historical Racism, General Racism, and Perpetual Foreigner Racism subscales were .87, .82, .73, and .84, respectively. Overall, the AARRSI is relativity new and requires future validity studies. Moreover, the utility and accuracy of the AARRSI might be limited because participants are asked to self-report perceptions of racism.

Almost Perfect Scale–Revised

The Discrepancy subscale of the Almost Perfect Scale–Revised (APS-R; Slaney, Rice, Mobley, Trippi, & Ashby, 2001) is a 23-item self-report measure that is designed to assess maladaptive perfectionism. The items are measured on a 7-point Likert scale ranging from 1 (*strongly disagree*) to 7 (*strongly agree*) and make up three subscales: High Standards, Order, and Discrepancy. Slaney et al. (2001) argued that the Discrepancy subscale assesses maladaptive perfectionism. Wei et al. (2007) found that the perceived discrepancy was a risk factor for distress in Chinese international students. The Discrepancy subscale measures the level to which individuals perceive themselves as failing to meet their personal performance standards—for example, "My performance rarely measures up to my standards." Wang, Slaney, and Rice (2007) found that the coefficient alpha was .88 for Taiwanese college students, whereas the coefficient alpha was .92 for American college students. The construct validity of the Discrepancy subscale was supported by the strong relationships with depression in American college students (Wei, Mallinckrodt, Russell, & Abraham, 2004) and Taiwanese college students (Wang et al., 2007) and with self-esteem for Taiwanese college students (Wang et al., 2007).

Loss of Face Scale

The Loss of Face (LOF) Scale was initially developed by Zane (1993) to measure loss of face, which was identified as a key factor in Asian interpersonal relations. Items were developed to assess loss of face related to social status, ethical behavior, social propriety, or self-discipline. Initial examinations of the LOF Scale demonstrated good validity, reliability, and sensitivity to cultural differences (Zane, 1993). The construct of face on the LOF Scale was later split into self-face and other-face by Mak, Chen, Lam, and Yiu (2009). *Self-face* refers to the preservation of one's face, and *other-face* refers to the preservation of others' face. Self-face was related to greater distress, whereas other-face was not related to as many adverse effects. Though this measure is the most commonly used measure for assessing LOF, the LOF Scale has been used primarily with Chinese American individuals, which may limit utility with other Asian American subgroups (Mak et al., 2009).

Academic Expectations Stress Inventory

The Academic Expectations Stress Inventory (Ang & Huan, 2006) was developed to assess expectations resulting in academic stress among adolescent Asian students. This inventory measures expectations from various sources such as self, parents, and teachers. The measure was established to be valid and reliable for use with adolescent Asian students. Although it targets expectations, which may result in stress in an academic setting, other aspects of academic-related stress are not assessed (e.g., academic stress related to bullying). In addition, the sample was limited to adolescents in middle and high school, which may affect generalizability to elementary and college students (Ang & Huan, 2006).

Interpersonal Shame Inventory

The Interpersonal Shame Inventory (ISI; Wong, Kim, Nguyen, Cheng, & Saw, 2014) is a measure of shame developed for Asian Americans. This measure includes two subscales assessing external shame, family shame, and the desire to escape shameful experiences. The inventory demonstrated satisfactory validity and reliability across studies during measure construction. Though this measure was developed using culturally salient features of shame specific to Asian Americans, some aspects of shame may be missing (e.g., vicarious shame) and may not be applicable to non-college-aged individuals or individuals with differing levels of acculturation (Wong et al., 2014).

Index of Life Stress and Index of Social Support

The Index of Life Stress (ILS) and Index of Social Support (ISS) were developed by Yang and Clum (1995) to predict cultural adjustment for Asian international students. The ILS measures six areas of stress, including language difficulties, cultural adjustment, perceived racial discrimination, academic concerns, financial concerns, and outlook for the future. The ISS measures both quantity and quality of connection with sources of social support, such as direct family, secondary family, old friends in the home country, new friends in the United States, churches, school organizations, the international student center on campus, and community activities. These measures were determined to be valid with acceptable reliability. Researchers found that these measures, relative to other commonly used measures, were successful in adding incremental validity predicting factors such as depression and hopelessness among this population. Due to limitations of inclusion and exclusion criteria for the validation of these measures (e.g., residing in the United States fewer than 7 years, individuals from Asian countries holding student visas), they may not be appropriate for second-generation Asian Americans, nonstudents, or individuals who have permanently immigrated to the United States (Yang & Clum, 1995).

Asian American Family Conflicts Scale

The Asian American Family Conflicts Scale (FCS; R. M. Lee, Choe, Kim, & Ngo, 2000) was developed to assess types of culturally specific family conflicts. These conflicts reflect familial disagreements in values and practices, which are often related to intergenerational and acculturation differences within families. The FCS is made up of two subscales: FCS-Likelihood and FCS-Seriousness. The FCS-Likelihood subscale addresses the likelihood that each of the conflicts listed on the FCS will occur between the reporter and the parents, and the FCS-Seriousness measures the degree of seriousness of the problems caused by conflicts within the family. Validation studies indicated that both the FCS-Likelihood and FCS-Seriousness subscales of the Asian American FCS are valid and reliable measures. However, R. M. Lee and colleagues (2000) recommended further research to confirm the validity and reliability of the FCS-Likelihood scale and noted that variations in familial conflict may occur over time.

Summary

Many generic and culturally specific measures of stress have been validated for use with Asian Americans. The only cultural adaptations of the generic stress measures are translations into an Asian language, and few generic measures integrate the various stress indicators unique to each Asian cultural group. Culturally specific measures are helpful for measuring specific types of stress, which often exist in the context of culture, acculturation, and intergenerational differences among Asian American populations. However, these assessments are likely limited in utility as outcome measures because administering many measures to assess the different types of stress is not realistic for clinical practice. Unfortunately, no measure exists that addresses both generic and culturally specific stress for Asian Americans.

COGNITIVE BEHAVIORAL APPROACHES FOR THE TREATMENT OF STRESS IN ASIAN AMERICANS

In light of cultural variations in the precipitating events, expression, and use of coping strategies for stress, it is important to attend to such cultural variations in examining cognitive and behavioral approaches for the treatment of stress among Asian Americans. In the following section, we examine the applicability of current and predominant approaches to the assessment and cognitive behavioral treatment of stress in Asian Americans. In addition, we review the research on cultural adaptations to cognitive behavioral treatments for stress to ensure a culturally competent approach with this underserved population. We organize our discussion of cultural considerations in cognitive behavioral treatments around the specific stressors and ways of coping among Asian Americans that have been identified in this chapter, such as addressing stigma and shame, the mind and body connection, collectivism, minority stress, perfectionism, acculturative stress, and family and intergenerational conflict.

It is important to note that although general cognitive and behavioral modifications exist for work with Asian American populations, cognitive behavioral treatments have not been traditionally researched or modified specifically for stress. Therefore, in the following sections, recommendations for cultural treatment adaptations for stress are extrapolated from research on related mental conditions such as posttraumatic stress disorder (PTSD) and depression.

APPLICABILITY OF COGNITIVE BEHAVIOR THERAPY FOR ASIAN AMERICANS

In many important ways, key components and approaches of cognitive behavior therapy (CBT) may be culturally congruent for application with Asian American populations. Hays (2009), for example, highlighted a number of similarities between CBT and multicultural therapy (MCT). First, both CBT and MCT emphasize the need to tailor treatment interventions to the individual. Second, both accentuate empowerment in therapy; MCT focuses on cultural identity as a strength, whereas CBT empowers clients to use specific skills. Third, both are easily adaptable for those speaking English as a second language because conscious processes are more easily assessed in CBT, whereas cultural assumptions are more easily articulated in MCT. Fourth, CBT uses assessment throughout the therapy process, which emphasizes communication and collaboration between the therapist and client. Fifth, both therapies integrate support and strength in the therapy process to facilitate change. Sixth and last, the behavioral component of CBT matches well with MCT's cultural influence emphasis.

Although these similarities suggest that CBT can be easily modified for cultural fit with Asian Americans, Hays (2009) described the significant limitations to the multicultural applications of CBT. First, CBT emphasizes the overt behaviors, conscious processes, and language that have been based on the values of dominant cultures. Thus, issues pertaining to stress (behavioral change, assertiveness, and personal independence) may contradict many Asian beliefs (e.g., assertiveness as a goal vs. communication). Second, CBT's focus on the present may lead to more errors when understanding a client's complete cultural and historical background. The third limitation relates to CBT's focus on an individual orientation, which may lead a therapist to overemphasize cognitive change rather than the social and physical environmental change that may be needed in situations of minority stress, acculturative stress, or other events within the ecological system. Given these limitations, it is important to account for literature that has addressed cultural considerations and treatment modifications when applying CBT with Asian Americans dealing with stress.

CULTURAL CONSIDERATIONS AND ADAPTATIONS TO COGNITIVE BEHAVIORAL APPROACHES

Clinicians and researchers should be aware of several cultural considerations and modifications for the cognitive behavioral treatment of stress among Asian American clients. The following discussion focuses first on treatment considerations specific to the cultural variations in stress pathways discussed earlier in this chapter, followed by other general modifications suggested in the literature.

Reframing Perfectionism

In addressing perfectionism, psychoeducation regarding the benefits of making mistakes throughout treatment and reframing errors would be helpful. Some individuals may bring perfectionism into treatment, aiming to be the "good" client. Rather than praising them for being such compliant or hard-working clients, addressing the drive for perfectionism and engaging in behavioral experiments in session targeting assumptions regarding personal failure would be more therapeutic. Relative to Lazarus and Folkman's (1984) transactional model, Zureck, Altstötter-Gleich, Gerstenberg, and Schmitt (2015) found that the most promising targets for intervention were primary and secondary threat appraisals for those with maladaptive tendencies. In other words, guiding clients through a cognitive restructuring of a stressful event (e.g., receiving a poor grade) may help to decrease anxiety, depression, and clinically significant stress symptoms (Zureck et al., 2015).

Family and Intergenerational Conflict

When adapting CBT to address family or intergenerational conflict, similar levels of acculturation in addition to strong attitudes toward valuing family relationships and closeness may prevent or reduce the effects of intergenerational conflict and promote overall well-being (Li, 2014; Tsai-Chae & Nagata, 2008). For example, cognitive behavioral interventions providing adolescents or young adults with exposure to traditional cultural values while providing parents with the skills that align with more of the mainstream culture in the United States may be effective in alleviating distress related to intergenerational conflict. In addition, educating parents and incorporating parental input with personal desires may be an effective strategy for reducing family conflict (Ma et al., 2014). In his adaptation of CBT for Asian Americans, Hwang (2009) recommended increasing emphasis on social conflict resolution in the face of family conflict.

Stress Due to Minority Status

Cultural competency literature has underscored that culturally competent therapists must account for cultural factors related to racial bias or differences between the therapist and client in majority–minority experiences. In fact, awareness of biases, attitudes, and assumptions toward other racial groups is a widely adopted core definitional component of cultural competency (e.g., D. W. Sue et al., 1982), with the American Psychological Association's (2003) *Guidelines on Multicultural Education, Training, Research, Practice, and Organizational Change for Psychologists* highlighting how detrimental cultural attitudes and beliefs by therapists can negatively affect therapeutic relationships with culturally different clients. S. Sue (2010) further discussed a need for therapists to focus on race relations in the therapeutic relationship because of difficulties that can arise from cultural differences in power or marginalization. D. F. Chang and Berk (2009) qualitatively studied differences between ethnic minority clients who reported a satisfied versus dissatisfied experience with Caucasian therapists. Unsatisfied ethnic minority clients more frequently perceived that their therapists did not convey an understanding of power and privilege issues clients encountered in their lives and in the therapeutic context and even downplayed clients' experiences of oppression or discrimination. In a series of studies, microaggressions, an "insidious" form of discrimination, were found to be related to negative outcomes such as client well-being (e.g., Owen, Imel, Tao, Wampold, Smith, & Rodolfa, 2011, p. 204; Owen, Tao, & Rodolfa, 2010, p. 94). This research indicates that therapeutic alliance and therapeutic outcome can be impaired when ethnic minority clients perceive therapists' behaviors as racially insensitive through discrimination, oppression, or microaggressions.

In regard to minority stress experienced by Asian Americans outside the therapeutic relationship (e.g., racism, discrimination, acculturative stress, socioeconomic stressors), it is particularly important for therapists to become aware and understand the impact of such cultural life experiences (Hwang, 2009). Because individuals may not immediately or directly disclose their experiences of minority and acculturative stress, therapists should listen for distress cues or difficulties adjusting to their new host country. Addressing such minority stressors may require a more ecological than individual approach to recognize the larger systemic forces at play. For example, rather than address perceptions of racism or unfair treatment as a cognitive distortion, the therapist may instead validate clients' experiences and empower them within the situation.

Engagement Strategies: Addressing Shame and Stigma

Asian Americans may fear being perceived as "weak" or "crazy," resulting in issues related to disclosure and low treatment-seeking behavior (Gee et al., 2007), and they may make efforts to "save face" by avoiding treatment and not disclosing symptoms or distress. Given these issues, individual engagement strategies of using gentler and normalizing language about stress and mental illness and providing reinforcement for seeking therapy may increase the likelihood of disclosure and reduce barriers to seeking or engaging in treatment. Hwang et al. (2006), for example, discussed differences in dropout rates and self-esteem between clients whose therapists normalized the experience of mental illness and praised clients' efforts in the therapeutic process, compared with control conditions. Leong and Lau (2001) suggested that when Asian Americans view their mental health symptoms as a result of being "weak" or "crazy," clinicians should be prepared to confront culturally influenced core schemas such as "I am weak because of my mental illness." Psychoeducation regarding the underlying cognitive behavioral theory and the many contributors to stress (e.g., biological, environmental, psychological) may also assist in reducing stigma, self-blame, and loss of face (Hwang et al., 2006).

Community engagement strategies, such as integrating the service provision of CBT with accepted and non-stigmatized entities (e.g., community centers, primary care settings, collaborating with religious leaders) or providing outreach as a standard component of CBT, may also serve to mitigate shame and stigma concerns for Asian Americans (e.g., Husain et al., 2011; Rathod, Kingdon, Phiri, & Gobbi, 2010).

Somatization and the Mind–Body Connection

When working with Asian American clients who feel more familiar with somatic symptoms of stress (e.g., headaches, gastrointestinal distress, rapid heart rate), cognitive behavioral treatment plans that address a physical health component would be beneficial. In fact, one study by Hinton, Pich, Chhean, Safren, and Pollack (2006) treated Cambodian refugees with PTSD with a treatment focused on somatic symptoms. Psychoeducation is critical for those who believe that their symptoms are solely based on physical causes to assist in clients' understanding of the link between the physical and psychological. Indeed, an integration of both emotional and physical health interventions may help clients be more comfortable addressing their cognitive symptoms of stress (Hwang et al., 2006), and emphasis on problem solving and behavioral activation may be particularly congruent with Asian Americans' focus on physical health (Hwang, 2009). Incorporating mindfulness and meditation may also be well received (Hall, Hong, Zane, & Meyer, 2011).

Other Cultural Expressions of Stress

When adapting one's CBT approach to account for an Asian American client's preference for emotional control, it may be important to understand that talk therapy as a primary modality to resolve one's problems may be more foreign than a more problem-solving or action-oriented approach (Hwang,

2009). Therapists may have to practice communication behaviors that are more culturally congruent with Asian American cultural practices (e.g., indirect or nonverbal communication) and allow clients more time and more psychoeducation to adjust to the process of talking through feelings versus thoughts (Hwang, 2009).

Balancing Collectivism and Individualism

Characteristics of many Asian worldviews include an external locus of control and responsibility—the belief that individuals are controlled by forces outside the self, such as luck, chance, or fate, and that people share a certain amount of responsibility for others in their community. Y. Lin (2002) recommended shifting the emphasis within CBT from an internal to an external locus of control to better match the Chinese worldview. While applying CBT to counsel Chinese clients, using a balance of collectivism and individualism may be helpful for raising clients' awareness about the effects of their culturally sanctioned external locus of control on their psychological distress. Y. Lin also recommended encouraging clients to develop their own decisions while balancing their family's expectations, social norms, group goals, and individual personalities. If therapists adhere solely to external worldviews, clients may be more likely to experience psychosomatic symptoms through frustration, anger, and. However, if therapists stick solely to the individualistic techniques typical of CBT, the therapeutic process may be ineffective. Y. Lin suggested that assertion training, confrontation, and exploration of personal problems early in therapy may be ineffective and advised using gentler forms of therapeutic interventions.

OTHER CULTURAL MODIFICATIONS TO CONSIDER WHEN TREATING STRESS IN ASIAN AMERICANS

Treatment Delivery: Strengthening the Client–Therapist Relationship

Studies on cultural adaptation of cognitive behavioral treatments have indicated that modifications to treatment delivery via the framework of the client–therapist relationship may be indicated with Asian Americans. These therapeutic relationship modifications are encompassed within three main considerations. First, cultural treatment adaptation studies have indicated that therapists gain credibility with Asian American clients when they emphasize their role as authority figures by providing advice, giving explicit directions, and teaching skills that provide immediate distress relief (Chu et al., 2012;

Hwang, 2009; Hwang et al., 2006). CBT has been more widely used and preferred over other psychotherapies among Asian Americans because of its more directive, symptom-focused, and structured approach (Chu et al., 2012; Hong & Domokos-Cheng Ham, 2001). This style dovetails nicely with the common Asian cultural emphases on social structure and hierarchical relationships (Zhang et al., 2002). A focus by clinicians on immediate symptom relief can play a role in preventing early dropouts, increasing perceived therapist credibility, and strengthening the client–therapist relationship (Hwang et al., 2006).

Second, researchers suggested adapting CBT for Asian American clients by discussing the limitations, roles, and expectations of therapy, which has been shown to reduce early terminations and increase overall satisfaction (Tseng, 2004). Hwang and colleagues (2006) suggested that CBT therapists should explicitly explain that therapy is not a miracle nor an immediate solution. Instead, therapists should remind Asian American clients that therapy will be helpful with careful practice and adequate time. Tseng (2004) found that clinicians who are explicit about therapeutic expectations have higher ratings of respect compared with their peers who did not explicitly discuss therapeutic outcomes.

Third, clinicians may adapt CBT by discussing any cultural differences or salient identities between the clinician and the client. One study by Tseng (2004) suggested that explicit conversations about identity divergences can improve treatment outcome. The authors found that incorporating culturally rooted proverbs and beliefs during session significantly improved client insight and the working alliance, compared with clients whose therapists used ethnocentric allegories in session (Tseng, 2004).

Highlighting Strengths and Respect

Another recommendation for cultural modification of CBT for Asian Americans centered on the emphasis on cultural strengths and the practice of interpersonal respect. Hays (2009) suggested that CBT for Asian Americans should emphasize the client's culturally related personal strengths such as pride in one's identity, religious spirituality or faith, and artistic or musical appreciation. Practicing culturally congruent behaviors of respect within treatment may be valued among Asian Americans more so than the rapport building that is highly emphasized in Western concepts of CBT (Iwamasa, Hsia, & Hinton, 2006). For example, as a directive process, cognitive behavioral assessment may include repeated questioning, which is considered disrespectful by many elders (Weisman et al., 2005). In these cases, therapists should slow down questioning and allow the client more control over the content discussed (Hays, 2006).

Awareness and Respect for Differences

The term *Asian American* encompasses a highly diverse group of individuals originating from very different countries (Hoeffel et al., 2012) with varying values and unique histories (Costigan et al., 2006). Many of these groups share similar cultural values, beliefs, and practices. However, research has also revealed significant differences in traditional Asian values and perceptions of others' behavior (Costigan et al., 2006; Kim et al., 2001). These within-group differences highlight the challenge of providing culturally competent services to such a diverse ethnic group. For example, Costigan and colleagues (2006) indicated that identification as Asian American does not necessarily guarantee the uniformity of perceptions across all individuals identifying within this category. In addition, D. W. Sue and Sue (1987) suggested that mental health providers of a different culture or language than those of clients may experience more difficulties with the therapeutic relationship. However, clinician identification as Asian American and assumption of a client's own ethnic identity and cultural beliefs based on appearance or indication of identifying as Asian American on the intake paperwork may also be detrimental given that this category is highly diverse. It is essential that clinicians are aware of within-group differences and become familiar with the specific cultural subgroup and individual variations within each cultural subgroup without making assumptions based on ethnic identification as Asian American (Costigan et al., 2006). It is also important for researchers to avoid generalizations across heterogeneous Asian American subgroups because some subgroups are more understudied than others (Choi, 2008).

CONCLUSION

Psychological stress is a well-known risk factor for a wide variety of health issues, such as anxiety, mood, behavioral, and physical health problems (Grant, Compas, Thurm, McMahon, & Gipson, 2004). Chronic stress can increase externalizing behaviors and internalizing symptoms, plummeting the overall mental health of an individual and leading to decreased functioning and long-term health and functioning effects (Hammen, 2015). Though much of the experience and treatment of stress for Asian Americans can be culled from research and practice within the general population, important cultural variations within models and measures of stress call for a culturally modified approach. In this chapter, we presented a comprehensive analysis of the ways in which cultural factors and variations affect the stress response and coping process along with measurement and treatment considerations for Asian American populations.

The chapter illuminated several key cultural factors: (a) stress in Asian Americans must be understood from models that are broader in context or account for culturally specific risk factors, (b) culturally specific stressors and events (e.g., perfectionism, loss of face, family or intergenerational conflict, stress related to minority status, acculturative stress, stigma and shame) have to be taken into account when assessing and treating Asian Americans, (c) culturally variant expressions and experiences of stress (between group and within group) must be integrated into the conceptualization, and (d) cognitive and behavioral differences in coping responses to stress among Asian Americans should be applied to treatment. These cultural considerations, along with other modifications to treatment delivery via the therapeutic relationship, attention to cultural strengths and interpersonal respect, and awareness and respect of within-group differences, can be incorporated into applications to treat stress in Asian American populations using a cognitive behavioral approach.

REFERENCES

Adam, E. K., & Kumari, M. (2009). Assessing salivary cortisol in large-scale, epidemiological research. *Psychoneuroendocrinology, 34*, 1423–1436. http://dx.doi.org/10.1016/j.psyneuen.2009.06.011

American Psychological Association. (2003). Guidelines on multicultural education, training, research, practice, and organizational change for psychologists. *American Psychologist, 58*, 377–402. http://dx.doi.org/10.1037/0003-066X.58.5.377

Amirkhan, J. H., Urizar, G. G., & Clark, S. (2015). Criterion validation of a stress measure: The Stress Overload Scale. *Psychological Assessment, 27*, 985–996. http://dx.doi.org/10.1037/pas0000081

Ang, R. P., & Huan, V. S. (2006). Academic Expectations Stress Inventory: Development, factor analysis, reliability, and validity. *Educational and Psychological Measurement, 66*, 522–539. http://dx.doi.org/10.1177/0013164405282461

Bedford, A., & Foulds, G. (1978). *Delusions-Symptoms-States Inventory state of anxiety and depression*. Windsor, England: NFER-Nelson.

Berry, J. W. (2005). Acculturation: Living successfully in two cultures. *International Journal of Intercultural Relations, 29*, 697–712. http://dx.doi.org/10.1016/j.ijintrel.2005.07.013

Bronfenbrenner, U. (1979). *The ecology of human development: Experiments by nature and design*. Cambridge, MA: Harvard University Press.

Carver, C. S. (2011). Coping. In R. J. Contrada & A. Baum (Eds.), *The handbook of stress science: Biology, psychology, and health* (pp. 221–229). New York, NY: Springer.

Chang, D. F., & Berk, A. (2009). Making cross-racial therapy work: A phenomenological study of clients' experiences of cross-racial therapy. *Journal of Counseling Psychology, 56*, 521–536. http://dx.doi.org/10.1037/a0016905

Chang, E. C. (2001). A look at the coping strategies and styles of Asian Americans: Similar and different? In C. R. Snyder (Ed.), *Coping with stress: Effective people and processes* (pp. 222–239). New York, NY: Oxford University Press.

Chentsova-Dutton, Y. E., Chu, J. P., Tsai, J. L., Rottenberg, J., Gross, J. J., & Gotlib, I. H. (2007). Depression and emotional reactivity: Variation among Asian Americans of East Asian descent and European Americans. *Journal of Abnormal Psychology, 116*, 776–785. http://dx.doi.org/10.1037/0021-843X.116.4.776

Choi, Y. (2008). Diversity within: Subgroup differences of youth problem behaviors among Asian Pacific Islander American adolescents. *Journal of Community Psychology, 36*, 352–370. http://dx.doi.org/10.1002/jcop.20196

Chu, J. P., Goldblum, P., Floyd, R., & Bongar, B. (2010). The cultural theory and model of suicide. *Applied & Preventive Psychology, 14*, 25–40. http://dx.doi.org/10.1016/j.appsy.2011.11.001

Chu, J. P., Huynh, L., & Areán, P. (2012). Cultural adaptation of evidence-based practice utilizing an iterative stakeholder process and theoretical framework: Problem solving therapy for Chinese older adults. *International Journal of Geriatric Psychiatry, 27*, 97–106. http://dx.doi.org/10.1002/gps.2698

Cohen, S., Kamarck, T., & Mermelstein, R. (1983). A global measure of perceived stress. *Journal of Health and Social Behavior, 24*, 385–396. http://dx.doi.org/10.2307/2136404

Conway, V. J., & Terry, D. J. (1992). Appraised controllability as a moderator of the effectiveness of different coping strategies: A test of the goodness of fit hypothesis. *Australian Journal of Psychology, 44*, 1–7. http://dx.doi.org/10.1080/00049539208260155

Costigan, C. L., Bardina, P., Cauce, A. M., Kim, G. K., & Latendresse, S. J. (2006). Inter- and intra-group variability in perceptions of behavior among Asian Americans and European Americans. *Cultural Diversity and Ethnic Minority Psychology, 12*, 710–724. http://dx.doi.org/10.1037/1099-9809.12.4.710

DeGraff, A. H., & Schaffer, J. (2008). Emotion-focused coping: A primary defense against stress for people living with spinal cord injury. *Journal of Rehabilitation, 74*, 19–24.

De Jong, G. F., & Madamba, A. B. (2001). A double disadvantage? Minority group, immigrant status, and underemployment in the United States. *Social Science Quarterly, 82*, 117–130. http://dx.doi.org/10.1111/0038-4941.00011

D'Zurilla, T. J. (1986). *Problem-solving therapy: A social competence approach to clinical intervention.* New York, NY: Springer.

D'Zurilla, T. J., Nezu, A., & Maydeu-Olivares, A. (2018). *Social Problem-Solving Inventory–Revised.* Ipswich, MA: PsycTESTS.

Eid, M., & Diener, E. (2001). Norms for experiencing emotions in different cultures: Inter- and intranational differences. *Journal of Personality and Social Psychology, 81,* 869–885. http://dx.doi.org/10.1037/0022-3514.81.5.869

Epstein, S. (1990). Cognitive-experiential self-theory. In L. A. Previn (Ed.), *Handbook of personality: Theory and research* (pp. 165–192). New York, NY: Guilford Press.

Epstein, S., & Meier, P. (1989). Constructive thinking: A broad coping variable with specific components. *Journal of Personality and Social Psychology, 57,* 332–350. http://dx.doi.org/10.1037/0022-3514.57.2.332

Folkman, S., & Lazarus, R. S. (1988). Coping as a mediator of emotion. *Journal of Personality and Social Psychology, 54,* 466–475. http://dx.doi.org/10.1037/0022-3514.54.3.466

Folkman, S., & Moskowitz, J. T. (2004). Coping: Pitfalls and promise. *Annual Review of Psychology, 55,* 745–774. http://dx.doi.org/10.1146/annurev.psych.55.090902.141456

Gee, G. C., Spencer, M., Chen, J., Yip, T., & Takeuchi, D. T. (2007). The association between self-reported racial discrimination and 12-month *DSM–IV* mental disorders among Asian Americans nationwide. *Social Science & Medicine, 64,* 1984–1996. http://dx.doi.org/10.1016/j.socscimed.2007.02.013

Grant, K. E., Compas, B. E., Thurm, A. E., McMahon, S. D., & Gipson, P. Y. (2004). Stressors and child and adolescent psychopathology: Measurement issues and prospective effects. *Journal of Clinical Child and Adolescent Psychology, 33,* 412–425. http://dx.doi.org/10.1207/s15374424jccp3302_23

Hall, G. C. N., Hong, J. J., Zane, N. W., & Meyer, O. L. (2011). Culturally competent treatments for Asian Americans: The relevance of mindfulness and acceptance-based therapies. *Clinical Psychology: Science and Practice, 18,* 215–231. http://dx.doi.org/10.1111/j.1468-2850.2011.01253.x

Hamamura, T., & Laird, P. G. (2014). The effect of perfectionism and acculturative stress on levels of depression experienced by East Asian international students. *Journal of Multicultural Counseling and Development, 42,* 205–217. http://dx.doi.org/10.1002/j.2161-1912.2014.00055.x

Hammen, C. (2015). Stress sensitivity in psychopathology: Mechanisms and consequences. *Journal of Abnormal Psychology, 124,* 152–154. http://dx.doi.org/10.1037/abn0000040

Hays, P. A. (2006). Introduction: Developing culturally responsive cognitive-behavioral therapies. In P. A. Hays & G. Y. Iwamasa (Eds.), *Culturally responsive cognitive-behavioral therapy: Assessment, practice, and supervision* (pp. 3–20). Washington, DC: American Psychological Association.

Hays, P. A. (2009). Integrating evidence-based practice, cognitive-behavior therapy, and multicultural therapy: Ten steps for culturally competent practice. *Professional Psychology: Research and Practice, 40,* 354–360. http://dx.doi.org/10.1037/a0016250

Henry, J. D., & Crawford, J. R. (2005). The short-form version of the Depression Anxiety Stress Scales (DASS-21): Construct validity and normative data in a large non-clinical sample. *British Journal of Clinical Psychology, 44,* 227–239. http://dx.doi.org/10.1348/014466505X29657

Hinton, D. E., Pich, V., Chhean, D., Safren, S. A., & Pollack, M. H. (2006). Somatic-focused therapy for traumatized refugees: Treating posttraumatic stress disorder and comorbid neck-focused panic attacks among Cambodian refugees. *Psychotherapy: Theory, Research, Practice, Training, 43,* 491–505. http://dx.doi.org/10.1037/0033-3204.43.4.491

Hoeffel, E. M., Rastogi, S., Kim, M. O., & Shahid, H. (2012). *The Asian population: 2010.* Retrieved from https://www.census.gov/prod/cen2010/briefs/c2010br-11.pdf

Hong, G. K., & Domokos-Cheng Ham, M. (2001). *Psychotherapy and counseling with Asian American clients: A practical guide.* Pacific Grove, CA: Sage.

Husain, N., Chaudhry, N., Durairaj, S. V., Chaudhry, I., Khan, S., Husain, M., . . . Waheed, W. (2011). Prevention of: self harm in British South Asian women: Study protocol of an exploratory RCT of culturally adapted manual assisted Problem Solving Training (C-MAP). *Trials, 12,* 159–165. http://dx.doi.org/10.1186/1745-6215-12-159

Hwang, W.-C. (2009). The Formative Method for Adapting Psychotherapy (FMAP): A community-based developmental approach to culturally adapting therapy. *Professional Psychology: Research and Practice, 40,* 369–377. http://dx.doi.org/10.1037/a0016240

Hwang, W.-C., & Ting, J. Y. (2008). Disaggregating the effects of acculturation and acculturative stress on the mental health of Asian Americans. *Cultural Diversity and Ethnic Minority Psychology, 14,* 147–154. http://dx.doi.org/10.1037/1099-9809.14.2.147

Hwang, W.-C., Wood, J. J., Lin, K.-M., & Cheung, F. (2006). Cognitive-behavioral therapy with Chinese Americans: Research, theory, and clinical practice. *Cognitive and Behavioral Practice, 13,* 293–303. http://dx.doi.org/10.1016/j.cbpra.2006.04.010

Iwamasa, G. Y., Hsia, C., & Hinton, D. (2006). Cognitive-behavioral therapy with Asian Americans. In P. A. Hays & G. Y. Iwamasa (Eds.), *Culturally responsive cognitive-behavioral therapy: Assessment, practice, and supervision* (pp. 117–140). Washington, DC: American Psychological Association. http://dx.doi.org/10.1037/11433-005

Jun, J. (2012). Why are Asian Americans silent? Asian Americans' negotiation strategies for communicative discriminations. *Journal of International and Intercultural Communication, 5,* 329–348. http://dx.doi.org/10.1080/17513057.2012.720700

Kaduvettoor-Davidson, A., & Inman, A. G. (2013). South Asian Americans: Perceived discrimination, stress, and well-being. *Asian American Journal of Psychology, 4,* 155–165. http://dx.doi.org/10.1037/a0030634

Kim, B. S., Yang, P. H., Atkinson, D. R., Wolfe, M. M., & Hong, S. (2001). Cultural value similarities and differences among Asian American ethnic groups.

Cultural Diversity and Ethnic Minority Psychology, 7, 343–361. http://dx.doi.org/10.1037/1099-9809.7.4.343

Kuo, B. C. (2011). Culture's consequences on coping theories, evidences, and dimensionalities. *Journal of Cross-Cultural Psychology, 42*, 1084–1100. http://dx.doi.org/10.1177/0022022110381126

Kuo, S. F., Chang, W. Y., Chang, L. I., Chou, Y. H., & Chen, C. M. (2013). The development and psychometric testing of East Asian Acculturation Scale among Asian immigrant women in Taiwan. *Ethnicity & Health, 18*(1), 18–33. http://dx.doi.org/10.1080/13557858.2012.676632

Landrine, H., & Klonoff, E. A. (1996). The Schedule of Racist Events: A measure of racial discrimination and a study of its negative physical and mental health consequences. *Journal of Black Psychology, 22*, 144–168. http://dx.doi.org/10.1177/00957984960222002

Lazarus, R. S., & Folkman, S. (1984). *Stress, appraisal, and coping.* New York, NY: Springer.

Lee, B. (2013). Ambivalence over emotional expression and symptom attribution are associated with self-reported somatic symptoms in Singaporean school adolescents. *Asian Journal of Social Psychology, 16*, 169–180. http://dx.doi.org/10.1111/ajsp.12005

Lee, D. S., & Padilla, A. M. (2014). Acculturative stress and coping: Gender differences among Korean and Korean American university students. *Journal of College Student Development, 55*, 243–262. http://dx.doi.org/10.1353/csd.2014.0025

Lee, E. H. (2012). Review of the psychometric evidence of the Perceived Stress Scale. *Asian Nursing Research, 6*, 121–127. http://dx.doi.org/10.1016/j.anr.2012.08.004

Lee, H., & Mason, D. (2014). Cultural and gender differences in coping strategies between Caucasian American and Korean American older people. *Journal of Cross-Cultural Gerontology, 29*, 429–446. http://dx.doi.org/10.1007/s10823-014-9241-x

Lee, J. K., & Park, H.-G. (2001). Marital conflicts and women's identities in the contemporary Korean family. *Asian Journal of Women's Studies, 7*, 7–28. http://dx.doi.org/10.1080/12259276.2001.11665913

Lee, R. M., Choe, J., Kim, G., & Ngo, V. (2000). Construction of the Asian American Family Conflicts Scale. *Journal of Counseling Psychology, 47*, 211–222. http://dx.doi.org/10.1037/0022-0167.47.2.211

Lee, R. M., Su, J., & Yoshida, E. (2005). Coping with intergenerational family conflict among Asian American college students. *Journal of Counseling Psychology, 52*, 389–399. http://dx.doi.org/10.1037/0022-0167.52.3.389

Leong, F. T. L., & Lau, A. S. L. (2001). Barriers to providing effective mental health services to Asian Americans. *Mental Health Services Research, 3*, 201–214. http://dx.doi.org/10.1023/A:1013177014788

Leung, D. Y., Lam, T. H., & Chan, S. S. (2010). Three versions of Perceived Stress Scale: Validation in a sample of Chinese cardiac patients who smoke. *BioMed Central Public Health, 10*, 513. http://dx.doi.org/10.1186/1471-2458-10-513

Li, Y. (2014). Intergenerational conflict, attitudinal familism, and depressive symptoms among Asian and Hispanic adolescents in immigrant families: A latent variable interaction analysis. *Journal of Social Service Research, 40,* 80–96. http://dx.doi.org/10.1080/01488376.2013.845128

Liang, C. T., Li, L. C., & Kim, B. S. (2004). The Asian American racism-related stress inventory: Development, factor analysis, reliability, and validity. *Journal of Counseling Psychology, 51,* 103–114. http://dx.doi.org/10.1037/0022-0167.51.1.103

Lin, S. Y. (2013). Beliefs about causes, symptoms, and stigma associated with severe mental illness among "highly acculturated" Chinese-American patients. *The International Journal of Social Psychiatry, 59,* 745–751. http://dx.doi.org/10.1177/0020764012454384

Lin, Y. (2002). The application of cognitive-behavioral therapy to counseling Chinese. *American Journal of Psychotherapy, 55,* 46–58.

Lovibond, P. F., & Lovibond, S. H. (1995). The structure of negative emotional states: Comparison of the Depression Anxiety Stress Scales (DASS) with the Beck Depression and Anxiety Inventories. *Behaviour Research and Therapy, 33,* 335–343. http://dx.doi.org/10.1016/0005-7967(94)00075-U

Lueck, K., & Wilson, M. (2010). Acculturative stress in Asian immigrants: The impact of social and linguistic factors. *International Journal of Intercultural Relations, 34,* 47–57. http://dx.doi.org/10.1016/j.ijintrel.2009.10.004

Ma, P. W., Desai, U., George, L. S., San Filippo, A. A., & Varon, S. (2014). Managing family conflict over career decisions: The experience of Asian Americans. *Journal of Career Development, 41,* 487–506. http://dx.doi.org/10.1177/0894845313512898

Mak, W. W. S., Chen, S. X., Lam, A. G., & Yiu, V. F. L. (2009). Understanding distress: The role of face concern among Chinese Americans, European Americans, Hong Kong Chinese, and Mainland Chinese. *The Counseling Psychologist, 37,* 219–248. http://dx.doi.org/10.1177/0011000008316378

McNeilly, M. D., Anderson, N. B., Armstead, C. A., Clark, R., Corbett, M., Robinson, E. L., . . . Lepisto, E. M. (1996). The Perceived Racism Scale: A multidimensional assessment of the experience of White racism among African Americans. *Ethnicity and Disease, 6,* 154–166.

Meyer, I. H. (1995). Minority stress and mental health in gay men. *Journal of Health and Social Behavior, 36,* 38–56. http://dx.doi.org/10.2307/2137286

Meyer, I. H., Schwartz, S., & Frost, D. M. (2008). Social patterning of stress and coping: Does disadvantaged social statuses confer more stress and fewer coping resources? *Social Science & Medicine, 67,* 368–379. http://dx.doi.org/10.1016/j.socscimed.2008.03.012

Mimura, C., & Griffiths, P. (2004). A Japanese version of the Perceived Stress Scale: Translation and preliminary test. *International Journal of Nursing Studies, 41,* 379–385.

Mui, A. C., & Kang, S. Y. (2006). Acculturation stress and depression among Asian immigrant elders. *Social Work*, 51, 243–255. http://dx.doi.org/10.1093/sw/51.3.243

Norton, P. J. (2007). Depression Anxiety and Stress Scales (DASS-21): Psychometric analysis across four racial groups. *Anxiety, Stress & Coping*, 20, 253–265. http://dx.doi.org/10.1080/10615800701309279

Ong, A. D., Burrow, A. L., Fuller-Rowell, T. E., Ja, N. M., & Sue, D. W. (2013). Racial microaggressions and daily well-being among Asian Americans. *Journal of Counseling Psychology*, 60, 188–199. http://dx.doi.org/10.1037/a0031736

Owen, J., Imel, Z., Tao, K., Wampold, B., Smith, A., & Rodolfa, E. (2011). Cultural ruptures in short-term therapy: Working alliance as a mediator between clients' perceptions of microaggressions and therapy outcomes. *Counselling & Psychotherapy Research*, 11, 204–212. http://dx.doi.org/10.1080/14733145.2010.491551

Owen, J., Tao, K., & Rodolfa, E. (2010). Microaggressions against women in short-term psychotherapy: Initial evidence. *The Counseling Psychologist*, 38, 923–946. http://dx.doi.org/10.1177/0011000010376093

Pan, D., Huey, S. J., Jr., & Hernandez, D. (2011). Culturally adapted versus standard exposure treatment for phobic Asian Americans: Treatment efficacy, moderators, and predictors. *Cultural Diversity and Ethnic Minority Psychology*, 17, 11–22. http://dx.doi.org/10.1037/a0022534

Phillips, M. R., & Pearson, V. (1987). Coping in Chinese communities: The need for a new research agenda. In M. H. Bond (Ed.), *Chinese psychology* (pp. 429–440). Hong Kong: Oxford University Press,

Phinney, J. S., Ong, A., & Madden, T. (2000). Cultural values and intergenerational value discrepancies in immigrant and non-immigrant families. *Child Development*, 71, 528–539. http://dx.doi.org/10.1111/1467-8624.00162

Pityaratstian, N., Piyasil, V., Ketumarn, P., Sitdhiraksa, N., Ularntinon, S., & Pariwatcharakul, P. (2015). Randomized controlled trial of group cognitive behavioural therapy for post-traumatic stress disorder in children and adolescents exposed to tsunami in Thailand. *Behavioural and Cognitive Psychotherapy*, 43, 549–561. http://dx.doi.org/10.1017/S1352465813001197

Rathod, S., Kingdon, D., Phiri, P., & Gobbi, M. (2010). Developing culturally sensitive cognitive behaviour therapy for psychosis for ethnic minority patients by exploration and incorporation of service users' and health professionals' views and opinions. *Behavioural and Cognitive Psychotherapy*, 38, 511–533. http://dx.doi.org/10.1017/S1352465810000378

Rottenberg, J., Kasch, K. L., Gross, J. J., & Gotlib, I. H. (2002). Sadness and amusement reactivity differentially predict concurrent and prospective functioning in major depressive disorder. *Emotion*, 2, 135–146. http://dx.doi.org/10.1037/1528-3542.2.2.135

Roubinov, D. S., Turner, A. P., & Williams, R. M. (2015). Coping among individuals with multiple sclerosis: Evaluating a goodness-of-fit model. *Rehabilitation Psychology, 60,* 162–168. http://dx.doi.org/10.1037/rep0000032

Rowell, L. N., Mechlin, B., Ji, E., Addamo, M., & Girdler, S. S. (2011). Asians differ from non-Hispanic Whites in experimental pain sensitivity. *European Journal of Pain, 15,* 764–771. http://dx.doi.org/10.1016/j.ejpain.2010.11.016

Rudmin, F. (2009). Constructs, measurements and models of acculturation and acculturative stress. *International Journal of Intercultural Relations, 33,* 106–123. http://dx.doi.org/10.1016/j.ijintrel.2008.12.001

Ryder, A. G., Yang, J., Zhu, X., Yao, S., Yi, J., Heine, S. J., & Bagby, R. M. (2008). The cultural shaping of depression: Somatic symptoms in China, psychological symptoms in North America? *Journal of Abnormal Psychology, 117,* 300–313. http://dx.doi.org/10.1037/0021-843X.117.2.300

Slaney, R. B., Rice, K. G., Mobley, M., Trippi, J., & Ashby, J. S. (2001). The Revised Almost Perfect scale. *Measurement and Evaluation in Counseling and Development, 34,* 130–145.

Smedley, B. D., Myers, H. F., & Harrell, S. P. (1993). Minority-status stresses and the college adjustment of ethnic minority freshmen. *The Journal of Higher Education, 64,* 434–452. http://dx.doi.org/10.1080/00221546.1993.11778438

Spencer-Rodgers, J., & Peng, K. (2014). Perceiving racial/ethnic disadvantage and its consequences for self-esteem among Asian-Americans. *International Journal of Psychological Studies, 6,* 117–127. http://dx.doi.org/10.5539/ijps.v6n2p117

Stoeber, J., & Otto, K. (2006). Positive conceptions of perfectionism: Approaches, evidence, challenges. *Personality and Social Psychology Review, 10,* 295–319. http://dx.doi.org/10.1207/s15327957pspr1004_2

Sue, D., & Sue, S. (1987). Cultural factors in the clinical assessment of Asian Americans. *Journal of Consulting and Clinical Psychology, 55,* 479–487. http://dx.doi.org/10.1037/0022-006X.55.4.479

Sue, D. W., Bernier, J. E., Durran, A., Feinberg, L., Pedersen, P., Smith, E. J., & Vasquez-Nuttall, E. (1982). Position paper: Cross-cultural counseling competencies. *The Counseling Psychologist, 10,* 45–52. http://dx.doi.org/10.1177/0011000082102008

Sue, D. W., Bucceri, J., Lin, A. I., Nadal, K. L., & Torino, G. C. (2009). Racial microaggressions and the Asian American experience. *Asian American Journal of Psychology, S,* 88–101. http://dx.doi.org/10.1037/1948-1985.S.1.88

Sue, S. (2010). Cultural adaptations in treatment. *The Scientific Review of Mental Health Practice, 7,* 31–33.

Sue, S., Cheng, J. K. Y., Saad, C. S., & Chu, J. P. (2012). Asian American mental health: A call to action. *American Psychologist, 67,* 532–544. http://dx.doi.org/10.1037/a0028900

Sun, C. L. (2016). Philosophical roots of Asian psychology: The place of Asia in world psychology. In C. Tien-Lun Sun (Ed.), *Psychology in Asia: An introduction* (pp. 45–78). Boston, MA: Cengage.

Terrell, F., & Terrell, S. (1981). An inventory to measure cultural mistrust among Blacks. *The Western Journal of Black Studies, 5*, 180–185.

Tsai, J. L., & Levenson, R. W. (1997). Cultural influences on emotional responding: Chinese American and European American dating couples during interpersonal conflict. *Journal of Cross-Cultural Psychology, 28*, 600–625. http://dx.doi.org/10.1177/0022022197285006

Tsai-Chae, A. H., & Nagata, D. K. (2008). Asian values and perceptions of intergenerational family conflict among Asian American students. *Cultural Diversity and Ethnic Minority Psychology, 14*, 205–214. http://dx.doi.org/10.1037/1099-9809.14.3.205

Tseng, W. S. (2004). Culture and psychotherapy: Asian perspectives. *Journal of Mental Health, 13*, 151–161. http://dx.doi.org/10.1080/09638230410001669282

Uba, L. (2002). *A postmodern psychology of Asian American: Creating knowledge of a racial minority.* Albany: State University of New York Press.

Uppaluri, C. R., Schumm, L. P., & Lauderdale, D. S. (2001). Self-reports of stress in Asian immigrants: Effects of ethnicity and acculturation. *Ethnicity & Disease, 11*, 107–114.

Wang, K. T., Slaney, R. B., & Rice, K. G. (2007). Perfectionism in Chinese university students from Taiwan: A study of psychological well-being and achievement motivation. *Personality and Individual Differences, 42*, 1279–1290. http://dx.doi.org/10.1016/j.paid.2006.10.006

Wei, M., Heppner, P. P., Mallen, M., Ku, T., Liao, K. Y., & Wu, T. (2007). Acculturative stress, perfectionism, years in United States, and depression among Chinese international students. *Journal of Counseling Psychology, 54*, 385–394. http://dx.doi.org/10.1037/0022-0167.54.4.385

Wei, M., Mallinckrodt, B., Russell, D. W., & Abraham, T. W. (2004). Maladaptive perfectionism as a mediator and moderator between adult attachment and depressive mood. *Journal of Counseling Psychology, 51*, 201–212. http://dx.doi.org/10.1037/0022-0167.51.2.201

Weisman, A., Feldman, G., Gruman, C., Rosenberg, R., Chamorro, R., & Belozersky, I. (2005). Improving mental health services for Latino and Asian immigrant elders. *Professional Psychology: Research and Practice, 36*, 642–648. http://dx.doi.org/10.1037/0735-7028.36.6.642

Wenzel, L., Glanz, K., & Lerman, C. (2002). Stress, coping, and health behavior. In K. Glanz, B. K. Rimer, & F. M. Lewis (Eds.), *Health behavior and health education: Theory, Research, and practice* (pp. 210–239). San Francisco, CA: Jossey-Bass.

Wong, Y. J., Kim, B. S. K., Nguyen, C. P., Cheng, J. K. Y., & Saw, A. (2014). The Interpersonal Shame Inventory for Asian Americans: Scale development and psychometric properties. *Journal of Counseling Psychology, 61*, 119–132. http://dx.doi.org/10.1037/a0034681

Wongpakaran, N., & Wongpakaran, T. (2010). The Thai version of the Perceived Stress Scale (PSS-10): An investigation of its psychometric properties. *Biopsychosocial Medicine, 4*, 1–6.

Yang, B., & Clum, G. A. (1995). Measures of life stress and social support specific to an Asian student population. *Journal of Psychopathology and Behavioral Assessment, 17,* 51–67. http://dx.doi.org/10.1007/BF02229203

Zane, N. (1993). An empirical examination of loss of face among Asian Americans. In R. Carter (Ed.), *Ninth annual cross-cultural winter roundtable proceedings* (pp. 1–6). New York, NY: Columbia University. Retrieved from http://aacdrpubs.faculty.ucdavis.edu/wp-content/uploads/sites/211/2015/03/zane002.pdf

Zeng, Z., & Xie, Y. (2004). Asian-Americans' earnings disadvantage reexamined: The role of place of education. *American Journal of Sociology, 109,* 1075–1108. http://dx.doi.org/10.1086/381914

Zhang, Y., Young, D., Lee, S., Zhang, H., Xiao, Z., Wei, H., . . . Chang, D. F. (2002). Chinese Taoist cognitive psychotherapy in the treatment of generalized anxiety disorder in contemporary China. *Transcultural Psychiatry, 39,* 115–129. http://dx.doi.org/10.1177/136346150203900105

Zigmond, A. S., & Snaith, R. P. (1983). The Hospital Anxiety and Depression Scale. *Acta Psychiatrica Scandinavica, 67,* 361–370. http://dx.doi.org/10.1111/j.1600-0447.1983.tb09716.x

Zureck, E., Altstötter-Gleich, C., Gerstenberg, F. X., & Schmitt, M. (2015). Perfectionism in the transactional stress model. *Personality and Individual Differences, 83,* 18–23. http://dx.doi.org/10.1016/j.paid.2015.03.029

10

COGNITIVE BEHAVIORAL MODELS, MEASURES, AND TREATMENTS FOR STRESS DISORDERS IN LATINOS

ESTEBAN V. CARDEMIL, LISA M. EDWARDS, TAMARA NELSON, AND KARINA T. LOYO

The tremendous growth in the Latino population in the United States has led to a surge of interest in understanding the mental health experiences of this population. This interest has also been spurred by the recognition that Latinos are affected by significant and persistent economic, educational, and mental health care disparities (Blanco et al., 2007; Gonzales & Papadopoulos, 2010). These disparities make it critical that the mental health community increase its understanding of the mental health experiences, approaches to assessment, and treatments that have strong evidence bases with Latinos.

Stress has long been an important area of focus for researchers interested in understanding Latino health and mental health, given the consistent associations found between exposure to stressful life events and poor mental health, including depression, anxiety, and posttraumatic stress disorder (PTSD; Cheng & Mallinckrodt, 2015; Cuevas, Sabina, & Picard, 2010; Kaltman, Green, Mete, Shara, & Miranda, 2010; Myers et al., 2015).

http://dx.doi.org/10.1037/0000091-011
Treating Depression, Anxiety, and Stress in Ethnic and Racial Groups: Cognitive Behavioral Approaches,
E. C. Chang, C. A. Downey, J. K. Hirsch, and E. A. Yu (Editors)
Copyright © 2018 by the American Psychological Association. All rights reserved.

Moreover, researchers have documented the numerous ways in which Latino populations have historically been exposed to stressful and traumatic events. These have included traumas in their country of origin, traumas associated with the migration process, and traumas that result from living in under-resourced communities in the United States (Cuevas, Sabina, & Picard, 2015; Eisenman, Gelberg, Liu, & Shapiro, 2003; Fortuna, Porche, & Alegría, 2008). As a result, PTSD has been a major focus of research in Latino mental health. In addition, researchers have expanded their focus on stress among Latinos to include the stressors associated with the process of adaptation to the United States, termed *acculturative stress* (Berry, 1970). Although much of this work has focused on immigrant Latinos, researchers have also begun to explore the stress experienced by more assimilated Latinos and second-generation Latinos. In this chapter, we review the various cognitive behavioral models that have explored, measured, and treated PTSD and acculturative stress among Latinos. Throughout our review, we focus on how these efforts have balanced the application of cognitive behavioral principles with attention to culturally relevant factors.

COGNITIVE BEHAVIORAL MODELS FOR UNDERSTANDING STRESS IN LATINOS

Posttraumatic Stress Disorder

Prevalence Rates and Phenomenology

Early research on PTSD among Latinos focused on refugees and immigrants, victims of disasters, and Vietnam veterans (Hough, Canino, Abueg, & Gusman, 1996). This research generated useful data regarding the phenomenology and experience of PTSD among Latinos but was limited by variation in measurement, sampling, and context across studies. More recent epidemiological studies have estimated lifetime prevalence rates of PTSD among Latinos to be in the range of 4.4% to 7.0% (Alegría et al., 2008; Roberts, Gilman, Breslau, Breslau, & Koenen, 2011). However, controversy exists regarding the relative risk of PTSD experienced by Latinos compared with individuals from other racial and ethnic backgrounds. Early research on PTSD among Latinos found evidence for elevated risk among Latino Vietnam veterans (Ortega & Rosenheck, 2000); this elevated risk was subsequently found in a number of studies that examined different samples and contexts, including police officers (Pole, Best, Metzler, & Marmar, 2005), physical injury survivors (Marshall, Schell, & Miles, 2009), and mothers receiving services at child welfare organizations (Chemtob, Griffing,

Tullberg, Roberts, & Ellis, 2011). In contrast, several well-designed studies, including two large-scale epidemiological studies, found no elevated risk of PTSD among Latinos compared with Whites (Adams & Boscarino, 2005; Alegría et al., 2013; Dohrenwend, Turner, Turse, Lewis-Fernandez, & Yager, 2008; Roberts et al., 2011).

To explore these conflicting findings, Alcántara, Casement, and Lewis-Fernández (2013) conducted a systematic review of research that compared the conditional risk of PTSD between Latinos and other racial and ethnic groups. Across the 28 studies identified, the authors found mixed support for the notion that Latinos have a greater risk of PTSD. In particular, although they found that 75% of the articles documented some significant differences between Latinos and other ethnic groups with regard to PTSD, there were inconsistencies depending on how PTSD was assessed. In particular, over 90% of the articles that examined PTSD symptom severity found higher scores among Latinos, and 75% of the articles that assessed PTSD onset following a discrete event found evidence of greater risk for Latinos. However, only 55% of the studies that assessed prevalence of PTSD documented elevated risk for Latinos, and only 40% of the articles that examined the persistence of PTSD found that it was worse among Latinos. Thus, although their review suggests that Latinos do exhibit some elevated risk of PTSD, particularly as it pertains to symptom severity, much more research is needed to understand the inconsistencies they identified.

Researchers have also found some evidence for variability in symptom presentation of PTSD among Latinos. For example, in addition to finding overall elevated PTSD symptoms among Latinos, Marshall et al. (2009) found that Latinos were more likely than Whites to report elevations in some symptoms of PTSD (e.g., hypervigilance, intrusive thoughts, flashbacks) but not others (e.g., sleep disturbance, restricted affect, memory impairment). Other research has found elevated levels of reliving, hyperarousal, guilt, and avoidance (Ortega & Rosenheck, 2000), emotional upset and distancing (Hoyt & Yeater, 2010), and psychotic symptoms (David, Kutcher, Jackson, & Mellman, 1999; Wilcox, Briones, & Suess, 1991). Again, these findings have not been consistently replicated across symptom clusters, and some research has not found significant symptom differences between Latinos and other racial and ethnic groups (e.g., Alegría et al., 2013; C'de Baca, Castillo, & Qualls, 2012; DeVylder, Burnette, & Yang, 2014).

In addition to research comparing PTSD between Latinos and other ethnic groups, some limited research has explored within-Latino variability. Although limited in scope, this work has found results consistent with the larger literature on the immigrant health paradox, whereby Latino immigrants, especially those of Mexican descent, demonstrate better health and mental health outcomes than both later-generation Latino residents and non-Latino White residents (Alegría et al., 2008). That is, the few studies that have examined PTSD among Latinos of Mexican descent have found elevated levels of PTSD symptoms among later generation and English-speaking Latinos (e.g., Heilemann, Kury, & Lee, 2005; Kataoka et al., 2009; although for an exception, see M. A. Rodriguez et al., 2008). However, research that has examined PTSD among Latinos from non-Mexican backgrounds has found less support for the immigrant health paradox. This work has found higher rates of PTSD among Spanish-speaking Latinos (e.g., Perilla, Norris, & Lavizzo, 2002) and among Latinos of Dominican and Puerto Rican backgrounds (Galea et al., 2004).

Theories and Models

Efforts to understand PTSD among Latinos can be grouped into two categories: those that explore differential exposure to trauma among Latinos and those that examine differential vulnerability among Latinos (Perilla et al., 2002). Research on differential exposure has recognized the different life experiences in which Latinos might be at greater risk to trauma exposure, including political and other violence in their countries of origin, trauma and stress during the migration process, and greater exposure to violence resulting from living in low resource communities (Fortuna et al., 2008). In support of this theory, Eisenman and colleagues (2003) found that over half of Latino primary care patients they sampled reported exposure to political violence. Of these, 18% had symptoms of PTSD, a significantly greater proportion than those who had not been exposed to political violence. The limited research that has directly compared Latinos with other racial and ethnic groups has also found some support for the differential exposure hypothesis. In a study of the psychological sequelae following Hurricane Andrew, Perilla and colleagues (2002) found that Spanish-speaking Latinos were more likely to be exposed to severe trauma from the hurricane and be more likely to reside in neighborhoods that had been adversely affected.

Research that has examined the possibility of differential vulnerability in Latinos has explored a number of possible factors, including greater emotional expressiveness (Ortega & Rosenheck, 2000), increased use of avoidant coping styles (Pole et al., 2005), and fewer social supports (Hurtado-de-Mendoza, Gonzales, Serrano, & Kaltman, 2014; Pole et al., 2005; Vásquez et al., 2012), compared with individuals from other ethnic groups. Some researchers have also examined the possible role of cultural values, including familism, fatalism, and masculinity (Cuevas et al., 2015; Herrera, Owens, & Mallinckrodt, 2013; Perilla et al., 2002) and religious coping (Cuevas et al., 2015). Some differential vulnerability research has looked at deficits in basic cognitive and emotional processes. For example, one study found memory and executive functioning deficits in Puerto Rican women who had been victims of childhood sexual abuse (Rivera-Vélez, González-Viruet, Martínez-Taboas, & Pérez-Mojica, 2014). These deficits were correlated with symptoms of PTSD and dissociation.

Although intuitively appealing, these differential vulnerability hypotheses have not generated consistent findings (e.g., Dohrenwend et al., 2008; Lewis-Fernández et al., 2008). In contrast, the two risk factors that have emerged as most consistently associated with greater risk of PTSD have been prior trauma exposure and peritraumatic dissociation. Several studies have noted that prior trauma exposure increases risk of PTSD following a subsequent traumatic experience (e.g., Dohrenwend et al., 2008; Eisenman et al., 2008; Fortuna et al., 2008; Pantin, Schwartz, Prado, Feaster, & Szapocznik, 2003; M. A. Rodriguez et al., 2008; Sumner, Wong, Schetter, Myers, & Rodriguez, 2012). Similarly, peritraumatic dissociation has also emerged as an intriguing risk factor for PTSD across several studies (Denson, Marshall, Schell, & Jaycox, 2007; Greenwell & Cosden, 2009). Researchers have speculated that peritraumatic dissociation might be of particular relevance to some Latino populations who experience culturally specific expressions of distress that include dissociation among the symptoms (e.g., *ataques de nervios*; Alcántara et al., 2013; Gutiérrez Wang, Cosden, & Bernal, 2011b). However, this focus on peritraumatic dissociation is still relatively nascent, and the links to aspects of Latino culture have not yet been conclusively made.

Acculturative Stress

History and Explication

Acculturative stress is closely related to, although distinct from, the broader construct of *acculturation*, which describes the process by which people adapt to, and effect change in, a broader cultural context (Berry, 1991). According to Berry's (1991) acculturation framework, there are large variations in how groups and individuals undergo acculturation. Individuals may opt to engage in different acculturation strategies, reflected in attitudes and behaviors related to (a) their preference to maintain their heritage culture and identity and (b) their preference to have contact with the larger society. This variation can produce considerable differences across individuals, with some individuals choosing to maintain their connections to their culture of origin and not engage with the host society, whereas others may choose to prioritize assimilating to the larger host culture over maintaining connections to their heritage culture. Recent attention has been given to bicultural individuals—those who work to maintain connections to both cultures.

As individuals undergo the process of acculturation, they may experience stress from negotiating different, sometimes conflicting, values and behaviors (Romero, Carvajal, Valle, & Orduña, 2007). Early conceptualizations of this strain were termed *culture shock* (Oberg, 1960); however, Berry (1970) later described this as *acculturative stress* to emphasize that this reaction might not necessarily be negative (as was implied by *shock*), that it involved more than one culture (as was implied by *culture*), and that it could be framed within a stress and coping theory. In recent years, the field of Latino psychology has also referred to these effects as *immigration-related challenges* (e.g., Arbona et al., 2010), *culture* or *ethnicity-related stress* (e.g., Cervantes, Padilla, & Salgado de Snyder, 1990), and *bicultural stress* (e.g., Romero & Roberts, 2003); however *acculturative stress* is still the most popular term.

Latino immigrants, as well as those who have been in the United States for several generations, can experience acculturative stress (Baker, Soto, Perez, & Lee, 2012). In fact, Arbona et al. (2010) found that although undocumented immigrants reported higher levels of challenges related to family separation and language, both documented and undocumented immigrants reported similar levels of fear of deportation. It is not difficult to imagine the myriad factors that influence the level of acculturative stress an individual might experience. For example, the type of acculturating group (e.g., refugee, immigrant) and their degree of willingness to migrate, as well as the nature of the host society (e.g., immigrant and intergroup policies and climate), can affect the level of strain, not to mention numerous personal, psychological factors (Lueck & Wilson, 2011). In an early study of psychosocial predictors of acculturative stress among Latino adults, Hovey (2000) found that family dysfunction, separation from family, low income, and negative expectations for the future were related to elevated levels of acculturative stress. More recently, in a nationally representative sample of over 2,000 Latino immigrants, Lueck and Wilson (2011) found that acculturative stress was lower for U.S. citizens, immigrants who wanted to migrate to the United States (vs. refugees), those with higher English proficiency, and those with less perceived discrimination.

In addition to the diverse factors that might influence the level of an individual's acculturative stress, there are also different types of stressors that Latinos experience. Authors have commonly described acculturative stress as being experienced in the form of discrimination, lowered expectations, language conflicts (e.g., pressure to be bilingual or not speaking English well), cultural orientation gaps between family members, and family disruption

(Barrera, Gonzales, Lopez, & Fernandez, 2004; Romero, Edwards, & Corkery, 2013; Romero & Roberts, 2003). Indeed, most of the acculturative stress measures that are reviewed later in this chapter assess the stress experienced in these areas.

Theories and Models

Although acculturation theory has guided most of the work in the area of acculturative stress, few frameworks exist beyond general stress and coping theory (e.g., Lazarus & Folkman, 1984) to describe acculturative stress in particular. In an attempt to better understand and distinguish acculturation and acculturative stress within the Latino context and to contribute to theory in this area, Caplan (2007) conducted a dimensional concept analysis using research articles and a few other media articles as a basis for clarifying and refining concepts (Rodgers, 2000). Caplan identified three primary dimensions of acculturative stress, each of which included subdimensions. Specifically, the Instrumental/Environmental dimension includes the following subdimensions of stressors: financial issues, language barriers, lack of access to health care, unsafe neighborhoods, unemployment, and lack of education. The Social/Interpersonal dimension includes loss of social networks, loss of social status, family conflict, intergenerational conflict, and changing gender roles. Finally, the Societal dimension includes discrimination and stigma, legal status, and political and historical forces. Within each of these dimensions, Caplan described several influential contextual variables, including (a) individual psychological characteristics and coping mechanisms such as self-esteem and religiosity, (b) documentation status, (c) socioeconomic status, (d) pre-emigration experience (voluntary or involuntary), and (e) level of acculturation. Each of these factors played a role in how Latino individuals perceived stress from the acculturation process and illustrate the complex and diverse pathways by which one might experience acculturative stress.

It is important to note that authors have found that although acculturative stress may be common, it may not necessarily be negative or lead to psychopathology (Iwamasa, Regan, Subica, & Yamada, 2013). Indeed, Berry (2006) noted that most people can cope with stressors that are acculturation related. Nonetheless, the perception of stress varies by the individual and can accumulate over time, which can lead to chronic stress and other mental health concerns (Romero et al., 2013). Research has noted the negative effects of acculturative stress on mental health among adults, including its relation to a greater risk of mood and anxiety disorders, externalizing symptoms, and substance use (Hovey & Magaña, 2002; Torres, 2010; Verney & Kipp, 2007). Importantly, researchers have found some buffers against the negative effects of acculturative stress, including family support (Crockett et al., 2007) and hopefulness regarding the future and financial resources (Hovey & Magaña, 2002).

All these studies, although informative regarding the correlates and nature of acculturative stress among Latinos, have tended to be cross-sectional. To move the field forward, more longitudinal studies are needed (Caplan, 2007). As an example, a recent longitudinal study of 405 Latino immigrants by Dillon, De La Rosa, and Ibañez (2013) explored acculturative stress and changes in family cohesion in the initial years following arrival in the United States. Results suggested that those who experienced more acculturative stress and those who did not have family in the United States experienced a greater decline in family cohesion over the initial 2 years. Although the authors noted that they could not establish a causal link between increases in acculturative stress and declines in family cohesion, the findings are promising because they shed light on common processes that might affect Latinos during immigration.

COGNITIVE BEHAVIORAL MEASUREMENT OF STRESS IN LATINOS

In this section, we describe some of the most commonly used measures to assess PTSD and acculturative stress among Latino populations. To identify these instruments we searched for recent research on PTSD and acculturative stress among Latino adults and focused on assessments that were most frequently used. We elected to review one measure that assesses PTSD symptomatology, as well as one broad measure of trauma-related symptoms. Finally, we make note of other measures that can be used to assess PTSD among adults. With respect to acculturative stress, we review two measures for adults.

Measures of Posttraumatic Stress Disorder

PTSD Checklist

The PTSD Checklist (PCL; Weathers, Litz, Herman, Huska, & Keane, 1993) is a self-report, 17-item measure designed to assess PTSD symptomatology as defined by the *Diagnostic and Statistical Manual of Mental Disorders* (fourth ed. [DSM–IV]; American Psychiatric Association, 1994). The PCL is available in a version for military and in two formats for civilians—specific and general (PCL-C)—however, we primarily discuss the PCL-C because it is the version most frequently used in Latino samples. Participants are asked to rate on a scale from 1 (*not at all*) to 5 (*extremely*) how bothersome each symptom has been in the past month in relation to a nonmilitary general event. In addition to the studies with predominantly European American samples, the PCL has also been widely used with adult Latinos of various ethnic backgrounds (e.g., Mexican Americans, Puerto Ricans, South Americans, Central Americans) as a screening tool for diagnostic status and treatment outcome measure. Reliabilities of the PCL-C with Latinos have been comparable to the original validation sample, with Cronbach alphas for the total scale ranging from .89 to .94 for adult male and female Latinos exposed to interpersonal violence (Sumner et al., 2012) and discrimination (Cheng & Mallinckrodt, 2015) and in studies examining culturally related variables on PTSD symptomatology mixed trauma (Cuevas et al., 2015; Hoyt & Yeater, 2010).

Trauma Symptom Inventory

The Trauma Symptom Inventory (TSI; Briere, 1995) is a self-report measure used to assess the pervasiveness of acute and chronic trauma-related symptomatology over the previous 6 months evaluated on a 4-point scale from 0 (*never*) to 3 (*often*). The TSI has a total of 100 items organized within 10 symptom categories that tap into symptoms of anxiety, depression, irritability, intrusive thoughts or memories, dissociation, and other difficulties that may arise after experiencing a potentially traumatic event. It includes three validity scales. The TSI has been used with Latino adult samples that have experienced various potential traumas—for example, domestic violence (Greenwell & Cosden, 2009) and multiple victimizations (e.g., physical and sexual assault, stalking, or witnessing such events) as an adult exclusively (Cuevas, Bell, & Sabina, 2014) or throughout the life-span (Cuevas et al., 2010). The latter two studies used four of the 10 clinical scales, which include Anxious Arousal, Depression, Anger/Irritability, and Dissociation and reported Cronbach alphas at or above .86, .86, .89, and .83, respectively. Gutiérrez Wang, Cosden, and Bernal (2011a) examined the effects of childhood abuse and dissociation on adult symptomatology in Puerto Ricans using the Spanish-language Trauma Symptom Inventory–Revised scale (Gutiérrez Wang et al., 2011a) and demonstrated a high Cronbach alpha of .97 for the total score.

Other notable scales not reviewed are used to make a PTSD diagnosis and have been used with Latino samples; these include the Clinician Administered PTSD Scale (Blake et al., 1995; C'de Baca et al., 2012; Meredith et al., 2014; Pérez Benítez, Zlotnick, Gomez, Rendón, & Swanson, 2013; Vera et al., 2012) and the Structured Clinical Interview for *DSM–IV* (David et al., 1999; Dohrenwend et al., 2008; First, Spitzer, & Gibbon, 1995;

Hinton, Hofmann, Rivera, Otto, & Pollack, 2011; Kaltman et al., 2010; Lewis-Fernández et al., 2008, 2010; Pérez Benítez, Sibrava, Zlotnick, Weisberg, & Keller, 2014).

Measures of Acculturative Stress

Societal, Attitudinal, Familial, and Environmental Stress

The Societal, Attitudinal, Familial, and Environmental Acculturative Stress Scale (SAFE; Mena, Padilla, & Maldonado, 1987) is a 24-item scale adapted from the original 60-item Familial, Attitudinal, Social, and Environmental Scale (Padilla, Wagatsuma, & Lindholm, 1985). The SAFE asks participants to rate each item from 1 (*not stressful*) to 5 (*extremely stressful*) in relation to social, attitudinal, familial, and environmental domains or 0 in the case that an item is not applicable to the participant. The range of possible scores is 0 to 120. The Cronbach alpha for total scale was .89 for an ethnically diverse, mixed-generation undergraduate student sample (Mena et al., 1987). Similar values for the SAFE (Spanish and English) have been found for Latin American student and community-based samples representing various Latin countries of origin. Cronbach alphas have ranged from .75 to .93 among studies investigating the role of acculturative stress on psychological functioning and adjustment (Cano, Castillo, Castro, de Dios, & Roncancio, 2014; Crockett et al., 2007; Hovey & Magaña, 2002; Negy, Hammons, Ferrer, & Carper, 2010) and eating disorder symptomatology (Perez, Voelz, Pettit, & Joiner, 2002; Kroon Van Diest, Tartakovsky, Stachon, Pettit, & Perez, 2014).

Multidimensional Acculturative Stress Inventory

The Multidimensional Acculturative Stress Inventory (MASI; N. Rodriguez, Myers, Mira, Flores, & Garcia-Hernandez, 2002) is a 36-item measure that taps into sources of stress experienced by immigrants and subsequent generations of Mexican origin who are adjusting to a new environment (i.e., United States). The MASI isolates acculturative stress from general or other sources of stress that may be relevant for this ethnic group. The MASI has four subscales that address issues of Spanish and English language competency and adjusting to Anglo and Mexican values. On the basis of their experiences in the prior 3 months, participants first evaluate whether an item *does not apply* (0); if it does, it is rated on a 6-point scale from 1 (*not at all stressful*) to 5 (*extremely stressful*). The MASI has shown strong psychometric properties, with Cronbach alphas ranging from .77 to .93 and test–retest coefficients ranging from .53 to .84 among a community-based Latino adult sample (N. Rodriguez et al., 2002). It was recently validated with a college student population that supported the original four-factor structure (Castillo et al., 2015). The MASI has been used widely among Latino adults, both in English and in Spanish, in studies investigating the role of acculturative stress on depressive symptoms, psychosocial functioning, and academic achievement and has shown internal consistency comparable to the validation sample, with Cronbach alphas for individual subscales and total scores between .73 to .92 (Driscoll & Torres, 2013; Rivera et al., 2015; Sarmiento & Cardemil, 2009; Torres, 2010; Wang, Schwartz, & Zamboanga, 2010).

COGNITIVE BEHAVIORAL TREATMENTS FOR STRESS IN LATINOS

Despite decades of research demonstrating the effectiveness of cognitive behavior therapy (CBT) for a number of mental health disorders, the role of ethnicity has received little attention in outcome research (Mak, Law, Alvidrez, & Pérez-Stable, 2007). The majority of treatment outcome research for stress disorders has been on PTSD, which has had a similarly limited focus on Latinos (Mason, Resick, & Rizvi, 2014). For instance, as recently as 2008, a review of the effectiveness of CBT with ethnic minority adults found that no studies had included a sufficiently large sample of Latino adults to allow for any conclusions about the efficacy of CBT with Latinos (Horrell, 2008). In this section, we review the few treatment studies that have sufficient numbers of Latino adults to allow for preliminary conclusions to be drawn about relative effectiveness.

Cognitive Behavior Therapy for Posttraumatic Stress Disorder

Two separate investigative teams have made efforts to develop culturally adapted CBT approaches to treating PTSD among Latino clients. In one approach, Hinton et al. (2011) randomly assigned Latina women to receive culturally adapted CBT (CA-CBT; $n = 12$) or applied muscle relaxation (AMR; $n = 12$) for treatment-resistant PTSD. Treatment was delivered via a manual-based protocol (Hinton et al., 2004, 2005) in a group format (i.e., two groups of six patients) over the course of 14 weeks. The authors were intentional in addressing common barriers to treatment. In addition, they specifically inquired about their patients' illness conceptualization and understanding of their symptoms. For example, treatment focused on concerns about *nervios* and *ataque de nervios*. The authors also identified how several key CBT techniques were culturally adapted. For example, culturally congruent imagery relevant to the expression of spirituality among Latinos was used to facilitate meditation. The authors found that the women in the

CA-CBT group reported significantly lower levels of PTSD, anxiety, and *nervios* symptoms than women in the AMR group at posttreatment and follow-up. Similarly, women in the CA-CBT group reported significantly greater levels of emotion regulation.

In a similar effort, Pérez Benítez et al. (2013) conducted an open pilot trial of a culturally adapted CBT in eight Latina adult patients with a current diagnosis of PTSD and medically unexplained psychological symptoms. Treatment consisted of short-term (approximately 10–14 sessions) manualized CBT for both PTSD and somatization delivered at a community clinic in a southeastern university campus. In general, sessions included the basic aspects of cognitive therapy (Beck, 2005), including collaborative agenda setting, homework, psychoeducation, and review of learned skills. Treatment included six modules, including cognitive restructuring, relaxation training, activity regulation, and communication skills.

Culturally sensitive techniques were prioritized. For example, therapists focused on *desahogar* (unburdening oneself by venting), which recognizes that some Latino patients may view treatment as a means to get everyday problems off their chest (Interian & Díaz-Martínez, 2007). In addition, key ingredients in CBT such as dysfunctional thoughts were conveyed in Spanish (*pensamientos dañinos*, or harmful thoughts) to enhance understanding of CBT concepts. Finally, familiarity with Latin American history, as well as legal and immigration issues, were also critical for establishing rapport. Findings revealed that half the patients who completed treatment did not meet criteria for a diagnosis of PTSD at the end of the treatment. Ratings by independent evaluators indicated that five (62.5%) patients also improved in somatization.

In addition to these two culturally adapted CBT approaches, Vera and colleagues (2011) conducted a small randomized controlled trial to examine the feasibility of culturally adapted prolonged exposure (PE) therapy among Spanish-speaking Puerto Ricans with PTSD. Cultural adaptations included the representation of language, idioms, and examples reflective of Latino culture, including the incorporation of family relationships and interdependence. Treatment consisted of 16 sessions delivered in a group format lasting for 90 to 120 minutes. The first session focused on information gathering and providing a discussion of the treatment rationale and program overview; an optional introductory session for family members was also included. This session was followed by information about common reactions to trauma and an introduction to repeated in vivo exposure followed by exposure. Results indicated that participants randomly assigned to the PE condition had significantly greater symptom improvement than those randomly assigned to the usual care condition. Moreover, at posttreatment, three of the five participants in the PE condition had a 25% or greater reduction in pretreatment PTSD symptoms, compared with only one out of seven participants in the usual care condition.

Cognitive Behavior Therapy for Stress

In one small open pilot study that was not focused specifically on PTSD but on stress more generally, Hovey, Hurtado, and Seligman (2014) developed a six-session cognitive behavioral group intervention for Latina migrant farmworkers. In addition to using standard cognitive behavioral strategies (e.g., psychoeducation, exposure, assertiveness training, problem solving, cognitive restructuring, positive activity scheduling), the treatment emphasized several critical cultural considerations. First, groups were co-led by a female licensed psychologist and a *promotora de la salud* (community health worker), both of whom were bilingual and bicultural. Second, sessions were conducted in Spanish and held at a local church, which was a setting familiar to the women, selected to decrease stigma. Third, clients were included in the decision-making process regarding what topics were covered. The authors noted that the group leaders emphasized the cultural values of *simpatía*, *respeto*, and *personalismo* to facilitate increased levels of comfort and trust. These cultural values have been described as guides for different types of interpersonal interactions (Edwards & Cardemil, 2015). *Respeto* (respect) refers to a formal interaction style that is used within hierarchical relationships, both within the family and with authority figures outside the family. *Personalismo* (personalism), by contrast, refers to a personable interpersonal interaction designed to convey warmth and promote connection, and *simpatía* (geniality) refers to an individual's likeability. Six Latina participants enrolled in the study; significant reductions in migrant farmworker symptoms of stress, depression, and anxiety were documented posttreatment.

Overall, although the literature is clearly in its early stages, initial returns are promising and can build on recent research showing that Latinos are open to receiving mental health treatment for PTSD, with a preference for counseling within their primary care center (Eisenman et al., 2008). Moreover, there is reason to be optimistic about the specific potential of cognitive behavioral approaches, given the growing body of research on cultural adaptations of cognitive behavioral interventions for Latinos (Cardemil & Sarmiento, 2009; Interian & Díaz-Martínez, 2007), as well as the work that has found that Latinos demonstrate a preference for supportive and cognitive behavior therapy (Kaltman, Hurtado de Mendoza, Gonzales, & Serrano, 2014).

THE FUTURE OF COGNITIVE BEHAVIORAL MODELS, MEASURES, AND TREATMENTS FOR STRESS IN LATINOS

Our review of the literature on stress among Latinos has highlighted the surge in research focused on this population. In particular, the last 15 years have witnessed a veritable explosion in basic research on PTSD and acculturative stress, the development and evaluation of numerous measures of both constructs, and the beginning stages of interventions developed specifically for Latinos. This increased attention to stress among Latinos is welcome, given the dramatic population changes that have been occurring in the United States. However, there remain considerable gaps in our knowledge base, particularly as they apply to cognitive behavioral models. We briefly summarize the main findings from our literature review, highlight the gaps in our knowledge, and make recommendations for future research.

Our review indicated that although there is some evidence for elevated risk of PTSD among Latinos and differences in symptom profiles, the research findings have been equivocal and inconsistent. Similarly, although the evidence indicates that Latinos may be at elevated risk of exposure to stress and trauma, it is much less consistent with regard to differential vulnerability, with the intriguing exception of peritraumatic dissociation. In contrast to the literature on PTSD, the research on acculturative stress has produced more consistent findings, with acculturative stress being associated with a range of negative outcomes and some preliminary research identifying important buffers of acculturative stress (e.g., family support). With regard to measurement, our review identified a number of well-established measures of both PTSD and acculturative stress. With regard to treatment, the research base is just beginning to be established. A few approaches have shown considerable promise, with several independent research teams advancing the work on culturally adaptive CBT for PTSD.

Taken together, there exist considerable gaps in the field's understanding of theories, measurement, and treatment of stress among Latinos. Much of the equivocal results stem from inconsistent methodological approaches used across studies. For example, Alcántara and colleagues (2013) identified a number of methodological factors that varied across the research they reviewed, including different definitions of PTSD (i.e., lifetime prevalence vs. conditional risk), different approaches to assessment (i.e., self-report vs. clinician administered), and different sampling approaches (i.e., convenience vs. random sampling). Thus, future research would do well to use multimethod approaches to assessing PTSD and to make greater use of random, nationally representative sampling approaches.

In addition to methodological inconsistencies, there has been a notable dearth of research exploring contextual influences on outcomes. For example, despite the research on the immigrant health paradox that has shown important differences between Latinos of different national origin, the paradox has not been consistently explored in the context of PTSD or acculturative stress. Similarly, as with research on ethnic minority populations more generally, more attention to socioeconomic context is critical to disentangle the complicated effects of socioeconomic status and ethnicity. Although the research on acculturation has more consistently considered contextual influences, given its grounding in acculturation theory, this work has been predominantly cross-sectional. More longitudinal research is critically needed to advance our understanding of the dynamic influences of context on stress.

We also note that despite the growth in attention to cultural variation in experience and symptom expression, particularly in the PTSD research, not enough of this research has been guided by theory. For example, although a few studies examined symptom variability from within a cultural framework, many others simply examined group differences in scores on particular measures. We remain skeptical of the ability of between-groups comparative research to advance the field's understanding of the reasons for differences. Moreover, we were struck by the relative dearth of research simultaneously examining PTSD and acculturative stress (see Rivera et al., 2015, for a notable exception). The absence of this integrative work is likely the result of an overly siloed approach to research; finding ways to encourage interdisciplinary research has considerable potential.

Finally, with regard to cognitive behavioral models specifically, we are encouraged by the initial efforts to examine stress among Latinos using these models; however, this work should be more widespread and carefully integrated with cultural considerations. For example, the intriguing possibility that some Latinos may be at greater risk of peritraumatic dissociation, which would, in turn, elevate their risk of subsequent PTSD, remains in need of considerable additional research to better understand the underlying mechanisms by which this link may exist. Understanding these mechanisms would have clear implications for the continued refinement of the treatments that have begun to show promise.

REFERENCES

Adams, R. E., & Boscarino, J. A. (2005). Differences in mental health outcomes among Whites, African Americans, and Hispanics following a community disaster. *Psychiatry: Interpersonal and Biological Processes*, 68, 250–265. http://dx.doi.org/10.1521/psyc.2005.68.3.250

Alcántara, C., Casement, M. D., & Lewis-Fernández, R. (2013). Conditional risk for PTSD among Latinos: A systematic review of racial/ethnic differences and sociocultural explanations. *Clinical Psychology Review, 33,* 107–119. http://dx.doi.org/10.1016/j.cpr.2012.10.005

Alegría, M., Canino, G., Shrout, P. E., Woo, M., Duan, N., Vila, D., . . . Meng, X. L. (2008). Prevalence of mental illness in immigrant and non-immigrant U.S. Latino groups. *The American Journal of Psychiatry, 165,* 359–369. http://dx.doi.org/10.1176/appi.ajp.2007.07040704

Alegría, M., Fortuna, L. R., Lin, J. Y., Norris, F. H., Gao, S., Takeuchi, D. T., . . . Valentine, A. (2013). Prevalence, risk, and correlates of posttraumatic stress disorder across ethnic and racial minority groups in the United States. *Medical Care, 51,* 1114–1123. http://dx.doi.org/10.1097/MLR.0000000000000007

American Psychiatric Association. (1994). *Diagnostic and statistical manual of mental disorders* (4th ed.). Washington, DC: Author.

Arbona, C., Olvera, N., Rodriguez, N., Hagan, J., Linares, A., & Wiesner, M. (2010). Acculturative stress among documented and undocumented Latino immigrants in the United States. *Hispanic Journal of Behavioral Sciences, 32,* 362–384. http://dx.doi.org/10.1177/0739986310373210

Baker, A., Soto, J. A., Perez, C. R., & Lee, E. A. (2012). Acculturative status and psychological well-being in an Asian American sample. *Asian American Journal of Psychology, 3,* 275–285. http://dx.doi.org/10.1037/a0026842

Barrera, M., Gonzales, N. A., Lopez, V., & Fernandez, A. C. (2004). Problem behaviors of Chicano/a and Latino/a adolescents: An analysis of prevalence, risk, and protective factors. In R. Velasquez, L. Arellano, & B. McNeil (Eds.), *Handbook of Chicano/a psychology and mental health* (pp. 83–109). Mahwah, NJ: Erlbaum.

Beck, J. S. (2005). *Cognitive therapy for challenging problems: What to do when the basics don't work.* New York, NY: Guilford Press.

Berry, J. W. (1970). Marginality, stress and ethnic identification in an acculturated Aboriginal community. *Journal of Cross-Cultural Psychology, 1,* 239–252. http://dx.doi.org/10.1177/135910457000100303

Berry, J. W. (1991). Understanding and managing multiculturalism: Some possible implications of research in Canada. *Psychology and Developing Societies, 3,* 17–49. http://dx.doi.org/10.1177/097133369100300103

Berry, J. W. (2006). Acculturative stress. In P. T. P. Wong & L. C. J. Wong (Eds.), *Handbook of multicultural perspectives on stress and coping* (pp. 287–298). Dallas, TX: Springer. http://dx.doi.org/10.1007/0-387-26238-5_12

Blake, D. D., Weathers, F. W., Nagy, L. M., Kaloupek, D. G., Gusman, F. D., Charney, D. S., & Keane, T. M. (1995). The development of a clinician-administered PTSD scale. *Journal of Traumatic Stress, 8,* 75–90. http://dx.doi.org/10.1002/jts.2490080106

Blanco, C., Patel, S. R., Liu, L., Jiang, H., Lewis-Fernández, R., Schmidt, A. B., . . . Olfson, M. (2007). National trends in ethnic disparities in mental health care. *Medical Care, 45,* 1012–1019. http://dx.doi.org/10.1097/MLR.0b013e3180ca95d3

Briere, J. (1995). *Trauma Symptom Inventory professional manual*. Odessa, FL: Psychological Assessment Resources.

Cano, M. Á., Castillo, L. G., Castro, Y., de Dios, M. A., & Roncancio, A. M. (2014). Acculturative stress and depressive symptomatology among Mexican and Mexican American students in the U.S.: Examining associations with cultural incongruity and intragroup marginalization. *International Journal for the Advancement of Counselling, 36*, 136–149.

Caplan, S. (2007). Latinos, acculturation, and acculturative stress: A dimensional concept analysis. *Policy, Politics, & Nursing Practice, 8*, 93–106. http://dx.doi.org/10.1177/1527154407301751

Cardemil, E. V., & Sarmiento, I. (2009). Clinical approaches to working with Latino adults. In F. A. Villarruel, G. Carlo, J. M. Grau, M. Azmitia, N. Cabrera, & T. J. Chahin (Eds.), *Handbook of Latino psychology* (pp. 329–345). Thousand Oaks, CA: Sage.

Castillo, L. G., Cano, M. A., Yoon, M., Jung, E., Brown, E. J., Zamboanga, B. L., . . . Whitbourne, S. K. (2015). Factor structure and factorial invariance of the Multidimensional Acculturative Stress Inventory. *Psychological Assessment, 27*, 915–924. http://dx.doi.org/10.1037/pas0000095

C'de Baca, J., Castillo, D., & Qualls, C. (2012). Ethnic differences in symptoms among female veterans diagnosed with PTSD. *Journal of Traumatic Stress, 25*, 353–357. http://dx.doi.org/10.1002/jts.21709

Cervantes, R. C., Padilla, A. M., & Salgado de Snyder, N. (1990). Reliability and validity of the Hispanic Stress Inventory. *Hispanic Journal of Behavioral Sciences, 12*, 76–82. http://dx.doi.org/10.1177/07399863900121004

Chemtob, C.M., Griffing, S., Tullberg, E., Roberts, E., & Ellis, P. (2011). Screening for trauma exposure, and posttraumatic stress disorder and depression symptoms among mothers receiving child welfare preventive services. *Child Welfare, 90*, 109–127.

Cheng, H. L., & Mallinckrodt, B. (2015). Racial/ethnic discrimination, posttraumatic stress symptoms, and alcohol problems in a longitudinal study of Hispanic/Latino college students. *Journal of Counseling Psychology, 62*, 38–49. http://dx.doi.org/10.1037/cou0000052

Crockett, L. J., Iturbide, M. I., Torres Stone, R. A., McGinley, M., Raffaelli, M., & Carlo, G. (2007). Acculturative stress, social support, and coping: Relations to psychological adjustment among Mexican American college students. *Cultural Diversity and Ethnic Minority Psychology, 13*, 347–355. http://dx.doi.org/10.1037/1099-9809.13.4.347

Cuevas, C. A., Bell, K. A., & Sabina, C. (2014). Victimization, psychological distress, and help-seeking: Disentangling the relationship for Latina victims. *Psychology of Violence, 4*, 196–209. http://dx.doi.org/10.1037/a0035819

Cuevas, C. A., Sabina, C., & Picard, E. H. (2010). Interpersonal victimization patterns and psychopathology among Latino women: Results from the SALAS study. *Psychological Trauma: Theory, Research, Practice, and Policy, 2,* 296–306. http://dx.doi.org/10.1037/a0020099

Cuevas, C. A., Sabina, C., & Picard, E. H. (2015). Posttraumatic stress among victimized Latino women: Evaluating the role of cultural factors. *Journal of Traumatic Stress, 28,* 531–538. http://dx.doi.org/10.1002/jts.22060

David, D., Kutcher, G. S., Jackson, E. I., & Mellman, T. A. (1999). Psychotic symptoms in combat-related posttraumatic stress disorder. *The Journal of Clinical Psychiatry, 60,* 29–32. http://dx.doi.org/10.4088/JCP.v60n0106

Denson, T. F., Marshall, G. N., Schell, T. L., & Jaycox, L. H. (2007). Predictors of post traumatic distress 1 year after exposure to community violence: The importance of acute symptom severity. *Journal of Consulting and Clinical Psychology, 75,* 683–692. http://dx.doi.org/10.1037/0022-006X.75.5.683

DeVylder, J. E., Burnette, D., & Yang, L. H. (2014). Co-occurrence of psychotic experiences and common mental health conditions across four racially and ethnically diverse population samples. *Psychological Medicine, 44,* 3503–3513. http://dx.doi.org/10.1017/S0033291714000944

Dillon, F. R., De La Rosa, M., & Ibañez, G. E. (2013). Acculturative stress and diminishing family cohesion among recent Latino immigrants. *Journal of Immigrant and Minority Health, 15,* 484–491. http://dx.doi.org/10.1007/s10903-012-9678-3

Dohrenwend, B. P., Turner, J. B., Turse, N. A., Lewis-Fernandez, R., & Yager, T. J. (2008). War-related posttraumatic stress disorder in Black, Hispanic, and majority White Vietnam veterans: The roles of exposure and vulnerability. *Journal of Traumatic Stress, 21,* 133–141. http://dx.doi.org/10.1002/jts.20327

Driscoll, M. W., & Torres, L. (2013). Acculturative stress and Latino depression: The mediating role of behavioral and cognitive resources. *Cultural Diversity and Ethnic Minority Psychology, 19,* 373–382. http://dx.doi.org/10.1037/a0032821

Edwards, L. M., & Cardemil, E. V. (2015). Clinical approaches to assessing cultural values in Latinos. In K. Geisinger (Ed.), *Psychological testing of Hispanics: Clinical and intellectual issues* (2nd ed., pp. 215–236). Washington, DC: American Psychological Association. http://dx.doi.org/10.1037/14668-012

Eisenman, D. P., Gelberg, L., Liu, H., & Shapiro, M. F. (2003, August 6). Mental health and health-related quality of life among adult Latino primary care patients living in the United States with previous exposure to political violence. *JAMA, 290,* 627–634. http://dx.doi.org/10.1001/jama.290.5.627

Eisenman, D. P., Meredith, L. S., Rhodes, H., Green, B. L., Kaltman, S., Cassells, A., & Tobin, J. N. (2008). PTSD in Latino patients: Illness beliefs, treatment preferences, and implications for care. *Journal of General Internal Medicine, 23,* 1386–1392. http://dx.doi.org/10.1007/s11606-008-0677-y

First, M. B., Spitzer, R. L., & Gibbon, M. (1995). *Structured Clinical Interview for DSM–IV Axis I disorders.* New York, NY: New York State Psychiatric Institute.

Fortuna, L. R., Porche, M. V., & Alegría, M. (2008). Political violence, psychosocial trauma, and the context of mental health services use among immigrant Latinos in the United States. *Ethnicity & Health, 13*, 435–463. http://dx.doi.org/10.1080/13557850701837286

Galea, S., Vlahov, D., Tracy, M., Hoover, D. R., Resnick, H., & Kilpatrick, D. (2004). Hispanic ethnicity and post-traumatic stress disorder after a disaster: Evidence from a general population survey after September 11, 2001. *Annals of Epidemiology, 14*, 520–531. http://dx.doi.org/10.1016/j.annepidem.2004.01.006

Gonzales, J. J., & Papadopoulos, A. S. (2010). Mental health disparities. In B. L. Levin, K. D. Hennessy, & J. Petrilla (Eds.), *Mental health services: A public health perspective* (3rd ed., pp. 443–464). New York, NY: Oxford University Press.

Greenwell, A. N., & Cosden, M. (2009). The relationship between fatalism, dissociation, and trauma symptoms in Latinos. *Journal of Trauma & Dissociation, 10*, 334–345. http://dx.doi.org/10.1080/15299730902956820

Gutiérrez Wang, L., Cosden, M., & Bernal, G. (2011a). Adaptation and validation of the Spanish-language Trauma Symptom Inventory in Puerto Rico. *Journal of Consulting and Clinical Psychology, 79*, 118–122. http://dx.doi.org/10.1037/a0021327

Gutiérrez Wang, L., Cosden, M., & Bernal, G. (2011b). Dissociation as a mediator of posttraumatic symptoms in a Puerto Rican university sample. *Journal of Trauma & Dissociation, 12*, 358–374. http://dx.doi.org/10.1080/15299732.2011.573759

Heilemann, M. V., Kury, F. S., & Lee, K. A. (2005). Trauma and posttraumatic stress disorder symptoms among low income women of Mexican descent in the United States. *Journal of Nervous and Mental Disease, 193*, 665–672. http://dx.doi.org/10.1097/01.nmd.0000180741.93635.ab

Herrera, C. J., Owens, G. P., & Mallinckrodt, B. (2013). Traditional machismo and caballerismo as correlates of posttraumatic stress disorder, psychological distress, and relationship satisfaction in Hispanic veterans. *Journal of Multicultural Counseling and Development, 41*, 21–35. http://dx.doi.org/10.1002/j.2161-1912.2013.00024.x

Hinton, D. E., Chhean, D., Pich, V., Safren, S. A., Hofmann, S. G., & Pollack, M. H. (2005). A randomized controlled trial of cognitive-behavior therapy for Cambodian refugees with treatment-resistant PTSD and panic attacks: A cross-over design. *Journal of Traumatic Stress, 18*, 617–629. http://dx.doi.org/10.1002/jts.20070

Hinton, D. E., Hofmann, S. G., Rivera, E., Otto, M. W., & Pollack, M. H. (2011). Culturally adapted CBT (CA-CBT) for Latino women with treatment-resistant PTSD: A pilot study comparing CA-CBT to applied muscle relaxation. *Behaviour Research and Therapy, 49*, 275–280. http://dx.doi.org/10.1016/j.brat.2011.01.005

Hinton, D. E., Pham, T., Tran, M., Safren, S. A., Otto, M. W., & Pollack, M. H. (2004). CBT for Vietnamese refugees with treatment-resistant PTSD and panic attacks: A pilot study. *Journal of Traumatic Stress, 17*, 429–433. http://dx.doi.org/10.1023/B:JOTS.0000048956.03529.fa

Horrell, S. C. V. (2008). Effectiveness of cognitive-behavioral therapy with adult ethnic minority clients: A review. *Professional Psychology: Research and Practice*, *39*, 160–168. http://dx.doi.org/10.1037/0735-7028.39.2.160

Hough, R. L., Canino, G. J., Abueg, F. R., & Gusman, F. D. (1996). PTSD and related stress disorders among Hispanics. In A. J. Marsella, M. J. Friedman, E. T. Gerrity, & R. M. Scurfield (Eds.), *Ethnocultural aspects of posttraumatic stress disorder* (pp. 301–338). Washington, DC: American Psychological Association. http://dx.doi.org/10.1037/10555-012

Hovey, J. D. (2000). Psychosocial predictors of acculturative stress in Mexican immigrants. *The Journal of Psychology*, *134*, 490–502. http://dx.doi.org/10.1080/00223980009598231

Hovey, J. D., Hurtado, G., & Seligman, L. D. (2014). Findings for a CBT support group for Latina migrant farmworkers in Western Colorado. *Current Psychology*, *33*, 271–281. http://dx.doi.org/10.1007/s12144-014-9212-y

Hovey, J. D., & Magaña, C. G. (2002). Cognitive, affective, and physiological expressions of anxiety symptomatology among Mexican migrant farmworkers: Predictors and generational differences. *Community Mental Health Journal*, *38*, 223–237. http://dx.doi.org/10.1023/A:1015215723786

Hoyt, T., & Yeater, E. A. (2010). Comparison of posttraumatic stress disorder symptom structure models in Hispanic and White college students. *Psychological Trauma: Theory, Research, Practice, and Policy*, *2*, 19–30. http://dx.doi.org/10.1037/a0018745

Hurtado-de-Mendoza, A., Gonzales, F. A., Serrano, A., & Kaltman, S. (2014). Social isolation and perceived barriers to establishing social networks among Latina immigrants. *American Journal of Community Psychology*, *53*, 73–82. http://dx.doi.org/10.1007/s10464-013-9619-x

Interian, A., & Díaz-Martínez, A. M. (2007). Considerations for culturally competent cognitive-behavioral therapy for depression with Hispanic patients. *Cognitive and Behavioral Practice*, *14*, 84–97. http://dx.doi.org/10.1016/j.cbpra.2006.01.006

Iwamasa, G. Y., Regan, S. M. P., Subica, A., & Yamada, A. (2013). Nativity and migration: Considering acculturation in the assessment and treatment of mental disorders. In F. A. Paniagua & A. Yamada (Eds.), *Handbook of multicultural mental health* (2nd ed., pp. 167–188). San Diego, CA: Elsevier. http://dx.doi.org/10.1016/B978-0-12-394420-7.00009-6

Kaltman, S., Green, B. L., Mete, M., Shara, N., & Miranda, J. (2010). Trauma, depression, and comorbid PTSD/depression in a community sample of Latina immigrants. *Psychological Trauma: Theory, Research, Practice and Policy*, *2*, 31–39. http://dx.doi.org/10.1037/a0018952

Kaltman, S., Hurtado de Mendoza, A., Gonzales, F. A., & Serrano, A. (2014). Preferences for trauma-related mental health services among Latina immigrants from Central America, South America, and Mexico. *Psychological Trauma: Theory, Research, Practice, and Policy*, *6*, 83–91. http://dx.doi.org/10.1037/a0031539

Kataoka, S., Langley, A., Stein, B., Jaycox, L., Zhang, L., Sanchez, N., & Wong, M. (2009). Violence exposure and PTSD: The role of English language fluency in Latino youth. *Journal of Child and Family Studies, 18,* 334–341. http://dx.doi.org/10.1007/s10826-008-9235-9

Kroon Van Diest, A. M., Tartakovsky, M., Stachon, C., Pettit, J. W., & Perez, M. (2014). The relationship between acculturative stress and eating disorder symptoms: Is it unique from general life stress? *Journal of Behavioral Medicine, 37,* 445–457. http://dx.doi.org/10.1007/s10865-013-9498-5

Lazarus, R. S., & Folkman, S. (1984). *Stress, appraisal, and coping.* New York, NY: Springer.

Lewis-Fernández, R., Gorritz, M., Raggio, G. A., Peláez, C., Chen, H., & Guarnaccia, P. J. (2010). Association of trauma-related disorders and dissociation with four idioms of distress among Latino psychiatric outpatients. *Culture, Medicine and Psychiatry, 34,* 219–243. http://dx.doi.org/10.1007/s11013-010-9177-8

Lewis-Fernández, R., Turner, J. B., Marshall, R., Turse, N., Neria, Y., & Dohrenwend, B. P. (2008). Elevated rates of current PTSD among Hispanic veterans in the NVVRS: True prevalence or methodological artifact? *Journal of Traumatic Stress, 21,* 123–132. http://dx.doi.org/10.1002/jts.20329

Lueck, K., & Wilson, M. (2011). Acculturative stress in Latino immigrants: The impact of social, socio-psychological and migration-related factors. *International Journal of Intercultural Relations, 35,* 186–195. http://dx.doi.org/10.1016/j.ijintrel.2010.11.016

Mak, W. W. S., Law, R. W., Alvidrez, J., & Pérez-Stable, E. J. (2007). Gender and ethnic diversity in NIMH-funded clinical trials: Review of a decade of published research. *Administration and Policy in Mental Health and Mental Health Services Research, 34,* 497–503. http://dx.doi.org/10.1007/s10488-007-0133-z

Marshall, G. N., Schell, T. L., & Miles, J. N. V. (2009). Ethnic differences in posttraumatic distress: Hispanics' symptoms differ in kind and degree. *Journal of Consulting and Clinical Psychology, 77,* 1169–1178. http://dx.doi.org/10.1037/a0017721

Mason, C. M., Resick, P. A., & Rizvi, S. L. (2014). Posttraumatic stress disorder. In D. H. Barlow (Ed.), *Clinical handbook of psychological disorders* (5th ed., pp. 62–107). New York, NY: Guilford Press.

Mena, F. J., Padilla, A. M., & Maldonado, M. (1987). Acculturative stress and specific coping strategies among immigrant and later generation college students. *Hispanic Journal of Behavioral Sciences, 9,* 207–225. http://dx.doi.org/10.1177/07399863870092006

Meredith, L. S., Eisenman, D. P., Green, B. L., Kaltman, S., Wong, E. C., Han, B., . . . Tobin, J. N. (2014). Design of the Violence and Stress Assessment (ViStA) study: A randomized controlled trial of care management for PTSD among predominantly Latino patients in safety net health centers. *Contemporary Clinical Trials, 38,* 163–172. http://dx.doi.org/10.1016/j.cct.2014.04.005

Myers, H. F., Wyatt, G. E., Ullman, J. B., Loeb, T. B., Chin, D., Prause, N., . . . Liu, H. (2015). Cumulative burden of lifetime adversities: Trauma and mental health in low-SES African Americans and Latino/as. *Psychological Trauma: Theory, Research, Practice and Policy, 7*, 243–251. http://dx.doi.org/10.1037/a0039077

Negy, C., Hammons, M. E., Ferrer, A. R., & Carper, T. M. (2010). The importance of addressing acculturative stress in marital therapy with Hispanic immigrant women. *International Journal of Clinical and Health Psychology, 10*, 5–21.

Oberg, K. (1960). Culture shock: Adjustment to new cultural environments. *Practical Anthropology, 7*, 177–182. http://dx.doi.org/10.1177/009182966000700405

Ortega, A. N., & Rosenheck, R. (2000). Posttraumatic stress disorder among Hispanic Vietnam veterans. *The American Journal of Psychiatry, 157*, 615–619.

Padilla, A. M., Wagatsuma, Y., & Lindholm, K. J. (1985). Acculturation and personality as predictors of stress in Japanese and Japanese-Americans. *The Journal of Social Psychology, 125*, 295–305. http://dx.doi.org/10.1080/00224545.1985.9922890

Pantin, H. M., Schwartz, S. J., Prado, G., Feaster, D. J., & Szapocznik, J. (2003). Posttraumatic stress disorder symptoms in Hispanic immigrants after the September 11th attacks: Severity and relationship to previous traumatic exposure. *Hispanic Journal of Behavioral Sciences, 25*, 56–72. http://dx.doi.org/10.1177/0739986303251695

Perez, M., Voelz, Z. R., Pettit, J. W., & Joiner, T. E., Jr. (2002). The role of acculturative stress and body dissatisfaction in predicting bulimic symptomatology across ethnic groups. *International Journal of Eating Disorders, 31*, 442–454. http://dx.doi.org/10.1002/eat.10006

Pérez Benítez, C. I., Sibrava, N. J., Zlotnick, C., Weisberg, R., & Keller, M. B. (2014). Differences between Latino individuals with posttraumatic stress disorder and those with other anxiety disorders. *Psychological Trauma: Theory, Research, Practice, and Policy, 6*, 345–352. http://dx.doi.org/10.1037/a0034328

Pérez Benítez, C. I., Zlotnick, C., Gomez, J., Rendón, M. J., & Swanson, A. (2013). Cognitive behavioral therapy for PTSD and somatization: An open trial. *Behaviour Research and Therapy, 51*, 284–289. http://dx.doi.org/10.1016/j.brat.2013.02.005

Perilla, J. L., Norris, F. H., & Lavizzo, E. A. (2002). Ethnicity, culture, and disaster response: Identifying and explaining ethnic differences in PTSD six months after Hurricane Andrew. *Journal of Social and Clinical Psychology, 21*, 20–45. http://dx.doi.org/10.1521/jscp.21.1.20.22404

Pole, N., Best, S. R., Metzler, T., & Marmar, C. R. (2005). Why are Hispanics at greater risk for PTSD? *Cultural Diversity & Ethnic Minority Psychology, 11*, 144–161. http://dx.doi.org/10.1037/1099-9809.11.2.144

Rivera, P. M., Gonzales-Backen, M. A., Yedlin, J., Brown, E. J., Schwartz, S. J., Caraway, S. J., . . . Ham, L. S. (2015). Family violence exposure and sexual risk-taking among Latino emerging adults: The role of posttraumatic stress symptomology and acculturative stress. *Journal of Family Violence, 30,* 967–976. http://dx.doi.org/10.1007/s10896-015-9735-5

Rivera-Vélez, G. M., González-Viruet, M., Martínez-Taboas, A., & Pérez-Mojica, D. (2014). Post-traumatic stress disorder, dissociation, and neuropsychological performance in Latina victims of childhood sexual abuse. *Journal of Child Sexual Abuse, 23,* 55–73. http://dx.doi.org/10.1080/10538712.2014.864746

Roberts, A. L., Gilman, S. E., Breslau, J., Breslau, N., & Koenen, K. C. (2011). Race/ethnic differences in exposure to traumatic events, development of post-traumatic stress disorder, and treatment-seeking for post-traumatic stress disorder in the United States. *Psychological Medicine, 41,* 71–83. http://dx.doi.org/10.1017/S0033291710000401

Rodgers, B. L. (2000). Philosophical foundations of concept development. In B. L. Rodgers & K. A. Knafl (Eds.), *Concept development in nursing: Foundations, techniques and applications* (2nd ed., pp. 7–35). Philadelphia, PA: W. B. Saunders.

Rodriguez, M. A., Heilemann, M. V., Fielder, E., Ang, A., Nevarez, F., & Mangione, C. M. (2008). Intimate partner violence, depression, and PTSD among pregnant Latina women. *Annals of Family Medicine, 6*(1), 44–52. http://dx.doi.org/10.1370/afm.743

Rodriguez, N., Myers, H. F., Mira, C. B., Flores, T., & Garcia-Hernandez, L. (2002). Development of the Multidimensional Acculturative Stress Inventory for adults of Mexican origin. *Psychological Assessment, 14,* 451–461. http://dx.doi.org/10.1037/1040-3590.14.4.451

Romero, A. J., Carvajal, S. C., Valle, F., & Orduña, M. (2007). Adolescent bicultural stress and its impact on mental well-being among Latinos, Asian Americans, and European Americans. *Journal of Community Psychology, 35,* 519–534. http://dx.doi.org/10.1002/jcop.20162

Romero, A. J., Edwards, L. M., & Corkery, S. (2013). Assessing and treating Latinos: Overview of mental health research. In F. Paniagua & A. Yamada (Eds.), *Handbook of multicultural mental health* (2nd ed., pp. 327–343). San Diego, CA: Elsevier. http://dx.doi.org/10.1016/B978-0-12-394420-7.00017-5

Romero, A. J., & Roberts, R. E. (2003). Stress within a bicultural context for adolescents of Mexican descent. *Cultural Diversity and Ethnic Minority Psychology, 9,* 171–184. http://dx.doi.org/10.1037/1099-9809.9.2.171

Sarmiento, I. A., & Cardemil, E. V. (2009). Family functioning and depression in low-income Latino couples. *Journal of Marital and Family Therapy, 35,* 432–445. http://dx.doi.org/10.1111/j.1752-0606.2009.00139.x

Sumner, L. A., Wong, L., Schetter, C. D., Myers, H. F., & Rodriguez, M. (2012). Predictors of posttraumatic stress disorder symptoms among low-income Latinas during pregnancy and postpartum. *Psychological Trauma: Theory, Research, Practice, and Policy, 4,* 196–203. http://dx.doi.org/10.1037/a0023538

Torres, L. (2010). Predicting levels of Latino depression: Acculturation, acculturative stress, and coping. *Cultural Diversity and Ethnic Minority Psychology, 16,* 256–263. http://dx.doi.org/10.1037/a0017357

Vásquez, D. A., de Arellano, M. A., Reid-Quiñones, K., Bridges, A. J., Rheingold, A. A., Stocker, R. P. J., & Danielson, C. K. (2012). Peritraumatic dissociation and peritraumatic emotional predictors of PTSD in Latino youth: Results from the Hispanic family study. *Journal of Trauma & Dissociation*, *13*, 509–525. http://dx.doi.org/10.1080/15299732.2012.678471

Vera, M., Juarbe, D., Hernández, N., Obén, A., Pérez-Pedrogo, C., & Chaplin, W. F. (2012). Probable posttraumatic stress disorder and psychiatric co-morbidity among Latino primary care patients in Puerto Rico. *Journal of Depression & Anxiety*, *1*(5). http://dx.doi.org/10.4172/2167-1044.1000124

Vera, M., Reyes-Rabanillo, M. L., Juarbe, D., Pérez-Pedrogo, C., Olmo, A., Kichic, R., & Chaplin, W. F. (2011). Prolonged exposure for the treatment of Spanish-speaking Puerto Ricans with posttraumatic stress disorder: A feasibility study. *BMC Research Notes*, *4*, 415. http://dx.doi.org/10.1186/1756-0500-4-415

Verney, S. P., & Kipp, B. J. (2007). Acculturation and alcohol treatment in ethnic minority populations: Assessment issues and implications. *Alcoholism Treatment Quarterly*, *25*, 47–61. http://dx.doi.org/10.1300/J020v25n04_04

Wang, S. C., Schwartz, S. J., & Zamboanga, B. L. (2010). Acculturative stress among Cuban American college students: Exploring the mediating pathways between acculturation and psychosocial functioning. *Journal of Applied Social Psychology*, *40*, 2862–2887. http://dx.doi.org/10.1111/j.1559-1816.2010.00684.x

Weathers, F., Litz, B., Herman, D., Huska, J., & Keane, T. (1993, October). *The PTSD checklist (PCL): Reliability, validity, and diagnostic utility*. Paper presented at the meeting of the International Society of Traumatic Stress Studies, San Antonio, TX.

Wilcox, J., Briones, D., & Suess, L. (1991). Auditory hallucinations, posttraumatic stress disorder, and ethnicity. *Comprehensive Psychiatry*, *32*, 320–323. http://dx.doi.org/10.1016/0010-440X(91)90080-V

11

COGNITIVE BEHAVIORAL MODELS, MEASURES, AND TREATMENTS FOR STRESS DISORDERS IN AFRICAN AMERICANS

TAWANDA M. GREER, ELIZABETH BRONDOLO, ELOM AMUZU, AND AMANDEEP KAUR

Over the past 20 years, a growing body of research has provided evidence of significant racial disparities in stress exposure. African Americans report higher levels of stress than White Americans when assessments include self-report indices of stress. African Americans also experience stress as a function of greater exposure to significant threats to safety, achievement, and belonging and reduced access to resources necessary to mitigate these threats. Racial and ethnic discrimination serves as an additional source of stress and contributes to disparities in other critical life areas. Interconnections among stressors (e.g., crime and unemployment) and bidirectional relationships among stressors and stress responses (e.g., crime, trauma, and revictimization) further exacerbate racial disparities in stress exposure.

Substantial research has suggested that across populations, greater perceptions of stress are associated with increased distress and risk of impairments in mental and physical health (Baum, 2002; Baum, Garofalo, & Yali,

http://dx.doi.org/10.1037/0000091-012
Treating Depression, Anxiety, and Stress in Ethnic and Racial Groups: Cognitive Behavioral Approaches,
E. C. Chang, C. A. Downey, J. K. Hirsch, and E. A. Yu (Editors)

1999; Chen & Miller, 2013; Clark, D'Ambrosio, & Ghislandi, 2016; Krieger 2010; Yoshikawa, Aber, & Beardslee, 2012). Due to the experience of high levels of overall stress, members of African American populations possess increased risk of allostatic load which, in turn, increases their risk of acquiring illnesses and exacerbates symptoms associated with chronic disease (e.g., hypertension), compared with members of other racial and ethnic groups (e.g., Geronimus, Hicken, Keene, & Bound, 2006; Greer, 2016).

Cognitive behavioral stress management techniques have often been used to assist persons in managing symptoms of stress, with the goal of mitigating symptoms and improving health and quality of life. Standard cognitive behavioral stress management (CBSM) training includes multiple components, such as psychoeducation about stress exposure and health, self-monitoring of stress exposures and stress responses, training and practice in relaxation exercises, identification and challenging of negative and distorted thoughts, development of coping skills, improvement of social skills (e.g., assertiveness, conflict resolution, anger management), and engagement with support networks (e.g., Antoni et al., 1991; Brown & Vanable, 2008).

Cognitive behavior therapy (CBT) has commonly been referred to as the gold standard of psychological interventions (e.g., Otte, 2011). However, African Americans have been less likely than White Americans to engage in CBT for mental health problems or CBSM (e.g., Kelly, 2006). Among African American individuals who are able and willing to engage, the limited literature suggests that CBSM, including culturally modified approaches to CBSM, and alternative stress reduction approaches (e.g., mindfulness-based stress reduction) show some promise, particularly when they are delivered in the context of integrated care for medical illness (e.g., Lechner et al., 2013). However, limited evidence exists on interventions that are effective for Africans Americans to reduce stress.

We propose that a careful consideration of the conceptualization of stress and its consequences for African American populations can improve both the design of CBSM interventions and, possibly, their receptivity among members of this population. The context within which individual-level stress exposure occurs has important implications for the nature of stress-reduction programs. When the sources of stress originate from cultural and institutional practices that are discriminatory and result in persistent social and economic disadvantages, interventions that emphasize individual-level effort to reduce stress may be problematic.

Further, racial discrimination, coupled with types of social and economic disadvantage, has substantial effects on many of the intrapersonal psychological processes involved in the stress response, including the development of negative schemas about others and the world at large and the formation of stress and threat appraisals (Brondolo et al., 2015). Discrimination-related changes to social cognition may increase the experienced frequency, intensity, and duration of threat exposure. Yet, as we examine later, some changes to social cognition may also be protective, at least in the short term. The complex effects of disadvantage and discrimination on social cognition may require modifications to the traditional cognitive approaches used in CBSM interventions. Alternative approaches to strengthening resilience may be needed.

In this chapter, we first review conceptualizations of stress and racial disparities in the level and type of stress exposure and then examine the effects of discrimination and social disadvantage on social cognition. We examine the implications of stress exposures and their social cognitive sequelae for CBSM interventions. Finally, we examine the evidence generated by existing CBSM and other interventions that have been implemented in African American populations. Throughout this chapter, we also articulate ethical and practical issues involved in stress management interventions for African Americans.

CONCEPTUALIZATIONS OF STRESS

There is a growing consensus that health disparities may derive from racial differences in stress exposure (Baum et al., 1999; Clark et al., 2016; Krieger, 2010; Sternthal, Slopen, & Williams, 2011). However, there is less clarity about the conceptualization of stress. In an early conceptualization, Cannon (1927) emphasized physiological and biochemical responses to environmental demands as opposed to cognitive processes, such as perception and interpretation of the events. In later models (e.g., Holmes & Rahe, 1967; Selye, 1956), stress was conceptualized as an event that poses both internal and external demands on individuals (i.e., life events), with the notion that increasing objective demands would be associated with increases in stress responses; however, individual differences in the perceptions of the consequences of demands were not emphasized.

In contrast, Lazarus and Folkman (1984), in their transactional theory, defined *stress* as "a particular relationship between the person and the environment that is appraised by the person as taxing or exceeding his or her resources and endangering his or her well-being" (p. 19). Lazarus and Folkman suggested that the experience of stress was not limited to physiological responding nor did it depend on the intrinsic nature of the specific types of demands presented by events or the objective quantity or quality of resources. Instead, they suggested that individuals experience stress when their internal calculations about the demands they face exceed their estimates of the resources they have available to cope with those demands. Therefore, individuals might perceive stress when they face high-intensity demands, particularly those that were unpredictable, uncontrollable, or threatening.

Lazarus and Folkman (1984) further theorized that subjective appraisal of experiences influences emotions and behaviors that relate to events. *Primary appraisals* reflect the degree to which an event is perceived as a threat, harm or loss, or challenge. *Secondary appraisals* reflect the individual's assessment of resources that are available to respond to an event (Lazarus & Folkman, 1984). Stress is the product of appraisals in which the demands of the situation or event are perceived as taxing or exceeding available resources (Lazarus & Folkman, 1984). Over the last few decades, several measures of stress have been developed to capture subjective appraisals, such as those designed to assess daily and chronic stressful events, including the Perceived Stress Scale (Cohen, Kamarck, & Mermelstein, 1983), the Daily Inventory of Stressful Events (Almeida, Wethington, & Kessler, 2002), and the Stress Appraisal Measure (Peacock & Wong, 1990). See the Macarthur Research Network on Socioeconomic Status and Health for an overview of commonly used measures of stress (http://www.macses.ucsf.edu/research/psychosocial/stress.php#chronic).

RELATIONSHIP BETWEEN RACISM EXPOSURE AND STRESS

Racism encompasses various forms of race-based mistreatment and has been conceptualized to occur on cultural, institutional, and interpersonal levels of society (J. M. Jones, 1997). *Cultural level racism* occurs when the values, worldviews, and cultural practices of persons of color are deemed by society as less valuable and inferior compared with those of White persons (J. M. Jones, 1997). Denigrating cultural messages about African Americans, for instance, can occur through media and biased reporting of perpetrators and victims of crime by race (Dalisay & Tan, 2009; Gilens, 1996; Mastro & Kopacz, 2006). Further, *institutional racism* can be defined as policies and practices embedded within institutions that serve to disadvantage persons on the basis of race (J. M. Jones, 1997). Bulhan (1985) defined *institutional discrimination* as a systemic effort that "inhibits human growth, negates human potential, limits productive living, and causes death" (p. 135). We, and other researchers, have viewed racial residential segregation as a form of institutional discrimination (e.g., Brondolo, Libretti, Rivera, & Walsemann, 2012; Williams & Collins, 2001). *Residential segregation* is defined as "the degree to which groups of people categorized on a variety of scales (race, ethnicity, income) occupy different space within urban areas" (Kramer & Hogue, 2009, p. 2). Across all income groups, large numbers of African Americans reside in more racially segregated areas than do White Americans; however, it is most pronounced among individuals with low levels of income and education (Williams & Collins, 2001). Race-based residential segregation can trigger a chain of events and other adverse consequences for residents that include poorer health, limited employment opportunities, and low quality of education for school-age children (e.g., Brondolo et al., 2012). Other forms of institutional discrimination which contribute to stress include inequalities in law enforcement, judicial, and correctional control practices; differential enforcement of voting laws; and differential access to quality health care and other services (e.g., Brunson & Miller, 2006; Greer, Laseter, & Asiamah, 2009).

Individual or *interpersonal racism* has been defined as "directly perceived discriminatory interactions between individuals whether in their institutional roles or as public and private individuals" (Krieger, 1999, p. 301). Racism occurring at the individual level can entail negative race-related experiences occurring within social interactions (e.g., racial slurs). It can be experienced as overt or subtle actions that influence social inclusion and threaten safety and opportunities and can include nonverbal behaviors that communicate disrespect and devaluation (e.g., Brondolo, Brady Ver Halen, Pencille, Beatty, & Contrada, 2009; Harrell, 2000). Studies on individual racism have revealed that members of Asian American, Latino(a) American, and African American populations are chronically exposed to forms of discrimination over the course of their lifetimes (e.g., Brondolo et al., 2005; Kwok et al., 2011). Some evidence has suggested that African Americans report more frequent exposure to this form of racism compared with members of other racial and ethnic groups in the United States (e.g., Paradies, 2006). Overall, individual, cultural, and institutional levels of racism often intersect in daily life and contribute to the insidious and deleterious effects of racism for persons of color.

RACE-RELATED STRESS AND MEASUREMENT

Like Lazarus and Folkman's (1984) conceptualization of stress, *race-related stress* is the product of race-related transactions that are perceived as taxing and/or exceeding available resources to address these experiences (Harrell, 2000; Outlaw, 1993). Given that African Americans are chronically exposed to racism, measures of race-related experiences and race-related stress should be included in CBSM interventions. A number of measures have been developed over the years, but many of them yield differences in dimensions of racism assessed, as well as differences in the assessment of cognitive, behavioral, and emotional experiences that relate to racism exposure. For instance, the Perceived Racism Scale (PRS; McNeilly et al., 1996) was developed with a sample of African American community and college adults. The PRS was designed to assess the frequency of racism exposure, as well as emotional and coping responses to racism-related experiences. The items reflect exposure to negative race-related experiences in several domains, including employment, school, and areas of public life (McNeilly et al., 1996). Aggregate subscale scores can also be calculated for emotional and behavioral responses. The PRS is one of the few measures designed to capture coping responses to race-related experiences. Another commonly used multidimensional measure is the Index of Race-Related Stress–Brief version (IRRS-B; Utsey, 1999). The IRRS-B was designed for African American adults and consists of three subscales that reflect individual, cultural, and institutional racism. A global racism score can be calculated with this measure. High scores reflect chronic exposure to types of racism, as well as high levels of stress associated with racism-related experiences (Utsey, 1999).

For CBSM interventions that include African American participants, as well as members of other racial and ethnic groups, measures designed to assess both racial and ethnic discrimination should be used. For instance, the Perceived Ethnic Discrimination Questionnaire–Community Version (PEDQ-CV; Brondolo et al., 2005) was designed to assess discrimination for members of various racial and ethnic groups in the United States. The PEDQ-CV consists of 70 items that make up five subscales: Lifetime Discrimination, Past-Week Discrimination, Discrimination in Different Settings, Discrimination in the Media, and Discrimination Against Family Members. A brief version of the measure consists of 17 items and subscales that assess exclusion, workplace discrimination, stigmatization, threat and harassment, and interactions with police (Brondolo et al., 2005). For the PEDQ-CV, Brondolo et al. (2005) reported adequate internal consistency estimates for each subscale of the measure, with African Americans reporting more experiences of lifetime discrimination than Latinos in the study. Overall, multiethnic discrimination measures can be particularly useful in determining racial and ethnic differences in the frequency of exposure to discrimination, as well as differences in overall stressfulness of discrimination experiences. See Utsey (1999) and Gamst, Liang, and Der-Karabetian (2011) for a comprehensive review of additional measures of racism and ethnic-related discrimination.

Stressors place a wide range of demands on individuals because they often result in loss, hardship, and/or the threat of loss of resources (Lazarus & Folkman, 1984). It is also important to note that although general stressors (e.g., parenting, busy work schedules) and race-related stressors are conceptually distinct, in daily life they can intersect or occur in tandem. For instance, low wages can be experienced as a source of stress for some African Americans, but low wages may also be attributed to racially discriminatory practices within institutions that serve to limit economic mobility for African Americans and other persons of color. Therefore, employment-related problems can be perceived both as a general source of stress and as a form of race-based maltreatment, with the emotional burden associated with perceiving unfair treatment compounding the stressors associated with insufficient income.

Overall, CBSM interventions designed to reduce stress and improve the mental health of African Americans will have to be developed in a manner that accurately reflects the effects of the range and nature of stressors facing African Americans. These stressors may require modifications to the CBSM intervention components designed to increase awareness of stress and stress reactions and to promote identification of triggers. When stress exposure is a function of discrimination, it is particularly important that racial and ethnic discrimination measures are included to assist in identifying the dimensions of discrimination exposure that greatly affect mental health.

STRESS AND COGNITION

CBSM further involves strategies to address cognitive components of stress. Cognitive interventions are intended to support the individual's efforts to reinterpret or reappraise the degree of threat and harm posed by events or situations, to reappraise one's capacity to cope with events that are appraised as stressful, and to develop problem-solving skills and activate stress-reduction techniques. The cognitive approaches typically used in CBSM interventions include psychoeducational strategies to help individuals become more aware of their cognitions and the role of cognitive processes in the experience and response to stressful events. CBSM can also include more directive strategies that are designed to aid individuals in challenging dysfunctional beliefs and developing effective cognitive strategies to reduce stress. However, the social threats of racism, discrimination, and socioeconomic disadvantage are chronic, insidious systemic stressors that are not extinguishable by individual efforts to cognitively reappraise and/or by activating individual-level coping efforts (Brondolo, Ng, Pierre, & Lane, 2016; Greer, 2011; Henson, Derlega, Pearson, Ferrer, & Holmes, 2013). Consequently, cognitive interventions in CBSM have to be tailored to accommodate cognitive components of stress that are related to persistent exposure to social and economic threats for members of African American populations.

Defined broadly, *cognitive processes* provide the structure and mechanisms through which individuals interpret and respond to the social world (Fiske & Taylor, 2013). *Schemas* are the underlying mental structures that provide an interpretative context for processing new experiences (McKenzie, Robinson, Herrera, Churchill, & Eichenbaum, 2013). Schemas play an important role in shaping appraisals of stress because they determine the types of events perceived as threatening and the extent of available coping resources.

Several conceptualizations of schemas exist in the research literature; however, in most clinical formulations, schemas are defined as mental structures that comprise a network of thoughts, attitudes, and affect about the self, the world, and others (J. S. Beck, 2005; Halvorsen et al., 2009). These schemas incorporate a positive or negative affective tone, incorporating a perception of the self as accepted or rejected, other people as supportive or hostile, and the world as safe or threatening (A. T. Beck, 1987; Markus & Wurf, 1987). Schemas also incorporate characteristics associated with the self and with others, including those involving one's identity, as well as the identities associated with one's racial and ethnic group (Oyserman, 2008).

Schemas develop over time through direct and vicarious experiences, including the observations of others in daily life and as presented in the media (Brondolo et al., 2016). An individual develops relational schemas (i.e., schemas about others and relationships with others) that reflect the degree to which the individual has experienced warmth and acceptance versus rejection, exclusion, and threat from others (e.g., James, Reichelt, Freeston, & Barton, 2007). Schemas also influence individual perceptions of the nature and meaning of events, as well as the perception of personal and environmental coping resources (James et al., 2007). Consequently, schemas guide appraisal processes and influence thoughts, emotions, behaviors, and/or decision making. In turn, appraisal processes serve to activate physiological systems (e.g., neuroendocrine, immune, and autonomic systems) that mediate the experience of stress (Gianaros & Wager, 2015).

Members of African American populations are often exposed to a variety of threats that may serve to foster the development of negative relational schemas, as well as negative schemas about the world (Brondolo et al., 2016). For instance, previous literature has demonstrated that African Americans are more likely than White Americans to experience early childhood adversity, crime victimization, and more frequent adverse interactions with members of law enforcement and other major institutions (e.g., health care, education; Evans & Kim, 2013; Greer et al., 2009). Such experiences shape negative schemas about others and the world at large. These schemas can manifest as negative beliefs about one's competence and acceptability, the likelihood of experiencing warmth and acceptance in interactions with others, and the degree to which the world operates in a fair and nonthreatening manner (e.g., Brondolo et al., 2016; Foa et al., 1999). Ultimately, such schemas may heighten appraisals of threat because individuals likely anticipate potential harm during social interactions and/or engagement with institutions.

Exposure to forms of discrimination has also been demonstrated to influence the development of negative schemas. Specifically, discrimination has been linked to race-based rejection sensitivity (Mendoza-Denton, Downey, Purdie, Davis, & Pietrzak, 2002), stigma consciousness (Pinel, 1999), and stereotype-threat concerns (e.g., Thames et al., 2013). These schemas can operate in complex ways and can increase the anticipation of unfair or unjust treatment. For example, African Americans who possess higher levels of cultural mistrust have been shown to display negative attitudes and expectations of others, especially toward White American clinicians and other health care professionals (e.g., Moore et al., 2013). The link between past racism-related experiences, schemas, and appraisal processes was also illustrated in a recent neuroimaging study. Greer, Vendemia, and Stancil (2012), using a sample of White American and African American adults, displayed pictures of both White and African Americans who were depicted in service-oriented occupations (e.g., health care, legal systems, retail, food service) and who also displayed neutral/ambiguous, angry/hostile, or happy/joyful facial expressions. African Americans exhibited increased activation in brain regions that are associated with fear, anxiety, and negative emotional memories (e.g., anterior cingulate cortex, amygdala) when exposed to White Americans with neutral/ambiguous facial expressions (Greer et al., 2012). Further, the authors found that, for African American participants, previous exposure to racism-related experiences was significantly associated with amygdala activation when exposed to White Americans, regardless of the emotional valence of facial expression. These findings suggest that when social situations are ambiguous and/or occur in settings that are closely tied to survival or well-being (e.g., health care), African American persons might rely on cognitive heuristics and schemas to interpret interpersonal interactions involving White Americans, and this may be particularly problematic for African Americans who have experienced chronic exposure to racism (Greer et al., 2012).

However, by focusing on the likelihood of exposure to negative treatment, discrimination-based schemas may also serve to mitigate some outcomes that relate to the unpredictability and uncontrollability of discrimination experiences. Greer, Brondolo, and Brown (2014) tested exposure to systemic racism as a moderator of the effects of provider racial biases on treatment adherence and mistrust of health care for a sample of African American adult hypertensive patients. The authors expected that high levels of exposure to societal-level racism would contribute to poor treatment adherence and high levels of health care mistrust. No significant influences were observed for mistrust, however, and contrary to expectations, patients who endorsed low levels of exposure to societal-level racism exhibited the greatest adverse impacts on treatment adherence. In particular, hypertensive patients who reported low levels of exposure to systemic racism demonstrated poor treatment adherence in relation to those with high levels of exposure to provider racial biases (Greer et al., 2014). These findings suggest that African American patients who perceived themselves as chronically exposed to racism most likely anticipated or expected to experience provider racial biases. Thus, these patients may have managed provider racial biases in ways that enabled them to recover and maintain adherence to treatment compared with those who viewed themselves as infrequently exposed to societal racism (Greer et al., 2014). Therefore, although discrimination exposure can contribute to the development of negative schemas about others, such schemas can also serve a protective function for some African Americans against adverse psychological consequences that are related to unfair treatment.

In addition to schemas that can develop through discrimination experiences, other schemas that can arise in the context of stress exposure for African Americans include *John Henryism* and *superwoman* ideas of self and attitudes. Both of these ideas incorporate beliefs that intense efforts on the part of the individual are necessary to overcome socially constructed barriers that are present in society for African Americans (e.g., Bennett et al., 2004; Greer et al., 2009). On one level these beliefs could serve to drive active coping and could maintain self-esteem. However, if circumstances are not, in fact, under individual control, these efforts could lead to exhaustion and a sense of personal defeat. The evidence from psychobiological studies has suggested that these schemas are associated with severe cardiovascular responding and overall negative health consequences (e.g., Clark & Adams, 2004).

Overall, African Americans are more likely than White Americans to experience a wide variety of threats in the social environment, many of which are related to discrimination. Each of these threats has been associated with the development of negative schemas. The context in which these cognitions (and their underlying schemas) develop should be considered as part of CBSM interventions.

Different approaches to the reappraisal of negative cognitions may be needed when they arise in the context of a social environment that presents substantial threats but does not provide sufficient resources to cope with these threats. Grier and Cobbs (1968) first introduced the idea of *cultural paranoia* to describe adaptive behaviors exhibited by many African Americans in response to injustices and inequalities experienced within society. They argued that negative cognitions that might seem maladaptive or would be maladaptive in other circumstances might have important functions in a hostile environment. For example, beliefs about the persistence or pervasiveness of unfair treatment can reduce the unpredictability of these events and ward off the consequences of disappointment or loss of hope. Anger, a natural response to injustice, can be stressful; however, anger can also provide energy for social change and can protect against feelings of powerlessness. CBSM intervention efforts that are designed to challenge an individual's perceived and lived experiences, and the experiences of members of their families and communities, will likely be viewed as invalidating and alienating.

Therefore, approaches and measures that are designed to assess negative cognitions and that allow individuals to explore how their experiences have shaped their understanding about themselves, others, and the world, may be helpful in CBSM interventions. The types of negative schemas we have discussed can be assessed with self-report measures such as the Race-Based Rejection Sensitivity Scale (Mendoza-Denton et al., 2002) and the Stereotype Confirmation Concern Scale (Contrada et al., 2001), which can help clarify the nature of the beliefs individuals hold about the world at large and the predictability and controllability of future outcomes. The Posttraumatic Cognitions Inventory (Foa et al., 1991) may also be helpful to clarify changes in beliefs following trauma exposure, and the scale items could be customized to prompt discussions about negative cognitions related to discrimination and the contexts in which these cognitions might develop. However, to our knowledge, there is no research evaluating the use of these scales in a therapeutic context; thus, their potential therapeutic benefits in CBSM interventions warrant empirical investigation.

Examining negative cognitions and their history may present some concerns. As individuals trace the development of their underlying schemas and related cognitions, they may reexperience the circumstances in which these underlying schemas were formed. When trauma is ongoing (i.e., when the threats are not truly abated), examining these cognitions can evoke strong, negative emotions. Clinicians who have experienced similar circumstances may find that their own concerns and pain are evoked by clients' discussion. Further, some clinicians may find it difficult to challenge their own assumptions about fairness and justice, and these difficulties can potentially erode the therapeutic alliance (Brondolo & Jean-Pierre, 2014).

As a consequence, the pace and timing of these discussions may have to be modified to provide both clients and clinicians the opportunity to process emotions evoked by efforts to examine relations between the social environment, negative schemas, and stress. It may be useful to frame the analyses of negative cognitions within the context of consciousness raising (Haslanger, 2013). Consciousness raising supports efforts to understand historical and current forces that affect the group as a whole, as well as the individual. In this context, an evaluation of negative cognitions can be seen as a way to remind individuals of their connection to others who have fought against injustice. Activating a sense of belonging and pride may buffer some of the negative effects of exposure to past trauma (e.g., Lee & Ahn, 2013). Overall, future research is needed to guide the development of strategies for providing an effective therapeutic alliance that can withstand the strains imposed on the relationship as individuals evaluate and attempt to mitigate stressors associated with chronic social disadvantage and discrimination.

STRESS AND COGNITIVE BEHAVIOR THERAPY: CULTURAL ADAPTATIONS

Cultural adaptation of empirically based treatments has been defined as any modifications in service delivery, treatment components, and strategies used to enhance therapeutic relationships that accommodate cultural values, attitudes, and behaviors of a specific population (Whaley & Davis, 2007). Some evidence has suggested that culturally adapted CBT interventions for mental health are more effective than less adapted interventions and that the benefits increase as more adaptations are included. However, despite consistent evidence that the chronic experience of societal inequity and exposure to racial injustices increases the overall burden of stress and poor health for African Americans, there are limited data on CBSM therapeutic strategies that are effective in alleviating stress and related health consequences for members of this population. Validation samples for CBSM have consisted mostly of middle-class, predominantly White Americans and individuals who do not reside in urban residential areas (e.g., Lechner et al., 2013).

CBSM approaches have been criticized for lacking cultural specificity for African Americans and members of other diverse cultural groups (e.g., Kelly, 2006; Lechner et al., 2013) and for being designed to emphasize individualism and autonomy (Kelly, 2006). However, many of the most problematic stressors facing African American populations include those associated with discrimination and social and economic barriers. Preventing exposure to these stressors and reducing their psychophysiological sequelae will require not only individual effort but also collective action. Therefore, a focus of stress-reduction efforts for African Americans should also include strategies to improve social support and social networking and to strengthen the capacity for collective problem solving. Interventions might be designed to improve the ability of participants to identify and articulate common goals and values, to generate and evaluate multiple approaches to achieving shared goals, to develop effective strategies for collaborative communication, and to learn to identify individual strengths and motivations that can contribute to collective efforts, as well as those at the individual level. Communication skills training emerging from traditions of conflict resolution and mediation, which are aimed at promoting individual autonomy and include assertiveness training, may be more relevant than broader communication interventions (e.g., Greer 2007; Kelly, 2006).

However, more research may be needed to guide the development of effective interventions to build social support. Many African Americans report using social support to address concerns about experiences of discrimination. However, there is limited evidence that social support is an effective buffer against the effects of discrimination on depression and some evidence that social support buffers physiological stress reactivity (i.e., blood pressure reactivity) only when individuals have experienced low levels of discrimination (Clark, 2006). As a whole, the data have suggested that there may be negative side effects to conversations about discrimination when individuals have experienced high levels of stress exposure (Brondolo et al., 2009). Social support and communication skills interventions to address the stress associated with injustice may have to be modified for individuals who have faced different levels of exposure.

Cognitive approaches that emphasize viewing negative cognitions as distorted or potentially dysfunctional may not be appropriate without considering the context in which these cognitions develop. Instead, cognitive interventions could be focused on strengthening resilience. For example, clinicians could use modified *values affirmation strategies*, interventions that create opportunities to articulate and strengthen positive values and to integrate these values into personal identity. Values affirmation strategies provide guidance for identifying positive values that can motivate action and the psychological resources needed for social change. Conducting these exercises in a group format could allow participants to identify common goals and can provide social resources to achieve these goals (Sherman & Hartson, 2011).

Strategies that focus on developing problem-solving and communication skills to address systemic-level stressors must be supplemented with interventions to reduce the individual-level consequences of sustained stress exposure. These interventions can include different components such as relaxation interventions or approaches that strengthen positive mood and motivation. To date, relaxation techniques, or those designed to improve mood, have been examined among African Americans diagnosed with hypertension and other chronic illnesses (e.g., Bell, 2015; D. L. Jones et al., 2010) and demonstrate the potential for effectiveness in reducing stress and other related symptoms (e.g., depression, blood pressure). Group-based relaxation interventions have also been demonstrated to be potentially effective for African American populations to reduce overall stress, particularly in conjunction with physical exercise (e.g., Webb, Beckstead, Meininger, & Robinson, 2006).

Overall, different interventions may be needed for individuals who have faced high versus low levels of discrimination-related stress. For individuals who have experienced highly threatening or unjust interactions, interventions focused on strengthening inner resources or positive mood may be needed before more direct discussion of highly threatening and unjust events. The timing and pace of discussion may also have to be flexible and unstructured to facilitate participation and processing of emotions related to injustice. Additional research is needed to evaluate the differential efficacy of interventions for individuals who have experienced high versus low levels of direct exposure to discrimination.

EFFECTIVENESS OF CULTURALLY ADAPTED COGNITIVE BEHAVIOR THERAPY APPROACHES

A limited number of studies have assessed the effectiveness of CBT approaches that were culturally adjusted for African American populations. The existing approaches to the cultural adaptation of CBSM interventions implicitly recognize the importance of acknowledging the systemic and severe stressors facing African Americans. Each of the intervention approaches described next incorporates a focus on recognizing significant stressors, including discrimination; supporting interdependence and collective efforts; and providing training in physical stress reduction and relaxation skills. Some interventions embed these strategies in an Afrocentric cultural orientation (Kelly, 2006). Overall, the limited literature on CBSM interventions has suggested that both tailored and standard approaches may be effective, but barriers to engagement remain.

Townsend, Hawkins, and Batts (2007) conducted one of the few investigations to examine the effectiveness of a standard group-based CBSM program versus an Afrocentric, female-centered stress-reduction program (a cultural adaptation of standard CBSM) that was also administered in group format. The Afrocentric stress-reduction program was designed to incorporate core values of spirituality, communalism, and interdependence. Its content reflected social and economic realities that were common for women in the investigation, including racial discrimination, sexism, and other daily stressors and challenges related to motherhood and intimate relationships (Townsend et al., 2007). Treatment was limited to a 7-hour, 1-day session for women in the standard CBSM condition, whereas treatment entailed an 8-hour, 1-day session for those in the Afrocentric program. Findings revealed reductions in levels of stress and severity of depressive symptoms for women in both groups, with no differences between groups. Women in the Afrocentric program experienced a reduction in negative affective coping (e.g., irritability, pessimism) compared with women in the standard CBSM group.

In a more recent investigation, Lechner et al. (2013) adapted a 10-week group-based CBSM intervention for African American women who had survived breast cancer. Changes were made to the didactic dimensions of the intervention, experiential exercises (e.g., role plays), and the treatment manual to ensure that the content was culturally congruent for women in the study. For instance, the Serenity Prayer was incorporated in the intervention to help match common core values of religiosity and spirituality as tools for coping with difficulties. In addition, church and other religious outlets were included as resources and as sources of social support. Stigma associated with breast cancer within the women's communities and families was also discussed during group meetings (Lechner et al., 2013).

The adapted intervention was compared with a control condition, a group-based breast cancer education program. The outcomes for this study were limited to participant ratings of program acceptability and its benefits. Results revealed that women rated both programs as acceptable and beneficial to them, and women from both groups demonstrated a high retention rate (Lechner et al., 2013). In a later investigation, Lechner et al. (2014) tested the psychological benefits of the culturally congruent CBSM program with African American women survivors of breast cancer. The control condition was a generic complementary medicine program. Findings revealed that over a 6-month period, women from both programs experienced decreases in severity of depression, intrusive thoughts, and overall stress levels, as well as improved quality of life, with no significant differences between the two interventions (Lechner et al., 2014). Overall, the findings in these limited studies suggest that when participants are able to engage in treatment, both traditional and tailored stress-management techniques may provide benefit.

These culturally tailored approaches incorporated group-based discussions of discrimination. These discussions may permit individuals to identify and examine stress exposures but in the context of strengthening group cohesion and belonging. These approaches recognize the systemic and unjust nature of the exposure and reinforce options for addressing the stressors that include a focus on coordinated and collaborative efforts (e.g., focusing on church involvement, encouraging interdependence). Group discussions can decrease the sense of individual isolation and stigmatization that discrimination can engender. However, only women have been included in these studies to date, and it remains unclear whether men will respond in the same way to these collaborative discussions. It is also unclear whether these interventions worked equally well for individuals with varying degrees of exposure to stress.

ALTERNATIVE TREATMENT APPROACHES

In addition to CBT-focused approaches to stress reduction, alternative intervention approaches, such as meditation and yoga, have received increased empirical attention (Burnett-Zeigler, Schuette, Victorson, & Wisner, 2016). The cognitive components of these approaches focus more on self-compassion rather than on modifying cognitions or directed problem solving. Other primary components include improving management of physical reactions to stress, providing guidance in reducing muscle tension, and regulating respiration, among other strategies.

In a review of mind–body approaches and their effectiveness in addressing mental health symptoms among members of historically disadvantaged groups, Burnett-Zeigler et al. (2016) reported that overall mind–body interventions were acceptable and showed some evidence of efficacy. However, a limited body of research was examined, with only 18 investigations included in their review. Many studies had methodological limitations, including small sample sizes, absence of a control group, and limited ability to examine diversity in effects among groups of Black individuals of varying ethnicity.

Overall, the reviewed studies demonstrated high retention rates for mindfulness-based stress reduction (MBSR) and interventions using related techniques (e.g., yoga, meditation, guided imagery)—about 60% to 70% retention across studies. Participants consistently practiced techniques on their own, and findings from some of the investigations suggested that offering services such as child care and transportation increased participant engagement. Across studies, the participants reported improvements in substance use, some mental and physical health symptoms, and quality of life (Burnett-Zeigler et al., 2016).

In particular, there is some evidence that MBSR is effective in reducing stress-related symptoms for members of diverse cultural groups. MBSR is a nonreligious intervention that was designed for persons managing chronic pain, stress, emotional and cognitive-related disorders (e.g., depression, anxiety), and chronic illness (e.g., Chiesa & Seretti, 2009; Kabat-Zinn, 1991). Participation in an MBSR program involves engaging in a 2.5-hour course for 8 consecutive weeks to acquire skills and attitudes that have been described by Kabat-Zinn (1991) as being nonstriving, being nonjudgmental of one's experiences, being oneself, being patient, and allowing one's thoughts to "come and go" in an uncensored fashion. Studies have shown that MBSR helps in the reduction of stress, improved pain management, reduction in alcohol use, smoking cessation, reduction of posttraumatic stress associated with intimate partner violence, and improved management of hypertension for African Americans (e.g., Adams et al., 2015; Dutton, Bermudez, Matas, Majid, & Myers, 2013; Woods-Giscombé & Gaylord, 2014).

The beneficial effects of MBSR for African Americans have been linked to cultural relevancy. Woods-Giscombé and Gaylord (2014) documented the cultural congruence of MBSR for African American adults. In their investigation, those who participated in a group-based MBSR intervention indicated that it helped them reduce stress and that the strategies improved their self-confidence in managing stress and chronic disease. Participants further expressed that MBSR was consistent with their cultural values, especially spiritual beliefs and worldviews. The group-based format also appeared to provide peer support for improved management of stress (Woods-Giscombé & Gaylord, 2014). Other mind–body approaches have been shown to be efficacious in alleviating stress and other mental health symptoms for African American populations. These treatment approaches include yoga, progressive muscle relaxation, biofeedback, autogenic training, guided imagery, diaphragmatic breathing, and transcendental meditation (e.g., Woods-Giscombé & Gaylord, 2014). Overall, the data suggest that MBSR and related treatment approaches are therapeutically beneficial in the treatment of stress-related dysfunction for members of African American populations. More research is needed to understand the degree to which these approaches are just as or more effective than standard CBSM in reducing stress for African Americans.

CONCLUSION

African Americans face significant and often unique stressors in their lives, and these stressors play a role in the development and course of mental and physical health impairments. These stressors, which may include oppression and discrimination based on race, also foster the development of a wide range of social cognitive changes that influence both the perception of stress and stress responses. The nature of stress exposure and the social cognitive changes that emerge from these stress exposures highlight the need for effective stress management approaches for African Americans.

CBSM techniques have not been consistently used by African Americans. The limited preliminary data have suggested that both tailored and standard CBSM approaches may have some benefit in reducing stress responses and improving quality of life. However, the ongoing nature of unjust stress exposure suggests that modifications to stress-monitoring procedures are needed. These interventions have only been tested with women, and it is not clear whether similar interventions aimed at identifying and recognizing the effects of discrimination on stress responses will be effective for men.

A limited body of data also supports the role of alternative approaches, including MBSR and other physical interventions such as yoga (Burnett-Zeigler et al., 2016). These approaches focus on strengthening resilience to the physical consequences of stress through the regulation of respiration or physical activity and can be administered in group formats that can generate solidarity and hope. Given the severity of the stressors facing African Americans, a focus on strengthening resilience and offsetting the physical complications of stress may be an important first step.

Culturally adapted cognitive behavioral approaches are receiving increased empirical attention. Additional studies are needed to determine their long-term benefits. These approaches may require new training for clinicians who have to develop different types of therapeutic alliances and engage in more multilevel interventions to address stress exposures in populations facing significant disadvantage and discrimination.

REFERENCES

Adams, C. E., Cano, M. A., Heppner, W. L., Stewart, D. W., Correa-Fernández, V., Vidrine, J. I., . . . Wetter, D. W. (2015). Testing a moderated mediation model of mindfulness, psychosocial stress, and alcohol use among African American smokers. *Mindfulness*, 6, 315–325. http://dx.doi.org/10.1007/s12671-013-0263-1

Almeida, D. M., Wethington, E., & Kessler, R. C. (2002). The daily inventory of stressful events: An interview-based approach for measuring daily stressors. *Assessment*, 9, 41–55.

Antoni, M. H., Baggett, L., Ironson, G., LaPerriere, A., August, S., Klimas, N., . . . Fletcher, M. A. (1991). Cognitive-behavioral stress management intervention buffers distress responses and immunologic changes following notification of HIV-1 seropositivity. *Journal of Consulting and Clinical Psychology*, 59, 906–915. http://dx.doi.org/10.1037/0022-006X.59.6.906

Baum, A., Garofalo, J. P., & Yali, A. M. (1999). Socioeconomic status and chronic stress: Does stress account for SES effects on health? In N. E. Adler, M. Marmot, B. S. McEwen, & J. Stewart (Eds.), *Socioeconomic status and health in industrial nations: Social, psychological, and biological pathways* (pp. 131–144). New York, NY: New York Academy of Sciences.

Baum, V. C. (2002). Cardiac trauma in children. *Paediatric Anaesthesia*, 12, 110–117. http://dx.doi.org/10.1046/j.1460-9592.2002.00702.x

Beck, A. T. (1987). Cognitive models of depression. *Journal of Cognitive Psychotherapy*, 1, 5–37.

Beck, J. S. (2005). *Cognitive therapy for challenging problems: What to do when the basics don't work*. New York, NY: Guilford Press.

Bell, T. (2015). Meditative practice cultivates mindfulness and reduces anxiety, depression, blood pressure, and heart rate in a diverse sample. *Journal of Cognitive Psychotherapy*, 29, 343–355. http://dx.doi.org/10.1891/0889-8391.29.4.343

Bennett, G. G., Merritt, M. M., Sollers, J. J., III, Edwards, C. L., Whitfield, K. E., Brandon, D. T., & Tucker, R. D. (2004). Stress, coping, and health outcomes among African-Americans: A review of the John Henryism hypothesis. *Psychology & Health*, 19, 369–383. http://dx.doi.org/10.1080/0887044042000193505

Brondolo, E., Brady Ver Halen, N., Pencille, M., Beatty, D., & Contrada, R. J. (2009). Coping with racism: A selective review of the literature and a theoretical and methodological critique. *Journal of Behavioral Medicine*, 32, 64–88. http://dx.doi.org/10.1007/s10865-008-9193-0

Brondolo, E., & Jean-Pierre, K. (2014). "You said, I heard": Speaking the subtext in interracial conversations. In A. Kalet & C. Chou (Eds.), *Remediation in medical education: A midcourse correction* (pp. 131–156). New York, NY: Springer. http://dx.doi.org/10.1007/978-1-4614-9025-8_8

Brondolo, E., Kelly, K. P., Coakley, V., Gordon, T., Thompson, S., Levy, E., . . . Contrada, R. J. (2005). The Perceived Ethnic Discrimination Questionnaire: Development and preliminary validation of a community version. *Journal of Applied Social Psychology, 35,* 335–365. http://dx.doi.org/10.1111/j.1559-1816.2005.tb02124.x

Brondolo, E., Libretti, M., Rivera, L., & Walsemann, K. M. (2012). Racism and social capital: The implications for social and physical well-being. *Journal of Social Issues, 68,* 358–384. http://dx.doi.org/10.1111/j.1540-4560.2012.01752.x

Brondolo, E., Ng, W., Pierre, K. L. J., & Lane, R. (2016). Racism and mental health: Examining the link between racism and depression from a social cognitive perspective. In A. N. Alvarez, C. T. H. Liang, & H. A. Neville (Eds.), *The cost of racism for people of color: Contextualizing experiences of discrimination* (pp. 109–132). Washington, DC: American Psychological Association.

Brondolo, E., Rahim, R., Grimaldi, S. J., Ashraf, A., Bui, N., & Schwartz, J. C. (2015). Place of birth effects on self-reported discrimination: Variations by type of discrimination. *International Journal of Intercultural Relations, 49,* 212–222. http://dx.doi.org/10.1016/j.ijintrel.2015.10.001

Brown, J. L., & Vanable, P. A. (2008). Cognitive–behavioral stress management interventions for persons living with HIV: A review and critique of the literature. *Annals of Behavioral Medicine, 35,* 26–40. http://dx.doi.org/10.1007/s12160-007-9010-y

Brunson, R. K., & Miller, J. (2006). Young Black men and urban policing in the United States. *British Journal of Criminology, 46,* 613–640. http://dx.doi.org/10.1093/bjc/azi093

Bulhan, H. A. (1985). *Frantz Fanon and the psychology of oppression.* New York, NY: Plenum Press.

Burnett-Zeigler, I., Schuette, S., Victorson, D., & Wisner, K. L. (2016). Mind–body approaches to treating mental health symptoms among disadvantaged populations: A comprehensive review. *The Journal of Alternative and Complementary Medicine, 22,* 115–124. http://dx.doi.org/10.1089/acm.2015.0038

Cannon, W. B. (1927). The James-Lange theory of emotions: A critical examination and an alternative theory. *The American Journal of Psychology, 39,* 106–124. http://dx.doi.org/10.2307/1415404

Chen, E., & Miller, G. E. (2013). Socioeconomic status and health: Mediating and moderating factors. *Annual Review of Clinical Psychology, 9,* 723–749. http://dx.doi.org/10.1146/annurev-clinpsy-050212-185634

Chiesa, A., & Seretti, A. (2009). Mindfulness-based stress reduction for stress management in healthy people: A review and meta-analysis. *The Journal* of *Alternative and Complementary Medicine, 15*, 593–600. http://dx.doi.org/10.1089/acm.2008.0495

Clark, A. E., D'Ambrosio, C., & Ghislandi, S. (2016). Adaptation to poverty in long-run panel data. *Review of Economics and Statistics, 98*, 591–600. http://dx.doi.org/10.1162/REST_a_00544

Clark, R. (2006). Perceived racism and vascular reactivity in Black college women: Moderating effects of seeking social support. *Health Psychology, 25*, 2–25. http://dx.doi.org/10.1037/0278-6133.25.1.20

Clark, R., & Adams, J. H. (2004). Moderating effects of perceived racism on John Henryism and blood pressure reactivity in Black female college students. *Annals of Behavioral Medicine, 28*, 126–131. http://dx.doi.org/10.1207/s15324796abm2802_8

Cohen, S., Kamarck, T., & Mermelstein, R. (1983). A global measure of perceived stress. *Journal of Health and Social Behavior, 24*, 385–396. http://dx.doi.org/10.2307/2136404

Contrada, R. J., Ashmore, R. D., Gary, M. L., Coups, E., Egeth, J. D., Sewell, A., . . . Chasse, V. (2001). Measures of ethnicity-related stress: Psychometric properties, ethnic group differences, and associations with well-being. *Journal of Applied Social Psychology, 31*, 1775–1820. http://dx.doi.org/10.1111/j.1559-1816.2001.tb00205.x

Dalisay, F., & Tan, A. (2009). Assimilation and contrast effects in the priming of Asian American and African American stereotypes through TV exposure. *Journalism & Mass Communication Quarterly, 86*, 7–22. http://dx.doi.org/10.1177/107769900908600102

Dutton, M. A., Bermudez, D., Matas, A., Majid, H., & Myers, N. L. (2013). Mindfulness-based stress reduction for low-income, predominantly African American women with PTSD and a history of intimate partner violence. *Cognitive and Behavioral Practice, 20*, 23–32. http://dx.doi.org/10.1016/j.cbpra.2011.08.003

Evans, G. W., & Kim, P. (2013). Childhood poverty, chronic stress, self-regulation, and coping. *Child Development Perspectives, 7*, 43–48. http://dx.doi.org/10.1111/cdep.12013

Fiske, S. T., & Taylor, S. E. (2013). *Social cognition: From brains to culture*. London, England: Sage. http://dx.doi.org/10.4135/9781446286395

Foa, E. B., Davidson, J. R. T., Frances, A., Culpepper, L., Ross, R., & Ross, D. (1999). The expert consensus guideline series: Treatment of posttraumatic stress disorder. *The Journal of Clinical Psychiatry, 60*(Suppl. 16), 3–76.

Foa, E. B., Rothbaum, B. O., Riggs, D. S., & Murdock, T. B. (1991). Treatment of posttraumatic stress disorder in rape victims: A comparison between cognitive–behavioral procedures and counseling. *Journal of Consulting and Clinical Psychology, 59*, 715–723. http://dx.doi.org/10.1037/0022-006X.59.5.715

Gamst, G., Liang, C. T. H., & Der-Karabetian, A. (2011). *Handbook of multicultural measures*. Thousand Oaks, CA: Sage.

Geronimus, A.T., Hicken, M., Keene, D., & Bound, J. (2006). "Weathering" and age patterns of allostatic load scores among Blacks and Whites in the United States. *American Journal of Public Health, 96*, 826–833. http://dx.doi.org/10.2105/AJPH.2004.060749

Gianaros, P. J., & Wager, T. D. (2015). Brain–body pathways linking psychological stress and physical health. *Current Directions in Psychological Science, 24*, 313–321. http://dx.doi.org/10.1177/0963721415581476

Gilens, M. (1996). Race-coding and White opposition to welfare. *The American Political Science Review, 90*, 593–604. http://dx.doi.org/10.2307/2082611

Greer, T. M. (2007). Measuring coping strategies among African Americans: An exploration of the latent structure of the COPE Inventory. *Journal of Black Psychology, 33*, 260–277. http://dx.doi.org/10.1177/0095798407302539

Greer, T. M. (2011). Coping strategies as moderators of the relationship between race- and gender-based discrimination and psychological symptoms for African American women. *Journal of Black Psychology, 37*, 42–54. http://dx.doi.org/10.1177/0095798410380202

Greer, T. M. (2016). Age influences the effects of provider racial biases on treatment adherence and blood pressure control for African American hypertensive patients. *Journal of Health Care for the Poor and Underserved, 27*, 604–621. http://dx.doi.org/10.1353/hpu.2016.0066

Greer, T. M., Brondolo, E., & Brown, P. (2014). Systemic racism moderates effects of provider racial biases on adherence to hypertension treatment for African Americans. *Health Psychology, 33*, 35–42. http://dx.doi.org/10.1037/a0032777

Greer, T. M., Laseter, A., & Asiamah, D. (2009). Gender as a moderator of the relation between race-related stress and mental health symptoms for African Americans. *Psychology of Women Quarterly, 33*, 295–307. http://dx.doi.org/10.1111/j.1471-6402.2009.01502.x

Greer, T. M., Vendemia, J. M. C., & Stancil, M. (2012). Neural correlates of race-related social evaluations for African Americans and white Americans. *Neuropsychology, 26*, 704–712. http://dx.doi.org/10.1037/a0030035

Grier, W. H., & Cobbs, P. M. (1968). *Black rage.* New York, NY: Basic Books.

Halvorsen, M., Wang, C. E., Richter, J., Myrland, I., Pedersen, S. K., Eisemann, M., & Waterloo, K. (2009). Early maladaptive schemas, temperament and character traits in clinically depressed and previously depressed subjects. *Clinical Psychology & Psychotherapy, 16*, 394–407. http://dx.doi.org/10.1002/cpp.618

Harrell, S. P. (2000). A multidimensional conceptualization of racism-related stress: Implications for the well-being of people of color. *American Journal of Orthopsychiatry, 70*, 42–57. http://dx.doi.org/10.1037/h0087722

Haslanger, S. (2013). Liberatory knowledge and just social practices. *Philosophy and Law, 12*, 6–11.

Henson, J. M., Derlega, V. J., Pearson, M. R., Ferrer, R., & Holmes, K. (2013). African American students' responses to racial discrimination: How race-based rejection sensitivity and social constraints are related to psychological reactions. *Journal of Social and Clinical Psychology, 32,* 504–529. http://dx.doi.org/10.1521/jscp.2013.32.5.504

Holmes, T. H., & Rahe, R. H. (1967). The Social Readjustment Rating Scale. *Journal of Psychosomatic Research, 11,* 213–218. http://dx.doi.org/10.1016/0022-3999(67)90010-4

James, I. A., Reichelt, F. K., Freeston, M. H., & Barton, S. B. (2007). Schemas as memories: Implications for treatment. *Journal of Cognitive Psychotherapy, 21,* 51–57. http://dx.doi.org/10.1891/088983907780493296

Jones, D. L., Ishii Owens, M., Lydston, D., Tobin, J. N., Brondolo, E., & Weiss, S. M. (2010). Self-efficacy and distress in women with AIDS: The SMART/EST women's project. *AIDS Care, 22,* 1499–1508. http://dx.doi.org/10.1080/09540121.2010.484454

Jones, J. M. (1997). *Prejudice and racism* (2nd ed.). New York, NY: McGraw-Hill.

Kabat-Zinn, J. (1991). *Full catastrophe living: Using the wisdom of your body and mind to face stress, pain, and illness.* New York, NY: Delta.

Kelly, S. (2006). Cognitive-behavioral therapy with African Americans. In P. A. Hays & G. Y. Iwamasa (Eds.), *Culturally responsive cognitive-behavioral therapy: Assessment, practice, and supervision* (pp. 97–116). Washington, DC: American Psychological Association. http://dx.doi.org/10.1037/11433-004

Kramer, M. R., & Hogue, C. R. (2009). Is segregation bad for your health? *Epidemiologic Reviews, 31,* 178–194. http://dx.doi.org/10.1093/epirev/mxp001

Krieger, N. (1999). Embodying inequality: A review of concepts, measures, and methods for studying health consequences of discrimination. *International Journal of Health Services, 29,* 295–352. http://dx.doi.org/10.2190/M11W-VWXE-KQM9-G97Q

Krieger, N. (2010). The science and epidemiology of racism and health: Racial/ethnic categories, biological expressions of racism, and the embodiment of inequality—An ecosocial perspective. In I. Whitmarsh, D. S. Jones, I. Whitmarsh, & D. S. Jones (Eds.), *What's the use of race? Modern governance and the biology of difference* (pp. 225–255). Cambridge, MA: MIT Press.

Kwok, J., Atencio, J., Ullah, J., Crupi, R., Chen, D., Roth, A. R., . . . Brondolo, E. (2011). The perceived ethnic discrimination questionnaire–community version: Validation in a multiethnic Asian sample. *Cultural Diversity and Ethnic Minority Psychology, 17,* 271–282. http://dx.doi.org/10.1037/a0024034

Lazarus, R. S., & Folkman, S. (1984). *Stress, appraisal, and coping.* New York, NY: Springer.

Lechner, S. C., Ennis-Whitehead, N., Robertson, B. R., Annane, D. W., Vargas, S., Carver, C. S., & Antoni, M. H. (2013). Adaptation of a psycho-oncology intervention for Black breast cancer survivors: Project CARE. *The Counseling Psychologist, 41*, 286–312. http://dx.doi.org/10.1177/0011000012459971

Lechner, S. C., Whitehead, N. E., Vargas, S., Annane, D. W., Robertson, B. R., Carver, C. S., . . . Antoni, M. H. (2014). Does a community-based stress management intervention affect psychological adaptation among underserved black breast cancer survivors? *Journal of the National Cancer Institute Monographs, 2014*, 315–322. http://dx.doi.org/10.1093/jncimonographs/lgu032

Lee, D. L., & Ahn, S. (2013). The relation of racial identity, ethnic identity, and racial socialization to discrimination-distress: A meta-analysis of Black Americans. *Journal of Counseling Psychology, 60*, 1–14. http://dx.doi.org/10.1037/a0031275

Markus, H., & Wurf, E. (1987). The dynamic self-concept: A social psychological perspective. *Annual Review of Psychology, 38*, 299–337. http://dx.doi.org/10.1146/annurev.ps.38.020187.001503

Mastro, D. E., & Kopacz, M. A. (2006). Media representations of race, prototypicality, and policy reasoning: An application of self-categorization theory. *Journal of Broadcasting & Electronic Media, 50*, 305–322. http://dx.doi.org/10.1207/s15506878jobem5002_8

McKenzie, S., Robinson, N. T., Herrera, L., Churchill, J. C., & Eichenbaum, H. (2013). Learning causes reorganization of neuronal firing patterns to represent related experiences within a hippocampal schema. *The Journal of Neuroscience, 33*, 10243–10256. http://dx.doi.org/10.1523/JNEUROSCI.0879-13.2013

McNeilly, M. D., Anderson, N. B., Armstead, C. A., Clark, R., Corbett, M., Robinson, E. L., . . . Lepisto, E. M. (1996). The Perceived Racism Scale: A multidimensional assessment of the experience of white racism among African Americans. *Ethnicity & Disease, 6*, 154–166.

Mendoza-Denton, R., Downey, G., Purdie, V. J., Davis, A., & Pietrzak, J. (2002). Sensitivity to status-based rejection: Implications for African American students' college experience. *Journal of Personality and Social Psychology, 83*, 896–918. http://dx.doi.org/10.1037/0022-3514.83.4.896

Moore, A. D., Hamilton, J. B., Knafl, G. J., Godley, P. A., Carpenter, W. R., Bensen, J. T., . . . Mishel, M. (2013). The influence of mistrust, racism, religious participation, and access to care on patient satisfaction for African American men: The North Carolina-Louisiana Prostate Cancer Project. *Journal of the National Medical Association, 105*, 59–68. http://dx.doi.org/10.1016/S0027-9684(15)30086-9

Otte, C. (2011). Cognitive behavioral therapy in anxiety disorders: Current state of the evidence. *Dialogues in Clinical Neuroscience, 13*, 413–421.

Outlaw, F. H. (1993). Stress and coping: The influence of racism on the cognitive appraisal processing of African Americans. *Issues in Mental Health Nursing, 14*, 399–409. http://dx.doi.org/10.3109/01612849309006902

Oyserman, D. (2008). Racial-ethnic self-schemas: Multidimensional identity-based motivation. *Journal of Research in Personality, 42*, 1186–1198. http://dx.doi.org/10.1016/j.jrp.2008.03.003

Paradies, Y. (2006). A systematic review of empirical research on self-reported racism and health. *International Journal of Epidemiology, 35*, 888–901. http://dx.doi.org/10.1093/ije/dyl056

Peacock, E. J., & Wong, P. T. (1990). The Stress Appraisal Measure (SAM): A multidimensional approach to cognitive appraisal. *Stress Medicine, 6*, 227–236. http://dx.doi.org/10.1002/smi.2460060308

Pinel, E. C. (1999). Stigma consciousness: The psychological legacy of social stereotypes. *Journal of Personality and Social Psychology, 76*, 114–128. http://dx.doi.org/10.1037/0022-3514.76.1.114

Selye, H. (1956). *The stress of life*. New York, NY: McGraw-Hill.

Sherman, D. K., & Hartson, K. A. (2011). Reconciling self-protection with self-improvement: Self-affirmation theory. In M. Alicke & C. Sedikides (Eds.), *The handbook of self-enhancement and self-protection* (pp. 128–151). New York, NY: Guilford Press.

Sternthal, M., Slopen, N., & Williams, D. R. (2011). Racial disparities in health: How much does stress really matter? *Du Bois Review, 8*, 95–113. http://dx.doi.org/10.1017/S1742058X11000087

Thames, A. D., Hinkin, C. H., Byrd, D. A., Bilder, R. M., Duff, K. J., Mindt, M. R., . . . Streiff, V. (2013). Effects of stereotype threat, perceived discrimination, and examiner race on neuropsychological performance: Simple as Black and White? *Journal of the International Neuropsychological Society, 19*, 583–593. http://dx.doi.org/10.1017/S1355617713000076

Townsend, T. G., Hawkins, S. R., & Batts, A. L. (2007). Stress and stress reduction among African American women: A brief report. *The Journal of Primary Prevention, 28*, 569–582. http://dx.doi.org/10.1007/s10935-007-0111-y

Utsey, S. O. (1999). Development and validation of a short form of the Index of Race-Related Stress (IRRS)–Brief Version. *Measurement & Evaluation in Counseling & Development, 32*, 149–167.

Webb, M., Beckstead, J., Meininger, J., & Robinson, S. (2006). Stress management for African American women with elevated blood pressure: A pilot study. *Biological Research for Nursing, 7*, 187–196. http://dx.doi.org/10.1177/1099800405283144

Whaley, A. L., & Davis, K. E. (2007). Cultural competence and evidence-based practice in mental health services: A complementary perspective. *American Psychologist, 62*, 563–574. http://dx.doi.org/10.1037/0003-066X.62.6.563

Williams, D. R., & Collins, C. (2001). Racial residential segregation: A fundamental cause of racial disparities in health. *Public Health Reports, 116*, 404–416. http://dx.doi.org/10.1016/S0033-3549(04)50068-7

Woods-Giscombé, C.L. & Gaylord, S.A. (2014). The cultural relevance of mindfulness meditation as a health intervention for African Americans: Implications for reducing stress-related health disparities. *Journal of Holistic Nursing, 32,* 147–160. http://dx.doi.org/10.1177/0898010113519010

Yoshikawa, H., Aber, J. L., & Beardslee, W. R. (2012). The effects of poverty on the mental, emotional, and behavioral health of children and youth: Implications for prevention. *American Psychologist, 67,* 272–284. http://dx.doi.org/10.1037/a0028015

12

COGNITIVE BEHAVIORAL MODELS, MEASURES, AND TREATMENTS FOR STRESS DISORDERS IN AMERICAN INDIANS AND ALASKA NATIVES

BETH BOYD AND RYAN HUNSAKER

American Indian (AI) and Alaska Native (AN) people (collectively referred to as *AI/AN people* and *Native people* in this chapter) experience disproportionately high levels of health and mental health problems, often resulting from various forms of stress. Although stress is frequently conceptualized as an acute physiological demand on the body resulting from attempts to cope with daily stressors, it is also important to understand it as the cumulative effect of prolonged experiences related to sociocultural history and status (American Psychological Association, 2011). Understanding this chronic, long-term stress is particularly important for the AI/AN population because of their experience of unresolved grief transmitted across generations; staggering health disparities; and devastating social issues, including poverty, oppression, and unemployment.

Attention to historical trauma is important for understanding the context in which stress occurs for AI/ANs. The systematic marginalization of

http://dx.doi.org/10.1037/0000091-013
Treating Depression, Anxiety, and Stress in Ethnic and Racial Groups: Cognitive Behavioral Approaches,
E. C. Chang, C. A. Downey, J. K. Hirsch, and E. A. Yu (Editors)

Native populations through traumatic losses related to genocide and colonialism, discrimination, racism, and oppression has been correlated with higher documented rates of health and mental health problems in AI/ANs (Brave Heart, Chase, Elkins, & Altschul, 2011; Manson et al., 2005). An "indigenist" stress-coping model articulated by Walters and Simoni (2002) links historical and resultant contemporary trauma to a number of adverse health (e.g., high rates of cardiac, respiratory, and liver diseases; malignant neoplasms; and substance abuse) and mental health outcomes (e.g., high rates of depression, anxiety, and posttraumatic stress disorder [PTSD]), whereas more proximal stressors include factors such as higher rates of poverty (Kelley & Lowe, 2012), unemployment (Sharpe, 2013), limited access to mental health services (Gone & Trimble, 2012), and acculturative stressors (Goldston et al., 2008).

WHO ARE AMERICAN INDIANS AND ALASKA NATIVES?

Health Disparities

AI/AN people face extraordinary health and mental health care challenges. Native people die at higher rates than other Americans from chronic liver disease and cirrhosis, diabetes mellitus, unintentional injuries, assault and homicide, intentional self-harm or suicide, and chronic lower respiratory diseases. More specifically, Native people are faced with alcoholism and tuberculosis at 6 times the national average; diabetes, accidents, PTSD, and poverty at 3 times the national average; and suicide at 1.7 times the national average. The average life expectancy for AI/AN people is more than 4 years less than that of the general U.S. population (Indian Health Service, 2015).

Health and behavioral health care for AI/ANs who are enrolled in federally recognized tribes are provided by the Indian Health Service, an agency within the U.S. Department of Health and Human Services (Indian Health Service, 2015). However, access to quality health and mental health care remains a far greater challenge for AI/AN people than for others in the United States (Gone & Trimble, 2012). Barriers include logistical issues such as geographically remote locations, lack of transportation, shortage of qualified providers, lack of culturally responsive care, concerns about confidentiality, communication about care issues (Lane & Simmons, 2011), and quality of health care that is sometimes harmful, resulting in death and/or endangerment (Kaufman, 2015). Compounding these challenges, and largely due to these issues, AI/AN people have a long-standing distrust of government services and Western medicine (Goodkind, Gorman, Hess, Parker, & Hough, 2015).

Historical Trauma

AI/AN issues cannot be separated from the unique sociopolitical history and the historical trauma experienced by each tribe, defined by Brave Heart and DeBruyn (1998) as the "cumulative emotional and psychological wounding, over the life span and across generations, emanating from massive group trauma experiences" (p. 7). It results from "a horrendous event that leaves indelible marks upon the consciousness of members of a collectivity, and changes their identity fundamentally and irrevocably" (Alexander, Eyerman, Giesen, Smelser, & Sztompka, 2004, p. 1). Such traumatic events overwhelm and alter the very structure of the cultural system, and the culture loses its ability to protect and support its members (deVries, 1996). Such cumulative historical trauma is thought to contribute to the high levels of substance abuse, suicide, depression, anxiety, low self-esteem, anger, difficulty recognizing and expressing emotions, and unresolved historical grief among AI/AN people (Brave Heart, 1999; Brave Heart & DeBruyn, 1998).

The historical trauma of AI/AN people began with contact with European people and continued through many years when federal Indian policy called for the extermination of the AI/AN people. Beginning in the early 1800s, federal policies of removal and assimilation contributed to the historical and cultural trauma of AI/AN people (Weaver, 1998). These policies included the seizure and reduction of territory (Kelly, 1990) and the forced removal of approximately five generations of Native children from their families and communities for placement in government-run or church-affiliated boarding schools (Weaver, 1998). The boarding schools often exposed Native children to physical, sexual, and emotional abuse, in addition to isolation from their families, communities, and cultures. Without family support and access to cultural forms of healing, they often developed coping styles that helped them to survive the boarding school but that proved to be maladaptive in the outside world as they became adults (e.g., learned helplessness, denial, repression, projection of blame, use of alcohol and drugs, suicide). When these young people returned to their communities, they were unable to relate to their Native culture, language, or traditions. In addition, they did not have the experience of growing up in families, living with siblings, or seeing parental role models, putting them at a serious disadvantage as they moved into adulthood and formed their own families (Brave Heart & DeBruyn, 1998; Garrett & Pichette, 2000). In addition, traditional spiritual and ceremonial ways of healing were outlawed by U.S. policy from 1883 until 1978, leaving Native people with no mechanism for healing from these traumatic experiences and devastating losses. This accumulation of traumatic experiences, combined with the lack of culturally resonant mechanisms of healing, has created unresolved historical grief

(Brave Heart & DeBruyn, 1998) and the high rates of health and behavioral health issues reported earlier.

In the following section, we present a brief overview of the major models of stress and how these models have been applied to conceptualize stress in AI/ANs.

STRESS

Regardless of whether stress is acute or chronic, it produces changes in many bodily systems and contributes to a variety of health and behavioral health problems, including cardiovascular, gastrointestinal, skin, immune, and respiratory diseases (S. Cohen, Janicki-Deverts, & Miller, 2007). Research has suggested that some individuals, especially from certain ethnic groups, are at greater risk of experiencing stress that is serious enough to overwhelm their ability to cope (Cokley, McClain, Enciso, & Martinez, 2013; French & Chavez, 2010). Factors most likely to result in stress-related health problems include an accumulation of persistent stressful situations, persistent stress after a severe acute response to a traumatic event, and acute stress accompanying a serious illness. Some of the in-person characteristics that influence how people respond to stress include quality of early nurturing (Farrell, Simpson, Carlson, Englund, & Sung, 2017; Miller, Chen, & Parker, 2011), individual personality traits (Villada, Hidalgo, Almela, & Salvador, 2016), genetic factors (DiGangi, Guffanti, McLaughlin, & Koenen, 2013), diseases of the immune system that may weaken the response to stress (Dougall, Wroble, Minhnoi, Swanson, & Baum, 2013), and the duration and intensity of stressors (Green et al., 1990). As with other health and behavioral health issues, populations who may be more vulnerable to the effects of stress include older adults, women, those with less education, those who experience financial strain, those who are lonely or isolated, and those who are the target of racial or sexual discrimination, experiences that AI/AN persons often encounter (Krieger, 1999).

Models of Stress

Stress is traditionally defined as any circumstance that threatens, or is perceived to threaten, one's well-being and, thereby, taxes one's ability to cope. Bernard and Krupat (1994) proposed a biopsychosocial model of stress, arguing that stress could be conceptualized in one of three basic ways that can be encompassed in three classic theories. First, stress can be conceptualized as a response to environmental factors (Selye, 1936), inclusive of the activation of physiological and somatic processes that attempt adaptation to the stressful situation, including the alarm or fight-or-flight stage, the adaptation stage, and the exhaustion stage. Stress can also be conceptualized as being a result of the impact of environmental factors or stressors (Holmes & Rahe, 1967), with more life changes related to greater incidence of mental or physical disease. The transactional model views stress as a continuous interaction (or adaptation) between the person and the environment (Lazarus & Folkman, 1984), in which the person thinks about, evaluates, and then responds to stressors. Appraisals of potentially stressful events are related to the controllability and predictability of events; the most stressful events are those that are perceived as uncontrollable and unpredictable. Finally, Dohrenwend and colleagues (1982) described a stress-paradigm model in which environmental and person factors are the antecedents of stressful life events. The interaction of internal mediators (e.g., aspirations, values, coping ability, biological strengths and vulnerabilities) and external mediators (e.g., material and social supports or deficits) with the state of stress would then determine positive, neutral, or negative effects on health. This model may be most useful for explaining the relationships between stress, coping, and physical and mental health in marginalized groups.

Native People and Stress

Walters, Simoni, and Evans-Campbell (2002) proposed an indigenist stress-coping model of AI/AN women's health based on Dingess and Joos's (1988) stress-coping model and Krieger's (1999) work on the health outcomes of discrimination and ecosocial theory. These views situate the health of Native people within the larger context of their status as a colonized people within the United States. However, development and nurturance of a strong, positive cultural identity, enculturation (e.g., immersion in traditional cultural practices), spiritual coping, and traditional health practices can serve as protective factors, strengthening psychological and emotional health and mitigating the effect of discrimination-based stressors.

Zimiles (2013) also used an indigenist framework to identify four types of stressors caused by the marginalization of AI/ANs. These are (a) the psychological strains of historical trauma, (b) environmental stressors (e.g., poverty, barriers to health care, lack of access to fresh foods or recreational facilities, high crime rates), (c) daily stressors arising from socioeconomic disparities (e.g., unsafe environments, challenges getting to school, homelessness), and (d) adversity resulting from personal and relational role conflicts (e.g., conflicts between indigenous and mainstream cultural values and expectations). These additional factors are important elements in understanding the effects of stress in AI/AN populations.

Bringing an integrative and applied perspective, Rivkin et al. (2010) reported on their work with ANs in the Yup'ik Experiences of Stress and

Coping Project. The goals of this ongoing project include understanding the experiences of stress and coping from the Yup'ik cultural perspective and the "development and implementation of community-informed and culturally grounded interventions to reduce stress and promote physical and mental health in rural Alaska Native communities" (Rivkin et al., 2010, p. 1). The conceptual framework for this project integrates models of stress physiology (Juster, McEwen, & Lupien, 2010; McEwen, 1998; McEwen & Seeman, 1999), ecological models (Dohrenwend, 1978; Hobfoll, 1988; Lazarus & Folkman, 1984), and specific models proposed for understanding stress and coping among AI/ANs (Dinges & Joos, 1988; Walters et al., 2002). In this integrated model, stressors (e.g., major life events and chronic stressors) and coping resources (e.g., social support, community integration, economic resources, traditional knowledge, spirituality, personal resilience) are viewed within a cultural and social context. The interaction of these stressors and coping resources influences perceptions of stress that, in turn, influences physical and mental health, both directly and indirectly. The direct effects of stress on psychological and physiological states (e.g., depression, blood pressure, stress hormones) are of concern, while the indirect effects of stress on health through its influence on harmful behaviors (e.g., smoking, alcohol use), can also contribute to development of chronic stress and associated disease.

CULTURALLY APPROPRIATE MEASURES OF STRESS WITH NATIVE PEOPLE

This review of the cognitive behavioral measures of stress is necessarily limited to explicating current needs. Bluntly stated, according to contemporary standards (Suzuki, Ponterotto, & Meller, 2001), the literature does not reveal any instrument that has been validated as a culturally appropriate assessment of stress for use with AI/ANs. The PTSD Checklist for the *Diagnostic and Statistical Manual of Mental Disorders* (Weathers, Litz, Herman, Huska, & Keane, 1993; PCL-5 is the most current version) is a widely accepted self-report instrument for tracking PTSD symptoms but does not have a version specifically for use with AI/AN people. The Adverse Childhood Experiences Questionnaire (Felitti et al., 1998) has been modified to examine early stressors in the lives of AI/ANs (De Ravello, Abeita, & Brown, 2008), but this measure is still being refined, and psychometric data were not readily available at the time of this review. Other potentially relevant measures include questionnaires about historical trauma (e.g., Balsam, Huang, Fieland, Simoni, & Walters, 2004; Whitbeck, Adams, Hoyt & Chen, 2004) and a number of traumatic stress inventories (e.g., Impact of Events Scale; Horowitz, Wilner, & Alvarez, 1979). The next sections explore the psychometric properties of these instruments, including their cultural appropriateness or lack thereof.

DSM-Based Measures and Assessment
of Posttraumatic Stress Disorder

The *Diagnostic and Statistical Manual of Mental Disorders* (fifth ed. [*DSM–5*]; American Psychiatric Association, 2013) attempts to assess stress-related disorders in a culturally appropriate manner through the use of a cultural formulation interview (CFI), a semistructured supplemental interview module. The use of the CFI with AI/ANs was reviewed by Fleming and Lim (2015), but there is no literature on the issue of assessing stress-related disorders specifically. Fleming and Lim noted that this measure shows promise for augmenting the assessment process when working with AI/AN people, but issues of cultural responsiveness or validity of results using this measure are less clear.

To determine whether an assessment practice is culturally resonant, it is necessary to understand the cultural explanations for the disorders being assessed. In AI/AN people, stress often results in psychological problems that are manifested as physical symptoms or spiritual malady. Csordas, Storck, and Strauss (2008) examined contemporary Native healing practices in several contexts and attempted to compare these in ethnographic fashion with *DSM* diagnoses. This study confirmed that PTSD in AI/ANs is often associated with physical symptoms and grief. The appropriateness of *DSM–IV–TR* diagnoses was not questioned in this study, but Csordas and colleagues suggested that traumatic stress disorders with Native people should be conceptualized as a "multilayered existential synthesis" (p. 595).

There are other assessment tools based on *DSM* criteria, both semistructured interviews and checklists, but none of them appear to have been validated specifically for use with AI/ANs. In reviewing the literature on PTSD for AI/AN people, Bassett and colleagues found that many studies simply used unstructured or semistructured interviews (see Bassett, Buchwald, & Manson, 2014, for a review). Other examples of measures used to assess PTSD with AI/ANs include the PTSD Checklist for the *DSM* (PCL-5), the PTSD Symptom Severity Interview (PSS-I; Foa, Riggs, Dancu, & Rothbaum, 1993), and the Composite International Diagnostic Interview (CIDI; World Health Organization, 1990). The PCL is a 20-item self-report measure that is widely used in both research and clinical settings. In its current iteration, the PCL-5 (revised for use with the *DSM–5*) is psychometrically sound in terms of internal consistency, test–retest reliability, convergent validity, and discriminant validity (Blevins, Weathers, Davis, Witte, & Domino, 2015), but it has not been specifically validated with AI/ANs. The PCL has been used in research with Native populations in several settings, including acute medical care (Santos et al., 2008) and a community setting (Stephens et al., 2010). The PSS-I is a 17-item semistructured interview that corresponds fairly directly with *DSM* diagnostic criteria. Although the PSS-I has been shown to have good reliability and validity compared with other similar measures (Foa et al., 1993), this measure has not been yet validated with an AI population, despite its use in research with AI/AN groups (e.g., Pearson et al., 2015). The CIDI has also been cited as a PTSD assessment tool that is based on *DSM* criteria. Andrews and Peters (1998) reviewed the use of this measure, noting its consistently good interrater and test–retest reliability. Yet, despite its use with AI/ANs (e.g., Duran et al., 2004), there is no extant literature that addresses its cultural appropriateness as a diagnostic measure with AI/ANs. These instruments all attempt to establish the presence of *DSM*-defined symptoms of PTSD. However, none of them allow for culturally specific variation in the expression of traumatic stress, particularly important for the extremely heterogeneous AI/AN population. Bassett et al. (2014) recommended an approach to assessment that is culturally tailored for the specific AI/AN tribe and/or community in which it will be used, developed in active collaboration with members of the community who understand the cultural expression of symptoms.

Other Stress-Related Measures

There are several instruments that measure other stress-related issues, including culturally informed adaptations of measures that assess adverse childhood experiences (ACEs) and the impact of historical trauma (Balsam et al., 2004; Whitbeck et al., 2004) and other stress-related inventories (e.g., Impact of Events Scale; Horowitz et al., 1979).

ACEs are measured in a number of studies and have been conceptualized in different contexts. Whitfield (1998) defined ACEs in terms of a "broad range of hurtful experiences, including traumas" (p. 361). ACE measures are similar to those that assess traumatic stress, but they are also broad enough in scope to include AI/AN childhood events such as attendance at boarding school (e.g., Koss et al., 2003). De Ravello et al. (2008) modified an ACE measure for use with Native populations, which resulted in categories such as experiencing physical neglect, having a dysfunctional family member, witnessing violence in the home, being physically abused by someone close to the victim, and being sexually abused by someone close to the victim. Although the authors did not describe how this measure was culturally adapted, the purpose of the study was to assess the relationship between adverse experiences in childhood and adult outcomes in an AI/AN female incarcerated population. De Ravello and colleagues (2008) noted that Robin, Chester, Rasmussen, Jaranson, and Goldman (1997) used an ACE measure with a child and adolescent Native population, with the measure consisting of seven standardized, semistructured interview questions interspersed into the Schedule of Affective Disorders and Schizophrenia–Lifetime version psychiatric interview sessions related to sexual trauma. Unfortunately, Robin et al. (1997) did not reference these data in their publication.

Several instruments address the AI/AN experience of historical trauma. The Historical Trauma Scale is first reported in the literature by Balsam and colleagues (2004), based on work by Walters and Evans-Campbell (2004). This measure notes whether the respondent reports affirmatively for self, parents, grandparents, great-grandparents, or great-great-grandparents to experiencing AI/AN-specific events such as "medical testing, experimentation," "desecration of traditional lands," being "forced to not speak native language or practice cultural expression," and being "forcibly removed by the US government from traditional homelands and relocated." Other measures of historical trauma include the Historical Loss Scale (Whitbeck et al., 2004) and the Historical Loss Associated Symptoms Scale (Whitbeck et al., 2004). The Historical Loss Scale assesses the degree to which the respondent experiences historical trauma on items such as "loss of land," "loss of traditional spiritual ways," and "loss of respect by children for traditional ways" on a Likert-type scale from *never* to *several times a day*. This measure has also been adapted for use with other indigenous populations (e.g., Native Hawaiians; Pokhrel & Herzog, 2014).

Numerous other stress-related inventories have been used with Native populations, though few attempts have been made to adapt measures specifically for use with AI/ANs. Some of these include the Perceived Stress Scale (Glass & Bieber, 1997); measurements of acculturative stress in the context of physical health outcomes (Myers & Rodriguez, 2003), alcoholism (Verney & Kipp, 2007), and suicide (Goldston et al., 2008); and inventories of stressful life events (e.g., De Coteau, Hope, & Anderson, 2003; Liberman & Frank, 1980). Examples of modifications made to existing scales include adding items or administering a scale orally, as was done for the Social Readjustment Rating Scale (Holmes & Rahe, 1967). Little information, aside from the psychometrics in individual studies, exists on the utility, reliability, or validity of such adapted measures for Native people. This underscores the need for future research focused on developing culturally responsive measures for use with tribally defined populations. In the meantime, development of local norms for psychometrically sound instruments may be the best alternative for the short term.

TREATMENTS FOR STRESS IN NATIVE POPULATIONS

In general, the literature for cognitive behavioral science has not yet integrated historical trauma into the assessment or treatment process for Native people experiencing stress-related disorders. In a review of the literature on cognitive behavior therapy (CBT) treatments for stress that have been adapted for use with AI/ANs, the most robust area to date relates to treatments for traumatic stress. However, knowledge of the course of PTSD treatment and treatment outcomes with AI/ANs is scant. In one recent meta-analysis of 37 articles, Bassett et al. (2014) noted that treatments for PTSD with AI/ANs yield no real conclusions beyond that PTSD rates are higher for this demographic group than the general population. This meta-analysis also noted a potential for large cultural, tribal, and regional differences between subgroups in this overall population, calling into question any broad generalizations on the subject of treatment efficacy and/or appropriateness of CBT interventions with AI/ANs.

With those cautionary remarks in mind, the following section explores cognitive behavioral interventions that have been adapted for use with Native populations. In addition, studies related to the treatment of other stress-related disorders and physical health interventions to manage disease and reduce stress in health care contexts are reviewed.

Treatments for Traumatic Stress

The Cognitive Behavioral Intervention for Trauma in Schools (CBITS; Morsette et al., 2009; Ngo et al., 2008) was adapted for use with AI/AN adolescents in school settings because of the paucity of research on treating AI/AN youth for PTSD in public clinic-based settings (Morsette et al., 2009). The CBITS program is a 10-week program intended for use with a small group of school-age children. Morsette and colleagues (2009) adapted the CBITS program for AI/AN children by consulting with Native health professionals, elders, teachers, and counselors. However, the data on this intervention are limited by the fact that only four children out of the original pool of 48 completed the CBITS intervention. Ngo et al. (2008) described an intervention by Stolle, Schuldberg, van den Pol, and Morsette (2007), which involved an adaptation of the CBITS intervention with groups of six AI/AN middle school students. The authors focused on the importance of understanding the children's cultural belief systems and levels of acculturation and offered some culturally specific guidelines for implementing treatment with AI/AN youth rather than reporting on treatment outcome.

Another trauma intervention that has been adapted for use with AI/AN children and adolescents, Honoring Children, Mending the Circle (HC-MC; BigFoot & Schmidt, 2010), focused on the cultural adaptation of evidence-based treatment approaches. This approach for managing the effects of trauma was adapted from trauma-focused cognitive behavioral therapy (TF-CBT; J. A. Cohen, Mannarino, & Deblinger, 2006). HC-MC was created in collaboration with tribal leaders, consumers of mental health services, traditional healers, local organizations such as schools and law enforcement, and mental health professionals in a reservation community. The circle is representative of the medicine wheel or other symbolic circles such as the cycle of life, sacred circle, or sacred hoop. Specifically, the HC-MC intervention emphasizes creating balance between the physical, mental, emotional, and spiritual aspects of the self. Adaptations include allowing flexibility for the "trauma narrative" to be told, not only in oral or written form but also, potentially, through a journey stick or traditional dance. In another example, familiar soothing traditional cultural images were used to augment TF-CBT practices such as deep breathing or progressive muscle relaxation. The practice of HC-MC includes assessing the Native child or adolescent in terms of affiliation with traditional beliefs and/or practices and recognizing that, in some cases, an AI/AN child or adolescent may be more comfortable with the original TF-CBT framework than with HC-MC. Although this approach has shown promise for the cultural adaptation of evidence-based treatments for traumatic stress, there have been no efficacy studies to date.

Similarly, BigFoot and Funderburk (2011) reviewed an adaptation of parent–child interaction therapy (PCIT; Eyberg, 1988) for AI/AN families entitled Honoring Children, Making Relatives. In this case, the *Parent Training Manual for American Indian Families* (BigFoot, 1989) was used as the basis for "cultural enhancement" of existing PCIT interventions with Native families. This intervention combines the basic social learning, family systems, and play therapy elements of PCIT with traditional tribal parenting practices and builds on the similarities of the approaches (behaviorally based, relational, and cognizant of developmental milestones). Adaptations to existing evidence-based practices have ensured that the intervention resonates with Native American worldview and philosophy by putting children at the center of the circle of the community and placing the program principles in a culturally familiar context. It can be made additionally responsive to specific tribal communities by integrating the local language, cultural stories, and cultural practices into the program. However, to date, there is no research that has addressed the efficacy of culturally adapted CBT parenting interventions for AI/ANs.

Some programs have sought to adapt mainstream approaches to more universal indigenous concepts such as the medicine wheel. Most AI/AN tribes make some use of the medicine wheel, which represents the unending circle of life, the four sacred directions, and the person or community at the center. Medicine wheel teaching involve a balance between the creator, the natural world, and the physical, mental, emotional and spiritual aspects of the self (Bassett, Tsosie, & Nannauck, 2012; Boyd & Thin Elk, 2008), and imbalances in any of these areas may result in individual or communal "dis-ease" or illness. Treatment approaches using this traditional model contend that culture is the treatment, emphasize local concepts of "wellness" and "healing," and privilege traditional cultural community worldviews relative to harmony and balance for healing (Cross, 1997; Gone & Trimble, 2012). Many of these approaches were grassroots projects originally developed for the treatment of substance abuse but have evolved to general approaches to wellness. For example, the Red Road approach, founded in 1989 by Gene Thin Elk and Rick Thomas, uses Lakota-centered concepts of wellness and healing but resonates for indigenous people everywhere and has been adapted in many communities. Similarly, the Wellbriety movement, founded by Don Coyhis (White Bison, Inc.) in 1988, uses a Native-centered approach to individual and community healing. These approaches have never been empirically evaluated, but for many Native participants, these are good examples of "practice-based evidence."

Treatments for Other Stress-Related Disorders

In reviewing the literature, no adaptations for other stress-related disorders were found that were specific to Native populations. If they exist, there are no data published in scientific journals about cognitive behavioral interventions for the treatment of adjustment disorders or reactive attachment disorders that are tailored for use with AI/AN populations.

Treatments for Stress in Primary Care Settings

Treatments for stress in primary care and other health care settings is a particularly relevant topic for AIs, for whom rates or severity of cardiovascular disease (CVD) and diabetes are greater than for non-Native groups (Sawchuk et al., 2005). Similarly, Huyser and colleagues (2015) noted that stress is a strong risk factor for diabetes amongst Native populations. Promoting health behaviors and disease management are critical outcomes that primary care providers seek through interventions that commonly have stress-reduction components. Some of these are outlined next.

Cardiovascular Disease

Several programs for reducing rates and/or severity of CVD in Native populations integrate elements of a larger intervention program for stress reduction. For example, A New Leaf . . . Choices for Healthy Living is a research-based intervention that seeks to improve a number of health-related outcomes, including diabetes (UNC Center for Health Promotion and Disease Prevention, 2013). One of the modules in this intervention is focuses on managing stress and depression, which Stefanich and colleagues (2005) reported was used in Southcentral Foundation's Traditions of the Heart program, a CVD prevention program for AN women. This program sought to both meet the cultural needs and take advantage of the strengths of a specific

Native group. There are also data from a pilot study for the same program (Witmer, Hensel, Holck, Ammerman, & Will, 2004), which, similarly, had a stress reduction component from the overall intervention. Unfortunately, these studies did not examine the impact of the stress reduction module of the overall intervention package in accounting for outcomes.

Another large intervention program, the Special Diabetes for Indians Healthy Heart Demonstration Project, addressed stress through the promotion of healthy exercise routines (Moore et al., 2014). Stress reduction was also emphasized in this program as a component of encouraging participants to stop smoking. Materials for this program were taken from the National Heart, Lung, and Blood Institute's Honoring the Gift of Heart Health program, a program that targets AI/AN populations for the reduction of CVD (Brega et al., 2013). This program also mentions stress management in the context of promoting exercise and discouraging smoking. The major outcome of this study was greater health literacy, and new programs targeting CVD are beginning to recognize stress reduction as part of health literacy for AI/ANs. Unfortunately, there is no evidence of the effectiveness of psychoeducation to reduce stress in AI/ANs populations.

The Healthy Hearts Across Generations project (Walters et al., 2012) attempted to evaluate a culturally appropriate CVD risk-prevention program for Native parents in the Pacific Northwest. This program used psychological interventions, including motivational interviewing and psychoeducation, to improve blood chemistry, blood pressure, body mass index, food intake, and physical activity outcomes, as measured at 4- and 12-month follow-ups. Although it was not a primary thrust of this program or the measurement of outcomes, stress reduction is mentioned in the programming.

Diabetes

Serious psychological distress is strongly linked to higher body mass index and diabetes (Huyser et al., 2015). Higher levels of stress may be a significant explanatory factor for higher rates of diabetes in AI/AN populations (Jiang, Beals, Whitesell, Roubideaux, Manson, & the AI-SUPERPFP Team, 2008). Namely, racial discrimination, residential segregation, poverty, lifestyle choices, and cultural issues have been enumerated in the literature as explanations of the higher rates of diabetes for AI/ANs (see Tashiro, 2005, for a review) and are all also associated with higher stress in this population. Tiedt and Sloan (2015) explained the phenomenon of higher rates of diabetes for AI/ANs in terms of the physiology of stress and the concept of allostatic load, or cumulative effect of chronic stressors eventually resulting in disease. Thus, the extant research seems to suggest that stress management should be an integral part of managing diabetes.

In another example, teaching stress-reduction skills was an element of the Partners in Care intervention (Sinclair et al., 2013) to address diabetes symptoms in a Native Hawaiian population. This module was part of an overall package of interventions that targeted skills building in other areas, such as health behaviors, diet, and exercise. This program was culturally adapted for Native Hawaiians from existing interventions with other minority groups and made culturally sensitive using focus groups, peer educators, and a steering committee. Positive outcomes from this study included healthier measurements of blood glucose, self-understanding of the disorder, and higher rates of diabetes self-care. However, because this study did not examine independent elements of the intervention, it is not possible to determine to what degree stress reduction contributed to the results.

Dreger, Mackenzie, and McLeod (2015) examined the use of a mindfulness-based intervention to affect Type 2 diabetes in a Native population. As an example of its content, the third session was themed "Air, Breath of Life," teaching breathing awareness and mindful movement practices. Other session themes included awareness, emphasis on other essential elements (i.e., earth, water, and fire), connection, and wholeness. Outcomes for this study included improved control of blood glucose levels and a reduction in blood pressure, as well as better self-rated health and well-being (Ware, Snow, Kosinski, & Gandek, 1993).

In the area of stress-reduction approaches for treating health conditions such as CVD and diabetes in AI/AN populations, not many studies have addressed questions related to the efficacy of these practices. Research might profitably be geared at dismantling studies that can properly address the impact of stress-reduction interventions on health outcomes in Native populations.

Overall, it is clear that research on assessments and interventions for stress-related disorders with AI/AN populations is still in an infancy stage. Culturally adapted assessments for AI/AN stress-related disorders, when they even exist, have not been systematically examined in terms of validity or reliability. There is an assumption that measures, such as those for traumatic stress, are appropriate for use with Native clients, but this assumption has not been properly explored. Interventions for stress-related disorders with Native individuals are also not adequately researched. There are some adapted CBT interventions, but these require more research to validate their utility with Native populations.

FUTURE DIRECTIONS

The broad class of interventions known as CBT has become the standard for modern empirically based practice. Moving forward, models for conceptualizing stress with AI/ANs will have to be more "integrative" (Wickrama,

Lee, O'Neal, & Kwon, 2015), meaning that new models should be developed that acknowledge issues such as historical trauma, ongoing social inequities, and discrimination as factors that contribute to the impact of stress on physical and psychological health outcomes with AI/AN people. In addition, with the rise of integrated care (Torrence et al., 2014), biopsychosocial developmental models incorporating multicultural competence are becoming increasingly important. Seeing that culture-specific assessments can enhance the impact and cultural sensitivity of cognitive behavioral interventions, establishing psychometrically strong and culturally sensitive measures of stress for AI/ANs is a current imperative. This review has established the paucity of research using culturally adapted assessments of stress, traumatic stress, or other stress-related physiological or psychological disorders with AI/AN populations. The current assumption appears to be that assessments used in the mainstream culture also have validity for use with AI/ANs, but this assumption appears unproven at best and contradictory at worst. Studies such as the Yup'ik Experiences of Stress and Coping Project in Alaska (Rivkin et al., 2010) hold much promise for setting out a process for learning to understand specific AI/AN perspectives on stress, its impact on health, and what is needed to lessen that impact. Without knowledge of those perspectives, we will never know whether the constructs we are attempting to measure are relevant or useful to AI/AN people or communities.

The future of cognitive behavioral treatments for stress with AI/ANs may lie in achieving an acceptable blend of CBT with traditional AI/AN healing practices. Blending CBT treatments with AI/AN beliefs and practices is vastly preferable to CBT treatments that feature little adaptation for AI/AN clients because CBT concepts are derived from a completely different cultural context (Nebelkopf et al., 2011). Simply using typical CBT protocols with Native populations has often led to challenges with language, homework compliance, and contrasting beliefs concerning causes of, and solutions for, physical and mental disorders (De Coteau, Anderson, & Hope, 2006).

Although there may be significant differences between the perspectives and practices of Indigenous healing practices and cognitive behavioral interventions (see Gone, 2010, for review), there is rich potential for the integration of Western mental health practices with traditional Indigenous concepts and practices. True integration, however, will require a culturally driven understanding of specific AI/AN community concepts of health, wellness, healing, and balance, in addition to AI/AN perspectives on stress and its impact on health and mental health (Boyd, Niemann, & Bazemore, in press). Moorehead, Gone, and December (2015) examined themes emerging from a series of roundtable discussions between traditional Native healers, clinically trained service providers, and cross-cultural mental health researchers, which included the importance of "relationships to all" (p. 388), the importance of personal qualities such as faith or self-discipline, an emphasis on spirituality, and emphasis on traditional life and culture. This type of dialogue requires trust, patience, and willingness to make meaningful relationships, but the results of such partnership and collaboration can have a powerful impact on the lives of Native people.

This review of the literature on stress and Native people ends on an optimistic note, with the thought that AI/AN culture and "CBT culture" need not be at odds. Many theoretical and practical roots of contemporary cognitive behavioral approaches for treating stress rely on practices such as mindfulness and finding a balance. AI/AN concepts, such as the teachings of the medicine wheel, similarly direct those in search of health to engage in mindfulness and meditative practices that seek to build balance and health in daily living (Coffman, 2013). Developing the common ground between these approaches could have important healing benefits for Native people experiencing the impact of stress.

REFERENCES

Alexander, J. C., Eyerman, R., Giesen, B., Smelser, N. J., & Sztompka, P. (2004). *Cultural trauma and collective identity.* Los Angeles: University of California Press. http://dx.doi.org/10.1525/california/9780520235946.001.0001

American Psychiatric Association. (2013). *Diagnostic and statistical manual of mental disorders* (5th ed.). Arlington, VA: Author.

American Psychological Association. (2011). *Stress: The different kinds of stress.* Retrieved from http://www.apa.org/helpcenter/stress-kinds.aspx

Andrews, G., & Peters, L. (1998). The psychometric properties of the Composite International Diagnostic Interview. *Social Psychiatry and Psychiatric Epidemiology, 33*, 80–88. http://dx.doi.org/10.1007/s001270050026

Balsam, K. F., Huang, B., Fieland, K. C., Simoni, J. M., & Walters, K. L. (2004). Culture, trauma, and wellness: A comparison of heterosexual and lesbian, gay, bisexual, and two-spirit Native Americans. *Cultural Diversity and Ethnic Minority Psychology, 10*, 287–301. http://dx.doi.org/10.1037/1099-9809.10.3.287

Bassett, D., Buchwald, D., & Manson, S. (2014). Posttraumatic stress disorder and symptoms among American Indians and Alaska Natives: A review of the literature. *Social Psychiatry and Psychiatric Epidemiology, 49*, 417–433. http://dx.doi.org/10.1007/s00127-013-0759-y

Bassett, D., Tsosie, U., & Nannauck, S. (2012). "Our culture is medicine": Perspectives of Native healers on posttrauma recovery among American Indian and Alaska Native patients. *The Permanente Journal, 16*, 19–27. http://dx.doi.org/10.7812/TPP/11-123

Bernard, L. C., & Krupat, E. (1994). *Health psychology: Biopsychosocial factors in health and illness.* New York, NY: Harcourt Brace.

BigFoot, D. S. (1989). Parent training for American Indian families. *Dissertation Abstracts International: Section A. Humanities and Social Sciences, 50,* 1562.

BigFoot, D. S., & Funderburk, B. W. (2011). Honoring children, making relatives: The cultural translation of parent–child interaction therapy for American Indian and Alaska Native families. *Journal of Psychoactive Drugs, 43,* 309–318. http://dx.doi.org/10.1080/02791072.2011.628924

BigFoot, D. S., & Schmidt, S. R. (2010). Honoring children, mending the circle: Cultural adaptation of trauma-focused cognitive-behavioral therapy for American Indian and Alaska native children. *Journal of Clinical Psychology, 66,* 847–856. http://dx.doi.org/10.1002/jclp.20707

Blevins, C. A., Weathers, F. W., Davis, M. T., Witte, T. K., & Domino, J. L. (2015). The Posttraumatic Stress Disorder Checklist for *DSM–5* (PCL-5): Development and initial psychometric evaluation. *Journal of Traumatic Stress, 28,* 489–498. http://dx.doi.org/10.1002/jts.22059

Boyd, B., Niemann, Y. F., & Bazemore, C. M. (in press). Mental health intervention with American Indians. In F. T. L. Leong, G. Bernal, & N. Buchanan (Eds.), *Clinical psychology of ethnic minorities: Integrating research and practice.* Washington, DC: American Psychological Association.

Boyd, B., & Thin Elk, G. (2008, August). Indigenous perspectives on healing [Special Section]. *Communique: Psychology and Racism,* 44–46.

Brave Heart, M. Y. H. (1999). Gender differences in the historical trauma response among the Lakota. *Journal of Health & Social Policy, 10*(4), 1–21. http://dx.doi.org/10.1300/J045v10n04_01

Brave Heart, M. Y. H., Chase, J., Elkins, J., & Altschul, D. B. (2011). Historical trauma among Indigenous Peoples of the Americas: Concepts, research, and clinical considerations. *Journal of Psychoactive Drugs, 43,* 282–290. http://dx.doi.org/10.1080/02791072.2011.628913

Brave Heart, M. Y. H., & DeBruyn, L. M. (1998). The American Indian Holocaust: Healing historical unresolved grief. *American Indian and Alaska Native Mental Health Research, 8*(2), 56–78.

Brega, A. G., Pratte, K. A., Jiang, L., Mitchell, C. M., Stotz, S. A., Loudhawk-Hedgepeth, C., . . . Beals, J. (2013). Impact of targeted health promotion on cardiovascular knowledge among American Indians and Alaska Natives. *Health Education Research, 28,* 437–449. http://dx.doi.org/10.1093/her/cyt054

Coffman, S. G. (2013). Cognitive behavioral therapy's mindfulness concepts reflect both Buddhist traditions and Native American medicine. *The Behavior Therapist, 36,* 156–157.

Cohen, J. A., Mannarino, A. P., & Deblinger, E. (2006). *Treating trauma and traumatic grief in children and adolescents.* New York, NY: Guilford Press.

Cohen, S., Janicki-Deverts, D., & Miller, G. E. (2007, October 10). Psychological stress and disease. *JAMA, 298,* 1685–1687. http://dx.doi.org/10.1001/jama.298.14.1685

Cokley, K., McClain, S., Enciso, A., & Martinez, M. (2013). An examination of minority status stress, impostor feelings and mental health among ethnic minority college students. *Journal of Multicultural Counseling and Development, 41*(2), 82–95. http://dx.doi.org/10.1002/j.2161-1912.2013.00029.x

Cross, T. (1997). *Understanding the relational worldview in Indian families*. Retrieved from http://oregon.4h.oregonstate.edu/sites/default/files/information/staff/inclusive/RelationalWorldView.pdf

Csordas, T. J., Storck, M. J., & Strauss, M. (2008). Diagnosis and distress in Navajo healing. *Journal of Nervous and Mental Disease, 196*, 585–596. http://dx.doi.org/10.1097/NMD.0b013e3181812c68

De Coteau, T., Anderson, J., & Hope, D. (2006). Adapting manualized treatments: Treating anxiety disorders among Native Americans. *Cognitive and Behavioral Practice, 13*, 304–309. http://dx.doi.org/10.1016/j.cbpra.2006.04.012

De Coteau, T. J., Hope, D. A., & Anderson, J. (2003). Anxiety, stress, and health in Northern Plains Native Americans. *Behavior Therapy, 34*, 365–380. http://dx.doi.org/10.1016/S0005-7894(03)80006-0

De Ravello, L., Abeita, J., & Brown, P. (2008). Breaking the cycle/mending the hoop: Adverse childhood experiences among incarcerated American Indian/Alaska Native women in New Mexico. *Health Care for Women International, 29*, 300–315. http://dx.doi.org/10.1080/07399330701738366

deVries, M. W. (1996). Trauma in cultural perspective. In B. A. Van der Kolk, A. C. McFarlane, & L. Weisaeth (Eds.), *Traumatic stress: The effects of overwhelming experience on mind, body, and society* (pp. 398–413). New York, NY: Guilford Press.

DiGangi, J., Guffanti, G., McLaughlin, K. A., & Koenen, K. C. (2013). Considering trauma exposure in the context of genetics studies of posttraumatic stress disorder: A systematic review. *Biology of Mood & Anxiety Disorders, 3*, 2. http://dx.doi.org/10.1186/2045-5380-3-2

Dinges, N. G., & Joos, S. K. (1988). Stress, coping, and health: Models of interaction for Indian and Native populations. *American Indian & Alaska Native Mental Health Research, Monograph No 1*, 8–64.

Dohrenwend, B. S. (1978). Social stress and community psychology. *American Journal of Community Psychology, 6*, 1–14. http://dx.doi.org/10.1007/BF00890095

Dohrenwend, B. P., Pearlin, L., Clayton, P., Riley, M., Hamburg, B., Rose, R. M., & Dohrenwend, B. S. (1982). Report on stress and life events. In G. R. Elliot & C. Eisdorfer (Eds.), *Stress and human health: Analysis and implications of research* (pp. 55–80). New York, NY: Springer.

Dougall, A. L., Wroble, B., Minhnoi, C., Swanson, J. N., & Baum, A. (2013). Stress, coping, and immune function. In I. B. Weiner (Ed.), *Handbook of psychology* (2nd ed., pp. 440–460). New York, NY: Wiley.

Dreger, L. C., Mackenzie, C., & McLeod, B. (2015). Feasibility of a mindfulness-based intervention for aboriginal adults with Type 2 diabetes. *Mindfulness, 6*, 264–280. http://dx.doi.org/10.1007/s12671-013-0257-z

Duran, B., Sanders, M., Skipper, B., Waitzkin, H., Malcoe, L. H., Paine, S., & Yager, J. (2004). Prevalence and correlates of mental disorders among Native American women in primary care. *American Journal of Public Health, 94,* 71–77. http://dx.doi.org/10.2105/AJPH.94.1.71

Eyberg, S. (1988). Parent child interaction therapy: Integration of traditional and behavioral concerns. *Child & Family Behavior Therapy, 10,* 33–46. http://dx.doi.org/10.1300/J019v10n01_04

Farrell, A. K., Simpson, J. A., Carlson, E. A., Englund, M. M., & Sung, S. (2017). The impact of stress at different life stages on physical health and the buffering effects of maternal sensitivity. *Health Psychology, 36,* 35–44. http://dx.doi.org/10.1037/hea0000424

Felitti, V. J., Anda, R. F., Nordenberg, D., Williamson, D. F., Spitz, A. M., Edwards, V., . . . Marks, J. S. (1998). Relationship of childhood abuse and household dysfunction to many of the leading causes of death in adults: The Adverse Childhood Experiences (ACE) Study. *American Journal of Preventive Medicine, 14,* 245–258. http://dx.doi.org/10.1016/S0749-3797(98)00017-8

Fleming, C. M., & Lim, R. F. (2015). Issues in the assessment and treatment of American Indian and Alaska Native patients. In R. F. Lim & R. F. Lim (Eds.), *Clinical manual of cultural psychiatry* (2nd ed., pp. 251–285). Arlington, VA: American Psychiatric Publishing.

Foa, E. B., Riggs, D. S., Dancu, C. V., & Rothbaum, B. O. (1993). Reliability and validity of a brief instrument for assessing post-traumatic stress disorder. *Journal of Traumatic Stress, 6,* 459–473. http://dx.doi.org/10.1002/jts.2490060405

French, E. S., & Chavez, N. R. (2010). The relationship of ethnicity related stressors and Latino ethnic identity to well-being. *Hispanic Journal of Behavioral Sciences, 32,* 410–428. http://dx.doi.org/10.1177/0739986310374716

Garrett, M. T., & Pichette, E. F. (2000). Red as an apple: Native American acculturation and counseling with or without reservation. *Journal of Counseling & Development, 78,* 3–13. http://dx.doi.org/10.1002/j.1556-6676.2000.tb02554.x

Glass, M. H., & Bieber, S. L. (1997). The effects of acculturative stress on incarcerated Alaska Native and non-Native men. *Cultural Diversity and Mental Health, 3,* 175–191. http://dx.doi.org/10.1037/1099-9809.3.3.175

Goldston, D. B., Molock, S. D., Whitbeck, L. B., Murakami, J. L., Zayas, L. H., & Hall, G. C. (2008). Cultural considerations in adolescent suicide prevention and psychosocial treatment. *American Psychologist, 63,* 14–31. http://dx.doi.org/10.1037/0003-066X.63.1.14

Gone, J. P. (2010). Psychotherapy and traditional healing for American Indians: Exploring the prospects for therapeutic integration. *The Counseling Psychologist, 38,* 166–235. http://dx.doi.org/10.1177/0011000008330831

Gone, J. P., & Trimble, J. E. (2012). American Indian and Alaska Native mental health: Diverse perspectives on enduring disparities. *Annual Review of Clinical Psychology, 8,* 131–160. http://dx.doi.org/10.1146/annurev-clinpsy-032511-143127

Goodkind, J. R., Gorman, B., Hess, J. M., Parker, D. P., & Hough, R. L. (2015). Reconsidering culturally competent approaches to American Indian healing and well-being. *Qualitative Health Research, 25*, 486–499. http://dx.doi.org/10.1177/1049732314551056

Green, B. L., Lindy, J. D., Grace, M. C., Gleser, G. C., Leonard, A. C., Korol, M., & Winget, C. (1990). Buffalo Creek survivors in the second decade: Stability of stress symptoms. *American Journal of Orthopsychiatry, 60*, 43–54. http://dx.doi.org/10.1037/h0079168

Hobfoll, S. E. (1988). *The ecology of stress.* Washington, DC: Hemisphere.

Holmes, T. H., & Rahe, R. H. (1967). The social readjustment rating scale. *Journal of Psychosomatic Research, 11*, 213–218. http://dx.doi.org/10.1016/0022-3999(67)90010-4

Horowitz, M., Wilner, N., & Alvarez, W. (1979). Impact of Event Scale: A measure of subjective stress. *Psychosomatic Medicine, 41*, 209–218. http://dx.doi.org/10.1097/00006842-197905000-00004

Huyser, K. R., Manson, S. M., Nelson, L. A., Noonan, C., Roubideaux, Y., the Special Diabetes Program, & the Indians Healthy Heart Demonstration Project. (2015). Serious psychological distress and diabetes management among American Indians and Alaska Natives. *Ethnicity & Disease, 25*, 145–151.

Indian Health Service. (2015). *Behavioral health.* Retrieved from http://www.ihs.gov/newsroom/factsheets/behavioralhealth/

Jiang, L., Beals, J., Whitesell, N. R., Roubideaux, Y., Manson, S. M., & the AI-SUPERPFP Team. (2008). Stress burden and diabetes in two American Indian reservation communities. *Diabetes Care, 31*, 427–429. http://dx.doi.org/10.2337/dc07-2044

Juster, R. P., McEwen, B. S., & Lupien, S. J. (2010). Allostatic load biomarkers of chronic stress and impact on health and cognition. *Neuroscience and Biobehavioral Reviews, 35*, 2–16. http://dx.doi.org/10.1016/j.neubiorev.2009.10.002

Kaufman, K. (2015, July 23), Report: Winnebago hospital neglect led to patient death, endangered 9 others. *Sioux City Journal.* Retrieved from http://siouxcityjournal.com/news/report-winnebago-hospital-neglect-led-to-patient-death-endangered-others/article_9b7ba036-3836-5cf0-8bea-50ebecb585e9.html

Kelley, M., & Lowe, J. (2012). The health challenge of stress experienced by Native American adolescents. *Archives of Psychiatric Nursing, 26*, 71–73. http://dx.doi.org/10.1016/j.apnu.2011.10.001

Kelly, L. C. (1990). *Federal Indian policy.* New York, NY: Chelsea House.

Koss, M. P., Yuan, N. P., Dightman, D., Prince, R. J., Polacca, M., Sanderson, B., & Goldman, D. (2003). Adverse childhood exposures and alcohol dependence among seven Native American tribes. *American Journal of Preventive Medicine, 25*, 238–244. http://dx.doi.org/10.1016/S0749-3797(03)00195-8

Krieger, N. (1999). Embodying inequality: A review of concepts, measures, and methods for studying health consequences of discrimination. *Interna-*

tional Journal of Health Services, 29, 295–352. http://dx.doi.org/10.2190/M11W-VWXE-KQM9-G97Q

Lane, D. C., & Simmons, J. (2011). American Indian youth substance abuse: Community-driven interventions. *The Mount Sinai Journal of Medicine*, 78, 362–372. http://dx.doi.org/10.1002/msj.20262

Lazarus, R. S., & Folkman, S. (1984). *Stress, appraisal, and coping.* New York, NY: Springer.

Liberman, D. B., & Frank, J. (1980). Individuals' perceptions of stressful life events: A comparison of Native American, rural, and urban samples using the Social Readjustment Rating Scale. *White Cloud Journal of American Indian/Alaska Native Mental Health*, 1(4), 15–19.

Manson, S. M., Beals, J., Klein, S. A., Croy, C. D., & the AI-SUPERPFP Team. (2005). Social epidemiology of trauma among 2 American Indian reservation populations. *American Journal of Public Health*, 95, 851–859. http://dx.doi.org/10.2105/AJPH.2004.054171

McEwen, B. S. (1998, January 15). Protective and damaging effects of stress mediators. *The New England Journal of Medicine*, 338, 171–179. http://dx.doi.org/10.1056/NEJM199801153380307

McEwen, B. S., & Seeman, T. (1999). Protective and damaging effects of mediators of stress: Elaborating and testing the concepts of allostasis and allostatic load. *Annals of the New York Academy of Sciences*, 896, 30–47. http://dx.doi.org/10.1111/j.1749-6632.1999.tb08103.x

Miller, G. E., Chen, E., & Parker, K. J. (2011). Psychological stress in childhood and susceptibility to the chronic diseases of aging: Moving toward a model of behavioral and biological mechanisms. *Psychological Bulletin*, 137, 959–997. http://dx.doi.org/10.1037/a0024768

Moore, K., Jiang, L., Manson, S. M., Beals, J., Henderson, W., Pratte, K., . . . Roubideaux, Y. (2014). Case management to reduce cardiovascular disease risk in American Indians and Alaska Natives with diabetes: Results from the Special Diabetes Program for Indians Healthy Heart Demonstration Project. *American Journal of Public Health*, 104(11), e158–e164. http://dx.doi.org/10.2105/AJPH.2014.302108

Moorehead, V. D., Jr., Gone, J. P., & December, D. (2015). A gathering of Native American healers: Exploring the interface of Indigenous tradition and professional practice. *American Journal of Community Psychology*, 56, 383–394. http://dx.doi.org/10.1007/s10464-015-9747-6

Morsette, A., Swaney, G., Stolle, D., Schuldberg, D., van den Pol, R., & Young, M. (2009). Cognitive Behavioral Intervention for Trauma in Schools (CBITS): School-based treatment on a rural American Indian reservation. *Journal of Behavior Therapy and Experimental Psychiatry*, 40, 169–178. http://dx.doi.org/10.1016/j.jbtep.2008.07.006

Myers, H. F., & Rodriguez, N. (2003). Acculturation and physical health in racial and ethnic minorities. In K. M. Chun, P. Balls Organista, & G. Marín (Eds.),

Acculturation: Advances in theory, measurement, and applied research (pp. 163–185). Washington, DC: American Psychological Association. http://dx.doi.org/10.1037/10472-011

Nebelkopf, E., King, J., Wright, S., Schweigman, K., Lucero, E., Habte-Michael, T., & Cervantes, T. (2011). Growing roots: Native American evidence-based practices. Introduction. *Journal of Psychoactive Drugs, 43*, 263–268. http://dx.doi.org/10.1080/02791072.2011.628909

Ngo, V., Langley, A., Kataoka, S. H., Nadeem, E., Escudero, P., & Stein, B. D. (2008). Providing evidence-based practice to ethnically diverse youths: Examples from the Cognitive Behavioral Intervention for Trauma in Schools (CBITS) program. *Journal of the American Academy of Child & Adolescent Psychiatry, 47*, 858–862. http://dx.doi.org/10.1097/CHI.0b013e3181799f19

Pearson, C. R., Kaysen, D., Belcourt, A., Stappenbeck, C. A., Zhou, C., Smartlowit-Briggs, L., & Whitefoot, P. (2015). Post-traumatic stress disorder and HIV risk behaviors among rural American Indian/Alaska Native women. *American Indian & Alaska Native Mental Health Research: The Journal of the National Center, 22*(3), 1–20.

Pokhrel, P., & Herzog, T. A. (2014). Historical trauma and substance use among Native Hawaiian college students. *American Journal of Health Behavior, 38*, 420–429. http://dx.doi.org/10.5993/AJHB.38.3.11

Rivkin, I. D., Lopez, E., Quaintance, T. M., Trimble, J., Hopkins, S., Fleming, C., . . . Mohatt, G. V. (2010). Value of community partnership for understanding stress and coping in rural Yup'ik communities: The CANHR Study. *Journal of Health Disparities Research and Practice, 4*(3), 2.

Robin, R. W., Chester, B., Rasmussen, J. K., Jaranson, J. M., & Goldman, D. (1997). Prevalence and characteristics of trauma and posttraumatic stress disorder in a southwestern American Indian community. *The American Journal of Psychiatry, 154*, 1582–1588. http://dx.doi.org/10.1176/ajp.154.11.1582

Santos, M. R., Russo, J., Aisenberg, G., Uehara, E., Ghesquiere, A., & Zatzick, D. F. (2008). Ethnic/racial diversity and posttraumatic distress in the acute care medical setting. *Psychiatry, 71*, 234–245. http://dx.doi.org/10.1521/psyc.2008.71.3.234

Sawchuk, C. N., Roy-Byrne, P., Goldberg, J., Manson, S., Noonan, C., Beals, J., & Buchwald, D. (2005). The relationship between post-traumatic stress disorder, depression and cardiovascular disease in an American Indian tribe. *Psychological Medicine, 35*, 1785–1794. http://dx.doi.org/10.1017/S0033291705005751

Selye, H. (1936). Thymus and adrenals in the response of the organism to injuries and intoxications. *British Journal of Experimental Pathology, 17*, 234–248.

Sharpe, M. (2013). The sorrows of Native Americans. *Challenge, 56*, 98–104. http://dx.doi.org/10.2753/0577-5132560407

Sinclair, K. A., Makahi, E. K., Shea-Solatorio, C., Yoshimura, S. R., Townsend, C. M., & Kaholokula, J. K. (2013). Outcomes from a diabetes self-management intervention for Native Hawaiians and Pacific people: Partners in Care. *Annals of Behavioral Medicine, 45*(1), 24–32.

Stefanich, C. A., Witmer, J. M., Young, B. D., Benson, L. E., Penn, C. A., Ammerman, A. S., . . . Etzel, R. A. (2005). Development, adaptation, and implementation of a cardiovascular health program for Alaska native women. *Health Promotion Practice, 6*, 472–481. http://dx.doi.org/10.1177/1524839904263725

Stephens, K. A., Sue, S., Roy-Byrne, P., Unützer, J., Wang, J., Rivara, F. P., . . . Zatzick, D. F. (2010). Ethnoracial variations in acute PTSD symptoms among hospitalized survivors of traumatic injury. *Journal of Traumatic Stress, 23*, 384–392.

Stolle, D., Schuldberg, D., van den Pol, R., & Morsette, A. (2007, November). *Trauma symptom reduction and academic correlates of violence exposure amongst Native American students, in school-based mental health programs for children exposed to trauma.* Paper presented at the meeting of the International Society for Traumatic Stress Studies, Baltimore, MD.

Suzuki, L. A., Ponterotto, J. G., & Meller, P. J. (Eds.). (2001). *Handbook of multicultural assessment: Clinical, psychological, and educational applications.* New York, NY: Wiley.

Tashiro, C. J. (2005). Health disparities in the context of mixed race: Challenging the ideology of race. *Advances in Nursing Science, 28*, 203–211. http://dx.doi.org/10.1097/00012272-200507000-00003

Tiedt, J. A., & Sloan, R. S. (2015). Perceived unsatisfactory care as a barrier to diabetes self-management for Coeur d'Alene tribal members with Type 2 diabetes. *Journal of Transcultural Nursing, 26*, 287–293. http://dx.doi.org/10.1177/1043659614526249

Torrence, N. D., Mueller, A. E., Ilem, A. A., Renn, B. N., DeSantis, B., & Segal, D. L. (2014). Medical provider attitudes about behavioral health consultants in integrated primary care: A preliminary study. *Families, Systems, & Health, 32*, 426–432. http://dx.doi.org/10.1037/fsh0000078

UNC Center for Health Promotion and Disease Prevention. (2013). *Intervention: A new leaf . . . Choices for healthy living.* Retrieved from http://centertrt.org/content/docs/Intervention_Documents/Intervention_Templates/A_New_Leaf_template.pdf

Verney, S. P., & Kipp, B. J. (2007). Acculturation and alcohol treatment in ethnic minority populations: Assessment issues and implications. *Alcoholism Treatment Quarterly, 25*(4), 47–61. http://dx.doi.org/10.1300/J020v25n04_04

Villada, C., Hidalgo, V., Almela, M., & Salvador, A. (2016). Individual differences in the psychobiological response to psychosocial stress (Trier Social Stress Test): The relevance of trait anxiety and coping styles. *Stress and Health, 32*, 90–99. http://dx.doi.org/10.1002/smi.2582

Walters, K. L., & Evans-Campbell, T. (2004, February). *Measuring historical trauma among urban American Indians.* Paper presented at the University of New Mexico, School of Medicine, Albuquerque, NM.

Walters, K. L., LaMarr, J., Levy, R. L., Pearson, C., Maresca, T., Mohammed, S. A., . . . The Intervention Team. (2012). Healthy hearts across generations: Development and evaluation design of a tribally based cardiovascular disease prevention intervention for American Indian families. *The Journal of Primary Prevention, 33,* 197–207.

Walters, K. L., & Simoni, J. M. (2002). Reconceptualizing native women's health: An "indigenist" stress-coping model. *American Journal of Public Health, 92,* 520–524. http://dx.doi.org/10.2105/AJPH.92.4.520

Walters, K. L., Simoni, J. M., & Evans-Campbell, T. (2002). Substance use among American Indians and Alaska natives: Incorporating culture in an "indigenist" stress-coping paradigm. *Public Health Reports, 117*(Suppl 1), S104–S117.

Ware, J. E., Snow, K. K., Kosinski, M., & Gandek, B. (1993). *SF-36 Health Survey: Manual and interpretation guide.* Boston, MA: The Health Institute, New England Medical Centre.

Weathers, F., Litz, B., Herman, D., Huska, J., & Keane, T. (1993, October). *The PTSD Checklist (PCL): Reliability, validity, and diagnostic utility.* Paper presented at the meeting of the International Society of Traumatic Stress Studies, San Antonio, TX.

Weaver, H. N. (1998). Indigenous people in a multicultural society: Unique issues for human services. *Social Work, 43,* 203–211. http://dx.doi.org/10.1093/sw/43.3.203

Whitbeck, L. B., Adams, G. W., Hoyt, D. R., & Chen, X. (2004). Conceptualizing and measuring historical trauma among American Indian people. *American Journal of Community Psychology, 33*(3-4), 119–130. http://dx.doi.org/10.1023/B:AJCP.0000027000.77357.31

Whitfield, C. L. (1998). Adverse childhood experiences and trauma [Editorial]. *American Journal of Preventive Medicine, 14,* 361–364.

Wickrama, K. K., Lee, T. K., O'Neal, C. W., & Kwon, J. A. (2015). Stress and resource pathways connecting early socioeconomic adversity to young adults' physical health risk. *Journal of Youth and Adolescence, 44,* 1109–1124. http://dx.doi.org/10.1007/s10964-014-0207-7

Witmer, J. M., Hensel, M. R., Holck, P. S., Ammerman, A. S., & Will, J. C. (2004). Heart disease prevention for Alaska Native women: A review of pilot study findings. *Journal of Women's Health, 13,* 569–578. http://dx.doi.org/10.1089/1540999041280981

World Health Organization. (1990). *Composite International Diagnostic Interview (CIDI), version 1.0.* Geneva, Switzerland: Author.

Zimiles, E. (2013). Suicide and soul wound: Stress, coping, and culture in the American Indian and Alaska Native youth context. *Columbia University Academic Commons, 4.* Retrieved from https://cswr.columbia.edu/article/suicide-and-soul-wound-stress-coping-and-culture-in-the-american-indian-youth-context/

IV

WHERE WE ARE AND WHAT WE NEED TO DO

13

DEVELOPING AN INCLUSIVE PATH FOR APPLYING COGNITIVE BEHAVIORAL MODELS, MEASURES, AND TREATMENTS TO EVERYONE

CHRISTINA A. DOWNEY, EDWARD C. CHANG,
JAMESON K. HIRSCH, AND ELIZABETH A. YU

On November 8, 2016, real estate developer and international businessman Donald J. Trump was elected president of the United States. Despite a personal history and electoral campaign littered with controversy, Mr. Trump amassed enough votes to achieve an Electoral College path to the White House (Flegenheimer & Barbaro, 2016). It is not an overstatement to describe this outcome as completely unexpected among members of the media, the political class, the academic sector, and the public (Hirsch et al., 2017). As the country prepared to inaugurate the 45th president, a self-described grandmother from Hawaii told her friends via social media that she planned to march on Washington, DC, the day after Inauguration Day in protest of a president she perceived as racist, misogynist, xenophobic, and dangerous to the fabric of American society (Riley, 2017). In a powerful social movement, millions of people around the world joined what became the Women's March on Washington, with total participation estimates

http://dx.doi.org/10.1037/0000091-014
Treating Depression, Anxiety, and Stress in Ethnic and Racial Groups: Cognitive Behavioral Approaches,
E. C. Chang, C. A. Downey, J. K. Hirsch, and E. A. Yu (Editors)

placing this protest among the largest single acts of civil demonstration in U.S. history—and perhaps in the recorded history of the world (Hartocollis & Alcindor, 2017).

Chief among the many themes that were expressed in the Women's March was the concept of *intersectionality*. Because of the wide range of progressive policies the new president had promised to rapidly overturn, the march brought together supporters of many until-then separate movements, such as the anti–police violence group Black Lives Matter, the National Organization for Women, groups concerned about wealth inequality such as Occupy Wall Street, supporters of the rights of immigrants and the undocumented such as Latino USA, supporters of LGBTQ rights and protections, environmental and anti–fossil fuel activists, and citizens concerned about the Affordable Care Act and health care policy generally (Hess, 2017). In doing so, important leading voices expounded on the ways in which individuals whose identities include multiple vectors of disempowerment (e.g., to be Black and gay, to be female and undocumented, to be a racial minority and in poverty) have an American experience that is drastically different from those with wealth, privilege, and power (such as Mr. Trump himself). To change society, the protesters were saying, we must recognize how intersectionality exacerbates the impacts of inequality (Garran & Werkmeister Rozas, 2013; Sen, Iyer, & Mukherjee, 2009) and how societal change would not be sustainable until each disparate group recognized how intertwined their concerns were.

That same theme and concern play out in individual American lives, as well as in mental health. While scholars and pundits are examining a rapidly changing political landscape associated with the new presidency, mental health researchers and practitioners with interests in culturally competent services are trying to discern how these changes will play out in the research laboratory and therapy room. As well, researchers are generating new questions about whether contemporary intuitions about intersectionality align with scientific findings on mental health. Given the findings and statements of the contributors to this volume, we anticipate many challenges ahead.

Although our contributors elaborated on different racial and ethnic groups and different mental health issues, a number of central ideas undergirded their collective discussion. This volume focused on cognitive behavioral approaches in particular. However, what seemed more important to our authors than the specific theory or modality was their wish to see the mental health establishment fully recognize how one's racial or ethnic identity—as defined by the individual in all his or her complexity—is a real and powerful factor in one's ability to live a fulfilling life in American society. Accordingly, we note these recurrent ways in which specific topics interact with one another to fundamentally shape conceptualization, measurement, and treatment of mental health in diverse groups:

- The interaction of culture with context: Acculturation, language, cultural history, historical trauma, discrimination, self-construal, stigma, and the like all affect the expression of depression, anxiety, and stress within proximal and distal contexts. They are not factors independent of context but are activated more or less under various circumstances. Understanding how to meaningfully measure those factors, within the framework of the surrounding circumstances within which we believe they operate, is necessary to the improvement of health outcomes in marginalized groups.
- The interaction of race and ethnicity (in its complexity) with social class: Access to treatment, particularly culturally sensitive treatment, is a great challenge for the populations covered in our volume, and this is a component of the larger social issue of class disadvantage. Race and ethnicity and class disadvantage compound one another to perpetuate mental health and social challenges for these groups.
- The fundamental relations between culturally driven conceptualizations of mental disorders and cognitive behavioral research, assessment, diagnosis, and treatment: Assumptions underlying cognitive behavior therapy (CBT) may or may not correspond to concepts of depression, anxiety, and stress in diverse groups, raising a barrier to complete and comprehensive understanding of these conditions and how to ameliorate them.

In this concluding chapter, we review the literature on each of these themes and make recommendations about how to make mental health care generally, and CBT in particular, more accessible and effective for diverse groups.

THE INTERACTION OF CULTURE WITH CONTEXT

Culture, when considered as a macro-level phenomenon, is believed to be an overarching social and historical context within which individuals operate. However, culture at the micro level is thought to be carried and expressed by individuals in their beliefs, customs, and teaching. Thus, culture is said to be dynamic and interactive and manifests as individual perceptions and practices collide with broader norms and understanding set by histories of power, influence, and oppression (Canino & Alegría, 2008;

Guarnaccia & Rodriguez, 1996; López & Guarnaccia, 2000; Sotero, 2006; Whaley & Davis, 2007). It is also thought to be pervasive, influencing the reaches of human experience, including mental health, at a profound and unavoidable level (Anderson, 2013; Bernal, Jiménez-Chafey, & Domenech Rodríguez, 2009; Canino & Alegría, 2008; Hernandez, Nesman, Mowery, Acevedo-Polakovich, & Callejas, 2009; Mossakowski, 2003; Sawyer, Major, Casad, Townsend, & Mendes, 2012; Sotero, 2006; Whaley & Davis, 2007).

Although definitions of culture such as these are commonplace in the academic literature, it should be acknowledged that they have been criticized as imprecise and perhaps impossible to measure (Barry, Elliott, & Evans, 2000; Koneru, Weisman de Mamani, Flynn, & Betancourt, 2007). This can be problematic when concepts such as cultural values and acculturation are raised as empirically related to the health of diverse group members. Even more problematic is how assumed characteristics of various cultures are frequently offered as explanatory factors when different health outcomes are discovered in research; however, those cultural characteristics are rarely themselves based on objective empirical measurement, perhaps reflecting unquestioned stereotypes about perceived cultural groups (Hunt, Schneider, & Comer, 2004). Accordingly, a number of researchers have worried about issues of inconsistency in measurement of concepts such as acculturation (Barry et al., 2000; Escobar, Nervi, & Gara, 2000; Koneru et al., 2007; Lara, Gamboa, Kahramanian, Morales, & Hayes Bautista, 2005; Salant & Lauderdale, 2003), discrimination (Anderson, 2013; Araújo & Borrell, 2006; Araújo Dawson, 2009; Gaylord-Harden & Cunningham, 2009; Mossakowski, 2003; Sawyer et al., 2012; Williams, Neighbors, & Jackson, 2003), and historical trauma (Evans-Campbell, 2008; Mohatt, Thompson, Thai, & Tebes, 2014; Sotero, 2006) and the subsequent consequences for our understanding of how culture and health may be related.

Still, authors stressed in this volume how the individual expression of one's cultural background and values interacts with the proximate social environment to drive the perceptions, beliefs, emotions, and behaviors that CBT seeks to explore and (where appropriate) adjust (Bernal et al., 2009). The concept of discrimination and its relation to poorer mental health demonstrates this assertion well (Araújo & Borrell, 2006; Smedley, 2012; Wei, Heppner, Ku, & Liao, 2010; Williams et al., 2003). *Everyday discrimination* is one such type of discrimination, subsuming a number of social experiences that reflect personal judgments of mistreatment by others. For example, "being treated with less courtesy than others" (Mossakowski, 2003, p. 320) or "being ignored or not receiv[ing] a service in a restaurant" (Araújo Dawson, 2009, p. 101) have been assessed as indicators of such discrimination. On reflection, it is clear that judgments of such experiences would be influenced by "internal" variables such as one's culturally driven understanding of what "courtesy" is and how individually sensitive one is to discerning degrees of difference in courtesy between the self and others, as well as by "external" variables such as how often one is treated differently in one's particular social environment.

Those external experiences of discriminatory events have also been examined in relation to health (e.g., "being unfairly fired or denied a promotion"; Araújo Dawson, 2009, p. 101), but again a certain amount of interpretation (related to one's expectations) would apply to each situation and, as well, one's expectations are significantly influenced by one's social geographic context. Should a study (or a measurement or an intervention) ignore differences in social environment by state, region, or neighborhood, conclusions about what members of a particular cultural group experience within the United States will likely be flawed or at least less powerful and applicable to interventions. Anderson (2013), for example, analyzed a large dataset to examine the relationships between perceived racism and health and found that racial minority status was uniquely related to poorer health. However, despite data coming from states as diverse as Arkansas, Colorado, Delaware, Mississippi, Rhode Island, South Carolina, Wisconsin, and the District of Columbia, no indicators of geographic location were entered into analyses as independent variables. Had geographic indicators been controlled for, her conclusion that racial minority status predicts poor health would likely have been even stronger and hard to discount. Clinically, it is also imperative to take the immediate context into careful account when making decisions about cognitions or behaviors to target for intervention. Beliefs about unfair treatment may be perfectly rational in some environments but less rational in others.

Another crucial aspect of context is time. In a contemporary example of the impact of time, reconsider the 2016 election: On November 7, 2016, anxiety about race relations in the United States was higher than it had been a year prior, and by the time the presidential race was called during the wee hours of November 9, 2016, reactions of shock and even horror about what a Trump presidency would mean for race relations (among other issues) suddenly spiked in many communities. Diverse racial and ethnic communities are well aware of the impact of time on their well-being, from the ways in which local, national, and global events can trigger shifts in their life experience to the "long view" of historical trauma (Brave Heart, Chase, Elkins, & Altschul, 2011; Brave Heart & DeBruyn, 1998; Evans-Campbell, 2008; Sotero, 2006; Walters & Simoni, 2002). *Historical trauma* is conceptualized as "cumulative emotional and psychological wounding across generations, including the lifespan, which emanates from massive group trauma" (Brave Heart et al., 2011, p. 283). In addition, historical trauma has been described as a present, public narrative about how past victimization and oppression have caused current distress, meaning that members of certain social groups propagate continuously developing perceptions of significant historical events and their relations to the present (Mohatt et al., 2014). Our authors made the argument that understandings of such collective historical experiences result in distinct reactions to events in their social environment, with members of traumatized minority groups tending to show more distress than members of the non-traumatized majority would.

If a clinician fails to appreciate the significance of this factor in individual and collective mental health, that distress might be pathologized and stigmatized (Evans-Campbell, 2008; Walters & Simoni, 2002; Wilkins, Whiting, Watson, Russon, & Moncrief, 2013) rather than tended to as an authentic trauma response in need of clinical care. Further complicating the picture for historically oppressed communities and cultures is the possibility that the concept of historical trauma itself will come to be taken as an indication of weakness among oppressed group members and thus become grounds for increased discrimination (Fast & Collin-Vézina, 2010), as has been reported for posttraumatic stress disorder. This is one example of how the present should not be assumed to be kinder than the past; the increased medicalization of mental health has led to stigmatizing medical labeling of the trauma response that may well not have occurred in the past (Jackson, 2002). Therefore, it is incumbent on researchers and practitioners of CBT to proceed with great sensitivity regarding this issue.

Developing sensitivity to issues of time, place, and cultural background in mental health practice is within the realm of what is called *culturally competent* practice. A comprehensive review of the concept of cultural competence concluded that it is best thought of as a fit—indeed, a "compatibility" (p. 1047)—between the mental health services and supports available to a particular group and the multileveled, multifaceted community context within which those services are delivered and used (Hernandez et al., 2009). One simple instance of such fit is language: For example, Sentell, Shumway, and Snowden (2007) found that English-speaking individuals with mental health conditions seeking services in the United States were more than 6 times as likely to obtain those services than were non-English speakers. These authors noted that this finding was, in part, driven by lessened willingness on the part of non-White individuals to seek mental health care (also described by researchers such as Shea & Yeh, 2008, and Woodward, Dwinell, & Arons, 1992)—thus, an interaction between the individual and contextual factors.

However, the ability to speak the language of another cultural group is not sufficient to overcome all cultural barriers between practitioners and clients; true cultural familiarity is another matter entirely (Paone & Malott, 2008). A more profound approach to cultural competence in mental health might involve educating racial and ethnic minority clients to embrace neglected, forgotten, or stolen aspects of their cultural experience as a means of promoting resilience against discrimination and recovery from personal and historical trauma (Brave Heart & DeBruyn, 1998; Gone, 2013; Wilkins et al., 2013). This kind of intervention can not only change the individual's beliefs, emotions, and behaviors but can also improve the well-being of the surrounding community as greater numbers of residents share and celebrate treasured aspects of their heritage. As more members of historically and presently disadvantaged communities come together in shared narratives about their strengths and challenges, the likelihood of any single member's cognitions and behaviors being seen as "irrational" or "pathological" is likely to decrease.

THE INTERACTION OF RACE AND ETHNICITY WITH SOCIAL CLASS

Our authors clearly believe that health outcomes differ along multiple demographic and social vectors simultaneously—that is, outcomes manifest the concept of intersectionality (Bowleg, 2012; Constantine, 2002; Hulko, 2009; Rosenfield, 2012; Seng, Lopez, Sperlich, Hamama, & Reed Meldrum, 2012). Although this concept has contributed meaningfully to the theoretical and empirical literature on social identity and social justice since its major appearance in the mid-1990s (Mahalingam, Balan, & Haritatos, 2008), the empirical research literature on this concept is still in its relatively early stages (Bowleg, 2012; Sen et al., 2009). Still, clinicians are beginning to discuss how membership in multiple social groups affects the experiences of clients and how these various social identities can and should be taken into account during one's clinical work (Constantine, 2002; Harley, Jolivette, McCormick, & Tice, 2002; Morrow & Weisser, 2012). Indeed, the concept of cultural competence has arisen in relation to intersectionality, with some arguing that current notions of competence are incomplete if intersectionality is overlooked (Garran & Werkmeister Rozas, 2013). Others have gone further in contending that counseling and other helping professions have actually been complicit in creating and promoting certain unipolar stereotypes (e.g., of race, gender, or class alone), leaving these professions ill prepared for the reality of how intersectionality plays out in mental health care (Harley et al., 2002; Morrow & Weisser, 2012).

The particular dimensions our authors mentioned most frequently in relation to inequitable mental health outcomes were race and ethnicity, crossed with social class (aka socioeconomic status [SES]). It is important to appreciate that scholars in this area urge us not to interpret racial/ethnic and social class health disparities as only resulting from individual-level miscommunication, stereotyping, or discrimination. Instead, they argue that fundamental structural realities, including structural stigma, affect trust, access, and empowerment of minority group members and contribute a detrimental role in bringing about poorer health outcomes (Bowleg, 2012; Morrow & Weisser, 2012). Too much focus on the interpersonal aspects of living as a minority group member in the United States can lead to a disregard for that deeper reality (Hulko, 2009; Morrow & Weisser, 2012; Smedley, 2012). As Mossakowski (2008) noted, "SES is essential for understanding mental health disparities because it structures unequal access to resources for health, such as knowledge, power, prestige, money, material assets, lifestyle, and social networks" (p. 650).

Kessler and Neighbors (1986) were among the first to demonstrate empirically that the effects of race and social class on mental health were multiplicative rather than additive. They found that differences between Whites and Blacks in depression were much greater at low incomes than at high incomes (with low-income Blacks showing significantly more distress than low-income Whites). Later studies found that low educational level interacted with race and ethnicity in predicting externalizing symptoms (with less-educated racial and ethnic minority group members showing particularly high levels of these symptoms; Rosenfield, 2012). Also, disadvantaged family background (by family wealth and race or ethnicity) and present wealth have been found to predict depressive symptoms beyond the impact of race and ethnicity alone; however, significant interactions between race/ethnicity and SES have not been found in all studies (Mossakowski, 2008). Some studies have even found that members of racial minority groups may be at lessened risk of psychological disorders such as depression and anxiety when SES is controlled (Rosenfield, 2012; Samaan, 2000). Such studies have the potential to reveal strengths and vulnerabilities in racial and ethnic minority populations, both of which are relevant to sound delivery of CBT.

Again, CBT is, at its base, a model of mental health practice that is dedicated to uncovering and articulating the irrational perceptions, thoughts, and behaviors that characterize and maintain psychopathology. Social disadvantage due to race/ethnicity and class status are, in fact, real and pernicious, intractable things (Morrow & Weisser, 2012; Smedley, 2012), so what is to be done with and for the client who perceives and responds to them? A first step, our authors have argued, would be to validate the client's perspectives and experiences and to refuse to discount them as "making excuses" or "playing the race, ethnicity, or class card." Then, the clinician has to help clients recognize their strengths and resources that have contributed to their enduring struggle for growth in the face of daunting social odds. Finally, the clinician must make a meaningful, tangible commitment to changing the structural factors that maintain mental health disparities. Social justice and advocacy are essential work for the CBT clinician who chooses to serve racial/ethnic and class minority clients; failing to do so is akin to a physician who treats dozens of patients experiencing the same debilitating ailment but never investigates or tries to contain the pathogen that causes the disease.

THE INTERACTION OF CULTURE WITH COGNITIVE BEHAVIORAL CONCEPTUALIZATIONS OF MENTAL HEALTH

It is taken as fact that culture influences the conceptual framework that constructs our individual and collective understandings of mental health (Carpenter-Song et al., 2010; Cheung & Park, 2010; Draguns & Tanaka-Matsumi, 2003; Kleinman, 1977; Leong, Kim, & Gupta, 2011; López & Guarnaccia, 2000; López & Núñez, 1987; Rathod & Kingdon, 2009; Sheikh & Furnham, 2000), though empirical examination of its specific impact on mental distress is methodologically challenging (Canino & Alegría, 2008; Kohrt et al., 2014). Still, our authors repeatedly referenced their confidence in the importance of culture in their discussions of cognitive behavioral theory, assessment, and therapy among racial and ethnic minority group members. CBT, taking as its main premise the idea that behavior is driven by rational, analytical thought and having been associated most closely with White and WEIRD (Western, educated, industrialized, rich, and democratic) culture (Henrich, Heine, & Norenzayan, 2010; Rathod & Kingdon, 2009), invariably raises questions about how aptly it can be applied to diverse racial and ethnic groups within the United States. At one level, CBT's focus on cognitions over (for example) somatic symptoms as indicative of mental health problems may reduce CBT's applicability to diverse groups. At another level, however, it could be that a given culture simply endorses a different set of cognitions as being characteristic of a mental disorder (Chen & Mak, 2008; Leong et al., 2011; Rathod & Kingdon, 2009), and CBT as typically practiced may fail to accommodate to those cognitive differences.

Draguns and Tanaka-Matsumi (2003) described vividly how culture affects the practitioner's challenges in carrying out various clinical activities:

> The more a person's cultural background is unfamiliar and baffling, the more difficult it is to experience empathically . . . [and then] stereotypes tend to be invoked. As a result . . . overlap between groups is disregarded, and the complexities of trait distribution within a group are overlooked. (p. 760)

If the CBT clinician—who him- or herself also tends to be White and WEIRD—encounters a client who is challenging to empathize with because of their nonconformity to the assumption that rationality should be the principal guide for behavior, the fallback position may indeed be stereotyping or even pathologizing of the ways of the other. Unfamiliar factors such as loss of face (Leong et al., 2011), collectivist self-construal (Markus & Kitayama, 1991), the immigration experience (López & Guarnaccia, 2000), unconsciously held assumptions about the fundamental causes of mental illness (Chen & Mak, 2008), or any number of others may contribute to mental distress in ways that majority group CBT clinicians or researchers might fail to understand. This might then contribute to both diminished comprehension of, and stunted empathy for, the client at hand.

Relatedly but in another vein, members of certain cultures may not expect clinician empathy in the treatment process (CBT or otherwise). Rather, they might view the clinician as a professional guide and authority on mental health matters, whose role it is to direct the client to appropriate, health-promoting action (Rathod & Kingdon, 2009). Alternatively, their cultural and personal history might lead to views of any clinician (White or non-White) as an agent of the White cultural power structure that is not to be trusted in the first place (Carpenter-Song et al., 2010; Schnittker, Freese, & Powell, 2000). Therefore, CBT clinicians may miss opportunities to positively influence the behavior of certain clients if they fail to appreciate these cultural values and beliefs. Indeed, the clinician might unintentionally harm clients should any deep beliefs about the bad intentions of the mental health establishment go unrecognized.

It has been persuasively argued in this volume and elsewhere that the values of cultural competence in mental health practice and of commitment to discovery and adherence to empirically supported treatment modalities for mental disorders must be simultaneously upheld (Canino & Alegría, 2008; Lakes, López, & Garro, 2006; Whaley & Davis, 2007). Therefore, it is important that we both increase our empirical understanding of how culture drives cognitive behavioral conceptualizations of mental health and improve our ability to customize cognitive behavioral treatments to accord better with diverse cultures while remaining empirically sound. Some authors have described specific recommendations for how to do this. For example, Lakes et al. (2006) presented a case involving a family treatment in which the therapist intentionally explored cultural meanings of various beliefs, feelings, and behaviors with family members, incorporating the clients' concepts into the process of the treatment itself. Though the case did not exclusively use CBT in the family treatment, this particular technique would be an excellent candidate for both application in CBT practice and also for empirical testing (e.g., in an experimental design comparing its use with CBT without its integration). CBT has a good track record of other such customization already (Bernal et al., 2009; Naeem, Ayub, Gobi, & Kingdon, 2009; Whaley & Davis, 2007), so continued exploration in this area can be expected to bear clinical and empirical fruit.

CONCLUSION

For many of us whose personal and professional mission is to bear witness to and help improve the well-being of people from all sectors of the cultural landscape, experiencing the political and social change that has come with the 2016 presidential election has been profoundly worrisome and challenging. However, many of us take our hope from the renewed conversations and commitment to progress that has emerged in the public sphere since November 2016. Suddenly members of the public are advocating strongly for science, for the social safety net, and for everyday tolerance and humanity in ways that have not been evident in decades. It reminds us that our values must be preciously guarded and shared widely and that we cannot assume that certain kinds of setbacks are in the long-ago past. It is our belief that by continuing to learn from the experiences of those who have always known oppression and challenge on this continent and globally, we can all grow in our determination, resilience, and solidarity—but now, we have an opportunity to do that while crossing traditional cultural lines and building new intersectional coalitions. The researchers and clinicians gathered in this volume and beyond are key foot soldiers in that fight, and for that we are grateful.

REFERENCES

Anderson, K. F. (2013). Diagnosing discrimination: Stress from perceived racism and the mental and physical health effects. *Sociological Inquiry, 83,* 55–81. http://dx.doi.org/10.1111/j.1475-682X.2012.00433.x

Araújo, B. Y., & Borrell, L. N. (2006). Understanding the link between discrimination, mental health outcomes, and life chances among Latinos. *Hispanic Journal of Behavioral Sciences, 28,* 245–266. http://dx.doi.org/10.1177/0739986305285825

Araújo Dawson, B. (2009). Discrimination, stress, and acculturation among Dominican immigrant women. *Hispanic Journal of Behavioral Sciences, 31,* 96–111. http://dx.doi.org/10.1177/0739986308327502

Barry, D., Elliott, R., & Evans, E. M. (2000). Foreigners in a strange land: Self-construal and ethnic identity in male Arabic immigrants. *Journal of Immigrant Health, 2,* 133–144. http://dx.doi.org/10.1023/A:1009508919598

Bernal, G., Jiménez-Chafey, M. I., & Domenech Rodríguez, M. M. (2009). Cultural adaptation of treatments: A resource for considering culture in evidence-based practice. *Professional Psychology: Research and Practice, 40,* 361–368. http://dx.doi.org/10.1037/a0016401

Bowleg, L. (2012). The problem with the phrase *women and minorities:* Intersectionality—An important theoretical framework for public health. *American Journal of Public Health, 102,* 1267–1273. http://dx.doi.org/10.2105/AJPH.2012.300750

Brave Heart, M. Y. H., Chase, J., Elkins, J., & Altschul, D. B. (2011). Historical trauma among Indigenous Peoples of the Americas: Concepts, research, and clinical considerations. *Journal of Psychoactive Drugs*, *43*, 282–290. http://dx.doi.org/10.1080/02791072.2011.628913

Brave Heart, M. Y. H., & DeBruyn, L. M. (1998). The American Indian Holocaust: Healing historical unresolved grief. *American Indian and Alaska Native Mental Health Research*, 8, 56–78.

Canino, G., & Alegría, M. (2008). Psychiatric diagnosis—Is it universal or relative to culture? *Journal of Child Psychology and Psychiatry*, *49*, 237–250. http://dx.doi.org/10.1111/j.1469-7610.2007.01854.x

Carpenter-Song, E., Chu, E., Drake, R. E., Ritsema, M., Smith, B., & Alverson, H. (2010). Ethno-cultural variations in the experience and meaning of mental illness and treatment: Implications for access and utilization. *Transcultural Psychiatry*, *47*, 224–251. http://dx.doi.org/10.1177/1363461510368906

Chen, S. X., & Mak, W. W. (2008). Seeking professional help: Etiology beliefs about mental illness across cultures. *Journal of Counseling Psychology*, *55*, 442–450. http://dx.doi.org/10.1037/a0012898

Cheung, R. Y., & Park, I. J. (2010). Anger suppression, interdependent self-construal, and depression among Asian American and European American college students. *Cultural Diversity and Ethnic Minority Psychology*, *16*, 517–525. http://dx.doi.org/10.1037/a0020655

Constantine, M. G. (2002). The intersection of race, ethnicity, gender, and social class in counseling: Examining selves in cultural contexts. *Journal of Multicultural Counseling and Development*, *30*, 210–215. http://dx.doi.org/10.1002/j.2161-1912.2002.tb00520.x

Draguns, J. G., & Tanaka-Matsumi, J. (2003). Assessment of psychopathology across and within cultures: Issues and findings. *Behaviour Research and Therapy*, *41*, 755–776. http://dx.doi.org/10.1016/S0005-7967(02)00190-0

Escobar, J. I., Nervi, C. H., & Gara, M. A. (2000). Immigration and mental health: Mexican Americans in the United States. *Harvard Review of Psychiatry*, 8, 64–72. http://dx.doi.org/10.1080/hrp_8.2.64

Evans-Campbell, T. (2008). Historical trauma in American Indian/Native Alaska communities: A multilevel framework for exploring impacts on individuals, families, and communities. *Journal of Interpersonal Violence*, *23*, 316–338. http://dx.doi.org/10.1177/0886260507312290

Fast, E., & Collin-Vézina, D. (2010). Historical trauma, race-based trauma and resilience of indigenous peoples: A literature review. *First Peoples Child & Family Review*, 5, 126–136.

Flegenheimer, M., & Barbaro, M. (2016, November 9). Donald Trump is elected President in stunning repudiation of the establishment. *The New York Times*. Retrieved from https://www.nytimes.com/2016/11/09/us/politics/hillary-clinton-donald-trump-president.html

Garran, A. M., & Werkmeister Rozas, L. (2013). Cultural competence revisited. *Journal of Ethnic and Cultural Diversity in Social Work, 22,* 97–111. http://dx.doi.org/10.1080/15313204.2013.785337

Gaylord-Harden, N. K., & Cunningham, J. A. (2009). The impact of racial discrimination and coping strategies on internalizing symptoms in African American youth. *Journal of Youth and Adolescence, 38,* 532–543. http://dx.doi.org/10.1007/s10964-008-9377-5

Gone, J. P. (2013). Redressing First Nations historical trauma: Theorizing mechanisms for indigenous culture as mental health treatment. *Transcultural Psychiatry, 50,* 683–706. http://dx.doi.org/10.1177/1363461513487669

Guarnaccia, P. J., & Rodriguez, O. (1996). Concepts of culture and their role in the development of culturally competent mental health services. *Hispanic Journal of Behavioral Sciences, 18,* 419–443. http://dx.doi.org/10.1177/07399863960184001

Harley, D. A., Jolivette, K., McCormick, K., & Tice, K. (2002). Race, class, and gender: A constellation of positionalities with implications for counseling. *Journal of Multicultural Counseling and Development, 30,* 216–238. http://dx.doi.org/10.1002/j.2161-1912.2002.tb00521.x

Hartocollis, A., & Alcindor, Y. (2017, January 21). Women's March highlights as huge crowd protest Trump: 'We're not going away'. *The New York Times.* Retrieved from https://www.nytimes.com/2017/01/21/us/womens-march.html

Henrich, J., Heine, S. J., & Norenzayan, A. (2010, July 1). Most people are not WEIRD. *Nature, 466,* 29. http://dx.doi.org/10.1038/466029a

Hernandez, M., Nesman, T., Mowery, D., Acevedo-Polakovich, I. D., & Callejas, L. M. (2009). Cultural competence: A literature review and conceptual model for mental health services. *Psychiatric Services, 60,* 1046–1050. http://dx.doi.org/10.1176/ps.2009.60.8.1046

Hess, A. (2017, February 7). How a fractious women's movement came to lead the left. *The New York Times.* Retrieved from https://www.nytimes.com/2017/02/07/magazine/how-a-fractious-womens-movement-came-to-lead-the-left.html

Hirsch, J. K., Kaniuka, A., Brooks, B., Hirsch, K. K., Cohn, T. J., & Williams, S. L. (2017, March). Postelection distress and resiliency in LGBTQ communities. *APA Division 44 Newsletter.* Retrieved from http://www.apadivisions.org/division-44/publications/newsletters/division/2017/03/index.aspx

Hulko, W. (2009). The time- and context-contingent nature of intersectionality and interlocking oppressions. *Affilia, 24,* 44–55. http://dx.doi.org/10.1177/0886109908326814

Hunt, L. M., Schneider, S., & Comer, B. (2004). Should "acculturation" be a variable in health research? A critical review of research on US Hispanics. *Social Science & Medicine, 59,* 973–986. http://dx.doi.org/10.1016/j.socscimed.2003.12.009

Jackson, V. (2002). In our own voice: African-American stories of oppression, survival and recovery in mental health systems. *International Journal of Narrative Therapy & Community Work, 2,* 11–31.

Kessler, R. C., & Neighbors, H. W. (1986). A new perspective on the relationships among race, social class, and psychological distress. *Journal of Health and Social Behavior, 27*, 107–115. http://dx.doi.org/10.2307/2136310

Kleinman, A. M. (1977). Depression, somatization and the "new cross-cultural psychiatry." *Social Science & Medicine, 11*, 3–9. http://dx.doi.org/10.1016/0037-7856(77)90138-X

Kohrt, B. A., Rasmussen, A., Kaiser, B. N., Haroz, E. E., Maharjan, S. M., Mutamba, B. B., . . . Hinton, D. E. (2014). Cultural concepts of distress and psychiatric disorders: Literature review and research recommendations for global mental health epidemiology. *International Journal of Epidemiology, 43*, 365–406. http://dx.doi.org/10.1093/ije/dyt227

Koneru, V. K., Weisman de Mamani, A. G., Flynn, P. M., & Betancourt, H. (2007). Acculturation and mental health: Current findings and recommendations for future research. *Applied & Preventive Psychology, 12*, 76–96. http://dx.doi.org/10.1016/j.appsy.2007.07.016

Lakes, K., López, S. R., & Garro, L. C. (2006). Cultural competence and psychotherapy: Applying anthropologically informed conceptions of culture. *Psychotherapy: Theory, Research, Practice, Training, 43*, 380–396. http://dx.doi.org/10.1037/0033-3204.43.4.380

Lara, M., Gamboa, C., Kahramanian, M. I., Morales, L. S., & Hayes Bautista, D. E. (2005). Acculturation and Latino health in the United States: A review of the literature and its sociopolitical context. *Annual Review of Public Health, 26*, 367–397. http://dx.doi.org/10.1146/annurev.publhealth.26.021304.144615

Leong, F. T., Kim, H. H., & Gupta, A. (2011). Attitudes toward professional counseling among Asian-American college students: Acculturation, conceptions of mental illness, and loss of face. *Asian American Journal of Psychology, 2*, 140–153. http://dx.doi.org/10.1037/a0024172

López, S., & Núñez, J. A. (1987). Cultural factors considered in selected diagnostic criteria and interview schedules. *Journal of Abnormal Psychology, 96*, 270–272. http://dx.doi.org/10.1037/0021-843X.96.3.270

López, S. R., & Guarnaccia, P. J. (2000). Cultural psychopathology: Uncovering the social world of mental illness. *Annual Review of Psychology, 51*, 571–598. http://dx.doi.org/10.1146/annurev.psych.51.1.571

Mahalingam, R., Balan, S., & Haritatos, J. (2008). Engendering immigrant psychology: An intersectionality perspective. *Sex Roles, 59*, 326–336. http://dx.doi.org/10.1007/s11199-008-9495-2

Markus, H. R., & Kitayama, S. (1991). Culture and the self: Implications for cognition, emotion, and motivation. *Psychological Review, 98*, 224–253. http://dx.doi.org/10.1037/0033-295X.98.2.224

Mohatt, N. V., Thompson, A. B., Thai, N. D., & Tebes, J. K. (2014). Historical trauma as public narrative: A conceptual review of how history impacts present-day health. *Social Science & Medicine, 106*, 128–136. http://dx.doi.org/10.1016/j.socscimed.2014.01.043

Morrow, M., & Weisser, J. (2012). Towards a social justice framework of mental health recovery. *Studies in Social Justice*, 6, 27–43. http://dx.doi.org/10.26522/ssj.v6i1.1067

Mossakowski, K. N. (2003). Coping with perceived discrimination: Does ethnic identity protect mental health? *Journal of Health and Social Behavior*, 44, 318–331. http://dx.doi.org/10.2307/1519782

Mossakowski, K. N. (2008). Dissecting the influence of race, ethnicity, and socio-economic status on mental health in young adulthood. *Research on Aging*, 30, 649–671. http://dx.doi.org/10.1177/0164027508322693

Naeem, F., Ayub, M., Gobi, M., & Kingdon, D. (2009). Development of Southampton Adaptation Framework for CBT (SAF-CBT): A framework for adaptation of CBT in non-western culture. *Journal of Pakistan Psychiatric Society*, 6, 79–84.

Paone, T. R., & Malott, K. M. (2008). Using interpreters in mental health counseling: A literature review and recommendations. *Journal of Multicultural Counseling and Development*, 36, 130–142. http://dx.doi.org/10.1002/j.2161-1912.2008.tb00077.x

Rathod, S., & Kingdon, D. (2009). Cognitive behaviour therapy across cultures. *Psychiatry*, 8, 370–371. http://dx.doi.org/10.1016/j.mppsy.2009.06.011

Riley, D. (2017, January 17). Grandmother who organized Washington march 'felt women needed to stand up.' *ABC News*. Retrieved from http://abcnews.go.com/US/grandmother-organized-washington-march-felt-women-needed-stand/story?id=44814367

Rosenfield, S. (2012). Triple jeopardy? Mental health at the intersection of gender, race, and class. *Social Science & Medicine*, 74, 1791–1801. http://dx.doi.org/10.1016/j.socscimed.2011.11.010

Salant, T., & Lauderdale, D. S. (2003). Measuring culture: A critical review of acculturation and health in Asian immigrant populations. *Social Science & Medicine*, 57, 71–90. http://dx.doi.org/10.1016/S0277-9536(02)00300-3

Samaan, R. A. (2000). The influences of race, ethnicity, and poverty on the mental health of children. *Journal of Health Care for the Poor and Underserved*, 11, 100–110. http://dx.doi.org/10.1353/hpu.2010.0557

Sawyer, P. J., Major, B., Casad, B. J., Townsend, S. S., & Mendes, W. B. (2012). Discrimination and the stress response: Psychological and physiological consequences of anticipating prejudice in interethnic interactions. *American Journal of Public Health*, 102, 1020–1026. http://dx.doi.org/10.2105/AJPH.2011.300620

Schnittker, J., Freese, J., & Powell, B. (2000). Nature, nurture, neither, nor: Black–White differences in beliefs about the causes and appropriate treatment of mental illness. *Social Forces*, 78, 1101–1132. http://dx.doi.org/10.1093/sf/78.3.1101

Sen, G., Iyer, A., & Mukherjee, C. (2009). A methodology to analyse the intersections of social inequalities in health. *Journal of Human Development and Capabilities*, 10, 397–415. http://dx.doi.org/10.1080/19452820903048894

Seng, J. S., Lopez, W. D., Sperlich, M., Hamama, L., & Reed Meldrum, C. D. (2012). Marginalized identities, discrimination burden, and mental health: Empirical exploration of an interpersonal-level approach to modeling intersectionality. *Social Science & Medicine, 75,* 2437–2445. http://dx.doi.org/10.1016/j.socscimed.2012.09.023

Sentell, T., Shumway, M., & Snowden, L. (2007). Access to mental health treatment by English language proficiency and race/ethnicity. *Journal of General Internal Medicine, 22*(Suppl. 2), 289–293. http://dx.doi.org/10.1007/s11606-007-0345-7

Shea, M., & Yeh, C. (2008). Asian American students' cultural values, stigma, and relational self-construal: Correlates of attitudes toward professional help seeking. *Journal of Mental Health Counseling, 30,* 157–172. http://dx.doi.org/10.17744/mehc.30.2.g662g5l2r1352198

Sheikh, S., & Furnham, A. (2000). A cross-cultural study of mental health beliefs and attitudes towards seeking professional help. *Social Psychiatry and Psychiatric Epidemiology, 35,* 326–334. http://dx.doi.org/10.1007/s001270050246

Smedley, B. D. (2012). The lived experience of race and its health consequences. *American Journal of Public Health, 102,* 933–935. http://dx.doi.org/10.2105/AJPH. 2011.300643

Sotero, M. (2006). A conceptual model of historical trauma: Implications for public health practice and research. *Journal of Health Disparities Research and Practice, 1,* 93–108.

Walters, K. L., & Simoni, J. M. (2002). Reconceptualizing native women's health: An "indigenist" stress-coping model. *American Journal of Public Health, 92,* 520–524. http://dx.doi.org/10.2105/AJPH.92.4.520

Wei, M., Heppner, P. P., Ku, T. Y., & Liao, K. Y. H. (2010). Racial discrimination stress, coping, and depressive symptoms among Asian Americans: A moderation analysis. *Asian American Journal of Psychology, 1,* 136–150. http://dx.doi.org/10.1037/a0020157

Whaley, A. L., & Davis, K. E. (2007). Cultural competence and evidence-based practice in mental health services: A complementary perspective. *American Psychologist, 62,* 563–574. http://dx.doi.org/10.1037/0003-066X.62.6.563

Wilkins, E. J., Whiting, J. B., Watson, M. F., Russon, J. M., & Moncrief, A. M. (2013). Residual effects of slavery: What clinicians need to know. *Contemporary Family Therapy, 35,* 14–28. http://dx.doi.org/10.1007/s10591-012-9219-1

Williams, D. R., Neighbors, H. W., & Jackson, J. S. (2003). Racial/ethnic discrimination and health: Findings from community studies. *American Journal of Public Health, 93,* 200–208. http://dx.doi.org/10.2105/AJPH.93.2.200

Woodward, A. M., Dwinell, A. D., & Arons, B. S. (1992). Barriers to mental health care for Hispanic Americans: A literature review and discussion. *The Journal of Behavioral Health Services & Research, 19,* 224–236. http://dx.doi.org/10.1007/BF02518988

INDEX

Family
  expectations of, 37–38
  integrating, into treatment, 216–217
  in Native model of wellness, 210
  structure of, 184
Family conflict
  adapting CBT to address, 247
  as stressor for Asian Americans, 234
Fava, M., 28
FCS (Asian American Family Conflicts
    Scale), 244–245
Fear of Negative Evaluation (FNE)
    scale, 189
Fear Survey Schedule (FSS-II), 190
Fiferman, L. A., 108
Fink, C. M., 194
Fleming, C. M., 319
Flexibility, in Native perspective,
    105–106
FMAP (formative method for adapting
    psychotherapy), 33–35
FNE (Fear of Negative Evaluation)
    scale, 189
Folkman, S., 231, 289, 290
Formative method for adapting
    psychotherapy (FMAP), 33–35
Four-factor model, of depressive
    disorders, 78–79
Friedman, S., 192, 193
FSS-II (Fear Survey Schedule), 190
Functional disability, 76
Funderburk, B. W., 323

GAD (generalized anxiety disorder),
    128, 194
Garcia, M., 53
García-López, L. J., 161, 169
Gary, F. A., 204
Gaylord, S. A., 302
GDS (Geriatric Depression Scale), 30, 80
Generalized anxiety disorder (GAD),
    128, 194
Geographic location, and
    discrimination, 343
Geological isolation, of American
    Indians, 103
Geriatric Depression Scale (GDS),
    30, 80
Gerstenberg, F. X., 247
Ghahramanlou-Holloway, M., 78

Giesen, B., 315
Gitlin, L. N., 76, 90
Glueckauf, R. L., 75, 84
Goldin, P. R., 162, 169
Goldman, D., 320
Gone, J. P., 327
Gore, K. L., 193
Gray, J. S., 212
Green, B. A., 190
Green, K. E., 81
Greer, T. M., 295
Gregory, V. L., Jr., 83
Gresham, R. L., Jr., 28
Grier, W. H., 296
Griner, D., 60
Group discussions, of discrimination,
    301
Group therapy, individual vs., 87
*Guidelines on Multicultural Education,
    Training, Research, Practice,
    and Organizational Change for
    Psychologists* (APA), 248
Gutiérrez Wang, L., 271
Guzman, J., 57–59

Halpern, B., 193
Hambrick, J. P., 188
Hamilton Depression Inventory (HDI),
    30
Hamilton Depression Rating Scale
    (HDRS), 31
Harmony, in Native model of wellness,
    209, 210
Hawkins, S. R., 300
Hays, P. A., 16, 246, 251
HC-MC (Honoring Children, Mending
    the Circle), 210–211, 322–323
HDI (Hamilton Depression Inventory),
    30
HDRS (Hamilton Depression Rating
    Scale), 31
Health care access
  for American Indians and Alaska
      Natives, 102, 103
  for Latin Americans, 150–151
Health care disparities
  for African Americans, 10
  for American Indians and Alaska
      Natives, 11
  for Latin Americans, 9

McDonald, J. D., 205
McLeod, B., 326
McNeil, D. W., 205
MCT (multicultural therapy), 246
MDD (major depressive disorder), 24–26
Medication, in treatment of depression, 58
Medicine wheel, 208–209, 218, 323–324
Melka, S. E., 189
Mendoza, D. B., 192
Mental health
    cognitive behavioral models of, and culture, 347–348
    Native perspectives of, 105–107
    psychoeducation session on, 35–36
Mental Health: Culture, Race, and Ethnicity (Surgeon General), 50
Mental health disparities
    for American Indians and Alaska Natives, 11, 103, 204, 220
    for Latin Americans, 150–152
MET (motivation and enhancement therapy), 109–110
Meta-analysis, of culturally adapted interventions, 60–61
Methodology, improving to include cultural considerations, 90
Meyer, I. H., 233
Microaggressions, 235
Miller, O., 189–190
Miller, W. R., 109
Mind–body approaches, to stress interventions, 301–302
Mind–body connection
    in Asian American cultures, 238
    and somatization, in treatment of stress, 249
Mindfulness-based stress reduction (MBSR), 302–303, 326
Mini International Neuropsychiatric Interview (MINI), 55
Minority status
    adapting CBT to address, 247–248
    stress related to, 235–236
Minority stress model, 233
Miranda, J., 57–59, 62, 167
Mitakuye Oyasin (Lakota term), 117
Mitchell, F. E., 138
Moitra, E., 189

Moorehead, V. D., Jr., 327
Morsette, A., 322
Mossakowski, K. N., 346
Motivation and enhancement therapy (MET), 109–110
Multiculturally Sensitive Mental Health Scale (MSMHS), 81
Multicultural therapy (MCT), 246
Multidimensional Acculturative Stress Inventory (MASI), 272–273
Muñoz, R. F., 57–59, 62, 84
Munoz, Aguilar-Gaxiola, and Guzman CBT protocol, 57–59
Munoz and Miranda CBT protocol, 57–59, 62

National Comorbidity Survey, 24
National Comorbidity Survey-Replication (NCS-R), 25
National Epidemiological Survey on Alcohol and Related Conditions (NESARC), 51
National Latino and Asian American Survey (NLAAS), 25, 51
National Survey of American Life (NSAL), 79
Native model of wellness, 209–210
Native perspectives
    CBT congruence with, 207
    of mental health, 105–107
Native traditionalists, 107
Nativity status
    and intergenerational conflict, 235
    and likelihood of psychiatric disorders, 126–127
NCS-R (National Comorbidity Survey-Replication), 25
Neal-Barnett, A. M., 195
Neck-focused panic attacks, 139
Negative schemas, 294–297
Neighbors, H. W., 346
Nervios, 52
Nervios Scale, 166
NESARC (National Epidemiological Survey on Alcohol and Related Conditions), 51
A New Leaf . . . Choices for Healthy Living, 324–325
Ng, J., 59
Ngo, V., 322

Nguyen, H. T., 79
Nierenberg, A. A., 28
NLAAS (National Latino and Asian American Survey), 25, 51
Norton, P. J., 211–212, 241
NSAL (National Survey of American Life), 79

Oden, T., 84
Oh Happy Day Class (OHDC; CBT intervention), 86–87
Okazaki, S., 128, 130
Olivares, J., 161, 169
Organista, K. C., 62, 87
Orthostatic panic attacks, 139
Other-face, 243
Otto, M. W., 139

Pace, D., 113
PAMF (psychotherapy adaptation and modification framework), 33–34
Pan, D., 138
PANAS-X (Positive and Negative Affect Schedule–Expanded Form), 187
Panic attacks, neck-focused and orthostatic, 139
Panic disorders, 192–193
Paradis, C., 192
Parent–child interaction therapy (PCIT), 323
Park, I. J. K., 131
Partners in Care, 57–58, 326
Pathological worry, 129
Patient Health Questionnaire-9 (PHQ-9), 30, 54
Pawlow, L. A., 78
PCIT (parent–child interaction therapy), 323
Pearlin, L. I., 75
PEDQ-CV (Perceived Ethnic Discrimination Questionnaire–Community Version), 292
Peer interactions, 85
Peng, K., 236
Penn State Worry Questionnaire (PSWQ), 187–188
Perceived Ethnic Discrimination Questionnaire–Community Version (PEDQ-CV), 292

Perceived Racism Scale (PRS), 291–292
Perceived Stress Scale (PSS), 241
Pérez Benítez, C. I., 160–161, 274
Pérez-Stable, E. J., 152
Perfectionism
    in Asian Americans, 234
    reframing, in treatment, 247
Perinatal depression, 58–59
Peritraumatic dissociation, 267
Personalismo (cultural value), 275
Peter, L., 320
PE (prolonged exposure) therapy, 274–275
Petrie, J. M., 187, 190
Petros, T., 212
Pettibone, J. C., 78
Phobias, 190–191
PHQ-9 (Patient Health Questionnaire-9), 30, 54
Pich, V., 249
Pollack, M. H., 249
Polo, A. J., 61
Porter, C. A., 205
Positive and Negative Affect Schedule–Expanded Form (PANAS-X), 187
Posttraumatic Cognitions Inventory, 297
Posttraumatic stress disorder (PTSD)
    in American Indians and Alaska Natives, 205, 210–211, 322
    assessment measures, 270–272
    cognitive behavior therapy in treatment of, 273–275
    culturally adapted CBT for, 161
    in Latin Americans, 168–169, 264–267
    prevalence of, 180–181
Poverty rates
    of African Americans, 10
    of American Indians and Alaska Natives, 11, 204
    of Asian Americans, 7, 236
    of Latin Americans, 9
Powers, M., 192
Powers, M. B., 126
Prevalence
    of anxiety disorders
        in African Americans, 180–181
        in American Indians and Alaska Natives, 204–205

Stereotype Confirmation Concern
    Scale, 297
Stewart, S. H., 205
Stice, E., 59
Stigma
    addressing, with CBT, 248–249
    of mental illness, 23, 32, 184, 195,
        204, 237
Stoicism, 238
Stolle, D., 322
Storck, M. J., 319
Strauss, M., 319
Strengths, cultural, 251
Stress
    biological indicators of, 229
    and cognition, 293–297
    cognitive behavior therapy in
        treatment of
        in Latin Americans, 275
    conceptualizations of, 289–290
    coping responses to, 238–240
    culturally variant expressions of,
        237–238
    defining, 316
    minority stress model, 233
    models of, 316–318
    moderated by acculturation, 24–25
    race-related, 291–293
    and racism exposure, 290–291
    related to acculturation. See
        Acculturative stress
    related to minority status, 235–236
    transactional model of, 231
Stress disorders
    in African Americans, 287–304
        alternative treatment approaches
            to, 301–303
        and conceptualizations of stress,
            289–290
        culturally adapted cognitive
            behavior therapy for
            treatment of, 298–301
        race-related stress, 291–293
        racism exposure and stress,
            290–291
        stress and cognition, 293–297
    in American Indians and Alaska
        Natives, 313–328
        assessment measures, 318–321
        future research on, 326–328

and health disparities, 314
and historical trauma, 315–316
models of stress, 316–318
treatments for, 321–326
    in Asian Americans, 229–253
        assessment measures, 240–245
        cognitive behavior therapy for
            treatment of, 245–250
        coping responses to stress, 238–240
        culturally specific stressors,
            234–237
        culturally variant expressions of
            stress, 237–238
        cultural modifications in
            treatment of, 250–252
        stress theories and culture,
            231–233
    in Latin Americans, 263–277
        assessment measures, 270–273
        cognitive behavioral models for
            understanding, 264–270
        cognitive behavior therapy for
            treatment of, 273–275
        future research on, 276–277
Stressors
    culturally specific, 234–237
    race-related, 298
Stressors, intergenerational, 101
Stress-paradigm model, 317
Stress process model, 75
Stress theories, 231–233
Structured Clinical Interview for
    DSM–5 (SCID-5), 31
Substance abuse, 109–110
Suchday, S., 189–190
Sue, D. W., 252
Sue, S., 248, 252
Suh, E. M., 136
Suicidal ideation, 25–26
Superwoman (schema), 296
Support groups, 195–196
Support networks, 216–217
Systematic review method, 152–156
Systematic review results, 156–160
Sztompka, P., 315

Tai chi diagram, 39–40
Takeuchi, D. T., 126
Tanaka-Matsumi, J., 347
Tang, D., 188

ABOUT THE EDITORS

Edward C. Chang, PhD, is a professor of psychology and social work and a faculty associate in Asian/Pacific Islander American studies at the University of Michigan, Ann Arbor. He received his BA in psychology and philosophy from the State University of New York at Buffalo and his MA and PhD degrees from the State University of New York at Stony Brook. Dr. Chang completed his American Psychological Association accredited clinical internship at Bellevue Hospital Center–New York University Medical Center. He serves as a program evaluator for the Michigan Department of Community Health–Social Determinants of Health, working with the Asian Center of Southeast Michigan. Dr. Chang also serves as an associate editor of *Cognitive Therapy and Research*. He has published nearly 200 empirical and scholarly works focusing on optimism and pessimism, perfectionism, loneliness, social problem solving, and cultural influences on behavior.

Christina A. Downey, PhD, is assistant vice-chancellor for academic affairs and student success and associate professor of psychology at Indiana University Kokomo. She received her BA in psychology from Purdue University in West Lafayette, Indiana, and her MS and PhD in clinical psychology from the University of Michigan, Ann Arbor. Dr. Downey completed her American

Psychological Association–accredited clinical internship at the University of Michigan Center for the Child and Family and the University of Michigan Psychological Clinic. Dr. Downey has published articles on various topics in journals such as *Eating Behaviors*, *Psychology & Health*, the *Scandinavian Journal of Psychology*, and *The Journal of Effective Teaching* and has published several chapters on positive psychology and its history. She also serves on the editorial board of *Cognitive Therapy and Research*. She was coeditor of the *Handbook of Race and Development in Mental Health* (2012) with Edward C. Chang and *Positive Psychology in Racial and Ethnic Groups: Theory, Research, and Practice* (2016) with Edward C. Chang, Jameson K. Hirsch, and Natalie J. Lin.

Jameson K. Hirsch, PhD, is an associate professor and assistant chair of the Department of Psychology at East Tennessee State University. He received his BS in psychology and MA in clinical psychology from East Tennessee State University and his PhD from the University of Wyoming. Dr. Hirsch completed his American Psychological Association–accredited clinical internship at State University of New York Upstate Medical University and his postdoctoral fellowship at the University of Rochester School of Medicine and Dentistry. He is on the editorial boards of *Suicide and Life-Threatening Behavior*, *Journal of Rural Mental Health*, *International Journal of Mental Health and Addiction*, and *Cognitive Therapy and Research*. Dr. Hirsch has made more than 300 presentations, published more than 100 articles, and coedited three books examining the role of sociocultural, cognitive-behavioral, and emotional characteristics, particularly protective factors, in psychological well-being and physical health.

Elizabeth A. Yu, MS, is a graduate student in the clinical science area in the Department of Psychology at the University of Michigan. She received her BA and MS in psychology and is working toward her PhD in clinical psychology from the University of Michigan, Ann Arbor. Ms. Yu has conducted, presented, and published research on a wide range of topics, including perfectionism, optimism and pessimism, hope, well-being, depression, suicide risk, and meaning in life. Key to her research interests is the consideration of culture and context, especially in ethnic minority populations.